The World and a Very Small Place in Africa

Sources and Studies in World History

Series Editor: Kevin Reilly

The World and a Very Small Place in Africa

A HISTORY OF GLOBALIZATION
IN NIUMI, THE GAMBIA
THIRD EDITION

Donald R. Wright

M.E.Sharpe
Armonk, New York
London, England

On the cover: "Early Morning, Ready for Departure," by Beverly Derrick.

The EuroSlavic and Transroman fonts used to create this work are © 1986–2010
Payne Loving Trust. EuroSlavic and Transroman are available
from Linguist's Software, Inc., www.linguistsoftware.
com, P.O. Box 580, Edmonds, WA 98020-0580 USA, tel (425) 775-1130.

Library of Congress Cataloging-in-Publication Data

Wright, Donald R.
The world and a very small place in Africa : a history of globalization in Niumi, the Gambia /
by Donald R. Wright.—3rd ed.
p. cm.—(Sources and studies in world history)
Includes bibliographical references and index.
ISBN 978-0-7656-2483-3 (cloth : alk. paper)—ISBN 978-0-7656-2484-0 (pbk. : alk. paper)
 1. Niumi (Kingdom)—Relations. 2. Niumi (Kingdom)—Social conditions. 3. Globalization—
Social aspects—Niumi (Kingdom)—History. I. Title.

DT532.23.W75 2010
966.51—dc22   2009038898

Printed in the United States of America

IBT (c)   10   9   8   7   6   5   4   3   2   1
CW (p)   10   9   8   7   6   5

For George Brooks;
and in memory of
Deyda Hydara, 1946–2004.

CONTENTS

LIST OF ILLUSTRATIONS

Maps

Photographs

LIST OF PERSPECTIVES

FOREWORD

In the pages that follow, Donald Wright gives us a history of Niumi, in The Gambia, West Africa, that is unabashedly a local history populated by local characters, but at the same time affords us a refreshing, engaging perspective on both African history and world history. Wright does not distract us with events upriver from Niumi or in the dry sahel of Senegal, nor does he divert us into a regional history of Sudanic kingdoms or the Atlantic diaspora; rather, he rivets our attention on a "very small place" and attunes us to its global echoes.

The "world-systems" theory of Immanuel Wallerstein provides Wright with a helpful paradigm of world history. Since the mid-1970s, Wallerstein has argued that the development of a modern capitalist "world system" has benefited the developed countries at the expense of the colonized and exploited "periphery." Wright works with this model but carefully avoids two pitfalls—ignoring precapitalist systems or understating the degree to which people on the periphery participate in the shaping of their own destinies.

Wright shows how Niumi, from 1000 to 1450, was drawn into a "restructuring world system," in which the great forces of Islam and Sudanic kingdoms had only a minor impact on the local salt trade and fisheries. After 1450, the emerging Atlantic plantation system and slave trade actually brought new opportunities and increased political stability for the people of Niumi.

Over the two centuries between 1600 and 1800, Niumi did not change as much as it did between 1800 and 1850, when it was increasingly incorporated into the world capitalist system as a producer of agricultural staples, especially peanuts, for industrializing countries. Consequently, the declining global price of peanuts would have more bearing on Niumi's twentieth century than the political vicissitudes of colonialism and its aftermath. Globalization has not been kind to the people of Gambia.

This third edition, which charts the changes that have marked the first decade of the twenty-first century, shines a brighter light on The Gambia's homegrown dictatorship, in power since a military coup in 1994. Wright's keen observations and vivid prose help the reader sort through some of the most perplexing of contemporary issues facing Niumi, and not only Niumi: the intransigence of political corruption, the impact of aid versus investment, the viability of traditional cultural values in the face of consumerism, human rights movements, and a new global diaspora.

Some of Wright's stories will both affirm your faith in humanity and break your heart, but the world of Niumi will become your own.

Kevin Reilly
Series Editor

PREFACE TO THE THIRD EDITION

I am still not sure whether this is a book of African history inspired by my study and teaching of world history, or a book of world history inspired by my study and teaching of African history. It is a history of the state of Niumi, which existed for seven or eight centuries on the north bank of the lower Gambia River, with an emphasis on how a long process of globalization—a continuing widening of Niumi's world and, through a good portion of its existence, its relationships with world systems—affected the lives of people living there. I elaborate on what the book is, and how this edition differs from the first two, in the Introduction. I simply wish to convey here that in addition to standard elements of economic, social, and political history, I continue to keep a focus on topics brought out in recent scholarship in world and African history: transnational and cross-cultural influences; environmental and biological issues; matters pertaining to women; and globalization's effects on the world's poor.

Because world history, with its breadth and theoretical basis, and African history, with its grounding in African cultures unfamiliar to American readers, can be complicated and confusing, I keep theoretical discussions minimal and simple, and I use words in foreign languages, especially Mandinka, only where I believe it necessary. Persons wanting more detailed discussion of world-systems theory or more varying opinions on globalization, for example, or wishing to know the Mandinka word for a term used in the book, will need to do further reading. I attempt to guide such reading in the citations.

I wish to make four points for the sake of honesty and clarity. First, although Mandinka-speaking Africans always referred to the state along the north bank of the Gambia River's estuary as Niumi, not everyone did. For a long time it was "Barra" in the Creole used by people trading in the river, and between the seventeenth and nineteenth centuries, British and French records use "Barra" or "Bar" more frequently than "Niumi" to refer to the state. In quotations from these records and published sources based on these records, I have changed "Barra" to "Niumi" to avoid confusion and continual inclusion of "[sic]" in quotations. Second, the official name of the modern West African country is The Republic of The Gambia; it is properly referred to as The Gambia, with both words capitalized. Before 1965, the British referred to their Gambia River colony as the Gambia (or, officially, the Gambia Colony and Protectorate), without capitalizing the article. I keep this distinction in the text. Third, because in the increasingly oppressive regime of Gambian president Yahya Jammeh speaking publicly about anything can land one in serious trouble, I have gone to some lengths to mask the Gambian individuals who provided me with information for this third edition. I have also altered information I include about any experiences I have had in Niumi since 2003 to make it impossible for a reader to determine what villages or institutions I visited and what people I talked to. I regret it is necessary to do this. Fourth, while in The Gambia working on the second and third editions of this book, I was accompanied by my wife Doris, who is neither Africanist nor historian by training, but is a wise and informed person, sympathetic with the difficulties that the world's poor face in their daily lives. Doris has traveled with me in The Gambia, participated in interviews, interviewed and written on her own, talked with me about issues affecting people in Niumi, and read the entire manuscript with a critical eye. She played an important role in the development of many of the ideas in the last chapters and in untold ways has made the book better than it otherwise would have been.

A long list of people and institutions have lent assistance across my career of study and teaching of African and world history, and in the preparation of the first two editions of this book—far more than I can recognize here—but some have been especially helpful in the preparation of this edition.

As always, the men and women living in Niumi hold a special place in my heart and mind. They again welcomed me into their villages and homes during a research trip in 2009 and spoke to me frankly about circumstances surrounding their lives. Finding it unwise to thank them publicly, I have done so privately. More than anyone, I know that this book would not exist without their assistance. I also again thank Dr. David L. Miller for the maps; and I am grateful to artist Beverly Derrick for allowing use of "Early Morning, Ready for Departure" on the cover, and to Joe DeLuca for use of his camera to photograph her lovely painting.

The dual dedication of the book is for good reason. George Brooks, who introduced me to African and world history, never stops being my mentor. For forty-three years he has kept me engaged with fresh ideas, new challenges, and kind (if not always warranted) encouragement. I have always thought of him as Chaucer's Oxford Cleric, who "would gladly learn, and gladly teach." Deyda Hydara, respected Gambian journalist, reasoned government critic, and staunch defender of press freedom, was shot and killed in December 2004 as he was driving home from the offices of *The Point* newspaper. The Gambian government never satisfactorily investigated the incident. May his murderers be brought to justice and his death not be in vain.

The World and a
Very Small Place
in Africa

INTRODUCTION

*The global web of communication that influences everyone and
every locality so strongly today is not new.*
—William H. McNeill, 2006

No condition is permanent.
—Slogan popular among African liberation groups, 1970s–1980s

The Gambia River may not be the calmest and most easily navigated of the world's
great waterways, but to seamen entering the river after a few weeks of tossing in
the choppy Atlantic, it may seem so. The Gambia flows into the ocean 115 miles
below Cape Verde, the westernmost tip of the African continent. The river's mouth
is surprisingly broad—twelve miles across at its entrance into the Atlantic—and
funnel-shaped as if designed to catch vessels coasting down around the cape from
the north. Inside the mouth, the river is a sailor's delight: its main channel is deep
and its strong tidal flow helps vessels move upriver. In the days of sail, most ships
could ride the winds and tides 120 miles eastward to a port on the river called Niani-
Maru. Smaller craft that could tack more easily between the narrowing banks were
able to pass another eighty miles eastward to Barokunda Falls, a series of laterite
ledges on which craft drawing a little more than three feet of water scraped bottom.
Large canoes could pass Barokunda and travel another 140 miles southeasterly
toward the edge of the Futa Jalon highlands. Thus, from as early as West Africans
put vessels on the water, the Gambia served as a highway into the interior.

On the north bank of the Gambia, at its mouth, lies a territory known locally
as Niumi. For 500 years it was a separate political unit—a state, or kingdom, in
Western terms—one of many such small units that spread across West Africa's
savannas over the centuries before European rule. Niumi was never large—it is
difficult to say how large, because African rulers were more concerned with control
of people than of land, and they seldom delineated political boundaries with much
care, especially in lightly populated parts of their realm. Still, historical records
and notions of local residents tend to agree that Niumi never comprised more
than about 400 square miles, and even that figure is deceptively large because
most of its population before recent times lived within a few miles of the river.
Thus, through most of its existence, Niumi was more a long strip of land along the
riverbank under a single political authority than a compact, squared-off territory.
At the height of its control, even including uninhabited forests with the populated
riverside, it was only about one-third the size of the Duchy of Luxembourg or the
state of Rhode Island.

3

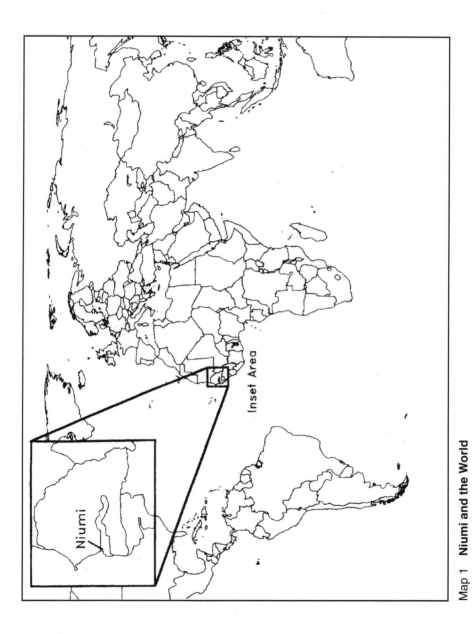

Map 1 **Niumi and the World**

I first saw Niumi in 1974 as I was coming into The Gambia by air. The plane made the short hop down from Dakar, Senegal, along the Atlantic Coast, and passed seaward of Niumi as it approached Gambia's airport, across the river. The farther south we flew, the brighter and whiter the coastal stretch appeared. In the vicinity of the Saloum River, north of the Senegal-Gambia border, great flats of land near the ocean were treeless and barren—a white moonscape, though without elevation. It was here that the tide spilled across huge, flat pans and then evaporated naturally, leaving a crust of salt that people gathered in baskets and exchanged for goods with people living in West Africa's salt-starved inlands. For 1,000 years, probably much longer, Niumi's residents had participated in, marshaled, and sometimes controlled the passage of salt up the Gambia River. It was a key to Niumi's power and wealth, and it would play an important role in much of the state's early history.

I could not spot the handful of buildings that served as the customs post on the border, but I knew from the coastline, having pored over maps for a year or more, about where Senegal stopped and The Gambia began. It was late August; the height of the rainy season, and everything was green. What immediately became evident was how Niumi was a combination of two landscapes: watery coast and rolling wooded grasslands. The northwestern part of the territory was a stretch of low, sandy, wooded islands separated from a mangrove-lined coast and crisscrossed by a maze of waterways. The mangroves hugged Niumi's riverbank in a sweeping arch from the Gambia's mouth down past Barra Point, around a big eastward bend, and they clogged the bank on up the river for 100 miles or more. Oysters clung to the mangrove roots and, when exposed at low tide, made fair picking. A few creeks and streams cut through the band of mangrove green and flowed a mile or two into the interior.

Inland from the coast and riverbank, savanna made up the rest. I was surprised at how much this reminded me of my eastern Indiana home: grasslands and tall trees, with little elevation, rolling on for what seemed like forever. It was thick and verdant, waving in the August breeze. By the next April, six months into the dry season when the *harmattan* wind blows hot off the Sahara, it would be crisp and dusty, everything tinted orange by the wind-blown soil.

From above, it all looked charming. Villages seemed to pop out behind the jet's wing, a mixture of thatch and metal roofs underneath canopies of majestic silk-cotton trees and fat baobabs. I thought I recognized Essau, Berending, and Bakendiki—old villages I had read about. I did not see many people—it was during the hottest part of the afternoon and the plane was still at several thousand feet—but I thought I spotted a few men in their peanut fields, a few children scattering birds from stands of millet. I saw the narrow scar of tarmac running down the fifteen miles from the Senegalese border to the ferry dock at Niumi's Barra Point. At Essau, near Barra, it intersected with a red-gravel road that struck off toward the far end of The Gambia, 200 miles dead east. A ferry full of people, cows, and a few cars was churning toward Barra from the river's south side, where The Gambia's capital, Banjul, is situated. Covered pickups and station wagons—the "bush taxis" (called by the onomatopoeic term *gellie-gellie* by Gambians) that convey people around West Africa's less-populated areas—were lined up near the terminal. It was all a pretty picture.

I would make the same trip by car a few days later. A problem with arrangements for my stay forced me to fly back to Dakar, and to save money returning to The Gambia, I joined a crowd of nine people in one of those station wagons riding down the tarmac road to the ferry. Close up, Niumi was not so charming. It was hot and humid, almost beyond belief. Just north of the Senegal-Gambia border we passed a couple of men working in fields of peanuts. They were squatting, and appeared to be weeding, chopping up clouds of dust with broad, flat, short-handled instruments. One of them stood as our vehicle approached. He wore a long shirt that I thought was a faded imitation of camouflage until I got closer and saw the reddish brown and black and olive blotches were soil and plant stains blended with perspiration. He did not wave, but just stared at us with a blank expression as sweat rolled down from beneath his stocking cap. We came upon a bicyclist, an older man wearing glasses and a short-brimmed hat, who, when he heard us approaching, got off the bike, picked it up, and walked a good five yards off the road. This was something I would see repeatedly. Cyclists had a history of bad experiences with automobiles.

We stopped longer than we wanted at the border station between Senegal and The Gambia, a handful of yellowish buildings with tin roofs built close to the road. Not far stood one of those massive silk-cotton trees I had spotted from the air. The Gambian border guards—nice-looking, officious young men in khaki shorts and knee socks—made us open our luggage. Arguments ensued. One female passenger did not want to retrieve a large, blue-plastic-wrapped package that the driver had tied snugly to the wagon's top. The guards were adamant. For a while she spoke loudly and waved her long arms. Other passengers spoke on her behalf. Then there was quieter talk. In the end she passed them a couple of small bills. Gambian officials accepted Senegalese currency. But the guards saved their most careful scrutiny for the driver's papers. They were just not in order, it seemed. Driver, passengers, and guards formed a tight huddle of loud discussion.

I took this opportunity to look around. Just down the road, vendors had set up shop. They knew that people did not cross the border speedily. Skinny young men were selling skinny loaves of bread; adolescents were offering sandwiches made with a spicy meat-and-oil mixture kept warm in enameled tubs; women were passively peddling green oranges; and two men, tall and dark with narrow, angular faces, were smoking animal carcasses—which looked like goats—over a slow-burning fire. They offered to cut off a strip of meat from one; I declined. There were flies everywhere. I walked another thirty yards to a low, roofed platform where old men were sitting. One of them had a milky-blue film over his eyes. The rest looked wan and listless. It was the "hungry season"—the months immediately preceding the harvest, when grain stores were low and few had cash, normally acquired by selling peanuts, to buy rice. It was also the time of year when mosquitoes bred in the standing water and then passed malaria among human hosts. Two women walked by slowly, balancing calabash bowls of greens on their heads. Each wore a long, wrapped skirt of colorful tie-dyed fabric, a T-shirt, and rubber flip-flops. Both had infants attached to their backs by cloth wraps. One child's red-tinged hair was the telltale sign of kwashiorkor, a disease resulting from protein deficiency. Like most of the children I encountered, these two had runny noses. Neither was asleep; their eyes silently followed me as their mothers walked past.

Once we got to Barra, I had time to kill. The noonish ferry had just left the pier—it was 100 yards out, had completed its pivot to face the south bank, and now was revving its old diesel engines into high speed for the four-mile crossing. It would not return for three hours. An engine breakdown in its twin had occasioned the long hiatus in the schedule. The Gambia Ports Authority did not have the part needed to repair the engine and was not sure it could turn one up. The other passengers were not surprised and did not seem to mind. They were content to sit and wait in the canopied pavilion. I wandered over to the Barra market, a small open-air gathering of people, tables, stools, and stalls where one could procure everything from fresh fish to woven baskets. I was not astute enough to consider the significance of all of the imported things for sale there—dry-cell batteries from France, rubber shoes from Spain, T-shirts from American colleges, pablumlike breakfast cereal in metal cans from Great Britain, and the ubiquitous Nescafé—but I did note a few oddities: huge bags of rice from Vietnam and Arkansas (in this rice-producing region); plastic bottles of peanut oil from France (in this country where peanut farming was the major economic enterprise); identical bars of soap in every stall, imported from England and selling for exactly the same price. As I stood sweating in the heat and humidity, 5,000 miles from my home—where there was no hungry season and no malarial languor, where (most) drivers did not aim at cyclists, where we extracted oils from the crops we grew, where we had parts to fix our cars, and where manufacturers of a dozen different brands of soap competed vigorously for my dollar—I recognized that something in that little place was awry.

What was wrong in Niumi, I eventually came to understand, was the same thing that was wrong in a good part of the world. I remained in The Gambia for nine months, interviewing oral traditionists so that I could, with additional archival work, reconstruct the precolonial history of Niumi for my doctoral thesis at Indiana University. About halfway through my stay in The Gambia, in late January 1975, George Brooks, my dissertation advisor, sent me a letter of encouragement and included a copy of Immanuel Wallerstein's new book, *The Modern World-System*. "By all accounts," Brooks wrote in typical understatement, "this book is very important." I was already acquainted with William H. McNeill's interpretive work on world history, *The Rise of the West*, and had taught a couple of world history courses, part time, at Auburn University at Montgomery, Alabama, so I was at least partially comfortable with the "global perspective." Now, I found plenty of time to read about the modern world system—all the more because I had to make frequent trips on the Barra ferry, which was forever under repair. I struggled with

Wallerstein's ideas of how events associated with the growth of European capitalism after the sixteenth century brought together increasing numbers of people of the world—brought them together not under a grand political authority but in a series of economic relationships he called the "modern world system." These economic relationships were more important than political ones, Wallerstein argued: how people fit into the world system, as participants from the stronger and wealthier "core" nations or as part of the weaker and poorer "periphery," determined important aspects of their lives. I suppose that reading was the beginning of my awareness of the influence of global events on local history. It is a perspective I have tried to maintain by following—sometimes at considerable distance—the evolution of arguments about world systems.

In 1976 I accepted a position in history with the liberal arts college at Cortland of the State University of New York; in 1978 I began the teaching of world history there; and I have taught African and world history ever since. It was the teaching and reading in both of these expanding fields, over a long time, combined with my experience of living in The Gambia (with trips back now and then) and studying its history, that gave me a sense of what has long been the key to problems in Niumi and much of the rest of the developing world. Specifically, I came to understand how dealings with large economic complexes and, eventually, incorporation into an ever-growing world market, or world economy, or world political economy, or, indeed, world system, had affected the way people lived for a long time in Niumi—this small place in Africa that I knew so well. It was this story I tried to tell in the first edition of this book, published in 1997.

The book's release occurred when the world was going through changes following the collapse of the Soviet Union and the end of the Cold War. A new wave of integration of the people, nations, and economies of the world was moving speedily toward a crest, and growing numbers of journalists and academics were using the term "globalization" to describe the process. By the late 1990s groups were beginning to call attention to globalization's effects on the lives of billions of people in the developing world. Protests at meetings of the World Trade Organization, the World Bank, and the International Monetary Fund brought international attention to the perceived personal, economic, environmental, and cultural harm these "globalizing" organizations were inflicting with their policies intended to break down barriers to human interaction and global integration.

As I considered these events, I realized that globalization was not so much a new phenomenon as an old process newly recognized; that, in fact, globalization had been going on for a long time—centuries, for certain. To my thinking, the coming into existence and restructuring of world systems that I had written about were parts—important parts, but, still, only parts—of the globalization process, which people living along the north bank of the Gambia River, near its entrance into the Atlantic, had been involved in for a very long time. Thus, in the fall of 2002, I began working on a new edition with the intention of having a greater emphasis on the globalization process, viewing Niumi's relations with world systems and the steady change its residents experienced through seven or eight centuries as a part of this process. I also recognized the importance of including a new chapter, discussing life in Niumi since the mid-1990s, when the most recent wave of globalization came bearing down on The Gambia like the tidal surge of a tropical storm. To that end, I spent two months, between January and March 2003, in The Gambia, in an effort to understand life in Niumi under globalization's influence. This was the added emphasis in the second edition.

Since the appearance of the second edition in 2004, events in The Gambia and the world have prompted me to reassess my thinking on the relative importance, through all circumstances, of global relationships and local influences. In December 2004, an acquaintance, the respected, veteran Gambian journalist Deyda Hydara, was murdered—shot and killed as he was driving home from his newspaper office. Many saw the hand of Gambian security forces in the murder, a suspicion heightened by the government's failure to investigate the crime in a serious manner. Since then, the country's president, Yahya A.J.J. Jammeh (who presently has his name and title written, "His Excellency President Sheikh Professor Alhaji Dr. Yahya Jammeh"), has brought tyrannous rule to the country, stifling the once-lively press, ignoring the country's constitution, disregarding human rights, and making Gambians live in fear of arrest, illegal detention, torture, and death. When the gravity of the 2008–2009 recession became apparent in the fall of 2008, I sensed that this economic downturn, though the worst since the Great Depression, was not nearly so harmful to people living in Niumi as was its own national government. In order to judge if this was the case, I went to The Gambia in January and February 2009. This third edition reflects this judgment as it includes a weighing of the effects of recent global and local circumstances on the lives of Niumi residents. It also offers a re-thinking of earlier ideas—or at least the strength of the earlier presentation of these ideas—in light of the present situation in the country. One thus may think of this book's first edition as emphasizing world systems, the second emphasizing globalization, and the third casting doubt on the emphases of the first two editions because of the harsh reality of local oppression.

Part I
BACKGROUND
Before A.D. 1446

In the late summer of 1446, nearly half a century before Christopher Columbus crossed the Atlantic, a Portuguese knight and adventurer named Nuno Tristão sailed an armed caravel down Africa's west coast and into the mouth of the Gambia River.[1] He had reason to expect a hostile reception. For several years prior to this, sailors such as Tristão had been capturing Africans along the Atlantic coast north of the Gambia and spiriting them back to Portugal. According to Gomes Eanes de Azurara, a contemporary Portuguese court chronicler, "the disposition and conversion of these prisoners occupied a good portion of [Prince Henry's] time."

Just inside the river's mouth, Tristão launched two boats, with twelve armed men (including Tristão) in one and ten in the other. They began to ride the tide upriver, intent on locating more "prisoners." Soon, however, they altered their route and, writes Azurara, "made for some habitations that they espied on the right hand." Their concentration on these habitations must have been intense, for they did not immediately notice the approach of twelve boats launched from the north bank, "in the which," Azurara records, "there would be as many as seventy or eighty Guineas, all Negroes, with bows in their hands." The men in one of the boats beached their craft, got out, and began to rain arrows on the Portuguese. The others came near and "discharged that accursed ammunition of theirs all full of poison upon the bodies of our countrymen." They chased the two Portuguese boats back to the caravel, where the seamen tied up to the larger vessel, the crew cut their anchor cables amid the hail of arrows, and the invaders limped away. Of the twenty-eight who had entered the river on the caravel, only seven remained alive two days later, because, Azurara notes, "that poison was so artfully composed that a slight wound, if it only let blood, brought men to their last end." Over several days, the survivors rolled twenty-one bodies into the Atlantic Ocean off Africa's west coast.

Because there was not a trained navigator among the remaining crew, the caravel's return to Portugal was long. Luck played a role, though Azurara credits "heavenly aid." After two months out of sight of land, sailing "directly to the north, declining a little to the east," the crew sighted a ship piloted by a Spanish pirate, who told them they were near Portugal's southern coast. They put in at Lagos and informed Prince Henry of the tragedy. Azurara writes that the prince "had great displeasure at the loss of the men," and "like a lord who felt their deaths had come to pass in his service, he afterward had an especial care of their wives and children."

Perspective 1   **A Sale of Slaves in Portugal**

Azurara was a strong court supporter, who took the side of his countrymen in disputes with Africans, but he was mindful of the pain associated with the commerce of slaves. Of some of the earliest Africans auctioned in Lisbon to work in the cane fields of southern Portugal, he writes:

> On the 8th of August 1444, early in the morning on account of the heat, the sailors landed the captives. When they were all mustered in the field outside the town, they presented a remarkable spectacle. . . . But what heart so hard as not to be touched with compassion at the sight of them! Some with downcast heads and faces bathed in tears as they looked at each other; others moaning sorrowfully, and fixing their eyes on heaven, uttered plaintive cries as if appealing for help to the Father of Nature. Others struck their faces with their hands, and threw themselves flat upon the ground. Others uttered a wailing chant, after the fashion of the country, and although their words were unintelligible, they spoke plainly enough the excess of their sorrow. But their anguish was at its height when the moment of distribution came, when of necessity children were separated from their parents, wives from their husbands, and brothers from brothers. Each was compelled to go wherever fate might send him. It was impossible to effect this separation without extreme pain.

Nothing is known of the immediate actions of the African bowmen, residents of a small political unit called Niumi, occupying the north bank of the Gambia's estuary, following the successful defense of their territorial waters. They must have returned up the creeks and backwaters of their homeland and, like the Portuguese, reported their exploits to their ruler, a person with the title of *mansa*. He was surely elated at the news. If true to later form, he led a celebration enhanced by palm wine and called in praise-singers—a *mansa*'s equivalent of court chroniclers—to extol the gallantry of the bowmen.

In time, though, however pleased he was with the defensive efforts, Niumi's *mansa* must have thought deeply about relations with the sharp-nosed intruders. Perhaps he recognized that the Portuguese would be as persistent as they were pugnacious, or gained respect for the fighting potential of crossbow men and caravels. More likely, with information trickling down of Portuguese trading with Africans along the Senegal River, to Niumi's north, providing access to horses, iron bars, and other valuable commodities, the *mansa* and his advisors recognized how their commercial interests intertwined. In any event, nine years later, in 1455, when the Venetian Alvise da Cadamosto, sailing for Portugal, brought three caravels into the Gambia River, Niumi traders advised him on products he could obtain there. A year later Niumi's *mansa* befriended Portuguese trader Diogo Gomes and mediated a dispute Portuguese merchants were having with coastal peoples north of Niumi.[2] What had begun as hostile relations turned friendly with prospects of trade; or, as Azurara concludes, after midcentury, "deeds in those parts involved trade and mercantile dealings more than fortitude and exercise of arms."

What brought the two groups—residents of the small southwestern European kingdom of Portugal on the one hand and the small West African kingdom of Niumi on the other—into conflict that summer day in 1446, to be followed within a decade by friendlier commercial contact, was a process of history that began centuries earlier and involved people across the central expanse of the Africa-Eurasian land mass. By the middle of the fifteenth century, Western Europe and West Africa were being drawn increasingly into a wider world or, more particularly, into a restructuring and expanding world economic system that forever after would alter the ways of life of the people living in each place.

1

THE GLOBAL SETTING FOR NIUMI'S HISTORY

BEFORE A.D. 1446

Somehow an appreciation of the autonomy of separate civilizations
(and of all the other less massive and less skilled cultures of the
earth) across the past two thousand years needs to be combined with
the portrait of an emerging world system, connecting greater and
greater numbers of persons across civilized boundaries.
—William H. McNeill, 1990[1]

Of all the phenomena that have affected the way groups of people have lived—anywhere, at any time through nearly all the human past—two are of particular importance for students of world history. One involves the relationship of groups of people with others who have different ways of thinking and acting. The other has to do with people's ways of relating to large-scale economic organizations—integrated trading complexes or commercial systems— because for thousands of years most people who appeared from afar, where people had new and different ideas and ways, were long-distance traders, and the two phenomena often were related.

The first of these is important because people have changed most thoroughly, in relatively short periods, by borrowing ideas or adopting technologies from others. Anthropologists call this process diffusion; examples of it abound. The native peoples of the Great Plains of North America altered their lifestyle once they adopted the horse, brought across the Atlantic by the Spanish in the sixteenth century, and a culture related to its use. Western Europeans changed over a longer time through the Middle Ages, but they used others' ideas and technologies to their advantage when, after 1500, they employed such Chinese inventions as gunpowder, printing, and the compass to help assert themselves economically and, eventually, politically on the rest of the world.[2] Today, contact and borrowing have led to such thorough change among groups of the world's people, as ideas have spread with ease across global communications networks, that we encounter others who have distinctly different ways with less frequency. We are moving toward a global culture where many people of the world do things alike. Such was not the case just a few hundred years ago, and sometimes people changed dramatically, over a short time, through contact with others having different ways.

The second phenomenon still holds in its effect on human lives, however. How any group fits into a larger network of commercial relations is an important determinant in the ways individuals within the group live. Today, people residing in centers of world finance and production—the United States, Western Europe, or Japan, for instance—live differently from those in countries that have little capital and industry and rely primarily on production of cash crops or raw materials for export. For an example of the latter, one can pick most countries of the developing world. Many now consider the major reason for the differences in the lives of people in the developed and underdeveloped worlds—differences in everything from income and productivity to caloric intake and life expectancy—to be how the groups have related to the larger economic systems of the last four or five centuries.

In recent years, more and more people have come to recognize diffusion and economic integration as major elements of what they tend to view, incorrectly, as a new phenomenon: globalization. Globalization is a process that has been occurring for a long time. An aspect of globalization having to do with the economic integration of peoples over large segments of the globe involves world systems.

Globalization and World Systems

In its broadest sense, globalization is the process of integration of the world's people, of their interacting more than before and thus developing closer economic, social, and cultural relationships.[3] The word "globalization" entered the English vocabulary in the 1960s to describe a phenomenon already under way and recognizable, but it did not come into common use for another three decades. It was in the 1990s that a need arose for a word to describe what people saw taking place that was affecting the way the world was working. With the decline of communism and the Cold War, a noticeable wave of economic and social integration was occurring. Capitalism was entering areas formerly under communist or socialist control or isolated from world trade for other reasons. Helping the process work more quickly and broadly than before were improved transportation and communication systems. People and products were moving over longer distances with more ease and speed, while individuals were finding it increasingly easy, fast, and cheap to get information from next door or the other side of the world, helping them place their investments around the globe where there was promise of the greatest or surest profits. So old processes that involved the integration of the world's societies and economies were happening again, only now they were working with unprecedented speed and involving people around much more of the globe's surface.

Thinking about globalization is maturing to the point that we are beginning to see agreement on its place in history. "[A]utonomy had been eroding long before 1850," writes William H. McNeill in a twenty-five-year retrospective of his path-breaking *The Rise of the West*, "long before 1500, and even long before 1000. The process, I now think, dated back to the very beginning of civilized history."[4] The worlds of 3000 B.C. and 500 B.C. were not "global" in the same sense as the world of A.D. 2000, but in the worlds that people knew at the time, the integration of its people and their economic efforts and cultural practices made up a formative process that may have seemed inexorable to those involved.

The worlds of human interaction grew into the first millennium A.D. as various

Perspective 2 **Terminology**

In the English language, words and phrases enter the vocabulary to fit new needs ("texting," "blog," and "download" being recent examples). In a book dealing with how a widening world affected people's lives in a small part of Africa, it is instructive to consider the origins of words relating to the subject. "Globalization," for instance, though describing a process that began long ago, first appeared in print only in 1962 and did not come into wide use until the 1990s, when the end of the Cold War and the spread of telecommunications broadened the integration of the world's people. More surprising is "imperialism"—the policy or practice of establishing and maintaining an empire. One would expect this to be among the oldest words in the language because imperialism was a part of history in the time of Cortes (and the Aztecs before he arrived in America), Genghis Khan, Alexander, Caesar, and the New-Kingdom pharaohs of the Nile. But "imperialism" with this meaning was not detectable until 1878, when Europeans were ready to take the practice to a new level in the "Scramble for Africa."

Other words come into use and then have their propriety questioned, sometimes resulting in their replacement. "Development," in the sense of "the economic advancement of a region or people," was used first in 1902 (in reference to needs in South Africa), and "underdevelopment" as development's antithesis appeared in 1927 (with H.G. Wells's noting the underdevelopment of regions of the Soviet Union). But in the 1960s social scientists gave "underdevelopment" a connotation of something purposeful that had been done to colonies or countries by the more powerful nations that controlled them. U.S. President Harry S Truman first used "underdeveloped" to describe such regions of the world in his 1949 State-of-the-Union speech, and the word quickly gained wide use because it was kinder sounding than its alternatives, including "backward." By the 1960s, the collective group of underdeveloped countries came to be referred to as the "Third World," a translation of the French *Tiers Monde*, a phrase used by French Premier Charles de Gaulle in 1948 to refer to the body of new nations aligned with neither the Soviet Union nor the United States. Eventually, however, "Third World" took on a pejorative connotation and development experts began shying away from referring to the "underdeveloped" or even "less-developed" world because the terms focus on what nations are not rather than on what they are. So, most recently, the world's poorer nations (which, incidentally, are sometimes referred to as "The South" or "The Global South" because most of them are south of the world's richest nations, which lie almost solely in the Northern Hemisphere) are referred to as "developing nations," even though many are not developing at a rate worthy of remark.

Oxford English Dictionary Online, 2d ed. (Oxford: Oxford University Press, 2003).

groups—Greeks, Romans, Bantu-speaking Africans, Muslims, Mongols, Vikings, East Asians—brought together people through conquest, new means of transportation, and growing trade. Integration broadened further with the exploits of Europeans after 1450. New technologies of shipbuilding and navigation eventually made possible human interaction on a scale surpassing anything yet known. By the start of the seventeenth century, people living on both sides of the Atlantic Ocean, on the one hand, and all around the Indian Ocean and China Sea, on the other, were involved in economic and social interaction that affected the lives of millions of people inhabiting parts of five continents. This interaction would only increase in scope and intensity in the ensuing centuries. There is little doubt about the emerging consensus: the roots of globalization run deep.[5]

World Systems

Immanuel Wallerstein early on recognized the political-economic aspect of globalization and offered a framework for understanding its importance in the human history of the last half millennium. In *The Modern World-System* (1974, 1980, 1988),[6] Wallerstein established a model for explaining how the world has come to be as it is today. This model rests on the rise of capitalism in Europe in the fifteenth and sixteenth centuries and the establishment of a Western-dominated capitalist economy involving people from all parts of the world in unequal relationships. According to Wallerstein, this "modern world system" remains in place, albeit with some structural change and "increasing instability." Several others have stretched Wallerstein's model to fit earlier periods and smaller "worlds."[7] For this book, an informed acquaintance with basic elements of world-systems theory, as an aspect of globalization's history, is useful for understanding the central argument—that events of a global scale affected the lives of people in a very small place in Africa for a very long time, and still do.

World Systems Based on Economic Relationships: The Standard Model

Through much of human history, groups of people have interacted with others some distance away through trade.[8] What they traded, primarily, were goods each produced that the other did not, or did not produce so well, or produced equally well but at much greater cost. The meeting places for exchange usually were towns or cities. Eventually, some of the trade goods were carried on to other sites, sometimes in other cultures, where they, in turn, were exchanged for products from elsewhere. Over time, those interacting in such economic arrangements came to exchange ideas and ways of doing things as well.

In some places these relationships became regular, systematic patterns of economic and cultural interchange—a form of interaction that lasted for long periods. Historians and others have come to call these broad and lasting patterns of exchange "economic complexes," "economic systems," "world economies," or, from Wallerstein's lead, "world systems." It is important to recognize that they were called *world* systems not necessarily because they involved people over the entire world—indeed, only the world system in place since the sixteenth century has done so—but because they involved people living in separate political units beyond the recognized boundaries of states, beyond empires, or even beyond what we have tended to call civilizations.

Why is it important to recognize the existence of past world systems? Simply because the way societies in different areas were involved in a world system determined much about how individuals in that society lived. In most world systems, relationships among the various involved groups were not equal. Some areas of competing cities or states slowly grew into more central, or "core," positions in the network by becoming particularly efficient producers, efficient users of resources, and effective accumulators of wealth. The core areas tended to grow strong politically and militarily, too. Other areas tended to remain in less central, or "peripheral," positions by becoming more suppliers of unprocessed resources to, and acquirers of processed goods from, the core or cores.[9] Indeed, one of the glaring ironies of such economic relationships is that groups on the periphery often found themselves trading for processed goods made from their own raw resources. In addition, peripheral areas remained weak politically and economically. Such wealth that people in the peripheral areas possessed tended to flow toward the core areas. The dissimilarities in production, labor, power, and wealth meant that persons living in core and peripheral areas of a world system lived differently: those in the core generally lived better in terms of material goods, security, and personal welfare than those on the periphery.

Such political-economic relationships often were long standing because the groups involved, especially on the periphery, were more or less trapped in them—not so much by deceit, stealth, or raw power as by circumstances. It was to the core areas' advantage to maintain their strong, central economic positions, so they tended to take what measures they could to do so. These might involve using their military to keep trade routes open or sending managers or advisors out to the peripheral areas to make more efficient the production of primary products. The circumstances, with wealth and resources flowing to the core, enabled the core areas to act in such a manner. On the periphery, the slow growth of production for the core areas became institutionalized. People who once put their efforts toward tasks vital to their own group's survival—food, tool, or clothing production—found themselves working to produce raw resources for the core and then obtaining food, tools, or clothing via trade with the core. The dependency for vital products made it difficult to quit. Abrupt alteration of the relationship was likely to lead to economic, social, and political problems—everything from hunger and starvation to social upheaval and political turmoil. For their well-being and even their survival, many on the periphery grew dependent on the relationship with the core.

As with most political or economic theories, one can take such generalizations to an unwarranted extreme. All people in the same locale did not necessarily have

similar living conditions, world systems notwithstanding, and there was uneven incorporation of people across the expanse of any world system. In addition, as recent
events in The Gambia show so well, relationships with the world system are not
behind all continuity and every facet of change.[10] Still, most of those living within
the loosely defined boundaries of a world system had their ways of life affected by
the relationships involved with the patterns of exchange. So, understanding these
relationships helps one understand much about how and why people lived as they
did in a particular place and time.

World Systems Based on Cultural Relationships: The Islamic Variant

In their application of world-systems theory, scholars have not always adhered
strictly to Wallerstein's outline, and as a result, useful variants of the theory have
appeared. Some include elements of the cultural diffusion model. One that is
relevant to this study comes from historians of Islam, who are in the best position
to recognize the overemphasis of Western civilization in historical study and who
smart over the past dismissal of Islamic history as something "Oriental" and thus
less important in global matters. Some of these historians believe that after the
thirteenth century, Muslims created their own kind of world system. According
to Richard M. Eaton, the Muslim world system did not link people through commercial relationships, but through "shared understandings of how to see the world
and structure one's relationship to it." Based on Muhammad's words in the Qur'an
and subsequent interpretations on how to build a religious community, Muslims
from West Africa to Southeast Asia were drawn together in their efforts to follow
the law on earth and make it possible to gain access to paradise after life.[11]

Muhammad had in mind a religious state and society based on law wherein a
person could readily achieve salvation through doing God's will. To clarify and
set out the law, a group of clerics studied and wrote for two centuries after the
Prophet's death, so that by the tenth century a largely agreed-upon body of law, the
Sharîa, was in existence. Further interpretation of the law fell to learned men, most
of whom lived in Islam's great central cities: Baghdad, Damascus, or Cairo. Their
interpretations tended to be conservative and the religious practice they authorized,
while conforming to their literate culture, had less appeal for Muslims outside the
urban centers of the Middle East. Eventually, a number of scholars found ways to
give Islam wider appeal through the growing popularity of religious practice that
emphasized Islam's spiritual and mystical dimensions. Such practice came to be
called *sufism*.

Incorporating the likes of saints, shrines, spirits, dreams, altered states of
consciousness, emotional frenzy, and ecstatic worship, *sufism* held appeal for the
less educated and could accommodate aspects of people's pre-Islamic religious
practices. Such worship made it easier for nonbelievers to enter the realm of Islam.
Sufi leaders, called *shayks*, formed brotherhoods, which used their own litany and
unique forms of worship. Some brotherhoods grew and spread widely with the

leader's popularity. One, the Qadiriyya, named after its founder, 'Abd al-Qādir, a twelfth-century Baghdad scholar, expanded around the Middle East and through North and West Africa; others had large numbers of adherents, too. In time these brotherhoods became the primary vehicles for spreading Islam beyond the large empires closer to the heart of the Muslim world.

Shayks and their followers spread their ideas mainly through travel and personal contact. These religious leaders came from a peripatetic tradition. Muhammad, himself a widely traveled merchant, had told the faithful they must "Journey in the land, then behold how He originated creation." Muslim scholars ever after took him at his word, and their traveling, whether to trade or teach or learn or perform religious pilgrimage, brought continuity to the vast realm of Islam. Eaton shows that in the fourteenth century, Ibn Battuta, the Moroccan who crossed seventy-odd thousand miles of Africa, the Middle East, central Asia, Southeast Asia, and China, "moved through a single cultural universe in which he was utterly at home" and "intuitively understood that the Muslim world of his day constituted a truly global civilization." The Islamic community of today may be divided into competing nation-states, but that is a function of recent history and is, as Eaton argues, "fundamentally hostile to the Islamic vision of the *umma*, the community of believers, the 'abode of Islam.'"[12] Even more than today, West African Muslims of several centuries ago believed themselves to be part of a vast community, an *intellectual* world system stretching across the desert they knew and into lands they could barely imagine, held together by scholars and saints and mystics and jurists and common folk all praying toward the same central shrine and living by the same law, parts of which they memorized in the same language. For this world system, economic unity was a factor, but not the major one. It was spiritual unity as much as anything that tied together peoples of the Muslim realm across the Afro-Eurasian landmass.

Restructuring World Systems

A valuable exercise for understanding general patterns in world history is to chart the progression of world systems over time. Several people have done so; one has identified thirteen world systems in existence before the rise of the "modern Central Civilization" in 1500 B.C.[13]; others count fewer. Naturally, such examinations never can be as precise as historians would like, because world systems are not established formally and given names. Also, world systems do not "rise" and "fall" as we commonly think when considering the history of nations, empires, or civilizations. Instead, as historian Janet L. Abu-Lughod argues, world systems evolve and sometimes restructure: "they rise when integration increases and they decline when connections along older pathways decay. . . . [W]hen the vigor of a given dynamic of integration dissipates . . . , the old parts live on and become the materials out of which restructuring develops, just as the earlier system inherited . . . a set of partially organized subsystems. By definition, such restructuring is said to occur when *players who were formerly peripheral* began to occupy more powerful positions in the system and when *geographic zones formerly marginal to intense interactions* become foci and even control centers of such interchanges."[14]

In recent decades we have witnessed a partial restructuring of the modern world system: Countries that once were core areas of capital, industry, and wealth— Great Britain and France, for instance—have become less important in the world economy, while countries once on the periphery, around the Pacific Rim, have become efficient producers of goods. World capital is flowing toward these emerging countries, their governments have the means to assert themselves more forcefully in internal matters and international affairs, and the ways of life of people living there are changing.

But this is a digression to modern times. According to some theorists, for the last several thousand years, world systems have been appearing, thriving, and restructuring. Generations of people in Europe, Africa, Asia, and the Americas lived better or worse lives depending in large part on how they were involved, at what time, in one or another of these large-scale economic complexes. One of those complexes, the biggest to its time, is a point of beginning for this study.

The World System of the Old World Before A.D. 1446

Historians, sociologists, anthropologists, archaeologists, and others have identified the existence of world systems of varying size and scope far into the past. Ancient Rome was part of an economic system, for example, that extended from modern England and Spain in the west to Mesopotamia and Egypt in the east and included all lands bordering the Mediterranean. Mesopotamia was in indirect commercial contact with China, India, Southeast Asia, and Africa's east coast. Even West Africa was connected via irregular trans-Sahara traders. Across thousands of miles of dusty Asian steppes, monsoon-blown waters of Asian oceans and seas, or balmy stretches of the Mediterranean, people passed goods and ideas back and forth in regular, perhaps even systematic, fashion. Rome's decline after the fourth century A.D. cut western regions from the system, but east and south of Europe a world system continued to operate.

The growth of this world system for a period after the mid-seventh century is related to the expansion of the Muslim world. Islam is a monotheistic religion, influenced heavily by Judaism, that evolved in the Middle East for several centuries before the time of Muhammad.[15] Over the century following Muhammad's death in A.D. 632, Muslim Arabs poured out of their homelands and conquered most of the Middle East, North Africa, and the Iberian Peninsula. Early in the eighth century, Muslim armies followed across the trade routes of central Asia and swept down into northern India, where they fought to establish themselves as purveyors of the fineries of the East. By the ninth century, Arab and Persian sailors were coming into direct contact with East Africa, India, Southeast Asia, and even China. The result was dramatic. The Muslim world, stretching from northwest Africa to India, was tied into a vast commercial complex that included the Pacific Rim. East Asian

23

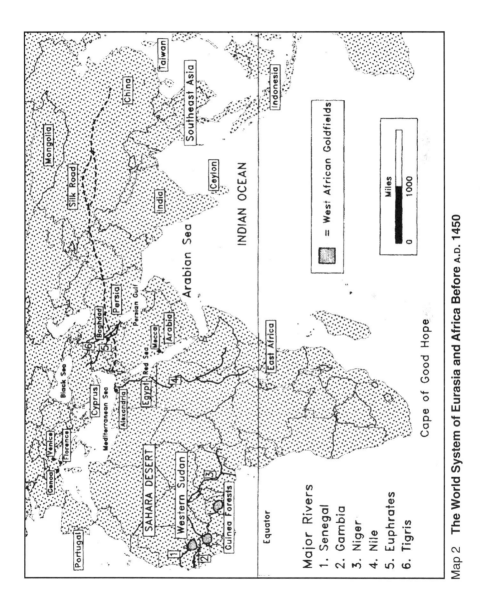

Map 2 **The World System of Eurasia and Africa Before A.D. 1450**

goods flowed westward in unprecedented amounts; East African goods moved north and eastward. A Persian geographer, al-Muqadassi, listed items one could obtain just prior to A.D. 1000 in Oman at the eastern tip of the Arabian Peninsula: drugs, perfumes, saffron, teakwood, ivory, pearls, onyx, rubies, ebony, sugar, aloes, iron, lead, canes, earthenware, sandalwood, glass, and pepper. Nearly every one of these commodities came to Arabia through the thriving Indian Ocean-East Asian-East African trade.[16]

To finance this commercial expansion and efforts at collateral political consolidation, Muslims needed bullion. They found it south of the Sahara Desert, in the gold deposits of Africa's western savannas; in gaining access to this gold in the eighth and ninth centuries, Muslim merchants established firmly the previously tenuous links that tied West Africa into the growing world system.[17] A trickle of trans-Sahara trade, with indirect commercial connections between the populated savannas of West Africa and the plains of North Africa, probably predated the Roman Empire, but such trade grew in the fourth century A.D. with the introduction of camels among North Africa's Berber population. Camels quickly replaced horses and pack oxen to become veritable ships of the desert, voyaging from oasis to oasis under the guidance of Berber masters, carrying slabs of salt from mines on the desert's north side to the continually salt-starved inhabitants of the savannas, along with dates, figs, woven cloth, and copper articles. They returned northward with gold, which West Africa had in greater supply than anywhere else in reach of the world system of the time, and also kola nuts, a popular stimulant from the Guinea forests, and ivory. Slaves usually accompanied the northward treks for sale in North Africa or the eastern Mediterranean. West Africa thus supplied a good part of the bullion that oiled the pre-Islamic commercial mechanisms between the Mediterranean and China. The Islamic stimulus to the trade across Eurasia increased the importance of the West Africa link and led to cultural transferrals back and forth across the desert accompanying the products of trade. This connection to the large economic system had important political and economic effects for the West Africans who were involved.

Interested parties could argue over which area or areas were cores of this world system. One could build a strong case for the Middle East–India corridor, where prior to A.D. 1000, Muslims controlled much of the international exchange that took place. Another could weigh China's growing land and sea connections with the world to its west and south after the end of the first millennium, in company with Southeast Asia's increasing involvement with the carrying trade of the East Indies, to argue that a restructuring was under way by the eleventh century and that eastern regions were more central to the system for several centuries thereafter.[18]

One thing seems more certain, however: before A.D. 1000, Europe was not a core in any economic network. When thinking of the vast Eurasian world system of the time, some of the isolated reaches of northern and Western Europe were barely peripheral. Through the several centuries when residents of these regions were tied to a narrow existence on the feudal manor, a network of economic inter-action existed from the southern and eastern rims of the Mediterranean, across the Sahara, down the East African coast, and over the expanse of central and eastern Asia that brought a material and cultural fullness to the lives of urban dwellers and the occasional lord of a manor. Northern and western Europeans were far removed from the commercial and cultural centers of this vast and thriving system.

Over the next several centuries, this situation would change. The world system that incorporated central parts of the Old World continued to grow after A.D. 1000. Across much of the central Eurasian landmass and extending to West and East Africa, production of agricultural and manufactured goods increased, short-distance trade continued to bustle, and long-distance trade grew, involving more merchants from different parts of the Old World. Growing in importance with the central Asian land trade was that of the Indian Ocean complex, which connected East Africa, the Red Sea and Persian Gulf, India, Malaysia, and China into one vast commercial network of production and exchange. The steady monsoon winds that reversed direction semiannually facilitated travel by sail across the system. Well known are the great voyages under the direction of Chinese mariner Zheng He that reached coastal East Africa early in the fourteenth century. But Arab, Persian, Indian, and Indonesian vessels operated across various parts of the network as well, and a peaceful coexistence enabled waterborne trade to pass back and forth in this grand operation.[19]

Abu-Lughod believes that this early Old World commercial system, with China, India, and central parts of the Muslim Middle East as core areas, reached its peak around A.D. 1300 and then began to restructure. "Indeed," she writes, "the century between A.D. 1250 and 1350 clearly seemed to constitute a crucial turning point in world history, a moment when the balance between East and West could have tipped in either direction. In terms of space, the Middle East heartland that linked the eastern Mediterranean with the Indian Ocean constituted a geographic fulcrum on which East and West were then roughly balanced."[20]

As we know, the balance eventually would tip toward the West. Slowly, the world system restructured after the middle of the fourteenth century, leading to the central-ity of Western Europe, by the sixteenth century, in a system that was expanding to include the continents of the New World as well as more parts of the old.

Western Europe in a Restructuring World System

It is not possible to point to a specific date when Western Europe began to move out of its provincial narrowness and become a more active participant in the globaliza-tion process. The long, slow movement of such activity probably began in the ninth century A.D. and became much more noticeable some time in the eleventh. By the fourteenth century, Western Europe was very different indeed: it was participating fully, and nearly equally, in the economic complex that spread goods and ideas across central parts of the Old World.[21]

Rising Western Europe

Here and there, even before A.D. 1000, venturesome European seamen began to sail farther from their ports, to come into contact with others from some distance away, and to exchange products to their advantage. European trade in the Baltic and North seas connected the Low Countries and northern Germany with the British Isles. To the south, growing numbers of Italian seamen were spreading across the eastern Mediterranean, meeting again with Byzantine and Muslim merchants, elbowing their way into the trade of the region. By the eleventh century, Venetian merchants were carrying a portion of Byzantium's seaborne trade.

The earliest Crusades, the drawn-out Christian efforts to recapture the Holy Lands from the Muslims that began at the end of the eleventh century, heightened European interest in the eastern Mediterranean and beyond.[22] The first part of the 1100s saw the appearance of a string of European crusader kingdoms—small city-states along the eastern Mediterranean coast—where enterprising Italians began producing foodstuffs and other marketable commodities to exchange for items that were available, through indirect contact, from East Asia. Europeans were awed by the products: spices were the main item—several hundred different flavors and scents that Europeans soon craved to enhance their almost tasteless cereals and often rancid meats—but there were also silk and cotton cloth, porcelain, cutlery, precious stones, and other luxury goods that European lords of the land and successful squires believed their due.

Yet, there was little future in relying on crusaders' booty as a source for these commodities. Northern and western Europeans recognized that if they wanted the luxuries, they would have to produce something in demand for the eastern Mediterranean and Middle Eastern market. So, ever slowly, but noticeably by the end of the twelfth century, people in parts of Western Europe were growing crops or mining metals or cutting trees or weaving woolens that could be traded south and eastward to Italian merchants, to the crusader states, or to anyone else who could provide access to the luxury products in demand.

The increasing trade stimulated Europeans to greater internal change. On the European manor, new events and activities were evident: a growing peasant population, the clearing of more land, and the production of more agricultural goods than the manor's population could consume. Lords acquired surplus foodstuffs and exchanged them at crossroads, which grew into towns. By the 1100s, commercial fairs dotted some areas of the European landscape; by the 1200s, the towns were centers of bustling market exchange and craft production; by the 1300s, the craft production was becoming more like small-scale industrial activity and urban merchants were casting their eyes further afield for commercial opportunities. As the Mongolian peace spread across central Asia in the fourteenth century, much of Europe was tied into the major commercial system of the Old World. Participation in the system was important in determining economic, social, and material aspects of their lives.[23]

Connecting the commercial and manufacturing centers of northwestern Europe with the markets of the eastern Mediterranean and beyond were the fleets of the great medieval Italian port cities: Genoa and Venice. These cities benefited greatly from the Crusades, carrying goods and supplies for the armies, trading for booty, and, in time, broadening their commercial activities into the Red and Black seas. By the time Muslims had retaken the last European crusader kingdom at the end of the thirteenth century, sailors from Italian ports were carrying a good part of the Mediterranean trade and venturing beyond Constantinople in an effort to get closer to the goods from the eastern markets. Back in the Italian cities, new methods of consolidating capital, both public and private, were behind financing of shipbuilding and trade. Abu-Lughod describes Genoa and Venice as "*almost* capitalist by the thirteenth century," and notes that "[i]n Marco Polo's Venice virtually every 'dandy' in the city had money invested in ships at sea."[24]

Fourteenth-Century Setback

Northern and Western Europe were on the political and economic rise at the start of the fourteenth century. Perhaps Europeans would have ventured earlier into the Atlantic, on their way to direct contact with West Africa and East Asia, had it not been for a series of economic and demographic setbacks they experienced in the difficult 1300s. At the root of these was the Black Death, which between 1348 and the end of the century carried off one-third to one-half of Europe's population.

It is ironic that Europe's economic woes and, in fact, its disastrous encounters with the Black Death came about in large part because of its participation in the existing world system.[25] Prosperity throughout the system rested on the efficient movement of goods across the entire network. When connections to an important part or parts broke down, the system declined. This seems to be what happened with the onset of the Black Death, the flea- and rat-transmitted bubonic plague that spread across the Eurasian landmass after 1330, killing without discrimination. From southwest China in the 1330s, the Black Death spread with Mongol horsemen, whose mounts carried infected fleas, across the steppes of central Asia to the shores of the Black Sea. There, rats carried fleas aboard ships bound for the resurgent Italian ports in the mid-1340s, and the disease then spread up trade paths through central and Western Europe by midcentury. Mongol unity in central Asia fell apart, and without the order that the Khan's army provided, goods ceased traveling smoothly across the Silk Road. The sea link to Southeast Asia and China continued to function—albeit with interruptions caused by individualized outbreaks of the Black Death—and Venetian merchants traded through Egypt and the Red Sea to India, but the spread of merchandise across the Indian Ocean from Southeast Asia fluctuated by decades. There was a brief resurgence of trade from China along the southern sea route, when the new Ming government took momentary interest in external trade, but following the dramatic voyages of Chinese fleets into and across the Indian Ocean to East Africa between 1403 and 1430, the Ming rulers decided that external contact was not for them.[26] Neither Arabs nor Indians were strong enough to fill the void the Chinese left. So there was, writes Abu-Lughod, a "Fall of the East" in the early fifteenth century that preceded, and was important in, the "Rise of the West."[27]

The Lure to Expand

Yet, there were difficulties in continental Europe that were separate from those caused by the Black Death or the fall of the East.[28] Agricultural productivity declined soon after 1300, the result of climate change, land exhaustion, and technological stagnation. Europeans needed new sources of food, new fishing grounds, new stands of timber for shipbuilding and other construction. Some historians argue, too, that lords of the European manor had reached the limit of their ability to extract surplus production from their serfs and that the serfs, or European peasants generally, were therefore becoming disruptive. Related to these difficulties was the ever-growing European need for bullion to finance the eastern trade. Muslims continued to have monopolistic access to West Africa's gold. Some Europeans began to wonder if expansion away from the continent, into new lands where agents of European lords could produce cheap foodstuffs, fuels, and new surpluses, might solve these problems. Such expansion might indeed enable Europeans to outflank the Muslims and get direct access to the West African gold—and maybe even the luxuries from the East. To some economically depressed Europeans of the fifteenth century, expansion loomed as their main hope for economic and social salvation.

Another kind of salvation brought Europeans by the 1400s to want to expand into new lands.[29] European Christians had been fighting Muslims for over half a millennium. The last crusader kingdom fell to Muslim advances in 1291, but that hardly signaled the end of Christians' desire to take on the infidel. Rumors of a Christian prince, Prester John, thought to possess a formidable force but to be surrounded and beleaguered by Muslims out in the lands beyond, fueled a general European desire to find new fields whereupon to resume the battle. A Christian missionary zeal that had been growing since the thirteenth century added strength to the religious motive for expansion.

So as the fifteenth century dawned—as the worst devastation of the plague faded into the past and Europe's population and economy slowly began to recover, and as the eastern realms of the Old World's commercial system were sending trade goods westward at irregular times, in insufficient amounts, and at high prices—kings and princes and lords and persons of means on the western side of Europe were wondering how they might get away from it all, literally, and find new lands to help bring about their economic, social, and spiritual recovery.

Portuguese Expansion Into the Atlantic

Well positioned to lead this effort were the Portuguese.[30] There has long been a notion that Portugal was always poor and backward, and that it was mainly Dom

Henrique ("Henry the Navigator" of many Western texts), a brother of Portugal's king, possessing funds from a wealthy religious order and a crusading and exploring spirit, who brought Portuguese and Italian seamen to make the discoveries that opened the Atlantic and soon the world to European commercial contact. But there is much more than Henry's activities behind the Portuguese maritime ventures of the fifteenth century. Portugal had finished winning back its lands from the Moors in 1249. Since then, Portuguese seamen had been ranging wide in their quest for trade—to Flanders and Ireland in the north, to the Canary Islands and the northwest African coast in the south. Supporting this quest after 1385 was a new dynasty of Portuguese rulers and a landed aristocracy ready and able to fight for glory, God, or loot. When it became clear by 1400 that Venice was in control of the trade of the eastern Mediterranean (and thus access to the products from the East) and able to prevent the participation of others, Genoese and Florentines looked west and brought their sailing know-how and mercantile instincts to the cities of coastal Spain and Portugal. All the elements that made up the commercial community of such ports as Lisbon in the fifteenth century hoped they could find a way to outflank Muslims and Venetians, who held the keys to the doors of African gold and Asian luxury goods.

But such outflanking was out of the question as long as the maritime technology and navigational wisdom available to Mediterranean and northern European mariners limited their ability to sail down Africa's west coast and return home.[31] Winds and currents were the root of the problem. Strong northeasterly winds blow steadily down from Morocco to Cape Verde, and the Canary current flows briskly in the same direction. Vessels could leave Portugal and sail down Africa's northwest coast with relative ease, but beyond a certain point not far into the voyage, returning home was nearly impossible. The square-rigged vessels could not sail close enough to the wind to allow them to make headway against the current. Sailors needed more maneuverable ships that were rigged differently and more knowledge of the Atlantic winds; without both, they were on a European tether.

Prince Henry did not single-handedly bring about a revolution in shipbuilding and ocean navigation. Instead, he played a small, but significant, role in bringing along the steady compilation of knowledge of construction, guidance, and mapmaking that had been going on for several centuries. Italian sailors, who had been in contact with seafarers in Europe's northern seas for over a century and knew also of such Muslim maritime advances as the triangular lateen sail, added to the effort to build more maneuverable ships that could haul bulkier cargo.[32] Equipped with the increasingly popular caravels, which sported lateen sails along with the traditional square rigs to allow for easier maneuvering and closer sailing to the winds, Portuguese sailors began venturing farther down the western coast of Africa. To return against wind and current, they had to make long and laborious tacks that took advantage of slight changes in wind direction, on and off shore, between morning and evening. In this fashion they sailed to Madeira in 1420, past Cape Bojador in 1434 and Cape Blanco in 1441. Arguim Island, just south of Cape

Blanco, quickly became a Portuguese base for fishing fleets and coastal traders, who were able to acquire enough gold and slaves to keep their attention. Then, in quick succession, Portuguese mariners passed the Senegal River in 1444 and Cape Verde a year later. Not long afterward, an unknown Portuguese captain discovered that he could leave the latitude of Cape Verde on a long northwesterly tack toward the Azores, and there pick up the strong trade winds blowing from the west that would bring him back toward continental Europe. It was a discovery as important as any for increasing contact among the world's humanity. From the middle of the fifteenth century, the south Atlantic and, essentially, all of the remaining oceans of the world were open to European shipping.

It was in this context that, in the summer of 1446, as part of a leapfrogging line of Portuguese adventurers advancing down Africa's west coast, Nuno Tristão sailed his caravel into the broad mouth of the Gambia River. As far as he knew, no European seaman had ever sailed that far southward and returned to tell of it. One can think of long-range ideals of reaching the Indies, finding beleaguered Christians, or tapping into West Africa's supply of gold, but goals of a more immediate nature drove men like Tristão.[33] As his predecessors had done, Tristão was intent on capturing Africans and taking them back to Portugal. Some could provide information on trade or belabored Christians, some could learn Portuguese and serve as interpreters on future voyages, and all could be put to work serving Portuguese lords or cutting cane on the expanding sugar plantations around the Mediterranean. Though he had no reason to be surprised by either fact, Tristão was probably not aware of the existence of the state of Niumi at the Gambia's mouth, nor of its relationship to the regional system of West Africa that connected, across the Sahara Desert, into the grand commercial complex of the Old World. That may be why, when he spied habitations on the river's south bank, he mistakenly believed he had easy picking.

West Africa in a Restructuring World System

The trans-Sahara trade, which had existed in the distant past in indirect form and had grown in volume and efficiency with the introduction of the camel in the fourth century A.D., received a new stimulus with the Muslim conquest of North Africa early in the eighth century. Muslim traders tied West Africa to the thriving economic complex that fanned out from the eastern Mediterranean. This alone brought a sharp rise in demand for sub-Saharan products. Then, as the world system grew in strength into medieval times, so did demand—especially for gold, the product needed for coinage and eventual shipment to India to pay for the spices and silks entering the Mediterranean trade, but also for slaves and lesser amounts of ivory and kola nuts. Export of gold from West Africa seems to have peaked at an annual average of considerably more than a ton in the thirteenth or fourteenth centuries.[34] It was the driving engine of the trade northward across the desert, just as salt occupied the same place for the caravans trekking south.

Islam's Movement Into West Africa

As Sijilmasa and other commercial centers developed on the Sahara's northern fringe, the Sanhaja Berbers, who inhabited such places and from there controlled desert trading, began to pay more heed to the Arabs' Islamic religion. By the tenth century nearly all Berbers were familiar with the religion's tenets, and many Sanhaja considered themselves part of the larger brotherhood of Islam. It was thus with Berber merchants at the head of camel caravans that Islam crossed the Sahara to the more heavily populated regions of West Africa's sahel and savanna.

As is often the case, the long-distance traders brought more than commodities intended for exchange. Once Arabs had conquered eastward and opened the door to extensive contact with India in the eighth century, they brought to the Middle East a host of agricultural products the likes of which people in the western half of the Old World never had seen. These included citrus fruits, eggplant, and watermelon, but also cotton. Production of the latter spread westward across North Africa, and then the idea of cotton cultivation, cottonseeds, and techniques of spinning and weaving passed southward across the Sahara with Berber caravans. In the heat of tropical West Africa, cotton cloth became a prized commodity. Between the upper Senegal and upper Niger rivers in particular, cotton production and weaving grew to be important segments of the regional economy by the tenth century.[35]

The Islam that crossed the Sahara was a far cry from the Sunni, or orthodox, Islam settled on generally by the learned followers of Muhammad after his death. Berbers seldom paid heed to orthodoxy of any kind, and they tended to prefer heretical versions of the Islamic faith that allowed for more emotional religious practice and inclusion of more local, pre-Islamic rites. This boded well for conversion of the masses in West Africa, for across the grasslands below the Sahara, people were involved in spiritual forces and the supernatural.

Yet throughout that area, peasants clung to animist practices and the veneration of ancestors that tied them to their land. The earliest West African converts to Islam and the ones who acted most effectively to spread the religion across the lands of their travels below the Sahara were itinerant traders, called wangara or jula. Detached from the peasant villages of their ancestors and thus not tied to spirits of the soil or local deities as were sedentary farmers, these merchants, like their Berber contacts before them, recognized the value that the sense of Islamic community provided them with fellow traders and among strangers in foreign lands. As they obtained trade goods from Berber caravans at cities serving as ports along the southern edge of the desert and then spread the goods with donkey and human caravans, they created a sophisticated commercial complex that stretched from the western Atlantic coast below the Sahara, eastward across the expanse of what Arabs called *Bilād al-Sūdān*—"the land of the blacks."

For a time these West African Muslims must have considered themselves on the distant periphery of the larger Islamic political and cultural realm. The militant Almoravid movement that swept many nonbelievers and loose practitioners before

32

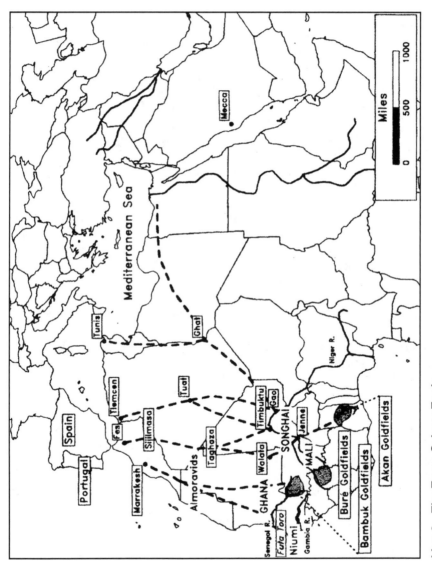

Map 3   The Trans-Sahara Trade

its armies in the eleventh and twelfth centuries was largely a Berber initiative with a focus on Morocco and Spain. Moreover, no matter what was going on among nominal Muslims as distant as sub-Saharan Africa in the west and the Indian sub-continent in the east, the political and cultural center of the Islamic world remained in Baghdad, where Arab culture held sway and Abbasid caliphs (successors of the Prophet) attempted to guide the vast Islamic state. But the once-great caliphate lost power and influence through the twelfth and thirteenth centuries, and the Mongol sack of Baghdad in 1258 effectively ended the political centralization of the world-wide Muslim community. What happened with Muslim civilization thereafter was not the steady decline that Western scholars long have pictured, however. With political fragmentation came a rapid cultural fluorescence and a slower but more steady spread of spiritual unity among Muslims. Those instrumental in this steadily growing and unifying Islamic identity were scholars and mystics, who, according to Eaton, "elaborated an immense corpus of rituals, dogmas, legal structures, social forms, mystical traditions, modes of piety, aesthetic sensitivities, styles of scholarship, and schools of philosophy that collectively defined and stabilized the very core and substance of Islamic civilization."[36]

For sub-Saharan West Africa, the process of Islam's spreading, gaining cohesiveness, and thereby tying the northern parts of the region into the greater Islamic world was long and fitful. It is indeed one of the fundamental themes of the history of West Africa north of the Guinea forests. Here and there, where trade routes crossed or exchange was particularly brisk, the itinerant Muslim traders sometimes settled separate villages. In such villages they supervised trade in the dry season of the year and set up practices of Islamic scholarship, teaching, mysticism, and healing through the months of the rains. Some members or branches of large families might eventually specialize in commerce, while others concentrated on divination, charm making, and healing. In this area Muslims had advantages over African practitioners of traditional magic and the supernatural, for the Muslims were inheritors of Indian, Iranian, and Greek systems of astronomy and mathematics. Their astute combination of science, numerology, astronomy, and aesthetic mysticism gave many Muslims deserved reputations as the best at their work.[37]

And there were practical advantages associated with the combination of trade and scholarship. Both traders and teachers could acquire slaves who could work their farms and provide for their families and passing caravans. Young Muslim scholars did agricultural work for their teachers, too. Enclave, Islamic-commercial villages operating in this fashion spread steadily throughout West Africa's savannas. They would be the nodes from which Islam, in later centuries, would spread or be assimilated by Africans from a variety of cultures and traditions.

State-Building in West Africa

The planting of an Islamic seed that would sprout and grow for a millennium was just one effect of the desert trade. As the commerce expanded through the

Photo 1   **The Great Mosque of Djenne, Mali, on the site of a mosque constructed in the thirteenth century.**

latter centuries of the first millennium A.D., and as the number and intensity of pastoralist raids on settled communities along the sahel and adjacent savannas increased, people south of the desert recognized a need to organize themselves in larger and stronger political units. Groups of agricultural people speaking one of the Mande languages and living in the heart of the savanna trading country between the upper Senegal and upper Niger rivers—whose basic unit of social and political organization and identity long had been the village of a few hundred to a few thousand inhabitants with its hinterland—began to combine their resources to protect themselves from raids and to enable them to control and tax the passing commerce.[38] The slow, gradual transition to political organization beyond the village level had been occurring as a reaction to necessity for a long time—back to the time of the introduction of the camel or perhaps even earlier. By the eighth century, an Arab geographer in Baghdad was writing about the territory of Ghana below the Sahara as "the land of gold," and by the tenth or eleventh century it is apparent that many Mande-speaking people were organized in states of varying size and complexity. The smallest and simplest consisted of handfuls of villages with the leading lineage of one providing the head of state; the largest was indeed Ghana, which held authority through much of the eleventh century and possibly longer over people occupying several thousand square miles of desert, sahel, and savanna.

After A.D. 1100, several things occurred that would change the focus of power in the western savannas. First was the onset of a long period of decreasing rainfall, which eventually made the existing sahel uninhabitable and forced herders and farmers to move south toward better-watered lands.[39] Also, by the thirteenth century, the Bambuk goldfields between the upper Senegal and Faleme rivers, long the major source for the trans-Sahara trade, were less productive, to be replaced by those of the Buré area, south and a little east, on the upper Niger. By the same time, aided by the dry period that reduced ground cover and forced tsetse flies southward, speakers of Mandinka, the mother tongue of the Mande languages, living along the upper Niger and its tributaries, found it possible to breed horses in number. Mandinka horsemen perfected tactics of cavalry warfare and the lightning-swift raid. Under the leadership of the great folk hero Sunjata, in the 1220s, Mandinka horsemen overcame the successors of Ghana and established the Mali Empire, greater still in the wealth and prestige of its rulers and the extent of its political and economic control.[40]

The Mali Empire

Regardless of its size—village, small state, or grand empire—at the center of a Mandinka political unit was a ruling lineage, or lineages, that were wealthy, powerful, and prestigious beyond all others. The ruler of a Mandinka state was a *mansa*, head of the lineage in power. It was the role of a *mansa* to settle disputes between lineages or villages, coordinate planting and harvesting, oversee relations with traders and other strangers, intercede with the ancestors or spirits of the land for the good of the living community, and organize forces for the state's protection and deal with matters related to warfare such as booty and captives.

Expenses of running such a state were considerable. To perform all of his functions efficiently, a *mansa* needed a large court establishment: a body of men who saw to it that state policies were executed and that the state was policed and defended. Taken away from normal tasks of food production, these specialized individuals had to be fed. Armies also needed weapons, supernatural protections that adorned each soldier and his mount and weapons, and horses, which required care, fodder, and tack. Also, as representatives of the state, the *mansa*, his court, and members of the royal lineage expected to enjoy a higher style of living than the rest of the population. This came mainly through access to luxury goods—various fineries of clothing and jewelry, alcohol, handsome saddlery, tasty foods—many of which were not produced locally but had to be obtained from outside.[41]

The *mansa* had basic ways to meet these expenses. One was to take a portion of the produce of the nonroyal lineages. As any taxing of a state's populace, this had obvious limits, so ruling families often established their own farms, worked at times by a draft of labor from the state's population, but more frequently by slaves, to provide food and fodder. Royal slaves also produced trade goods, especially woven cloth. Such slaves were usually captives from state warfare or organized raids. When such activity was frequent and successful, the *mansa* increased his wealth by selling or trading some of the captives.

Taxing trade was the other important element in financing the state. Rulers levied tolls on caravans and taxed commercial transactions in markets. Wise rulers understood that they could greatly increase their revenues by stimulating trade in lands under their control or by gaining control of areas where trade was already flourishing. Indeed, the latter seems to be what Mandinka lineages did from villages on the upper Niger in the early thirteenth century: They conquered and gained control of some of the most commercially important areas of West Africa, with active trade routes leading to and from the Sahara and passing horizontally across the western Sudan. They then set up rulers in these areas who would be loyal, assessed payments of tribute on the people under their rule, and taxed the brisk trade to the extent it would bear. This large conquest state was the Mali Empire.

Over time, rulers of Mali extended their control of commerce south of the desert's edge—from Hausaland in the east, to the forests in the south, and to the Atlantic border of the savannas in the west. At the Gambia's mouth, Niumi existed at the western edge of this regional trading complex. There was an increase in trade over this vast region through the thirteenth and fourteenth centuries, as Mande-speaking merchants fanned out from their homelands between the Senegal and Niger rivers to connect salt producers along the Senegambian Atlantic, kola-nut producers of the southern forests, and cotton-cloth and slave producers from all across the western Sudan into a large commercial network. All of it tied into the trans-Sahara trade, through cities near the desert edge, and thus connected West Africa to the major world system that spread out across central parts of the Old World.

Mali extended its control to incorporate many parts of the Sudanic trading complex. Its ruling lineages may have considered Niumi the empire's westernmost extension, though not enough evidence exists to determine this with precision. Some rulers of Gambian states acknowledged Mali's authority, but were far enough away from the empire's center that such control had to be indirect, sporadic, and not too taxing. The primary relationships were probably economic and cultural.

Mali's Decline

For a variety of reasons that included declining productivity of the Buré goldfields, Mali's power began to wane in the fifteenth century. Another Sudanic empire, Songhai, with its center on the port cities of Timbuktu and Gao on the big bend of the Niger River, eclipsed Mali by about the time the Portuguese were sailing down the West African coast. Mali did not disappear entirely, however; it pulled in its imperial tentacles and held on as the political, cultural, and spiritual center for Mande-speaking peoples throughout West Africa. As Mali's control declined, a smaller, but still powerful, empire emerged among Mandinka-speaking peoples to the west of the old Mali heartland on the upper Niger. Called Kaabu and centered on several Mandinka states south of the Gambia, this empire assumed some of Mali's authority toward the Atlantic and remained politically strong for some time. But after the fifteenth century Mali was a shadow of its former imperial self and most of the far-flung states it had once controlled, at least indirectly, while still thinking of the upper Niger region as the center of their cultural world, owed Mali little more than nominal allegiance.

Political decline did not mean a falling off of trade, however. The trans-Sahara trade continued as Songhai marshaled its southern connections; in fact, the trade of the western Sudan extended farther south toward goldfields deeper into the Guinea forests. And out on the western edge of West Africa's commercial complex, the very small state of Niumi continued to function as it had for some time. Mali's fall and Songhai's and Kaabu's rise were less important to ways of life in Niumi than the state's connections to the larger world. Its leaders controlled the exchange of much-needed salt toward the interior and received products and cultural influences from as far away as Timbuktu, Muslim North Africa, and a part of the world beyond.

2

NIUMI IN A RESTRUCTURING WORLD SYSTEM

Before a.d. 1446

Strangers make the village prosper.

—Old Mandinka proverb

People living in Niumi, on the north bank of West Africa's Gambia River, have been involved in the exchange of goods and ideas with people some distance away for as long as there is any record. From the eighth century a.d., if not earlier, West Africa was connected to the commercial complex of the central part of the Old World through the trans-Saharan trade, and Niumi was part of a commercial network of considerable scope and sophistication that was tied to that exchange. The increasing importance of West African gold and slaves to the Mediterranean and the expanding Eurasian trade in the thirteenth century affected West African history in general and Niumi in particular. By the fifteenth century it is likely that residents of the small coastal and riverine kingdom were as eager as Europeans to find access to greater and more direct participation in the expanding market of the world system.

The Physical Setting

The most striking physical feature of Niumi is not its mundane landscape, but its glistening water. Atlantic breakers lap against the northern shore of the territory, and the Gambia River's broad estuary, sometimes with good-size waves of its own, flows past the rest. Only here and there along Niumi's shore or riverbank, where man has slashed and cut and carved away and dug and built, can one see the distinct point where land meets water. The rest is covered with the spiderlike roots and woven branches of mangroves, a green wall at high tide and a maze of gnarled, skeletal obstructions at low. Upsetting the mangrove line along the Atlantic is a series of creeks, estuaries, lagoons, sandbars, and tidal islands, all connected by water, that Niumi's residents used effectively. The various barriers protected the waterways from the rougher Atlantic and facilitated fishing, gathering of mollusks, and rendering of salt by solar evaporation. The sheltered watercourses also made possible the transport of goods by boat, an activity Niumi's residents were involved in for as long as there is any historical or archaeological record.[1] No matter who ruled Niumi—1,000 years ago or the day before yesterday—a good proportion of its residents found a livelihood from products of the river and sea or trade that the waters facilitated.

Photo 2   *Pirogues* along Niumi's riverside near Barra Point.

Photo 3   **Brush and trees, typical of the landscape in central parts of Niumi.**

Niumi's other physical feature—its flat or barely rolling, wooded terrain—played an equally important role in its history. Niumi was located at a point where western Africa's savannas stretched out to the continent's edge. British colonial officers occupying posts in similar savanna regions sometimes referred to the landscape as "M.M.B.A."—"miles and miles of bloody Africa"—a reference to how across vast stretches holding few signs of human activity the rolling brush, grasses, and trees seemed to run on forever, meeting the wide sky at the distant horizon and passing beyond. The expanse of grass and scrub, tree and thorn, anthill and stalking animal, and more grass and scrub seemed to boggle the British mind, so foreign was it to the confines of hedgerows and stonewalls in the England they knew. This was what Mandinka bards called the "bright country," the agriculturally productive lands that have always held a good part of West Africa's population.[2] These savannas lie between latitude 12 and 16 degrees north—deep in the tropics, where it is hot and humid for a little less than half the year, roughly June through October, and hot and dry for the rest.

The north bank of the Gambia River lies on a boundary that, according to more technical geographers, separates pure savanna from savanna-woodland.[3] This means simply that in the rolling savanna country north of the line, there are progressively fewer trees until one encounters the sahel, or marginally habitable desert edge, in the vicinity of the Senegal River, and in the rolling savanna country south of the line, there are progressively more trees until one begins to encounter the galleried vegetation of true tropical rainforest after about 100 miles. This is not to suggest that Niumi lacked trees. Before the twentieth century, when increasing peanut cultivation prompted more people to come to Niumi and clear more land, there were forests across the whole central core of the state. In fact, Niumi's Mandinka inhabitants knew a good half of the 400-square-mile area as "the bad-devil place," a region where *jinns*, or evil spirits, ruined the lives of anyone attempting to settle there. Some still do not care to venture across Niumi's middle stretches, though in the twentieth century a good number of Wolof have built and sustained villages there. Colonial Medical Officer Emilius Hopkinson found Niumi's midsection much more wooded and less healthy than its coastal regions. He reasoned it was the diseases of the forests that brought the Mandinka to think of the land as being inhabited by bad devils.[4] These forests held occasional elephants and lions, more baboons and warthogs, and an abundance of smaller wild game. Just as important for Niumi's commerce with Europeans, they were homes to bees that provided honey and wax. But in terms of habitable area, this meant that until recent times, Niumi was more a strip of land along the Gambia River and the adjacent Atlantic, under the single political authority of several ruling lineages, rather than a carefully delineated, confined state as most of the early Gambian histories, full of maps with tidy boundaries, would have us believe.[5]

Creating the north-south differences in vegetation is the amount of rain that falls—less as one moves north from the Gambia and more as one travels south. Niumi lies in an east-west band that receives, on average, about forty inches of

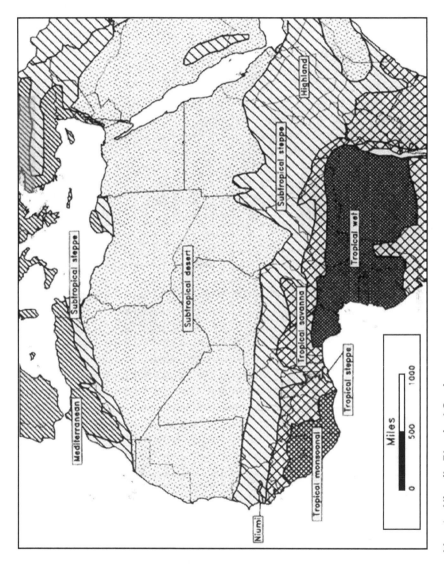

Map 4 **Niumi's Physical Setting**

rain each year, or as much as some of the best farmlands of the American Midwest. However, all of Niumi's rain falls within about five months, from June through October. This is the crop-growing season, the time when men and women for ages had to produce what their families would consume through the seven- or eight-month dry season that followed. It was never an easy task. The soils of the region lack fertility; they are similar to the reddish clays of the American South, impregnated with iron oxide, and they are alternately leached by the heavy rains and cooked by the sun until a thin, heavy crust is all that remains to nurture plants. The lower Gambia region has another agricultural cross to bear: high salinity of soils that makes farming more difficult. Niumi's residents had to practice shifting cultivation, rotating crops frequently and allowing long periods of fallowing between plantings, if they were to coax crops out of the soil and nurse them toward harvest. The food crops Niumi's farmers grew in these soils for hundreds of years before they had contact with Europeans were the savanna grains—several varieties of early- and late-ripening millet and sorghum—which before the late-nineteenth century provided the majority of calories in their diet. Up some of the small streams that enter the Gambia, where there is slightly less salt in swampy areas, people grew wet rice, and they broadcast rice onto lands above the swamps for dry-rice cultivation. Niumi's farmers also grew cotton, which had been introduced into West Africa across the Sahara back in the first millennium A.D. Women spun the cotton into thread; men wove it into cloth on narrow looms. Once the Portuguese had substantial contact with West Africans, they introduced a number of crops from Asia and the New World that gradually altered agriculture and nutrition across the region.[6]

In addition to marking the geographer's artificial division between savanna and savanna-woodland, the forty-inch rainfall line sets the approximate northern limit of the thick brush that supports the tsetse fly, the vector for trypanosomiasis ("sleeping sickness"), a disease that is fatal to most large animals.[7] Because of its heavy vegetation, Niumi was one of the worst areas along the river for the disease. Until recent years, as Niumi's population has grown and people have cleared more land for human habitation, neither cattle nor horses lived well there, or long—they had to be kept away from areas of heavy undergrowth—and it was nearly impossible to breed them there. This had important implications for agriculture, for in other parts of West Africa, where cattle thrived, residents used dung to return fertility to exhausted soil. In Niumi this was hardly possible. It meant that crop production was less successful there than in other areas not far away; it probably meant that, for a long time, people in Niumi relied more on trade, exchanging products they could obtain from the sea for foodstuffs that others could grow in greater abundance. Also, people in Niumi who were intent on making use of such large animals as horses knew they would have to have a steady supply from outside the state, particularly from areas to the north that were free of the tsetse fly.

Other diseases endemic to the region shortened people's lives and affected Niumi's history.[8] Malaria was the most important. West Africans inherited immunities to the disease from their parents, but these were mostly weak and thus not significant. Transmitted between hosts by the anopheles mosquito, malaria infected humans as infants and, if they survived the experience, infected them again, though with progressively less serious results, throughout their lives. With high fevers, headaches, and chills that could last for weeks, the disease is particularly debilitating. Because the mosquito population breeds in puddles, pools, and swampy areas created during the months of heavy rains, malaria is a seasonal disease. It is unfortunate that malaria's season is also the farming season, when success requires hard work. Yellow fever was another disease plaguing Niumi's residents. Also mosquito-borne, it came in epidemic waves, and it, too, was debilitating. Surviving yellow fever left victims with a longer period of immunity before contracting the disease again.

West Africans gained an ironic benefit from malaria and yellow fever: coming from an environment free of such diseases, Europeans had no immunities to either one. Thus, in West Africa's tropics, they acquired the diseases easily and frequently died. Annual death rates of Europeans living in West Africa before the middle of the nineteenth century, when quinine came into regular use to prevent malaria, varied between 250 and 500 per thousand per year. That was enough to keep the European presence small and weak.

Of course, Niumi's residents lived with more tropical diseases: dysentery, yaws, and snail fevers, for instance. All of them combined to give the region an unhealthy cast and a high rate of mortality, especially among infants and children. As late as 1960, life expectancy at birth in The Gambia was only thirty-two years, and over one of three children died before age five.[9] These figures were worse several centuries ago. The adult population had to produce about twice as many offspring as they would end up with as adults in the future, and many youngsters had to be fed who would never become productive members of society. Also, most men and women carried with them microbes for these diseases, which flared up now and again. The situation brought about lethargy when it did not bring an early end to life.

The fact that the natural habitat for humans changed relatively quickly, from north to south, and that what people could produce in each habitat was different, meant that exchange of products from one region to another was a regular aspect of people's lives. With the desert edge a few hundred miles to its north and the rainforest a few hundred miles to its south, and with the ocean and its abundant supply of seafood on its border and a river connecting it to the seasonally dry interior, Niumi was ideally situated to be an active participant in regional commerce. Long before any Europeans sailed into the Gambia River with products of their own to exchange, residents of Niumi were trading with persons from long distances away to get items they wanted or needed but did not produce.

The Cultural Setting

Today's population of 1.7 million in the tiny Republic of The Gambia is an ethnic mixture.[10] A person traveling the length of the country on either side of the river might encounter people speaking six different languages as their primary mode of communication. Yet, official ethnic classifications and linguistic differences mask the fact that today, and for a long time in the past, many aspects of people's ways of life in the region—and in a larger portion still of West Africa—were similar. These similarities made it easy for persons from different linguistic or ethnic backgrounds to live together, mix, intermarry, and move about within and through whatever boundaries a sense of ethnicity imposed.[11]

Chief among the similarities was the role of kinship in identity. As for nearly all West Africans at most times in the past, kinship provided individuals their sense of who they were and provided families the formal connections to others that tied together local groups and enabled the formation of larger political, social, and cultural groupings. The extended family, two or three generations of male relatives with their wife or wives and children, was society's building block.[12] An extended family lived together in a compound—a section of a village that was fenced off from others in which there were separate dwellings; several compounds of extended families formed a village; village members had rights to use surrounding land and they cooperated in projects that would benefit all. Groupings of villages often joined under formal agreements to form state structures, with one or several lineages providing the rulers. Niumi was such a grouping.

Kinship was important in chronically underpopulated Africa because it was through the family that offspring were produced to ensure group survival. This made marriage a critical social function. Marriage alliances linked lineages and, through mutual obligations, merged many of their interests. Bride wealth, a payment from the male's family to the female's family to compensate the latter for the loss of a productive worker and reproducer, cemented the interfamily relationships. This payment often was substantial; frequently it was in a form of wealth that was recognized throughout West Africa, such as pieces of woven cotton cloth or decorative personal items. It could include much else, however, from the popular stimulant kola nuts and storable foodstuffs to gold and slaves. As a way to maximize fertility, multiple marriage was nearly universal: if a man, through the resources of his family or the assistance of his age-mates, could amass sufficient bride wealth, he could marry two, three, four, or a dozen or more different women at the same time. In the centuries before the coming of Islamic law, which limits a man's wives to four, wealthy men—especially rulers, who generally had access to the greatest wealth and used marriage ties for reasons of state, cementing relationships with allies—might have a substantial household of wives and their children. Of course, the greater the wealth in the society, the greater the number of wives men tended to have, and the broader and stronger tended to be the kinship ties across village and state lines.

There probably was a time in Niumi when most lineages could intermarry. Before Serer and Mande influences grew strong in the region, people living there may not have recognized status groupings. According to a handful of studies of the population, they were more egalitarian than most other West Africans. Age, knowledge, and talent were the factors that differentiated among individuals.[13]

Perspective 3   **The Problem of Evidence for Precolonial African History**

Writing or speaking about the way Africans lived over 500 years ago requires a disclaimer related to the certainty of what we know. Stated simply, there is not much good evidence for studying African cultures so far back in the past and, thus, one cannot be as certain as one would like of many statements one wishes to make about them. Anthropologists have done historians of Africa great service with their cultural studies, but often they have lent confusion to historical study by their reference to societies in the cultural present, treating them as if they never had different ways of doing things until fairly recent times (which was, normally, the first time the anthropologist came into contact with the culture). In such studies there is an implied sense that only the complex world of the twentieth century brought change to "traditional ways." Of course, this is not historical, not an appropriate way to consider cultures through time. As all people in all cultures, African societies changed. The difficulty is that for most of those societies there is not sufficient evidence of the way things used to be.

For historians, though, it is important to know the way things were. Historians of recent years have argued, for example, that the Atlantic slave trade altered many aspects of society and polity along coastal West Africa. But in most cases they do so without good or complete evidence of the way people lived, and lived together, before the Atlantic trade began. It is a frustration for all concerned. The best one can do, it seems, is to use such evidence as is available, draw analogies from comparable societies under similar circumstances, and make inferences from regional cultural patterns of the time to reconstruct, in general terms, the relevant cultural setting. Such an effort is what appears in this book.

An excellent study that deals with these issues in a fresh way is Charles Piot, *Remotely Global: Village Modernity in West Africa* (Chicago: University of Chicago Press, 1999).

But influences of groups that came to dominate Senegambian society after A.D. 1000—the Mandinka, Serer, and Wolof—gradually put an end to whatever egalitarianism existed in the earlier population and brought limits on relationships of marriage. For a long time into its past, Niumi's population had levels of rank and regard—groupings of people, with boundaries more rigid than those of ethnicity. (A "freeborn" Mandinka might marry a freeborn Serer, for instance, but no freeborn Mandinka would marry a person belonging to the group of skilled artisans or slaves, regardless of the person's language or ethnic identity.) Students of African cultures often call such divisions social *classes*; it is not clear that West Africans thought of them as such. George Brooks argues that it was the Mande-speaking peoples who imposed their tripartite social structure on other groups in much of

West Africa when they infiltrated and sometimes conquered others several centuries ago.[14] It is clear that a stratified social structure has existed among a number of West African groups for a long time.

Persons occupying the highest level of Niumi's social structure were those whom Western social scientists often term simply "freeborn," and sometimes identify as "farmers and nobility."[15] These were not African concepts, however; they conformed to European notions of what the highest classes ought to be. Actually, a member of the so-called freeborn group was not necessarily a farmer or a nobleman, nor was the person always independent, since certain individuals or even extended families of the freeborn group lived as clients among nonrelated families or among other ethnic groups, depending on their hosts for food and shelter, at least until they harvested a crop or fulfilled some other economic function. The freeborn group might better be defined by what it was not: it did not include persons who were members of skilled occupational groupings or slaves. Rulers as well as common farmers, traveling merchants as well as Muslim clerics were "freeborn." At some point in the past—in the sixteenth century in Niumi, it seems—ruling lineages set themselves apart from the rest of society to the extent that they formed an elite sur-class making the rest of the freeborn families clearly in a second rank. Universally, birth and personal accomplishment combined to establish an individual's position among the freeborn population. One could be born into a lineage that provided rulers of a state, but if the individual did not prove himself successful at those things expected of male members of the ruling lineage—riding, performing brave deeds, gaining a large and influential nuclear family with numerous offspring, garnering wealth, dressing opulently, owning slaves—he would never become a ruler and indeed might not have much status at all. Conversely, a person born into a nonroyal freeborn family could elevate his status through hard work, economic success, increasing the size of his family, and being generally wise in word and deed. The most respected freeborn persons of nonroyal lineages were persons with whom all others had to reckon, but they could never become rulers of a state.

A second social category in Niumi consisted of lineages whose members performed skilled activities.[16] Blacksmiths, potters, leatherworkers, and bards were the major ones. Because these groups were endogamous, lived separately, and were often spoken of with contempt by members of the freeborn grouping, students of West African cultures sometimes refer to them as "castes." It is not an entirely appropriate term. The blacksmith was a necessary adjunct to farmers and warriors, for he alone knew how to fashion cultivating tools, spearheads and arrowheads, and swords. He also served as a diviner, pre-Islamic religious specialist, and manufacturer of protective charms. And blacksmiths were the traditional leaders of secret societies that did everything from ensuring social order to perpetuating Mande culture.[17] Women in blacksmith lineages were potters, and they, too, had special relationships with the earth wherein resided the powerful spirits of the potter's materials. The leatherworker used special ingredients to tan hides and then turn them into saddles and bridles, sandals, and pouches, and he covered with leather the charms and amulets, made by

Muslim diviners or traditional spiritualists, that nearly everyone in society wore on the body or attached to weapons, tools, saddles, or garments. The bard (popularly called a *griot*) was necessary because he kept the histories of clans, families, and individuals; served as diplomat, advisor, and confidant of common patrons and rulers; and entertained all elements of society. Bards also had a teaching role, for it was they who passed along real and fabricated genealogies and knowledge of the past that helped provide personal, family, and state identity, and political legitimacy.

Members of these occupational groupings filled an odd niche in society, one that we still do not completely understand. It was typical for a farmer, warrior, or trader to hold a skilled artisan in outward contempt but to recognize his usefulness to society and maintain an inward respect for the person and his skills. Because artisans had access to special knowledge and skills, feelings toward them could combine fear and awe of their mastery of the occult and access to spiritual and worldly powers with resentment, for artisans kept to themselves and guarded selfishly the knowledge of their skill that was essential to their economic well-being. Lineages of artisans often were wealthier than typical freeborn lineages, too. Blacksmiths and leatherworkers were revered for their craft secrets and expertise: both worked with trees and minerals from the earth, the dwelling places of spirits. Their dealings involved spiritual rituals that others were incapable of performing and just as glad to leave to the artisans. Perhaps because they were entertainers, who are set apart in many societies, but just as likely because they often had intimate ties with persons at the heart of political power, bards were regarded as social separates. They often were constrained to live on the edge of villages, physically detached from the residences of others. Bards were normally associated with a specific lineage for patronage, but blacksmiths and leatherworkers were more independent. They moved about to find the materials they needed for their work—ore, wood, hides, fruits and berries—and settled when it was to their advantage, sometimes allying themselves to a freeborn lineage through a system of varying-term credit whereby the artisans would perform services on promise of sustenance and protection through the following year or longer. Such relationships, continually renewed, appeared permanently binding to foreign observers, and in a sense they were, though in theory either party could break them when it had fulfilled its part of the bargain.

Slaves, who made up the third social grouping, are the most difficult to describe and, with artisans, the most misunderstood by outside observers of precolonial African society.[18] Before the twentieth century many slaves existed in states like Niumi. Estimates made from the late eighteenth century into the colonial period suggest that from two-thirds to three-fourths of some societies in West Africa consisted of slaves, and there is no good proof that this proportion had increased significantly from earlier times.[19] Today there is no doubt: most precolonial African societies, even before they had contact with Europeans, had large slave populations and participated in a trade of slaves. Why they did so and what slavery in precolonial West African societies was like are questions that have perplexed outside observers for a long time.

The nature of African slavery varied considerably and differed from forms of the institution familiar to Europeans. This has prompted students of the subject, like the blind men and the elephant, to stress only the aspects of its nature that they encountered. Some prefer to emphasize that African slavery was a property relationship;[20] others stress how, in a society where kinship defined the individual's place, slaves were those without kin.[21] It is clear that, for the continent as a whole, slavery encompassed a range of relationships of dependency.

Historian John Thornton provides a clear and logical discussion of slavery across much of West Africa in the early years of Atlantic commerce.[22] "Slavery was widespread in Atlantic Africa," writes Thornton, "because slaves were the only form of private, revenue-producing property recognized in African law."[23] Almost nowhere in precolonial Africa did the law recognize individual, private land holding; land was owned communally, by the state in some settings and by the village or the large clan in others, and parceled out to lineages for their use according to need. That need was based on the number of laborers the lineage had to work the land. So to increase production, lineages had to invest in more laborers. They could do this by paying the bride price for sons to marry, benefiting from the woman's productive efforts, and then waiting for the offspring of the marriage to mature, but this was an investment that might never pay off, and not for over a decade at best. They could, however, invest in a slave, who could be put to work almost immediately and bring rapid return on the investment. Women slaves could also bear children, who eventually would add to the size of the labor force. Thus, slavery was, according to Thornton, "possibly the most important avenue for private, reproducing wealth available to Africans."[24]

Who owned or sought to acquire slaves?; all those who had wealth and an interest in increasing it. Agriculturalists obtained slaves to augment crop production. Rulers owned slaves to do their routine work, grow their crops, tend their horses, weave cloth, mine ores, and more. When societies became more militaristic and required larger armies for protection or offensive raiding, rulers obtained slaves and made them soldiers of the state. Traders used slaves to provide foodstuffs for them and their families as they indulged in nonagricultural pursuits and to serve as porters on commercial forays. Muslim clerics had slaves who produced food while they and their male offspring conducted religious training or did any of a variety of supernatural work for their clientele.

Given the varied circumstances in which slaves might live, it is easy to understand that the lot of West African slaves varied considerably from one circumstance to another. One role that varied less than others, however, was that of women. A majority of slaves in West Africa during precolonial times were women, and typically they brought a higher price than men. This was for the obvious reason that women produced useful offspring, but also because females tended in many ways to be the main producers in the society. They also had the advantages of being more easily assimilated into a society than men and less likely to escape.[25] Besides sex differences, slaves associated with a lineage often did the same variety of tasks as other family members, though sometimes they specialized in a single craft such as weaving. Over several generations, and increasingly with marriage and childbirth, slaves could become recognized members of the household, no longer liable for sale and movement. Slaves of royal lineages might serve as soldiers or administrators and become particularly important in such matters. The difference was that slaves and their descendants were always outsiders, making them liable for exploitation by the original family members. Although slaves' fortunes rose with the wealth and position of the family, they never entirely lost their personal status as persons other than kin.

As in most places where slavery existed, West African societies obtained slaves by more or less violent means. Warfare, including raids, banditry, and kidnapping, was the most common method. Even wars not fought to gain slaves had that effect, for prisoners of war were normally enslaved and sold or put to work to help defray the war's cost. If ransom was impossible, there were other considerations. Young boys could train as future soldiers; girls and women could become concubines; and slaves of either sex could be given as gifts to religious persons or shrines. But captives were not of greatest value near their place of capture, close to home and likely to escape. Wise captors moved prisoners rapidly and sold them away quickly if there were no pressing needs for their labor. Even if the need for labor was strong, it was often better to sell local captives and buy slaves from some distance away. For these reasons African armies often had a following of merchants eager to buy prisoners at low prices and then march them off to more distant markets where their value would be greater.[26]

Less violent methods of enslaving involved condemnation through judicial or religious proceedings for civil crimes or religious wrongdoing. As the slave trade in western Africa grew heavy, slavery probably became a punishment for an increasing number of offenses.[27] Finally, there is evidence of individuals voluntarily enslaving themselves, almost always because they could not feed or otherwise care for themselves or their families.[28] In the worst of times, people chose dependence over starvation.

In the stratified societies here described, elements besides kinship lent them cohesion. One of these was the age grade. Groupings of adolescents went through several-month-long periods of training for adulthood and then were initiated together into the society. Such "bush schools" took place every few years. Those initiated at the same time formed a body of individuals of the same approximate age with particularly close ties. Members of age groups had obligations that ranged from serving as a labor brigade on communal projects to looking after elderly villagers. They lent assistance to one another at various stages in life, helping poorer members accumulate bride wealth, for instance, or joining to build dwellings for spouses.[29]

Secret societies, sometimes called power associations, also cut across lines of class and kin and helped keep social order. Among Mande speakers, blacksmiths were the principal keepers of cultural tradition, and where they settled, they established local chapters of secret societies.[30] Masked in public to hide their worldly identity, leaders of secret societies provided for social order, arbitrated disputes between lineage members, saw to it that trade routes were protected and free of banditry, and, writes Brooks, "influenced other—possibly all—matters of consequence in communities under their purview."[31] Secret societies probably played a role in the spreading of Mande culture and the assimilation of peoples to a hegemonic culture by inducting children of host societies and teaching them Mande ways. Also, over time they adopted and then perpetuated local beliefs and practices.

One other institution that was common throughout much of West Africa made possible the free movement of travelers and traders in foreign societies with minimal regard for protection, food, and lodging and provided a way for foreigners to assimilate into a new society. This was an age-old custom of reciprocity that anthropologists call the landlord-stranger relationship.[32] Even today, most West Africans of any means provide food and shelter, without question or fanfare, for visitors. For those staying for a few days, a farming season, several years, or permanently, the relationship with a family, village, or larger group is institutionalized. A person coming to a West African village without the ability to subsist or succeed alone obtains a host, or landlord, who agrees to provide food and lodging. The landlord also provides introductions and serves as the stranger's connection with local society, taking the stranger's side in disputes, guaranteeing debts, or serving as guardian for the stranger's children. In these societies where kinship ties are necessary for having a place, kin of the landlord become kin of the stranger, and the responsibilities of kinfolk and landlord become similar.

For their part, strangers must get along in the village on the landlord's terms, following local customs carefully and providing services for the landlord—perhaps working in the landlord's fields several days a week or, if appropriate, trading on the landlord's account. If the stranger is successful, the landlord can expect gifts in a quantity related to the stranger's prosperity. Because one of the landlord's assumed responsibilities is to assist the stranger in amassing bride wealth and finding a suitable marriage partner, it often happens that the stranger who remains for a long period marries into the family of the landlord and thus becomes a part of the family and community. Wealthier strangers might marry into other, more prosperous or prestigious families—maybe even into families of rulers. In such ways, onetime outsiders integrate themselves into local communities.

The landlord-stranger relationship played a particularly important role in Niumi's society, where for a variety of reasons alien peoples were forever coming to farm, fish, trade, proselytize, or otherwise attempt to prosper. Indeed, Niumi's history, early or late, is in large part the story of individuals or groups coming to live from some distance away and bringing with them material goods, cultural values, or religious practices that altered the circumstances of life for people in the region. Before the nineteenth century, when Europeans used force to bring about change in Niumi, it was the landlord-stranger relationship for accommodating strangers that made possible this cultural melding.

Niumi's Early Residents, the Commercial Milieu, and the Niumi State

It is not possible to determine a great deal about the earliest inhabitants of the coastal regions around the lower Gambia. Evidence that exists for the period before Europeans sailed down Africa's west coast and began leaving a written record is from archaeology (with only a few sites investigated), linguistics, or oral traditions and is limited in what it can tell us. We know that the region long had natural advantages that lured migrants, in good times and bad, so Niumi's population was a mixture of people from different ethnic backgrounds. This was typical of a wide area of West Africa. When Alvise da Cadamosto spent fifteen days at a commercial entrepôt sixty miles up the Gambia in 1456, he found "each day fresh people of various tongues down at the ship" and generally people "constantly journeying from place to place up and down the river in their canoes."[33]

A study of Senegambian place-names suggests that the earliest inhabitants might be identified most closely with one of several related groups—Bainunk, Kasanga, Beafada—who once populated a much larger area than they do today between the more arid lands to the north of the lower Gambia and the more humid lands to the south.[34] To these were added Serer, who moved southward during the first millennium A.D. from the Senegal River valley, and Mande-speaking peoples, who arrived later still from the east.[35]

Several residential and occupational tendencies characterized people's lives in early Niumi. Nearly everyone who lived there before the mid-nineteenth century resided near water, either ocean or river. The interior that today holds a sizable population of farmers was overgrown with forests and did not have permanent residents. Cadamosto found the lands along the Gambia "covered with numerous and very large trees which are everywhere throughout the country"—so much so that they stifled the breeze and made travel on the river less comfortable than on the Atlantic. He reported on an elephant hunt in Niumi's forests wherein men "advanced scrambling and jumping from tree to tree," shooting the elephant with arrows and throwing poisoned spears.[36]

Those inhabiting the sixty or seventy miles of islands and seacoast stretching north from the Gambia's mouth were long identified as "Niuminka," which means simply "the people of Niumi." They were a mixture of the earliest residents, the Bainunk and others, with Serer and Mandinka. The language and customs of Serer seemed to predominate to the north, but after the sixteenth century, more Mandinka customs entered into their ways. The sea was their livelihood; they were excellent boatmen in dugout canoes of varying sizes, some large enough to hold scores of men, and they fished, gathered mollusks, and extracted salt from the Atlantic's waters. They grew some of the savanna grains, too, and up the coastal rivers, into West Africa's interior, they traded what they obtained from the sea for cotton cloth, gold, and agricultural products.[37]

A small number of villages, primarily commercial in nature, were set along

52

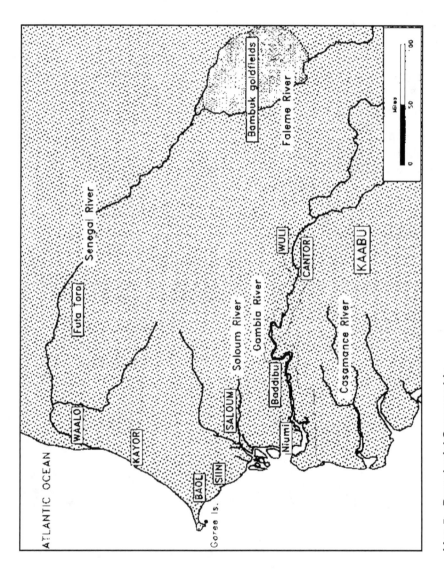

Map 5 **Precolonial Senegambia**

Perspective 4   **Ethnicity**

Ethnicity as we think of it—identity with, and strong loyalties to, an ethnic group—almost certainly did not exist in precolonial West Africa. Europeans, who developed national loyalties and intense feelings about ethnic and national identity in recent centuries, brought their notions of ethnicity, nationhood, and national loyalty to Africa in the late nineteenth and early twentieth centuries and applied them to Africans. Europeans assumed that Africans had the same identity with a "tribe" as Europeans had with an ethnic grouping—English, Irish, French, Italian, and German. For the benefit of order, colonial authorities attempted to label each African man, woman, and child as a member of one or another ethnic group. There was no room for multiethnicity. It did not matter if a person in colonial Gambia had a personal, primary identity as "Mandinka," "Jola," or "Serahuli": early in the twentieth century, he or she became such on the books—formally and officially. Gambia's British administrators could state the exact percentage of the colony's "native inhabitants" who were Mandinka or Jola or Serahuli. Then, the development of African nationalisms, which came into existence in the anti-Western, anticolonial culture of the first half of the twentieth century, heightened many of these prescribed ethnic divisions, especially when colonial political parties came to be based largely on ethnic designations and rendered Africans, indeed, downright "tribal."

But Africans did not always think of themselves as members of tribes or ethnic groups. Before the nineteenth century, ethnicity in Senegambia was much more fluid than we tend to think of it—a permeable membrane through which passed marriage partners, members of secret societies or occupational groupings, magico-religious figures (Muslims and non-Muslims), and just about everybody else. People frequently reached adulthood speaking several languages and existing comfortably among persons who did things differently from the way they did them. Thus, there is little doubt—and oral traditions bear this out—that Niumi's early population was a conglomeration of people who had various individual and group identities and who lived together without many of the troubles that today we identify as "ethnic conflict."

Donald R. Wright, "What Do You Mean There Were No Tribes in Africa? Thoughts on Boundaries—and Related Matters—in Precolonial Africa," *History in Africa: A Journal of Method* 26 (1999): 409–426.

---

the riverbanks south of the Niuminka settlements. These were outposts of a trade diaspora, the initial element of what would grow into a dominating presence of Mande-speaking peoples along the banks of the middle and lower Gambia by the seventeenth century.[38] Explaining the existence of these Mande commercial enclaves in an alien Niuminka polity were the patterns of trade in and around the lower Gambia. It was a commercial milieu that had long been among West Africa's most active, but, like most of the rest of the region, it became more active in the thirteenth and fourteenth centuries with the growth of a western Sudanic trading complex, tied into the trans-Saharan trade and the rise of the Mali Empire.

The Gambia River had long been an artery for trade between the Atlantic and the interior.[39] The commodity that made the river trade brisk was salt—the same one that had always been key to the desert trade, that had brought Berbers across the Sahara with slabs of it tied to camels, that had prompted West Africans to exchange gold for it. For the Niuminka, salt did not move in hundred-pound slabs, but in peck-size baskets. Extracting the salt from seawater was never easy. The activity required flooding large basins with tidal waters, closing off dikes and waiting for the tropical sun to evaporate the water, and scraping up the residual salt from the basin floor. Yet, it was an ideal activity for the dry season, when crops were in and there was less work of other kinds. Because of greater humidity and cloud cover, people living in areas south of the Gambia could not produce salt as efficiently as those living along the Atlantic coast north of the river.[40] So it was, in the coastal lands north of the Gambia's estuary, that residents extracted the creamy reddish mineral, put it in baskets made from woven palm fronds, loaded the baskets into large canoes, and conveyed the salt upriver. Beyond the Gambia's headwaters and off across several thousand miles of West Africa's savannas, there was almost no salt except that which was imported from the mines north of the Sahara. Thus, the river was a salt highway, running eastward and southeastward to areas of considerable demand. The traders took with them dried seafood and kola nuts (obtained from areas some distance to the south) for the eastward trade, returning with savanna grains—millets and sorghums—that people in the rice-producing regions to the south of the Gambia could not grow so efficiently.[41]

Wherever along the river the coastal canoe men met traveling merchants from distant places, they exchanged their products. For a long time the state of Cantora, on the Gambia's south bank at the head of navigation, was a regional center for such exchange.[42] From Mande-speaking merchants in Cantora, the coastal traders obtained cotton cloth, especially, but also iron, copperware, and gold; from Banyun merchants in the river's southerly tributaries—especially Vintang Creek, which enters the Gambia from the southeast some fifty miles upriver from the mouth—they received kola nuts, malaguetta pepper, and rice. Overland, from the north, came a trickle of horses, more cloth, and leather goods. And captives from one or another episode of local or regional warfare were an important part of this trade. These slaves carried goods as they marched and were sold along with them to end up working in the fields of a state's ruling lineages, working to produce crops for a nonroyal lineage, or marching across the Sahara for sale in Mediterranean markets.

Over the years of such heavy commercial activity, a trade diaspora came into being along the Gambia's banks. Initially, small numbers of Mande traders, perhaps Soninke speakers originally, from the region between the middle Senegal and upper Niger rivers, traveled toward the Gambia's mouth to trade and remained in one or another village along the river. In time, more of such traders, perhaps relatives of the original ones, followed and settled in the same villages. As rapidly as possible they would learn the languages, cultural nuances, and commercial ways of the people among whom they were living. Such villages thus became nodes of a trading network that stretched its arms some distance from the traders' original homes. The settled merchants served as cross-cultural brokers, facilitating trade between local people and the alien merchants.

By the fourteenth or fifteenth century, a dozen or more of such commercial enclaves of a Mande trade diaspora stretched from Mali's political and economic center on the upper Niger to the Gambia's mouth and tied people and polities along the river to the trading complex that reached across the savannas toward Lake Chad and connected into the trans-Saharan trade. *Julakunda*, the "place of the traders," these villages were called, and they caught the attention of the earliest Europeans to visit the Gambia because they were the points of exchange of products of all types, for all comers.[43]

But the villages were not only commercial centers: they were known also as *morakunda*, the "settlement of the Muslims," and, indeed, they were the places where Soninke, Fulbe, and Mandinka merchants who spread southward from the Senegal and westward from the Niger had established themselves as practitioners of Islam. Trade could take up a good part of these villagers' dry-season activities, when roads and paths were passable and travelers tended to stay healthier; then *moriya*, the magico-religious works of Muslim holy men, constituted their work through the rains, when slaves could be growing crops to sustain them all. If for some Africans and Europeans the villages were primarily the locus of trade, for many Africans from a surrounding region they were the places where ascetic and wealthy Muslims divined, made charms, and worked to cure people of their maladies.

This mixture of more numerous, coastwise settlements of Niuminka with a smaller number of mixed-Mandinka commercial and Islamic villages along the Gambia's banks was organized into a state that, into the sixteenth century, was ruled by a lineage of the more numerous Niuminka.[44] The lack of evidence makes it difficult to determine much about the state, and one forever must be wary of applying Western notions of states as carefully bounded territories under one government. Rulers of early West African states seem to have been concerned more with control and protection of people than of land.[45] In the fourteenth and fifteenth centuries, the Niumi state may have had more in common with the Wolof or Serer polities to the north than it would several centuries later, when Mandinka political influences were stronger. It had a hereditary ruler—the title *mansa* that Cadamosto and Gomes use for Niumi's ruler in the 1450s shows either a borrowing from the Mandinka that indicates, again, how mixed were customs, practices, and language, or more simply that the Portuguese relied on an interpreter who spoke one of the Mande languages. One suspects that Niumi's ruler had officials in the commercial villages to oversee and tax trading activities there.

The Niumi state was apparently independent at the time of the Portuguese arrival.[46] On the south bank of the Gambia, some distance upriver, several states owed at least nominal allegiance to a Mandinka *farim*, or governor, located, writes Cadamosto, "towards the south-south-east, . . . at nine or ten days journey," and this governor "was subject to the Emperor of Melli, the great Emperor of the Blacks."[47] The earliest Portuguese did not report Niumi as being subject to imperial Mali or any particular overlord. This may have been true because it was farther away from the center of Mandinka authority, on the upper Niger, or because its ruling lineage was more powerful and bellicose than those of the upriver states. Or maybe the Portuguese simply failed to make note of some hierarchical political situation involving Niumi.

Of course, differences existed in the first half of the fifteenth century between little Niumi and mighty Mali. A major one was the nature of their military forces. The key to Mali's power was cavalry. Horses had been important to West African rulers for centuries, but often more for the prestige they conferred than for their tactical use in battle. But by the thirteenth century, perhaps aided by a long dry period that reduced ground cover and, hence, disease-bearing tsetse flies along the upper Niger, Mandinka elites found it possible to sustain large herds, Mandinka horsemen perfected raiding tactics, and Malian horse warriors gained command of the battlefield. The men of Mali's royal lineages were horsemen, who rode and raided and defended on horseback.

This was not the case in early Niumi, where any lifestyle based on horses remained a problem. The lower Gambia had enough seasonal rain to keep brush growing, so tsetse flies were there to spread the deadly trypanosomiasis among large animals. And unlike Mali, Niumi did not have a steady source of horses through trade. So while Niumi's royal lineages may have clung to the trappings of horsemanship, keeping a few mounts about for use on ceremonial occasions, they were not able to marshal a cavalry force sufficient to raid others for slaves or to protect themselves from alien raiders. Instead, they had a different medium to command—the coast and river—and a different means of conveyance: the dugout canoe. If Mali remained master of the western savannas' overland trade routes into the fifteenth century with its cavalry, Niumi controlled the ocean and riverine trade routes in and around the lower Gambia with its fleet of large canoes, each capable of holding two or three scores of warriors wielding bows that fired arrows tipped with deadly poison. One can suppose that Niumi's rulers used the wealth they garnered from the aquatic trade to acquire slaves, whom they employed in household production, the rendering of salt, and the manning of the canoes that were so important to the state's power.

When Nuno Tristão entered the Gambia River and tried to acquire slaves by force, he experienced the power of Niumi's riverine forces and the efficacy of their weapons. The lessons the Portuguese learned from Tristão's experience were ones that Europeans trading in West Africa were loath to forget over the next three and one-half centuries: surrounding them were complex societies that were active participants in a sophisticated regional commerce that was growing in response to a restructuring world system. In virtually every situation, power was in the hands of the Africans; the vulnerability of the alien Europeans, who were outmanned and eternally dependent on local peoples for water, food, shelter, and cultural and commercial mediation, was palpable. Survival and success depended not on force of arms, but on finding a mutuality of interests and then fostering these to the benefit of African states and foreign traders alike.[48] This is precisely what the Portuguese did in dealing with Niumi and others, once they understood the circumstances of cross-cultural trade along Africa's west coast, toward the end of the fifteenth century.

Part II

THE PRECOLONIAL PERIOD

1446–1816

For 400 years following the opening of the Atlantic to European shipping, a group of merchants, planters, shippers, and bankers constructed and maintained an economic system that affected people on all four continents bordering the ocean. This system's primary purpose was to produce commodities for the European market, but also it involved obtaining and transporting laborers—mostly slaves—for staple-producing plantations in the tropical and subtropical Americas, supplying the laborers with their basic needs, and maintaining ancillary trade around the rim of the Atlantic basin.

People in Niumi had been involved in trade along West Africa's Atlantic coast long before the Portuguese arrived. They controlled a part of the regional exchange of salt, dried seafood, and kola nuts with their canoes and boatmen, and they were on the edge of the desert-side trade that connected them, across the Sahara, to the economic system of central parts of the Old World. But the appearance of Portuguese sailors in the Gambia in the middle of the fifteenth century marked Niumi's entrance into the trade of the growing Atlantic complex, an international economic network that Niumi would continue to be involved in for more than 350 years. In numerous ways, over several centuries, participation in the Atlantic economy altered politics and society in the state. Europeans active in the Atlantic commerce brought new means for political control, providing access to horses and later to firearms, to new markets for what people in Niumi could produce, including slaves, and to new sources to tap for revenue. The trade also brought new residents to Niumi—Africans, Europeans, and mixtures of the two. Some of the Africans would come to take advantage of the new means to political control, and their descendants would participate in ruling Niumi for the remainder of its existence as a sovereign state. Most of the Europeans would come to trade and then, to the degree Niumi's residents allowed, their offspring would assimilate into the society. Eventually, European private companies and governments established permanent commercial outposts on Niumi territory that would benefit Niumi's rulers. Over time, as Niumi was fully integrated into the Atlantic commercial network, it came to have an economy, polity, and society that were dependent on connection to the Atlantic trade. When the plantation complex or Niumi's relationship to it changed significantly, the lives of everyone in the state faced change as well.

3

NIUMI BETWEEN TWO SYSTEMS

Waxing Atlantic Trade, Continuing Sudanic Trade
1446–1600

When you go to a new land and find the people all hopping on one leg, you, too, must raise a leg.
> —*griot* Unus Jata, during an interview
> in The Gambia, September 1974

A steady globalization process brought partial reorientation for Niumi between 1446 and 1600. Portuguese merchants came by sea and connected westernmost sub-Saharan Africa to a growing plantation complex centered on the Atlantic Ocean. Among other things, this meant a significant heightening of the trading of slaves. Before Portuguese arrival, people in Niumi may have sent slaves northward toward the Sahara, but the numbers were not large and the importance of the trade to Niumi's economic well-being was not great. The state's main commercial activity was the trading of salt from the Atlantic toward the savanna hinterland of the upper Gambia, mainly for cloth, iron, and gold. But within a few decades of the appearance of Portuguese caravels in the Gambia River, Niumi, with other states along and near the Senegambian coast, became a supplier of commodities for the Atlantic economy: gold, hides, beeswax, foodstuffs, and slaves. The rulers of Niumi, more than the others, taxed the trade passing through the state and into and out of the river's mouth. Participation in the Atlantic commerce did not diminish the amount of trade taking place across the western savannas, however. If anything, it heightened that trade, and Niumi continued to exchange goods between the Atlantic, the upper Niger River, the southern edge of the Sahara, and the Guinea forests.

The growing trade led to gradual change for Niumi's residents. The heightening demand for slaves meant more slave raiding and associated political and social instability. Over half a century or more, people across coastwise Senegambia had to find new political institutions and social structures that would enable them to live with a reasonable level of security. People in Niumi found it necessary to change a number of their basic institutions, from the nature of the state to the form and structure of villages. But the new trade brought something besides instability: it provided some residents of Niumi with access to new wealth and new products, and it brought new people with fresh ideas from different parts of the world. Each of these would play a role in a century and a half of political, economic, social, and cultural change in the state.

Western Europe and the Rise of the Plantation Complex

From the perspective of world history, a series of events that occurred over the century following 1450 sped the process of globalization that had been bringing together people of the world. The steady Portuguese exploration of Africa's west coast, Bartolomeu Dias's 1488 rounding of the Cape of Good Hope, Vasco da Gama's voyage to India in 1497–1499, and subsequent Portuguese efforts to wrest control of the Indian Ocean spice trade from Muslim merchants are widely known events of "European expansion." By early in the sixteenth century, Portugal had gained control of key points of access to the Indian Ocean, defeated a strong Arab fleet, and established trading posts in East Africa, India, Indonesia, and China. Each year Portuguese fleets sailed to "the Indies" and returned primarily with spices, but also Indian cottons, East Asian silks, and foods and plants that were entirely new to most Europeans. Iberian and northern European cities became important suppliers for the European market, at the expense of trade through eastern Mediterranean and southern European ports.

In the other direction, the Genoese sailor Christopher Columbus enlisted Spanish rulers to back his 1492 voyage to the West to reach the same Indies, but he underestimated the earth's size and located what to Europeans was a new world in the Americas. With considerable speed Spanish conquistadors wrested control of central and southern regions of the Americas from the resident Indians, gaining access to an enormous expanse of land that held vast quantities of silver and gold and on which grew scores of plants entirely foreign to Europeans. The Spanish did not hesitate to begin exploiting the mines of Mexico and South America's highlands. Using Indian labor primarily, Spain mined from the earth and transported home nearly 20,000 tons of silver and over 200 tons of gold between 1503 and 1660. It was bullion that would grease the wheels of capitalism and international trade throughout Western Europe.

Spices, cottons, silver, and gold were not all that flowed from one region to another in greater abundance after 1450 and affected the lives of people around the world. With slightly less speed, perhaps, but inexorably nevertheless, the Portuguese, Spanish, and eventually other northern and western Europeans began spreading new plants and animals (and sometimes more simply new strains of the same plants) to parts of the world where they were unknown. Over time, wheat and most common barnyard animals for the Americas; maize and potatoes for Europe; maize and sweet potatoes for East Asia; maize, cassava, and peanuts for Africa— to name a few—would alter the caloric and nutritional basis of populations and enable regions to sustain larger numbers of people with less labor. Such changes, often overlooked, would underlie much of the history that transpired around most of the world over the last half millennium.[1]

For a century and more after 1450, as most of these events were taking place, Portuguese and Portuguese-African (Luso-African) sailors and entrepreneurs focused attention on West Africa, where they found riches of their own to exploit.

63

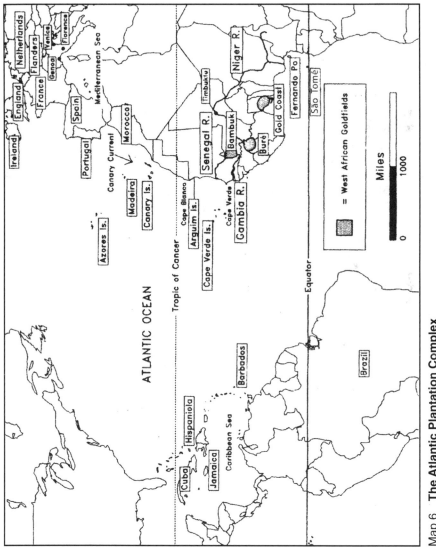

Map 6 The Atlantic Plantation Complex

What interested the Portuguese most in Africa south of the Sahara was gold. For several centuries word of rich West African potentates had been circulating around the Mediterranean, causing ambitious south Europeans to dream of reaching the lands below the Sahara. Rumors gave way to fact once Malian ruler *Mansa* Musa took 100 camels laden with gold on a pilgrimage to Mecca in 1324–1325 and reduced the value of gold in Cairo with lavish spending and giving.[2] When crusading Portuguese knights wrested Ceuta in Morocco from the Moors in 1415 and learned greater details about the gold-bearing lands of West Africa, their dreams became more vivid. Gold was a commodity in great demand around the Mediterranean in the late middle ages, where polities of all sizes had been minting gold coins for several centuries. Portugal did so for a while but was forced to stop in 1383 for want of bullion.[3] On a 1442 Atlantic voyage past Cape Blanco, Portuguese merchant-seamen traded for gold with Tuaregs; then, as Alvise da Cadamosto ascended the Gambia River in 1456, he bartered with an African ruler for gold—not a lot of it, he reported, but "they traded it cheaply, taking in exchange articles of little value in our eyes."[4]

The Gambia River turned out to be one of two important points of Portuguese access to West African gold—the other, after 1470, being El Mina on the Gold Coast. The river, which flowed toward the Bambuk and Buré goldfields, permitted oceangoing vessels to reach within 100 miles or a little more of Bambuk and 250 of Buré. Besides that, African merchants for a long time had been bringing down gold to ports along the Gambia to exchange primarily for salt. Diogo Gomes was duly impressed at Cantor, 250 miles up the Gambia, where he saw African merchants "come loaded with gold" and learned of a "lord of all the mines" toward the east, who "had before the door of his palace a mass of gold just as it was taken from the earth, so large that twenty men could scarcely move it, and [to which] the king always fastened his horse."[5] Quickly, Portuguese and Cape Verdean traders ascended the Gambia and began exchanging their "articles of little value" for gold, and the result in Portugal was almost instantaneous: in 1457 the Lisbon mint began issuing the *cruzado*, which Charles R. Boxer labels "a coin of almost pristine purity, which underwent no debasement until 1536." According to Philip D. Curtin's estimates, by the beginning of the sixteenth century, the Portuguese were obtaining, on average, about seventy-five pounds of gold per year from Senegambia.[6] A good portion of that they acquired in trade along the banks of the Gambia River.

If the amount of gold obtainable in West Africa was not as great as the Portuguese wished, the metal's availability captured their interest and brought them to recognize, in Curtin's words, "a fortuitous and unexpected by-product of the gold trade"[7]: the availability of slaves. What the Portuguese did with slaves initially was take them home to serve Europe's royalty, tending to the knights and squires who served as marginally productive members of European courts. Within decades of obtaining the first slaves from West Africa, however, new markets for them appeared. These were tied to an expanding economic complex of slave-worked plantation agriculture that was spreading into the Atlantic in the wake of Portuguese explorations. It was an enterprise that would have enormous and lasting consequences not just for West Africans, but also for people residing today on all four continents bordering the Atlantic.

The origins of this grand, modern, intercontinental economic system, the Atlantic plantation complex, go back, once more, to the formative time of the Crusades.[8] As European crusaders marched across Muslim lands bordering the eastern Mediterranean, they encountered a variety of products they never had seen or tasted. One they found particularly appealing was cane sugar, a product of central Asian origin that Muslims for many years had been growing for an Asian market. When they could, Italian merchants bought sugar from Muslim producers and imported it into southern Europe, where even the wealthiest people had only honey to add sweetness to their foods. Once Christian entrepreneurs acquired land as part of the crusading effort, they began altering feudal customs regarding land tenure and labor use so they could concentrate productive efforts on growing cane for export.

Curtin explains the properties of sugarcane that lend it to plantation agriculture and an export market. It requires considerable labor for its cultivation and harvest and it is so heavy and bulky that it must be concentrated, through pressing and boiling, into crystalline sugar and molasses before it can be moved any distance. Once concentrated, though, it has a high value relative to its bulk—qualities ideal for long-distance trade. With such heavy labor demands for growing and processing, and with such concentrated value in a product that was a dietary luxury rather than a nutritional staple, widespread plantation growth of sugar for export was not long in coming.

Indeed, by the start of the twelfth century a sugar-growing plantation complex was in existence on Christian holdings in the Levant and on the eastern Mediterranean islands of Cyprus and Crete. Capital and management for the plantations came from southern Europe, as did shipping. Labor was mostly servile, but in a different sense than on the feudal manor. At certain times of the year, workers on sugar plantations were required to work extraordinarily long hours under the most difficult circumstances. Feudal laws and customs did not contain obligations for such work on the part of serfs. Fortunately for the plantation owners, the old Roman legal status of *servitus*, or chattel slave, still existed around the Mediterranean, as did an active slave trade. So owners of the prototype plantations began buying laborers. Many of the early slaves on these plantations were captives from struggles between Christians and Muslims that were taking place on either end of the Mediterranean. With the opening of the Black Sea to European traffic at the start of the thirteenth century, more of the plantation slaves came from the sea's northern shores. Many spoke Slavic languages, from whence comes the word "slave" (*esclave, esclavo*) in several European languages. By the fifteenth century traders even were selling small numbers of black Africans in the Mediterranean slave trade, after a crossing of the Sahara. But on the sugar plantations, race or color were not of primary importance. Highest values were on strength and longevity.

Europe's growing population and its development of a commercial infrastructure of towns, roads, banks, and regular markets meant increasing demand for sugar and better methods of supply, so the Mediterranean plantation complex expanded. Sicily and Tunisia in the central Mediterranean became sugar producers; then southern Spain, southern Portugal, and northern Morocco. The fifteenth-century opening of the Atlantic to European shipping enabled the spread of sugar plantations to several ocean islands, where the warmer and wetter conditions were better still for growing cane. On Madeira after 1455 and São Tomé near the equator in the 1470s, plantation managers took over and quickly made the islands the major sources for sugar for the European market. Spain wrested the Canaries from Portugal after 1480 and established plantations there, too. For these new, rapidly growing, labor-intensive agricultural enterprises in the Atlantic, and for some of the older ones around the Mediterranean, the Portuguese obtained slaves from Africa's west coast, below the Sahara, in exchange for commodities in local demand: horses, iron, cloth, metalware, and more.

Columbus took sugarcane with him on his second voyage to North America in 1493 and made at least a halfhearted attempt at growing the crop in the Caribbean, but this and more concerted Spanish efforts at cane production through the sixteenth century were not as successful as later. A major problem was that the laborers for these plantations, local Arawak Indians, did not live long enough in captivity to be productive, for they had no immunities to the diseases—smallpox, measles, chicken pox, whooping cough, and several more—that came to the New World with the Europeans.[9] Once Spaniards located silver and gold deposits in Central and South America, mining held their attention, and they used local Indians and some imported African slaves for this enterprise. But purely African slave-based plantation agriculture was still some years away in 1600 in Spain's American empire.

It was the Portuguese, with access to African slaves, who moved plantation-based sugar production to South America after the middle of the sixteenth century. Africans had much the same inherited immunities as Europeans, and most adult Africans had some degree of immunity to malaria and yellow fever, largely because they had survived the tropical diseases in childhood. They could live longer in the American tropical environment of the sixteenth century than anyone else, and this factor, more than others, made the difference for Portuguese planters. Between 1550 and 1600, African slaves poured into Brazil, and by the latter date, Brazil had replaced the Atlantic islands as the major source for Europe's sugar. Slaves also were being taken to some of the Caribbean islands, Hispaniola especially, where planters continued their efforts to grow the crop.

Thus, whether for the West African, Atlantic-island, western-European plantation complex of 1500 or the West African, Brazilian, western-European plantation complex of a century later, most patterns and institutions were the same. Capital, know-how, management, and shipping all came from Europe, where the market lay. The laborers on the plantations were enslaved, and nearly all of them came from Africa's west coast and lands a reasonable distance inland from there.

Early Atlantic Trade and Political Change in Niumi

Senegambia was the first region of sub-Saharan Africa to become a major exporter of slaves into the Atlantic economy. The Atlantic trade picked up rapidly following Portuguese arrival: when Gomes made a second voyage to Senegambia in 1460, he found two Portuguese vessels anchored and trading peacefully not far north of Niumi. Though records for the trade and its timing are spotty, it is clear that by the start of the sixteenth century Africans living along Senegambia's Atlantic coast and its major rivers were fully involved in supplying captives, gold, hides, beeswax, and foodstuffs in exchange for horses, cloth, metals, and beads.[10]

This increase in trade was taking place at a time when Senegambia's long-stable political situation was beginning to change. What role the Portuguese and their demand for some products and supply of others played in altering Senegambian politics remains open to debate, but several historians believe that the increased access foreign traders provided persons living along the Gambia River and southward to valuable commodities, horses in particular, helped bring about and sustain the regional upheaval of the late fifteenth and sixteenth centuries. Such commodities were important in the social and political change that occurred in Niumi.[11]

As we know, when the first Portuguese arrived in the Gambia River just before the middle of the fifteenth century, they found Niumi existing on the river's north bank, a political unit populated largely by Niuminka, some closer culturally to their Serer kin in the northern coastal regions and others under more Mandinka influence toward the Gambia's mouth. The state was ruled by a prominent Niuminka lineage. Prosperous families living in the state owned slaves, who worked to increase food production. Existing at several locations within the state were separate commercial and religious enclaves, villages inhabited by Muslim, Mande-speaking traders and holy men, who had settled in the lower Gambia sometime earlier as part of a Mande trade diaspora, drawn from West Africa's interior by the availability of salt, dried fish, and kola nuts. Niumi's rulers derived revenue from tolls charged for the coastal and river trade and from taxes on state residents. The ruling lineages may have owned a small number of horses and displayed or ridden them for the prestige the animals provided for their position as heads of state, but Niumi in those years was not good territory for horse owning or for military pursuits involving cavalry. The backbone of Niumi's military force, as Tristão and his crew found out the hard way, was a fleet of war canoes, manned by poison-arrow-firing archers. This force allowed Niumi's rulers to command access to the waters of the lower Gambia and to control its trade.

North and east of the lower Gambia, the political and military situation was different.[12] A vast Jolof Empire, populated by Wolof-speaking peoples, had controlled much of the inland region between the Senegal and Gambia rivers since the thirteenth century. Along the Atlantic coast from the Senegal River to south of Cape Verde, smaller tributary states of Wolof speakers held sway. The Mali Empire, larger still, had been the dominant force through the vast interior lands east of the navigable Gambia for about the same length of time. Mali, too, had subsidiary and tributary states that at times of the empire's greatest power stretched to the banks of the Gambia.

The key to the military strength of Jolof and Mali alike was horse cavalry.[13] Elite Wolof and Mandinka forces used horses primarily for mobility: they specialized in the lightening-quick raids, galloping in on poorly defended villages and rounding up captives, whom they exchanged for slaves from elsewhere to work in royal fields or traded toward the Sahara for more horses and luxury items. The threat of raids from Jolof or Mali horsemen usually was enough to make people on the empires' peripheries render tribute payments. Access to a continuing supply of horses was necessary for the cavalry states because of the epidemiologically harsh savanna environment: Trypanosomiasis (sleeping sickness) was the major scourge of large animals, but other tropical diseases added to the fact that horses did not live long in Africa's more wooded grasslands. In addition, it was difficult to breed horses very far to the south of the sahel, and it was all but impossible to do so in the latitudes of the Gambia River and southward. So Jolof and Mali maintained a brisk trade toward the desert. Mali had access to gold and kola nuts, in addition to slaves, that it could exchange for the horses (and salt, figs, and dates), but Jolof, cut off from nearby goldfields by more powerful Mali, traded mostly captives. Indicative of the importance of horses for the savanna empires was their price: Cadamosto reported that desert traders in the 1450s were getting from ten to fifteen slaves per horse, and the Portuguese received similar prices when they began importing horses into Senegambia soon thereafter.[14]

In the second half of the fifteenth century, Senegambia and probably a good portion of the western savannas experienced a cavalry revolution.[15] The Jolof Empire quickly built its cavalry force to more than 8,000 horses, and other states tried to keep up. What brought this about was the combination of widespread adoption of the Arab stirrup, which made the beast much more effective as a tool of warfare; increasing numbers of horses imported from the desert edge; and the new supply of horses from the Portuguese. Use of the Arab stirrup, rather than riding bareback, enabled warriors to use their legs and upper bodies to thrust spears. It thus allowed for the combination of the mobility of the horse with the killing capability of the spear and made it possible for states with cavalries to acquire better means still to conquer and dominate agricultural communities. This caused demand for horses to rise, so Berber merchants all the way to North Africa responded with more mounts. At the same time, Portuguese traders began importing horses into Senegambia, originally from North Africa but eventually from herds developed on their newly acquired Cape Verde Islands.[16]

The Portuguese horse trade to the western savannas never eclipsed that from across the Sahara and the desert frontier, but it increased the supply of horses in areas where they could not be bred and thus played a role in altering the power relationships of some West African states. After 1500 there were enough horses in Senegambia and a sufficient supply for replacements that states could afford to risk more of their mounts in bigger battles. Small political units that were peripheral to the largest cavalry states rushed to find ways to increase the size of their horse-borne forces—usually by acquiring slaves to exchange for horses—to avoid total dominance or to come up with tribute payments that overlord states demanded in horses or slaves. By the sixteenth century, across Africa's westernmost savannas, the rush to mount was on, and a key to obtaining horses was obtaining slaves.

All of this occurred at a time when the Mali Empire, plagued by ineffective leadership, declining productivity from the Buré goldfields, and the growing strength of a new rival, Songhai, to its northeast, was in a state of decline. Taking advantage of Mali's weakness, a new group of Fulbe cavalry warriors gained control of the Senegal River valley in the first years of the sixteenth century and effectively cut off Jolof from its desert-side supply of horses. Jolof was experiencing internal warfare at the time, which its loss of horse supply might have exacerbated. Jolof power declined rapidly as its coastal tributaries—Walo, Kajor, and Baol—with horses from the Portuguese and the westernmost sahel, achieved independence. Other tributary and peripheral regions of Mali began to pull away as well.

Around the beginning of the sixteenth century a series of political realignments occurred among Mandinka-speakers living between the south bank of the Gambia and the Futa Jalon highlands.[17] Most noteworthy, with access to horses from Portuguese traders in the Gambia, Casamance, and Geba rivers, a number of Mandinka lineages broke from Mali and joined their separate, small political units to form a larger state called Kaabu. In form and substance, Kaabu took from its Malian heritage. The elite lineages of Kaabu, the *nyancho*, championed a Mandinka ethos that spurred young men to find areas of their own where they could command cavalry forces, dominate others, and rule. There were too many *nyancho* princes to achieve this in the dozen or so substates of Kaabu, so young, proud, ambitious, elite Mandinka warriors did what their types had tended to do far into the past: they cast about for states where their lineages could take or share political control. Prime targets were those where sufficient production and trade enabled them to maintain their elite lifestyle based on expensive cavalry. This meant that access to horses was essential. Sitting at the end of a major artery for trade into the interior, with agricultural and salt production of its own, with enclaves of Mande and Portuguese merchants already paying for the right to participate in the commerce of the region, and with Portuguese ships regularly bringing horses, iron, cloth, and other useful martial and luxury commodities, the region around the lower Gambia was a prime target for Mandinka conquest and settlement.

Evidence for what happened in Niumi during this formative period comes almost solely from oral data—stories collected in and around Niumi as told by family elders and *griot*s.[18] Because traditionists do not have sufficient ways of describing processes of change, their tales probably telescope into a short period events that occurred over a longer time. Still, as most African traditions, they contain a core of truth, which fits into a pattern of events that was taking place across the region.

In the last decade of the fifteenth century, a group of *nyancho* lineages from

Kaabu moved north of the Gambia River and took over an area on the southern edge of the weakening Jolof Empire.[19] From a settlement near the mouth of the Saloum River, these lineages soon mixed with the existing Wolof and Serer population and established the state of Saloum. Access to horses via overland trade to the north and the Portuguese in the Saloum River enabled the rulers of Saloum to assemble a strong cavalry. To obtain commodities to exchange for horses, Saloum warriors rode into neighboring lands plundering and taking captives. One of these lands immediately to the south was Niumi. Jolof bands might have done this earlier, on rare occasions, but Niumi's traditions suggest that the incursions became more frequent and damaging once the Saloum state was in place.

Niumi's existing rulers, whose military emphasis had long been on boatmen and canoes, could not alone assemble sufficient force to deter Saloum's land-based cavalry raids. So some time during the first half of the sixteenth century, these rulers either invited or, at a minimum, welcomed the arrival of several good-size Mandinka *nyancho* lineages from two of the states of Kaabu: lineages with the surname Manneh and Sonko. Then, from Portuguese merchants Niumi enhanced its cavalry force with new mounts and, with the combined strength of the three clans, fought to hold off the raids from Saloum.

The result of these events was the gradual strengthening of the Niumi polity. What had been a largely Niuminka state with an orientation to ocean and river, with Mande commercial and Muslim enclaves, slowly became a Mande-style state with a cavalry force adding to its water-based military backbone. Niumi's cavalry never was as large as those of many other savanna states because its dense interior forests and its more southerly setting meant that disease factors prevented horses from breeding easily there and shortened their lifespans. Still, the state's increased cavalry strength permitted Niumi to establish a relationship with Saloum more to its favor that would last for more than two centuries. It was not always a peaceful relationship, but one characterized by raiding and reprisals, arrangements to limit raiding so as to prevent serious disruption of trade and farming, and sometimes tribute payments. Niumi's cavalry served less as a defensive force and more as an offensive threat that brought about deterrence: its ability to launch a damaging raid of reprisal into Saloum brought about a relatively peaceful and prosperous standoff between the states. At times when Saloum felt strong enough to raid within Niumi's borders and then meet Niumi's reprisals with equal force, Saloum demanded tribute from Niumi—a kind of protection payment. And while marshaling human and material resources to build a cavalry force to maintain security, Niumi's rulers did not lose focus on their bread and butter: control of traffic on the lower Gambia with a body of armed boatmen that allowed them to levy customary taxes on trade passing between the Atlantic and upper river.

The Mandinka lineages that provided the state's new military strength took up residence in Niumi and gradually intermarried with important lineages already present. They were not the state's founding families and thus could not rule the state on that account, but in return for their efforts they desired the elite status of the state's rulers, so some arrangement had to be worked out. With three groups wanting power, it is not surprising that it was not settled peacefully. Niumi traditionists speak of conflict among the competing royal lineages that resulted in warfare so intense that the shallow valley running north from Barra Point toward Jinak Creek "ran red with blood." Before civil war destroyed the state, however, wise counselors intervened. An old woman from a clan of blacksmiths residing in a remote Niumi village supposedly advised one of the royal warriors, "Have peace. If you kill everyone you will have to work for yourself. The head that rests in the shade is supported by those heads that are under the sun. If you kill the rest of them off, no head will sit in the shade."[20] What came out of the tumult was a way of sharing political leadership and the elite lifestyle that accompanied it with a rotating system of succession.

Rotating succession was not unique to Niumi. A number of states of the western Sudan circulated political authority among prominent lineages. This was the case because the cavalry warfare that dominated fighting in the grasslands required considerable investment in horses, training for horsemanship, and slaves to care for the horses, produce subsistence crops for the royal lineages whose members did not farm, and add soldiers when necessary and possible to the state's forces. Lineages did not make such investment without a payoff: a share of political control. Succession to high office was the lineage's opportunity to reap the material and emotional rewards of its investment in that state's military pursuits. Patterns of successional rotation among lineages usually reflected their relative levels of investment.[21]

In Niumi, no single lineage dominated the state after its political consolidation in the sixteenth century. The Sonko clan seems to have been the most populous, meaning it would have made greater contribution to Niumi's cavalry force and owned more slaves, but traditional evidence is overwhelming that the Sonko alone were not strong enough to deter foreign forces or to provide a level of control sufficient to enable the state to benefit fully from the river trade.[22] The Manneh clan, whose members to this day guard most religiously their reputation as descendants of *nyancho* and the fiercest of horsemen, provided important numbers to Niumi's cavalry, and the Jammeh clan, besides being the territory's "owners" by right of precedence, controlled Niumi's formidable fleet of canoes that made possible participation in the salt and fish trade and the monitoring of river traffic. Each contributed enough to the communal welfare that, by political custom, it could expect to participate in ruling the state.

The pattern of circulating succession that came out of Niumi's sixteenth-century restructuring—two Jammeh, two Manneh, and three Sonko lineages rotating political authority—was honored religiously thereafter. Succession disputes that took place over the years occurred *within* lineages, usually among brothers; royal lineages did not challenge others out of turn. It was a practical matter: the weight of force of the six other families, who would suffer if another broke the sequence and ruled out of turn, kept the system functioning as established.

As with most things, those who had the worst experience from the changing political structure were slaves. Before the political consolidation and the coming of the Mandinka royal lineages to share political authority, Niumi's rulers, like other free lineages in the state, used slaves primarily for household production—to grow crops to help the lineage subsist—and reproduction—to produce offspring to add to the number of laborers supporting the lineage. Such persons would eventually be incorporated into the lineage as household slaves and, as such, treated better and less likely to be sold. But with the change in the nature of warfare and political control came a corresponding change in the nature of slavery in the state. Royal lineages and others acquired slaves to serve particular functions for the state or the family. Those producing subsistence crops so members of the lineage could engage in other activities—cavalry pursuits, trade, artisanal work, Islamic clericalism—tended to be kept separate from the lineage and were less likely to be assimilated. Many male slaves simply became soldiers, canoe men, or other functionaries for the state, never to be assimilated. Women were more likely to be assimilated, especially if they became concubines of freeborn men, but even the offspring of women slaves tended to remain separate, forever holding the badge of slave identity.

Trade Diasporas and New Identities

The increasing trade of Senegambia in general, and the Gambia River in particular, brought changes beyond the political. Among other things, it brought a new set of commercial specialists to travel to and settle in enclaves along the Gambia's banks. These merchants developed personal and group identities—colonial officials in the twentieth century probably would have thought of them as separate "tribes"—with distinct professions, languages, religions, and social customs. However much they differed from Niumi's indigenous population, they were welcome for their value to the state and its ruling lineages and their ability to bring material improvements to the lives of persons already residing there. It was customary to allow such groups to form villages on Niumi's soil, where they could live under their own laws and customs as far as they did not conflict seriously with those of the state's majority. The two main groups of these resident strangers were Muslim traders and Christian Portuguese (and Luso-Africans).

Muslim Traders

One group of new settlers in Niumi were people who identified themselves with the Torodbe, a religious grouping mostly of former slaves among the Fulbe, who took on characteristics approximating those of a large clan. Once residents of the Futa Toro region of the middle valley of the Senegal River, these Muslim clerical lineages spread southward and eastward, taking with them their own forms of worship and religious mysticism. The earliest Torodbe lineages came to Niumi around the beginning of the sixteenth century. The timing of their arrival and placement of their villages along the Gambian riverside suggest they came with commerce in mind.

A second, related group was that of Mandinka long-distance traders, called *jula* by Mandinka speakers, who ventured down to the Gambia's mouth in larger numbers than ever before to participate in the waxing commercial exchange there. Nearly all of these merchants were Muslims and a good many were clerics, for they came out of the tradition of long-distance trade of West Africa's interior where Islam and commerce walked together. Islamic clericalism provided the merchants an identity separate from those among whom they settled, and their religious beliefs and specialty in trade brought them a sense of solidarity with other merchant clerics across the region.[23]

The forerunners of these traders were Soninke-speaking merchants long associated with the trade of cotton textiles. Because they dealt with Muslim Berber traders from the Sahara and because they were itinerant folk, detached from agricultural communities whose members were tied to animist spirits of the soil and trees, they were among the earliest West Africans to accept Islam. Desire to learn Muhammad's word made some of them literate, and the literacy helped them with their commercial dealings, made them valuable to rulers wanting to keep careful state accounts, and gave them another calling in the manufacture of protective charms out of written script.[24] With the long dry period that set in gradually after about A.D. 1100, forcing cotton cultivation and weaving along with habitation generally southward, these trading lineages moved south and west to new lands along the upper Niger and upper Senegal rivers. From there they spread gradually across more of the western savannas, purveying trade goods and establishing merchant-clerical communities. They set up schools to teach the Qur'an when the rainy season kept them from venturing out in long-distance trade.

Some *jula* families, lured by the salt trade, had descended the Gambia River from its head of navigation prior to the fifteenth century. The earliest Portuguese met "Mauri" men—Muslim Mandinka—interested in selling them cotton cloth and pepper, and Niumi's *mansa* had a Muslim among his entourage when he came to the riverside to speak with Gomes in 1457.[25] The arrival of European traders in the Gambia and the heightening of trade that followed lured more *jula*. Over the course of the sixteenth century, they positioned themselves where they could most effectively participate in the trade that was blossoming along the Atlantic coast and between the lower Gambia and the savannas to the eastward. By the end of that century, they were tied through their trading interests and a sense of cultural solidarity with a group identified as Jahanka, the "people of Jaha," a village on the Bafing River east of the Gambia, who were known as much for their specialized Islamic clericalism as for their commercial acumen and who dominated the overland trade between the upper Gambia and the upper Niger. Influenced by the Jahankas' avoidance of involvement in the political or religious affairs of their hosts, Muslim *jula* lineages in Niumi were not driven to proselytize. From their enclaves in one or two villages near Niumi's waterside, they traded—probably a great deal more than one recognizes in European records; did "Muslim works," which included divination, making protective charms, and practicing medicine for others; and conducted schools of Islamic learning. From this time on, albeit quietly, Niumi would be one of several centers of Islamic clericalism and magico-religious practice, as well as trade, existing along the Gambia River. There would be prestigious and wealthy settlements of Muslims on Niumi territory some centuries later, when disaffection with the state's rulers became general and Islamic revivalist sentiments would be spreading throughout the region.[26]

Christian Portuguese and Luso-Africans

New Mandinka rulers and merchant clerics were not the only groups the economic situation lured into Niumi. Along the state's southern riverbank, in the neighborhood of the *jula* settlements where riverine trade seemed focused, other new and very different faces appeared. These were Portuguese or, before long, the offspring of unions between Portuguese men with African women, who quickly became the cultural brokers between traders from the African and European societies.[27]

This was not the way the kings of Portugal envisioned the African trade taking place. They intended to have their subjects explore and exploit Africa's western coast directly from ports in Portugal, and this happened as long as Prince Henry managed Atlantic activities. But in 1455 Portuguese mariners sighted the Cape Verde archipelago, a dozen small, uninhabited islands lying 350 miles northwest of Cape Verde, and it was soon evident that the volcanic islands could serve as an advance base for Portuguese trading with the nearby coast. Henry died in 1460, just as European mariners were reaching the coast of Sierra Leone; two years later, Henry's cousin arranged for the first shipload of colonists to settle one of the Cape Verde Islands; and to stimulate further settlement of the archipelago, in 1466, Portugal's King Afonso V granted Cape Verde colonists the right to trade along Africa's western coast. Within a few years, the land lying along that coast between the Senegal River and Sierra Leone became, in Portuguese eyes, the "Guinea of Cape Verde"—the northern part was "Senegambia" and the southern, below the Casamance, the "Southern Rivers." For the next century and a half, Portuguese and Cape Verdeans would operate out of a handful of the islands' ports to tie into the brisk African trade of the coast and vast hinterland of the Guinea of Cape Verde.

That commerce showed real potential. From the earliest voyages the Portuguese had learned of the great demand throughout Senegambia for horses. With the buildup of Jolof herds in the middle of the fifteenth century, followed by the growth of competitive cavalries among smaller states, Portuguese traders had their hands full trying to meet the demand, especially since one caravel could carry no more than ten horses on a single voyage.[28] In the beginning they brought animals from home or purchased them along the coasts of Morocco and Mauritania, but after about 1480 Cape Verde colonists began breeding horses on several of the islands, and soon the Cape Verdes became the major supplier for the Portuguese horse trade. Profits rolled in from the start. The earliest traders reported getting from nine to fourteen slaves per horse and making profits of between 500 and 700 percent per voyage.[29]

Of course, slaves were not the only commodities the Portuguese wanted, any more than horses the only items in demand in Senegambia. In a visit with traders in Niumi in 1455, the Portuguese learned of the availability of gold and malaguetta peppers up the Gambia River, and within a decade others recognized the profits available competing with African merchants in transporting kola nuts from Sierra Leone coastal regions northward. Africans had a variety of needs and wants themselves. Besides horses, caravels soon began bringing raw cotton and woven cotton cloth—much of it after the 1470s woven on the Cape Verde Islands, using African techniques and slaves to do the weaving—as well as iron (some from elsewhere in Africa), copperware, and tobacco to exchange along Senegambia's coast and riverbanks.[30]

The earliest of this new group of foreign traders in Senegambia were from Portugal (with a few Genoese and one or two other south Europeans), but that was not the case for long. Portuguese men settled the Cape Verde archipelago. To grow their crops, tend horses, weave, and do most of the other work on the islands, these settlers imported slaves from Africa's west coast. The slave population of the islands soon outnumbered the free, eventually by a ratio of six or seven to one. Other coastal Africans immigrated to the Cape Verdes, some of them members of ruling elites. Once the inevitable unions between Portuguese men and African women occurred, a sizable population of mixed parentage came into being on the islands. These Luso-Africans had the advantage of familiarity with Portuguese and African cultures and languages; they would be the ones, largely, who would conduct the growing trade of the Guinea of Cape Verde of the late fifteenth and sixteenth centuries.[31]

The first generation of Portuguese and Cape Verdeans in the Gambia River were content to trade from their ships. After a short period of initial wariness, African merchants ventured to the caravels or longboats with their trade goods. In Niumi, once Gomes had worked out satisfactory arrangements with the ruler in the mid-1450s, shipboard trading proceeded smoothly for two decades. Then, Spaniards got involved and muddied the waters. Having gotten wind of the brisk trade and respectable profits that Portuguese merchants were taking, a Spanish captain led several caravels down the coast and into the Gambia in 1475. Not recognizing the Spanish as different from the Portuguese and assuming the vessels' arrival meant more friendly discourse, with gifts for dignitaries and prospects for profit, Niumi's *mansa* led his retinue aboard one of the Spanish ships. As the Portuguese had tried thirty years earlier, the Spaniard had his crew detain the ruler and his people; then he sent a force on land and rounded up another 140 men and women to take back to Cartegena in southern Spain. King Ferdinand of Aragon eventually heard of the incident and ordered the *mansa*'s return, but the others were sold into Spanish slavery. Not surprisingly, it was a while before Niumi's riverside villages were again receptive to Iberian visitors.[32]

But the lure of horses, inexpensive cloth, and iron bars eventually broke down suspicions, and the shipboard trade began again, as was happening all along West Africa's Atlantic coast. It was not long in Niumi and elsewhere before a disgruntled Portuguese merchant here or a venturesome Cape Verdean trader there turned his back on the islands and cast his lot on shore among the local population. Termed *lançados* (from the Portuguese verb, *lançar*, to cast or throw [oneself]), these men and their descendants settled and became permanent members of West Africa's coastwise trading communities. Their numbers mounted rapidly—by early in the sixteenth century, there were *lançado* groups in nearly every commercial village of coastal and riverine Senegambia. They married local women, produced offspring, and added to their kinship groups with slaves and other dependents. They would serve as the linguistic and cultural intermediaries for African-European commercial relations for several centuries.

When the first renegade Portuguese or Cape Verde Islanders came to live on Niumi soil, probably in the last decades of the fifteenth century, it was necessary for them to establish relationships with their African hosts that would enable them to fit into local society and exist in a way that would prove beneficial to themselves and the Africans alike. The *lançados* were not entirely familiar with Niumi's language and culture, and it was their task, as rapidly as possible, to adopt customs and norms of local residents. What simplified this adoption and assimilation was the existence of the institutional landlord-stranger relationship. It allowed *lançados* entry into the society and monitored the synthesis of Portuguese (or Cape Verdean) and African ways of living.

The first *lançados* would have needed to make initial arrangements with the *mansa*, the state's ultimate landlord. Niumi's ruler, or perhaps it was more than one *mansa* over several decades, sanctioned *lançado* settlement in a line of villages along the then-sparsely populated southern riverbank—Tubab Kolong (which means, in Mandinka, "white man's well"), Lamin, Juffure, San Domingo (no longer in existence), and Sika. The villages were founded by a combination of Africans and Portuguese (or Luso-Africans) for the specific purpose of becoming settlements for Niumi's growing population of "strangers," most of whom were advanced elements of one or another trade diaspora. Knowledgeable informants in Juffure say that their village was founded as a "stranger village" by members of an Islamic commercial and clerical lineage named Tall between 1495 and 1520. This lineage came to Niumi from Futa Toro on the Senegal River, possibly as horse traders. Descendants of the Talls admit, however, that their ancestors founded the village with the assistance of "some Portuguese," who already had settled San Domingo nearby.[33] Evidently, there was a symbiosis between enclave settlements of African, Portuguese, and Luso-African merchants.

These early *lançado*-African settlements quickly became the points of contact among Niumi's ruling families, its growing number of merchant lineages, and Europeans seeking trade in the Gambia River. They symbolized the partial reorientation of the state's commercial focus from the seaside, where Niumi's boatmen controlled the salt trade, to the riverbank, where rulers would have to exert other kinds of control over a different sort of trade in the hands of merchants from new locations.

It is important to recognize, however, that the upper hand in these cross-cultural, commercial relationships remained in the hands of the Africans. Europeans who came to the Gambia River to trade in the sixteenth century did not have overwhelming power at their disposal. Some of the caravels mounted cannon, but the most effective fighting the Portuguese did was with the crossbow, and they always were badly outnumbered. Those settling on African soil had to rely on local rulers to ensure conditions for safe passage of trade goods and protection of merchants from outside forces. The Portuguese also came with more obvious, basic needs—water and food were the most important—and they required help with everything from navigating over shoals and shifting sandbars to communicating with African rulers and traders. So, after the initial episodes like Tristão's, when they learned just how vulnerable they were, these early Europeans came to Niumi in an accommodating mode, ready to do what they must to work out a mutually beneficial trading relationship. Their lone trump cards were access to commodities that people in Niumi wanted and growing wealth from the lucrative trade that Niumi's ruling families desired to tax.[34]

Wherever Niumi's *mansa* might decide to settle a *lançado*, the person had to attach himself to a local landlord, a host who would oversee the person's dealings with others. The landlord would allocate a plot of land on which the *lançado* would be allowed to construct a dwelling and would see to it that the individual had food—at least until the newcomer could make his own arrangements. Besides help with essentials, the landlord would represent the stranger in local councils and defend him in disputes. He would vouch for the *lançado* when commercial dealings might require trust or credit and do what he could to ensure the stranger's success in the foreign setting. Over time, the landlord might assist the *lançado* in finding a spouse, one of his own daughters, perhaps, or another woman with good kinship connections. It was all an institutional way of integrating the stranger into Niumi's society.

Of course, Niumi's rulers did not allow strangers to settle, and landlords did not perform beneficial tasks for their strangers, merely out of the goodness of their hearts or an ingrained sense of hospitality. The stranger was long on liabilities and short on assets, but as he became successful, he had something valuable to offer and an informal obligation to see that his landlord and Niumi benefited from his success. This was done normally through the giving of gifts, with values commensurate to the stranger's success, and the payment of more regular fees and taxes to the family of the reigning *mansa*. No records exist for the size of such rents and fees until late in the seventeenth century, but by then Euro-African traders settled in Juffure on Niumi's riverbank paid the *mansa* an annual rent of fifty *écus* (the equivalent of 150 francs) and had to render a tax of one-tenth the value of all commodities traded.[35] Contemporary reports claim (in the fashion of complaint) that a *mansa* could enter a Euro-African dwelling and take from the resident whatever he wanted, but Europeans who wrote of such incidents were probably biased in favor of the Euro-African intermediaries and may have been witnessing rulers coming to take their unpaid due.[36] In any event, reports of such activity on the part of rulers show the dependent status of Europeans and Euro-Africans on foreign soil.

Over the course of the sixteenth century, the *lançado* population gained acceptance as part of Niumi's society. Much as the Muslim *jula* had done, *lançados* developed their own identity, based not on their physical appearance, for soon they had none that was different from anyone else in Niumi, but on several cultural characteristics they shared.[37] They referred to themselves as Portuguese because they retained outward elements of their Portuguese background: They constructed and lived in square dwellings with walls whitened with lime; wore European-style clothing; sported crucifixes and claimed to be Catholic, though many never had seen a cleric; kept Portuguese names; and considered themselves "white." Among other languages, *lançados* spoke Crioulo, a language with a Portuguese vocabulary and grammar but also a syntax largely from West African languages, which developed on the Cape Verde Islands and spread as a commercial lingua franca along Africa's west coast and up its rivers. Finally, as many did throughout West Africa, the *lançados* identified with their profession: one way or another, they were engaged in activities involving trade.

The most successful *lançados* were able to head sizable families and to gather about them slaves and retainers who could help in their commercial dealings. The retainers most noteworthy in European eyes were those they called *grumetes* (or *gromettas*), whom ship captains employed to serve as navigational guides, oarsmen, translators, and brokers. Successful Luso-African families in Niumi also might have hunters, praise-singers, blacksmiths, boatbuilders, fishermen, leatherworkers, African diviners, or Muslim holy men attached to their extended families. The longer they existed on Niumi soil, the more these extended families looked and acted like their hosts.

New Ways of Life

Over the several generations of heightened economic activity and political consolidation, everyday life in Niumi rolled on: men and women farmed; women pounded grain, gathered wood, cooked meals, and supervised childrearing; artisans busied themselves with their skills; Muslim merchants went about their commercial or religious activities, the former with increased vigor; and slave men and women worked in fields, wove cloth, extracted salt, or, if royal slaves, served as boatmen or cared for horses. But few aspects of that life were the same in 1600 as they had been 100 years earlier. Over the course of the sixteenth century, foreigners associated with the new commercial contacts brought a range of new material goods, new products, and alien ways of doing everything from propelling boats to building houses that altered the lives of the state's residents.

From the time of the consolidation and strengthening of the state around the mid-1600s, residents of Niumi benefited from ruling lineages' ability to marshal force enough to keep foreign raiders from their fields and villages. When effectively protected, most probably did not chafe at having to provide a portion of their produce to the royal families.

By the time the rulers had acquired such force, people in the state were residing in different kinds of villages. In the new setting, individual compounds were tucked behind palisades and entire villages were ringed by stockades. Valentim Fernandes, a German residing in Portugal who compiled information about the Gambia-Geba region in 1506, describes the compound of a "Mandi Mansa" in the lower Gambia as consisting of several dwellings inside six rings of stockades with archers guarding the opening of the inner ring. André Alvares de Almada, a Cape Verdean who made frequent trips up and down the Gambia, wrote in 1594: "Along the [Gambia] river and its creeks are certain military fortifications . . . made of very strong wooden stakes, their pointed ends embedded, and a rampart of earth behind . . . [each with] guard-towers, bastions, and parades." It seems reasonable to assume that the increased raiding for captives that appeared in response to heavy demand for slaves along the Atlantic coast and the fighting that accompanied the political reshuffling throughout the region—all affected by the increased supplies of horses—heightened insecurity in Niumi and brought its villagers to take these evident defensive measures. From the start of the sixteenth century until an effective *pax colonia* descended on the Gambia at the start of the twentieth century, residents of Niumi would feel safe only behind palisade walls.[38]

Over time, the look of dwellings inside the villages changed, too—this because Portuguese and Luso-Africans brought with them their own architectural notions of form and function and blended them with materials, construction techniques, and styles they found in their new homes.[39] The sixteenth century saw the development of a housing style that European chroniclers referred to as "à la portugaise." This was a square dwelling rather than a round one, constructed of stone in the early years but eventually of African-style mud bricks. The exterior walls were covered with chalk or white clay, roofs were of thatch, and inside was a vestibule for receiving guests and transacting business. Such houses appeared first in Luso-African quarters of commercial villages, but because their occupants had the elevated status of traders, a position often associated, rightly or wrongly, with material wealth, the houses themselves came to be symbols of high status. It was not long before Niumi's rulers, Muslim merchants, and persons of means from other callings constructed their houses "in the Portuguese style."

Boatbuilding went through similar changes. Over the course of the seventeenth century, boatbuilders in Niumi picked up elements of European construction styles and propulsion techniques and blended them with the traditional dugout canoe to come up with an entirely new type of coastal and riverine trading vessel: the pirogue. This had a dugout as its basis, but had reinforced planking up the sides, husky wave breakers extending front and back, and sails. By 1600 the vessels were ubiquitous in the Gambia and up and down the Atlantic north and south of there. From then until the middle of the twentieth century, when motorized barges came to play a bigger role, the pirogue, in one form or another, was the primary vessel used to convey people and commodities about the region.[40]

Yet, the new products or adaptations that had the most far-reaching implications for life in Niumi were living things. Over the course of 150 years Portuguese and Luso-Africans introduced a host of new plants and animals—from Europe and from the more distant continents with which Europeans were recently in contact—that would greatly alter the diets and affect the health and well being of Niumi's residents.

Newcomers naturally wanted to eat and drink what they were accustomed to, so some of the earliest short-term visitors from Portugal or the Cape Verdes attempted to grow things that grew back home.[41] For one reason or another, many of their experiments ended in failure: European grains, grapes, peaches, olives, lettuce, cabbage, onions, and garlic failed test plantings. But from their homes in southwestern Europe and contacts around the Mediterranean rim, Portuguese sailors obtained and successfully introduced melons, figs, eggplants, and chickpeas. They also brought pigs and a healthier strain of chickens, both of which reproduced adequately. More important still, after the European voyages to East Asia and to the New World at the end of the fifteenth century, Portuguese and Cape Verdeans introduced other fruits and vegetables: coconuts, bananas, plantains, and a more productive strain of rice from East Asia; maize, cassava, chili peppers, peanuts, papayas, guavas, and tobacco from the Americas. It was fortunate that these plants happened to arrive in Niumi during a period of abundant rainfall, between 1500 and 1630.[42] The new crops grew well and the results were significant. Within a few generations, the Asian rice had replaced indigenous rice, making rice growers more important as providers for society. Local residents never took to maize as a staple of their diet—they preferred rice and millet—but they grew it eventually to sell to Europeans and in time recognized its importance in ripening early and thus serving as a suitable food at the end of the growing season ("the hungry season"), before rice and millet were harvested. They did like the new chilies, however, and perhaps enjoyed better health from the vitamin C the fiery peppers provided. Relatively quickly, Gambian stews took the place they hold today among the spiciest foods eaten on the continent.[43]

Farmwork was made easier, too, by the importation into Niumi of iron bars. Local blacksmiths had long been able to smelt iron and fashion tools appropriate for agricultural needs, but obtaining ore and producing charcoal were expensive operations that took time. Early European traders brought flat iron bars, the raw material for the blacksmiths to produce tools and weapons. Some came directly from Europe and some from local manufacture at other points along the West African coast. Before long, Niumi blacksmiths could turn out many more hoes for cultivating and machetes for beginning and maintaining farm plots and kitchen gardens, and they could do it more cheaply than before. When combined with the new crops and the more productive varieties of old crops available to farmers, access to inexpensive iron contributed to a rise in food output, improvement of the diets of the Niumi residents, and an ability to support a larger population. This combination of factors also made possible the production of sufficient surplus goods to provide for alien garrisons on European outposts in the seventeenth and eighteenth centuries and to stock slavers with grain as they left for the new world.[44]

The growing importation of iron bars had implications for Niumi's rulers and their offensive and defensive aspirations as well. As the sixteenth century progressed, Niumi's ruling elites could much more easily obtain the raw material for their blacksmiths to fashion weapons—spears, arrows, daggers, swords, and harpoons—so they could arm a greater military force, on land or water. This prompted them to seek more fighting personnel. The quickest way to do so was to purchase captives. They could obtain slaves in the traditional manner, by exchanging salt or dried fish for men and women from the interior lands, or, with their expanding cavalry, they could capture slaves in the region and trade them to lands farther away in exchange for slaves from some distance. (Slaves were of limited value near their point of capture, because they could easily escape and return home. Slave values increased with their distance from home.) In this fashion the internal capture and flow of slaves grew within a century of the beginning of western Africa's participation in the Atlantic economy.[45]

Thus, Europeans, mostly Portuguese, and Luso-Africans provided residents of Niumi access to a new economic endeavor, an Atlantic commercial complex. At the same time, Muslim African traders linked the land of Niumi more thoroughly to the trans-Sahara, sahel, and savanna commercial network that had been in existence for centuries. Through steadily increasing participation in these economic systems between 1446 and 1600, people in Niumi gained new methods of control, new means to enhance and broaden old forms of social and political relationships, new sources of raw materials, new products, new residents in the state, and new ways of doing things. Rulers, artisans, merchants, and many freeborn farmers benefited from the novelties. Others, many (though not all) slaves in particular, found life more difficult, with new kinds of work and new punishments for not doing it. In all these ways, over that century and a half, life in Niumi changed considerably. The Niumi of 1600 was different politically, socially, culturally, and religiously from the Niumi that existed before Nuno Tristão's caravel poked into the river in 1446. For the next two centuries, however, change would come at a slower pace.

NIUMI AT THE HEIGHT OF
THE ATLANTIC COMPLEX

Seventeenth and Eighteenth Centuries

*The great number of canoes and men employed in this commerce
gives great influence and respect to the king. Indeed, he is the most
powerful and terrible of all the kings of the Gambia; he has imposed
considerable duties on the ships of all nations.*

—J.B.L. Durand, c. 1806[1]

A body of mythology surrounds and confounds our understanding of West African
societies that participated in the Atlantic slave trade. One myth of long standing is
that powerful and wily European captains sailed their ships along Africa's western
coasts, sent longboats ashore, and grabbed unsuspecting African men and women to
fill their vessels and, eventually, to sell in the Americas as slave labor. The absurdity
of this portrayal of Africans—as hapless folk unable to stop the kidnapping and
as passive ciphers in the cross-cultural commercial dealings—has not reduced its
tenacity in the minds of generations of people.

A similar and equally inaccurate myth is what Curtin terms "the old stereotype
of gewgaws for slaves": the misconception that Europeans traded mostly worth-
less goods to Africans for the heart of their most productive manpower, implying
that "the Europeans hoodwinked a group of ignorant savages into parting with
something of considerable value in return for nothing, or even for goods that were
positively harmful."[2]

Unfortunately, historians of a generation ago did little to dispel such myths. It
is in the nature of those who write history to bring the ideas of their own culturally chauvinistic place and time to consideration of others, and the mid-twentieth
century was the end of a long period of strong racist notions among Western intellectuals. Many of the time were unable to recognize anything resembling order
and rationality in precolonial African state and social structures. As late as 1963,
a noted historian stated on British television that African history before the late-
nineteenth-century takeover by Europeans amounted to the "unrewarding gyrations
of barbarous tribes in picturesque but irrelevant corners of the globe."[3] In such an
intellectual climate, accurate assessment of African societies that participated in
the Atlantic economy was not likely to occur. There was no reason for Niumi to
be an exception. Although the state existed in the same locale for half a millennium and its residents dealt with Europeans from a position of strength through

most of the period, John M. Gray in his 1940 *History of the Gambia* termed Niumi and the other Gambian states "petty districts" that "lacked the unity and stability which really qualifies a territory for the title of kingdom." Gray described these states' rulers as nothing more than "war lords, who rose and fell very often with astonishing rapidity."[4]

Niumi was considerably more than a petty district commanded by warlords. Through the seventeenth and eighteenth centuries, when the state's participation in the Atlantic trade was at its height, Niumi was a stable state with a typical Mandinka political and social structure that, over the decades, its rulers modified to meet new necessities brought about through participation in the Atlantic complex. Europeans trading in the Gambia recognized the state's strength and curried favor from Niumi's *mansa* and scores of the state's other prominent people. Africans never dictated terms of the trade—the global market and laws of supply and demand did that—but Niumi's rulers determined much about how the cross-cultural exchange took place and controlled European access to Gambian commerce sufficiently to ensure the state's profit into the early years of the nineteenth century.

Furthermore, there is an element of irony in Niumi's history through the two centuries of its most active participation in the Atlantic trade. It is a natural assumption that slave trading was disruptive to local politics and society—that raiding, capturing, defending, and dealing with acquisitive foreigners were activities that led to a breakdown in established polity and society. This simply does not appear to have been the case through the seventeenth and eighteenth centuries in Niumi. People in the state experienced change over the first century and more of participation in the waxing Atlantic trade, before 1600, and as its position in the huge economic complex declined after 1800, the state's viability came under serious threat and its society changed considerably. But the two centuries or more when Niumi was engaged most fully in the Atlantic-oriented commerce (which we tend to think of only as slave trading) was a period of relative political and social stability in the state. People in Niumi's villages in 1800 lived more like their ancestors had lived in 1600 than like their children or grandchildren would exist in 1850. That seems to be the case for most of the states along the Gambia River: by 1600, ways of dealing with foreign merchants and shippers had become institutionalized, and the institutions would not come under serious threat and require drastic alteration until several decades after the end of slave trading toward the Atlantic. By then, much in the rest of the world was changing and people in Niumi would experience the full, disruptive effects in many aspects of their lives.

Niumi's Expanding World

Three different kinds of events had the greatest effect on the ways people lived in Niumi in the seventeenth and eighteenth centuries. One was natural: the steady drying of the climate, forcing a gradual alteration of lifestyles of those who relied on crop growing and animal breeding. The second was driven by human hands and involved further incorporation into a world economic system: it was the expansion of the Atlantic complex, fueled by a growing European craving for sugar, that heightened demand on New World plantations for laborers and raised demand in West Africa for commodities from Europe, Asia, the Americas, and other parts of Africa in exchange for them. The third was less dramatic than the others: it involved the increasing acceptance by people from all levels of Niumi's society of some of the ways of living, thinking, and acting of Muslim clerics and mystics living in enclave villages in their midst. None of these events was entirely disruptive. Niumi's rulers found ways to adapt the polity, economy, and society to meet the changing circumstances. But taken together, the events made Niumi a different place to live in 1800 than it was two centuries earlier.

The Ecological Base

Historians who have studied climate phases in West Africa do not agree on when long wet or dry periods occurred in different places.[5] Data are not sufficient for careful climatic reconstruction by years or decades, and rains have always fallen unevenly and unpredictably across West Africa's savannas. But James L.A. Webb, Jr., calls attention to one climatic fact that seems unassailable: since about 1600, with only minor regional fluctuation and short-term variance, West Africa's sahel and savanna have experienced a "marked trend toward increasing aridity." When he compared older maps of the region with more recent ones, Webb noticed "bodies of water [that] evaporate from the cartographic record," and from historical data on rainfall in Senegal he concludes that the same amount of annual precipitation judged "below-average" in the mid-eighteenth century was considered "above average" for a typical year in the mid-twentieth century.[6] There is no doubt that over the past several centuries West Africa, including the land of Niumi, has dried out.

One can imagine the effects this gradual alteration of rain-based ecological underpinnings had on the lives of people in Niumi. Among the effects for farming communities of reduced rainfall are more difficult circumstances for the production of food crops and, more often than before, periods when there is not enough grown locally to eat. As rainfall declined, the season of rain shortened and such rains that fell came more frequently in storms. This meant that erosion was more prevalent, that rain tended to run off rather than be absorbed into the soil, and that crop yields in the less-nourishing soil diminished. Fallowing did not replenish soils as efficiently as in times of heavier rainfall, too, so farming villages probably moved more frequently than before. Evidence exists of regular movement of Niumi's villages, perhaps of only a few miles at a time, through recent centuries.[7] Plus decisions about which crops to grow seem to have changed. The Portuguese had introduced maize to Senegambia during the wetter sixteenth century, and Niumi's farmers grew the crop to sell to the English garrison on James Island and to the slave ships heading for the Americas. But by the mid-twentieth century it was difficult to find a stalk of maize growing in Niumi. For staple food crops, Niumi farmers today plant millet, sorghum, or rice. While these grains do not approach the yield of maize when there is sufficient rainfall, millet and sorghum have greater yields in seasons of low rainfall or drought.[8]

The gradual decrease of rainfall and changing ecological base also affected the ability of the state's rulers to enhance cavalry forces. Because the tsetse fly that spreads trypanosomiasis requires thick foliage for coverage, reduced brush associated with drier conditions means healthier conditions for horses, resulting in longer lives for mounts, easier breeding, and more effective crossbreeding. So as rainfall diminished in West Africa through the seventeenth and eighteenth centuries, the zones of horse breeding north of the Senegal River moved south. While Niumi never became a place where horses had long lives or where one could breed horses effectively, the sources of horses through overland trade moved closer.[9] When they desired to do so, Niumi's ruling elites could more easily, and perhaps more cheaply, obtain horses from African sources. Such access to horses would be important in the enhancement of Niumi's military aristocracy as the eighteenth century wore on.

The Growth of Mercantile Capitalism and the Expanding Atlantic Complex

The expansion of the Atlantic economic complex that took place in the seventeenth and eighteenth centuries was part of a larger phenomenon associated with a pulling together of European wealth and its investment in worldwide commercial ventures. All of this led to greater European participation in an expanding global trade.[10]

Through the sixteenth century, Portugal and Spain remained masters of economic complexes that spanned a great portion of the globe, but by the century's end their domination of commercial networks would come under increasing challenge from other Europeans. The Dutch, English, and French rose to be important participants in world trade through the course of the seventeenth century. The Dutch, who were masterful seamen, were the first to encroach on Hispanic monopolies. Individual Dutch merchants could not amass enough wealth to compete directly with Spain, however, so they found ways to pool their wealth for collaborative ventures through the institution of the joint-stock company. With broad investment in a company run by a board of directors responsible to its stockholders, they could mount grand trading expeditions to markets about the world and stick their noses into far-flung Iberian business. Thus, with the resources of the East and West India Companies (established in 1600 and 1621, respectively), Dutch entrepreneurs ventured in trade for spices in the East and worked to wrest a share of the carrying trade of the Atlantic. Because merchant ships were armed for protection, a fine line separated commercial competition and military encroachment. The Dutch were inclined toward whichever seemed more prudent at the time. Through the first half of the seventeenth century, the Dutch captured Portuguese outposts in East Asia, West Africa, and Brazil, and it was clear they had scant regard for any Spanish notion of monopoly in the Americas. England and France were weaker maritime powers, so their nationals moved more slowly overseas, but by the middle of the seventeenth century, they, too, were manning outposts in India, West Africa, and on Caribbean islands where they could gain a greater share of the thriving trade.

As noted, the slave trade from Africa to the Americas was solidly in place by 1600. In a typical year of the early seventeenth century, Europeans would acquire some 5,000 slaves along Africa's west coast and ship them across the ocean to sugar plantations in Brazil or mining operations in Peru. But the entire Atlantic commercial complex was to expand greatly for the next two centuries. In terms of shipment of slaves, the system reached a peak between 1740 and 1810, when every year, on average, over 67,000 slaves were imported into staple-producing plantations that stretched from British North America, through the islands of the Caribbean, to Brazil and beyond.[11] It was an intercontinental economic complex on the largest scale yet and it held great significance not only for people living on lands bordering the Atlantic, but for others around the world as well.

The biggest stimulus to growth of the Atlantic complex was the increasing ability of English and French traders to accumulate capital and participate on larger and more favorable terms in the expanding world market. "Adventurers" (as the English referred to those who risked capital in commercial enterprises) from England and France settled islands in the eastern Caribbean and then, in the 1640s, turned the settlements toward plantation agriculture on a larger scale than ever before. For the Caribbean it was a sugar revolution, stimulated by Dutch shippers who cared less about who owned the plantations and more about profiting from the carrying trade of slaves and cane. To the English and French settling Caribbean islands in the first half of the seventeenth century, Dutch carriers gave instruction on production techniques and offered to sell machinery and slaves and to purchase sugar. The movement was rapid. On Barbados, the early leader in the sugar revolution, for example, no sugar was produced in 1637, but by 1645, 40 percent of the island was planted in sugar, and by the 1670s Barbados was producing 65 percent of all the sugar consumed in England. The English and French Antilles followed Barbados's lead, and once European mariners solved problems of catching appropriate winds for the eastbound, trans-Atlantic voyage, Jamaica and Cuba became big sugar producers. By the start of the eighteenth century, the Caribbean was one massive enterprise that exported sugar and imported laborers and foods to feed them from all around the Atlantic.

Factors in the growth of the Atlantic plantation complex and the slave trade that supported it were Europe's population expansion and disease-related demographic factors on both sides of the ocean. After a setback from the Black Death in the fourteenth century, Europe's population recovered and began growing more rapidly, aided by new food crops from the Americas. Although relatively free of large animals and many of the diseases associated with them that shortened human life, the Americas were loaded with foodstuffs from which they alone had benefited.

Coming to Europe over the course of the sixteenth century was a cornucopia of vegetables that included most varieties of beans, squash, tomatoes, and, by far of greatest importance, maize and potatoes. Relatively easy to grow and full of carbohydrates and important vitamins, these plants, when combined with European technological improvements and the clearing of more land for agriculture, added greatly to the European diet. With more and better food, Europe's population led a worldwide trend toward steady increase. In Europe the number of people went from 70 million in 1500 to 90 million in 1600, 100 million in 1650, and 180 million by the end of the eighteenth century. There were simply more people to consume sugar, and do a host of other things, every year.[12]

Furthermore, as wealth flowed to Europe because of its expanding economy, more people had money to buy products that heretofore had been luxuries. Sugar was one. And the price of sugar went down steadily because of improved production techniques and cheaper freight rates that resulted from increasing European shipping capacity. This increased demand even more. Per capita sugar consumption in Britain was only four pounds a year in 1700, but it doubled by 1750 and more than doubled again, to eighteen pounds, by 1800. More people wanting more sugar meant the continuing quest to increase production on more cleared land across a greater extent of the tropical Atlantic.

Yet, this alone did not account for the growing demand for African slaves. By 1700 between 1.5 and 2 million Africans had been carried to the Americas, most to work on sugar plantations. With a growth rate reasonable for the time, this population could have provided sufficient labor for the expanding tropical plantations. But it experienced no growth rate at all; in fact, the slave population in the Americas could not sustain itself through procreation. A lack of acquired immunities to some tropical diseases kept death rates of slaves high. Moreover, a notion held by some planters that it was less expensive to purchase a mature slave direct from the Atlantic passage than it was to rear a slave in the Americas (meaning that many planters did not encourage, and often actively discouraged, childbirth among their slaves) led to birth rates among the plantation labor force that were lower than normal. Thus, in a coldly economic sense, the plantations scattered across the American tropics consumed manpower. Figures supporting this phenomenon are startling: on the island of Jamaica, 750,000 slaves were imported between 1640 and 1834, when slavery there ended. On the latter date, the island's black population numbered only 350,000.[13] Simply maintaining the labor force required importing slaves every year, but to meet the increasing demand for sugar, more and more laborers were required. West and West Central Africa would continue to be the source for such captive laborers.

Because northern European maritime powers had used force in their competition with Spain and Portugal—and eventually with one another—and because the Dutch had already begun seizing Portuguese outposts along the African coast by the 1640s, European governments began seeing to it that their nationals built fortified trading posts to protect their share of the African trade. Ideal spots for such

Perspective 5   **The African Diaspora**

For over four and one-half centuries, African slaves were transported across the Atlantic to work as laborers. In round numbers, some 10 million Africans were sold as slaves in the Americas. Until the beginning of massive European migration in the last half of the nineteenth century, more Africans than Europeans crossed the Atlantic each year. The largest numbers were taken to the Caribbean islands and Brazil, but many also went to Spanish Central and South America and British and French mainland North America. Historians refer to this movement of people outside the African continent and their population of most parts of the Americas as the African Diaspora. In terms of everything from commerce and production to cultural heritage, the African Diaspora is one of the most important phenomena in the history of North and South America.

When considering numbers of slave imports in relative perspective, British mainland North America (later the United States) was a smaller part of the Atlantic plantation complex, and of the African Diaspora, than many other regions. Fewer than half a million African slaves came directly to British ports on the North American mainland, one-third fewer than were imported onto the small Caribbean island of Jamaica. But for a variety of reasons, the slave population of the United States grew more rapidly than elsewhere, so today the country has one of the largest African American populations in the Americas.

Slaves from around the Gambia River were involved in the Diaspora from its beginnings until early in the nineteenth century. Relatively large numbers of Gambian slaves crossed the ocean in the first century of Atlantic slaving— they were important in early Spanish mining operations in Peru and sugar production on Hispaniola—and the numbers did not fall off so much as those from other places along the African coast grew much larger. Gambian slaves played important roles in the history of the United States. In her book, *Black Rice*, Judith Carney shows that slaves from the Gambia River region were among those who transferred a culture of rice growing from their homelands to coastal South Carolina, where landowners established a long-lasting plantation system based on the technology. And it was along the banks of the Gambia River—in a Niumi village, in fact—where Alex Haley, author of *Roots* (see Chapter 7), claimed to have found his maternal ancestor.

Judith Carney, *Black Rice: The African Origins of Rice Cultivation in the Americas* (Cambridge, MA: Harvard University Press, 2001).

fortifications were easily defended, and from the European viewpoint marginally healthier, islands near the coast. The Dutch fortified Gorée island, off Cape Verde, in 1647, and in 1651 the duke of the Baltic duchy of Kurland sent an expedition into the mouth of the Gambia River with the intention of building a settlement to

Photo 4   **James Island, in the Gambia River, off Juffure. The island holds the ruins of James Fort, outpost of English trading concerns between 1661 and 1779.**

foster and protect what he conceived to be his land's economic calling in West Africa. The Kurlanders liked the looks of an island twenty-five miles upriver from the mouth, a small, anvil-shaped body almost centered in the river off Niumi's southern riverbank. The duke's agent negotiated with Niumi's *mansa* for the right to occupy the otherwise useless island and to have access to a small plot on Niumi's riverbank where the island's garrison could gather wood and draw water in return for an annual payment. For the next decade, amid regular threats from rival European privateers (some of which Niumi's boatmen helped deter), the Kurland garrison held the island and traded in the river.[14]

Kurland's chances of keeping its outpost in the face of challenges from stronger European competitors were slim, but they were made slimmer by notions in England that there were mountains of gold up the Gambia River and an abundance of slaves there for the English islands in the Caribbean. In 1661, an English chartered company, the Royal Adventurers of England Trading into Africa, sent an expedition to set up an outpost in the Gambia. Its leaders negotiated with Niumi's *mansa* and then gave the seven remaining Kurlanders on the island a choice between safe passage home or certain death. They took the former. On March 19, 1661, employees of the Royal Adventurers occupied the island, named it James Island for James, the Duke of York, and began an English presence in the river that would be longer lasting than that of any other European nation. In the 1670s, the Royal African Company, with a grant of monopoly over Gambian trade from the English government, took over James Island (and on it by then, James Fort) from the defunct Adventurers and attempted to wring profits out of the trade.

The English would never be free of European competition in the Gambian trade, however. In 1677, during one of many mercantile wars of the period, the French took Dutch forts at Gorée and on the adjacent mainland, effectively ending Dutch trading along the upper Guinea coast. In 1681 the French Compagnie du Sénégal obtained the trading rights in West Africa of an older French chartered company and then sent an agent to negotiate with Niumi's *mansa* for a plot of land for an unfortified trading post at Albreda, on Niumi's riverbank, in eyesight of James Island. The French occupied Albreda and stayed there (with some hiatuses) until 1857, and French merchants would remain important in Niumi's ties to the Atlantic trade and the world market for a longer time. Thus, within a generation after 1660, Niumi's rulers became landlords for trading diasporas of the two European nations that would figure most prominently in worldwide commerce for the next two centuries.

The Long March of Islam

Not all cultural and economic influences on people of the Upper Guinea coast in the seventeenth and eighteenth centuries came from the Atlantic. Some arrived overland, as ever, from the savannas that stretched eastward between the southern edge of the Sahara and the northern reaches of the Guinea forests. For the lower Gambia, because the majority of the region's people looked to the Mandinka heartland along the upper Niger River for their spiritual and cultural home, these influences included a strong element of Mandinka culture. But over several centuries following the demise of the Mali and Jolof empires, Islamic cultural influences, particularly from the Senegal River valley, continued to bear, and more heavily still, on the lives of people on all levels of Niumi's society. The period that saw people along the Gambia River participating more fully than ever in the Atlantic economy also saw the spreading of more Muslim merchants, scholars, and mystics, and the slow assimilation of parts of their spiritual outlook by more than just the commercial elements in African societies.

Such a steady assimilation of Islamic cultural practices was hardly unique to Niumi or West Africa; it was taking place across far-flung parts of the Eurasian landmass and Africa's east coast. Grand Islamic empires between the Mediterranean Sea and India captured the attention of seventeenth- and eighteenth-century Europeans, but these empires' conquering armies were not the principal agents of Islam's spread. The major purveyors of the Arabic language and a greater Islamic civilization were the lone mystics and scholarly clerics, consumed by spiritual affairs and thus no threat to rulers of states or heads of armies among whom they traveled. These individuals or lineage groups studied the Qur'an and other bodies of Islamic literature; moved about; settled enclave villages; set up informal schools; sold their ability to divine the future, protect persons from harm, and heal bodily ills; and generally created small fountains of an Islamic lifestyle in ponds of foreign culture that were the wonder and envy of the surrounding non-Muslim majorities.

Gradually, some of the Muslims' ways became the ways of others. In specific instances the distinction between who was a Muslim and who was not became blurred. It was not love of Allah and respect for Muhammad that was spreading so much as it was certain ways of life and thought practices of those who loved Allah and revered the Prophet. Some of the culture of the Islamic world, or, in a grand sense, a part of Islamic civilization, was being adopted by people who still communicated with deities through their ancestors and sacrificed animals to appease spirits of the soil. This assimilation was a critical part of what African historians call "The Long March of Islam," the slow spreading of Islamic culture and then, ultimately, the Islamic faith among people of the West African savannas.[15]

This assimilation was manifested in Niumi by Fulbe and Mandinka lineages, which moved to the lower river's north bank in the sixteenth century and after. Commerce brought them to settle in the villages of Juffure, Albreda, and Sika, where they fit comfortably with the Africans and Luso-Africans participating in trade. By the eighteenth century, Muslim lineages were establishing villages in Niumi away from the river and close to villages of ruling groups, locating themselves where they could benefit from the protection of rulers and, just as important, perform magical and spiritual functions for those in the state with the greatest ability to pay for their services. Rulers whose position of leadership was rooted in ties to traditional spirits and deities began appearing in public with Muslim advisors, wearing charms containing words from the Qur'an, and seeking maraboutic divination before taking major courses of action. Islam's march was under way through the years of heaviest slave trading, and European observers who kept records noticed. They simply failed to pay it much attention.

The Niumi Polity

Elders in Niumi and oral traditionists from around the lower Gambia have a good laugh, mostly, when they tell the story of Nandanko Suntu Sonko. Old Nandanko, the fifth *mansa* of Niumi from the Sonko lineage residing in Berending, tried to stop the flow of the Gambia River. He did it by getting his subjects to throw rocks into the river along the state's southeastern riverbank, near Sika. Something to that effect seems really to have happened. Resident traders on James Island wrote in December 1760: "The king . . . is on a scheme of stopping some Part of the River, in order to prevent large vessels from passing his country and of course to bring the [slave] coffles down. We look upon it as chimerical and what cannot be effected." The reason the English regarded the effort as absurd is the same reason people today shake their heads and chuckle when they tell the story: the river is more than three miles wide at the spot of all the rock throwing.[16]

Sonko, however, was not bereft of his senses. At least in a figurative way, or one that would send an appropriate message to European shippers, he was reaffirming his claim to control of traffic that tied the Gambia and its hinterland into the Atlantic complex. Long before the middle of the eighteenth century, Niumi's rulers had institutionalized their method of gaining wealth from the river trade. Shippers wanting to obtain slaves or other commodities had to do so on Niumi's terms. Masters of vessels entering the river had to pay fees for anchorage and taking on wood or water. Those wanting to sail upriver, where access to slaves was more direct and prices more favorable, had to employ extra crewmembers, brokers, and interpreters from Niumi's mixed populace; and Niumi's rulers collected ad valorem duty on all transactions. The wealth that allowed the ruling families to enjoy their elite lifestyle; to maintain their strategically important cavalry; to dress in finery, eat well, drink spirits of their choice, and marry sons and daughters to other prestigious families around the region and thus maintain collective security came largely from the river trade. Sonko wanted to make sure everyone knew that Niumi's rulers were serious about keeping control of flow along the river—not of water toward the ocean, as the English noted, but of river traffic in the other direction.

State Structures

One thing above all others was the key to Niumi's stability and prosperity through the seventeenth and eighteenth centuries: the ability of the state's rulers to control and tax the busy trade between the western savannas and the Atlantic complex that passed along its shores and through the state. Those who controlled political and social functions of the state recognized this and developed institutions to maintain order and ensure state revenues through the period when the slave trade, and the no-less-significant trade of other commodities, was going on all around. By the time of the state's thorough incorporation into the Atlantic economic complex, Niumi had developed an efficient, systematic, manageable, and adaptable political apparatus. Its basis was the Mandinka village and state structure long in place across the Mande-speaking savanna world. But Niumi's ruling families gradually altered and expanded elements of the structure to meet the new circumstances surrounding the state's involvement with Atlantic commerce.[17]

The basis of Niumi's administration was the hierarchical system of Mandinka polities involving family, village, and state. People at each level had progressively broadening functions. The nuclear family—a man, his wife or wives, and their children—was a basic social grouping, but several related nuclear families in the same village lived together and operated as a unit. Such extended families varied in size; large ones might make up half or more of one village. Generally, the eldest male of the original family group was the extended family's head. With the advice of other male family elders, he supervised matters pertaining to birth, death, marriage, circumcision, divorce, inheritance, interfamily affairs, and relations with dependents—slaves, visitors, or wards.

A village was a collection of between four and a dozen extended families. Again, one of the eldest male members of the village's founding lineage was normally the village head, or *alkalo*; heads of the other lineages and prosperous individuals served as a council. These men decided when to plant and harvest, how to regulate

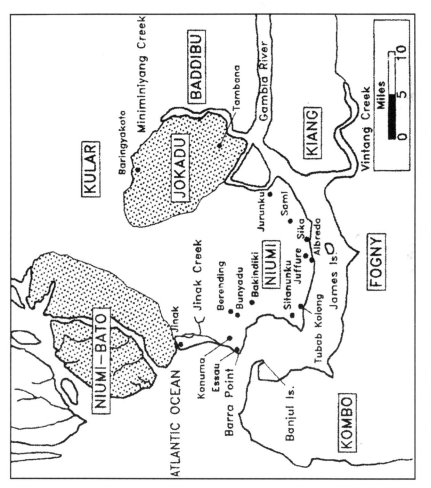

Map 7   The Niumi State, Seventeenth and Eighteenth Centuries

bush fires and care for livestock, where to locate family compounds, and which plots of land the different families could use. Village leaders also looked after public works—construction and maintenance of wells, granaries, paths, and the like—and supervised public ceremonies and celebrations. The village head was the principal adjudicator in disputes among the village's lineages. In masked form, to hide symbolically and help eliminate conflicting loyalties involving kin and friends, the village leaders meted out justice. Finally, the head of the village worked with, though not specifically for, Niumi's ruling lineages in collecting taxes, summoning manpower for military pursuits, policing the village and its approaches, and taking other action that would help maintain peace and state security. Village elders gave rulers counsel when asked. The frequency of this depended on the strategic or commercial importance of the village or the relationship, through marriage, among village families and the ruling lineages.

The state, then, was a collection of lineages in a group of villages. The *mansa*, as head of state, represented the figure of leadership of all the state's separate lineages and the formal link with their collective group of ancestors. People addressed him as "grandfather," the symbolic authority figure of every lineage in the state. He was the spiritual leader of all the non-Muslim residents, and as such, he played a key role in the communal worship of Niumi's spirits that resided in the ground and tall trees. As head of the hierarchy of authority he had a range of responsibilities: keeping order; defending the state, and thus raising armies for defense or deterrence; levying taxes and controlling commercial exchange; and supervising relations with persons outside the state and with other states.

Beyond his responsibilities, the *mansa* was the embodiment of the state. His well-being and that of Niumi were the same and his actions represented the state. For these reasons, people expected him and those around him to live a life they could speak of in superlatives. When the *mansa* ate, he ate the best food and lots of it; when he drank, he drank the most of the best spirits. When he rode it was on the finest horse fitted with the best-worked saddle. He owned the most slaves and had the most wives—sometimes more than a score, many from leading families in various Niumi's villages and other states, with political connections in mind. His granaries were the most numerous, the first filled, and the last emptied. And, literally, his drum beat loudest.

Court Officials

Officials in the *mansa*'s court assisted in administration. Most were physically close to the *mansa*—the English called them "the King's people": they included attendants, advisors, and assistants, though some typically were hangers-on. Most were from an entourage built over the years. Niumi's ruling lineages gradually modified the duties of these officials to accommodate dealings with the broadening commercial world.

In everyday affairs, the *mansa* had a chief of staff, frequently his closest advisor. Contemporary Englishmen called him the "King's Key Keeper."[18] His primary duty was to filter visitors. For those not allowed access, he conveyed messages (as the *mansa* often remained in his dwelling or behind a screen) and returned with replies. He also managed the ruling household. This official was selected from among the trustworthiest of the ruling lineage's royal slaves. His rewards were related to how much he could enhance the *mansa*'s position and prestige, and in personal remuneration through receipt of a "dash" when the *mansa* received a gift, rather than social advancement.

Still closer physically to the *mansa* were several bodyguards, called *satalama*, who ensured proper treatment of the ruler as well as his personal safety. People in Niumi still speak of the two stout bodyguards, dressed in black head ties, who sat on either side of the state's next-to-last reigning *mansa*. "If you wanted to kill Mansa Wali," one man said, "you had to kill them first."[19] Records of the Royal African Company from the 1680s show a bodyguard in action. The company's chief agent, Alexander Cleeve, came onto Niumi soil to resolve a dispute involving an assault committed by an English trader named Hodges on a Niumi resident. *Mansa* Jenung Wuleng Sonko had seized the company's agent at Juffure and would not release him without compensation for the assault. The haughty Cleeve found Sonko "at the foot of a great tree," records read, surrounded by bodyguards and courtiers. Cleeve strode up and said to Sonko, "How now, old Gennow, how is it?'" Quickly, he realized the impropriety of his casual conduct. The record continues: "But one of the grandees, by name Sambalama, taught him better manners by reaching him a box on the ears, which beat off his hat, and a few thumps on the back, and seizing him, disarmed him together with the rest of his attendance, amongst which was Benedict Stafford, commander of the *Margaret*, now in London (who made his escape and ran like a lusty fellow to his ship) and . . . several others, who together with the agent were taken and put into the king's pound and stayed there three or four days till their ransom was brought, value five hundred bars."[20]

The bodyguards were royal slaves, also. Their dependence on the *mansa* was the key to their position. If he died they would lose everything—prestige, comfortable surroundings, and perhaps their lives—and gain nothing.

Other court members included bards, diviners, magical practitioners, and royal slaves performing a further variety of tasks. One or more bards accompanied the ruler wherever he went, announcing his presence, communicating with large audiences, speaking for the *mansa*, and regularly singing his and his family's praises. Accounts from James Island regularly show gifts given to the *mansa*'s "drummers" and "singing men." Magical practitioners were among the most important court members. No successful Niumi man would be far from a trusted worker of magic. Such individuals divined the future, practiced healing, interpreted dreams, and made amulets and charms for most conceivable reasons: to protect the individual, to ensure bountiful crops, to help hunters at the hunt or warriors in battle. A special group of practitioners were the intermediaries between the *mansa* and the spirits of the land, normally worshiped or shown respect through icons or fetishes. These men prepared sacrifices—often fowls, or for greater occasion, cattle—and read the spirits' wishes in their acceptance or rejection of the sacrifice. In return for their services, magical workers' families received food and slaves. Successful warfare often brought captives and the *mansa* would designate some for the diviners who predicted success or the makers of amulets that protected soldiers and horses. Over the seventeenth and eighteenth centuries, Muslim clerics, with the generic label of "marabout," came to play an increasingly important role in magical practice in Niumi. At least one of Niumi's royal lineages, the Sonko of Berending, had a marabout lineage, the Fati of Aljamdu, just a few miles away, attached permanently to them in a patron-client relationship. Marabouts won a reputation for being the best at certain kinds of magic, particularly at making charms to protect from wounds and for prophesying. They were allowed to lead separate lives and worship as they wished, so long as they assisted the *mansa*. As with others, their rewards were in slaves or booty.

A body of royal slaves—a broadly inclusive term—performed most routine court duties. Some were captives who had proved themselves loyal; some were men or women offered to the state for service by families in Niumi or elsewhere with whom the ruling lineages had marriage ties. Royal slaves cooked, tended children, cared for horses, worked in fields, delivered messages, wove cloth, guarded food stores, and did the hundreds of other things necessary to secure the properties of the ruling lineages and make their households operate efficiently.

Finally, at court there were a number of people who appeared in many states around the world as adjuncts to royalty. Foremost were soldiers. Some of these were from Niumi's ruling lineages; some were young members of ruling families of other states, who came to learn the arts of war and effective rule (and to distance themselves from intrigue in their own courts); some were itinerant soldiers of fortune, who traveled with followers in pursuit of the exciting, male-dominated, high-living existence associated with the seats of rule in West African states; and some were slaves. Also, forever at the court were persons from Niumi villages seeking the *mansa*'s favors and official and unofficial representatives from the ruling courts of other states.

The size of the *mansa*'s entourage varied with the ruler's reputation and wealth. In the days of heavy commercial activity and large royal revenues, followings were substantial. When traveling, the *mansa* may have pared his retinue, as in 1702, when Niumi's ruler visited the French frigate *Mutiné* anchored in the Gambia's estuary: only one of his "tributary rulers," his "pope [*sic*]," several marabouts, and a dozen "princes" accompanied him onto the vessel.[21] But English and French officials who visited royal villages found that the *mansa* lived surrounded by a throng, most finely attired, who added greatly to the splendor of the court.

State Administration

Beyond the ruler's attendants and court following were officials whose major concern was state business. The most important for internal affairs was an official called the *suma*. Each of the royal villages had a special slave family, the head of which was the *suma*. As with others, slave status enabled the *suma* to deal directly with the highest levels of authority without posing a threat to them. A primary function of this official was to provide continuity during the potentially disruptive transition period between one *mansa*'s death and the investiture of another. The *suma* of the village of the previous ruler took care of state affairs, while the *suma* of the village of the next *mansa* oversaw selection of the new ruler and his installation. The second important function of the *suma* was the organization of Niumi's fighting forces. Helping him in this regard were several "war-leaders," who were members of the ruling family, and a person in charge of Niumi's powerful canoe fleet (to whom the English referred as Niumi's "Admiral"). Royal African Company officials on James Island occasionally sent spirits across the water for "the Comma and King's brothers with the rest of the army to drink."[22]

Another group of officials dealing with external affairs were those called *falifo*. In other Gambian states a *falifo* was any prosperous foreigner residing in the state, but in Niumi the position became an institution of state, reserved for members of a family originally from elsewhere whose patriarch had married a woman, or women, of one of Niumi's ruling lineages. They were, thus, royal nephews. Their status was unique: as outsiders they could not claim political authority; yet, as relatives through marriage, they had state interests at heart more than ordinary foreigners. As a consequence, they were suited to fill positions where the potential to acquire wealth, prestige, and power was great.

These are the reasons why a lineage named Tall, initially maternal nephews of the Jammeh royal lineage, settled in Juffure and gained the political plum of being tax and toll collectors at that major locus of trade. From some time in the sixteenth century, Juffure's Tall family played a growing role in the administration and control of the commercial and social exchange among Portuguese, Luso-Africans, other Europeans, other Africans, and the people of Niumi. State residents regarded the leader of Juffure's Tall lineage as the "state *falifo*." In addition to customs and tolls, he collected taxes on exchanges made in Niumi and received foreigners' gifts to the *mansa*, his court, and lesser officials. Yet, no matter how prosperous the Tall family became—and there were times when the "Alcaide of Gillifree" (as the English sometimes referred to the *falifo*) was among the most influential persons in the region—its members remained outsiders, related to the rulers only through marriage and thus no threat to usurp hereditary political authority.[23]

Dependent Territories

Much of Niumi's population lived in about fifteen villages within a mile or two of the ocean or river, where the state's economic interests were focused. Distances and difficulties of travel through heavy forests made it hard for rulers to control people living very far away. Especially independent were people on the state's peripheries, which served as buffer areas with surrounding states. In such regions,

Niumi's rulers found it advantageous to vest local lineages with state authority. These families administered, taxed, and defended people in the area with Niumi's backing. Europeans called such subrulers kings and Africans called them *mansa*, but they were subordinate to, and invested by, Niumi's ruling lineages.

The area for which there is the earliest evidence of subordinate status is Jokadu, along Niumi's east side. Jokadu is one of the best farming regions along the Gambia. It was likely settled permanently after the middle of the seventeenth century, when families established villages there to grow grain to sell to Europeans at James Island and Albreda and to slaving vessels in the river. Niumi sometimes fought with its eastern neighbor, Baddibu, over control of Jokadu, and after a time the region's population preferred independence from either state so they could benefit from their own production and trade. Niumi maintained a senior-subordinate relationship with Jokadu until the middle of the nineteenth century, when, under altered circumstances, Jokadu succeeded after a long struggle in winning its independence from a weakened Niumi.[24]

Niumi's *mansa* also invested persons with the state's authority in the salt-producing regions northward along the Atlantic coast. These held a central focus for the state when salt production and its shipment eastward, up the Gambia was its primary commercial activity. But in the sixteenth century, when operations of the Atlantic trade in the river's estuary captured more state interest, Niumi's direct control over the "Salt Islands" waned. Sovereigns of the states of Siin and Saloum to Niumi's north coveted the islands, making them a frequent focus of interstate hostilities. When in control there, Niumi's ruler kept a subordinate in charge. In the 1730s the English gave gifts to "Lassora Sonko, King of the Salt Islands," probably a royal slave of Niumi's *Mansa* Dusu Koli Sonko (r. 1727–1736).[25] Niumi maintained greater or lesser control of the area until 1860, when Muslim revolutionary forces defeated Niumi's army there.

A third region where Niumi supported a dependent ruler was around the village of Kular, on the edge of a sparsely populated buffer area between Niumi and Saloum. Eighteenth-century maps show a separate territory of Kular, and English officials noted that Niumi maintained a "tributary king" there through the first third of the nineteenth century, after which people in Kular allied with Jokadu in its effort to secure independence.[26]

Examination of dependent regions underscores that Niumi was less a carefully delineated territory and more the area where people resided who admitted allegiance to Niumi's *mansa*. The state's boundaries were as fluid as its people's social relationships. The social ties and arrangements of reciprocity the state's leading families had with other lineages throughout the lower part of Senegambia were more important than control over sparsely inhabited land. At times these relationships spread widely, making Niumi seem to observers with mindsets about territorial ownership as if it comprised a good-size piece of land. At other times they were more restricted, or concentrated with different groups (traveling merchant families or Luso-African traders, for instance) in different directions, making it seem to

Europeans as if the state had much narrower geographical confines and was not very strong at all.

State Revenues

Niumi's ruling lineages had two primary sources of revenue: the agricultural surplus produced by farmers in the state and the trade that passed along the Gambia River and through the state. By taxing grain and supervising growing their own, and by exacting taxes, tolls, and gifts from a variety of traders, the rulers obtained revenue they needed for the function of the government and the maintenance of their social position. Each was important. If production of commoners and slaves enabled male members of Niumi's ruling class to glorify themselves with personal finery, good food, strong drink, and ostentatious display (on and off horseback), and to live the sometimes idle, sometimes dangerously active lives of marauding horsemen, it also supported effective administration and provided for the forces that kept the people of the state reasonably secure from invasion. All elements of society accepted this last aspect as one of the primary reasons for the state's existence.

Agricultural surplus was at the heart of Niumi's existence. The state's ruling lineages obtained surplus grain and cotton through taxation and slave production. Following harvest, village heads supervised collection of about one-tenth of village production and conveyed it to the *mansa*'s village. Farmers recognized their need for protection and knew that when famine or other hard times beset them they could turn to their rulers for food. The ruling lineages used some of the wealth to create and maintain reciprocal ties, mostly through marriage, with wealthy lineages in the region so they could call for assistance—food in times of famine, soldiers or horses in times of war—when necessary.[27]

Rulers also supervised slave production of grain and cotton: royal fields were reputed to be the largest because the ruling lineages were able to marshal the greatest labor force. A *mansa* could call on the young men's age group to work in the fields at critical times, but slaves did most of the work. Produce from these crops provided food and trading commodities; surplus added to the *mansa*'s wealth.

A major way to increase state wealth was to increase production, and the only way to do that given the technology of slash-and-burn, hoe agriculture, was to increase the amount of land under cultivation. This required more people to work the land. Every immigrant family, attracted by the protection afforded by Niumi's royal lineages, increased state production and, thus, state revenues. Yet, another way rulers could increase the size of the state's labor force was to purchase slaves (and slaves arriving from inland when demand from Europeans was low at the river's mouth often sold for less) or to capture persons from outside the state and bring them back to live and work as royal slaves. Male members of the ruling lineages tended to be avid plunderers, inclined to make periodic horseborne raids that brought in human booty. Some captives could be ransomed and some sold for horses, grain, or other items of value, but the rest joined the rulers' workforce.

The other major source of state revenue was commercial exchange. Merchants passing along or through a West African state customarily paid tolls to ensure protection and rights to trade, gather provisions, and take up temporary residence. From as early as there are records, Niumi derived revenue from the passage of salt between the Atlantic and the upper river. With the opportunity of the waxing Atlantic commerce at its shores, Niumi's rulers adapted such requirements as necessary to deal with European merchant vessels.[28] Ships entering the Gambia out of the Atlantic steered for Jinak Point, where large trees marked what old coasters called "The King's Pavillion." There they fired a salute to announce their arrival. The ship's master then dispatched a longboat to Niumi's shore to obtain a pilot, who would guide the vessel past shoals near Barra Point and on to Juffure, where the *falifo* conducted business. Masters had to provide gifts for the *mansa*, the *falifo*, and from two to seven or eight other lesser officials. Vessels remained at anchor off Juffure while the *falifo* conveyed the gifts to the *mansa* and returned with word that they were satisfactory. The *falifo* then set a date when the master would be obliged to pay set tolls for anchorage and passage, and for the privilege of taking on wood, water, and provisions. European merchants intending to proceed upriver then had to hire a pilot, several "linguisters" for pending commercial transactions, and a number of crewmen to help with the strenuous work of tacking and rowing against the current. Each of these auxiliaries received a standard rate of pay.

After the English and French established permanent posts on Niumi's riverside, their agents arranged annual customs payments with Niumi's ruling lineages. In return, the *mansa* regularized payments required of company-affiliated trading vessels and speeded proceedings, the latter always a concern for shipmasters. Private traders continued to pay higher tolls and charges. These annual customs rose over the years with expanding trade and rising prices. English customs nearly quadrupled in the century after 1665. In addition to providing revenue, they bound and renewed the established relationships of local landlord and European stranger as well as specific agreements on trade.

Greater still than revenues from customs and tolls were rulers' tariffs on transactions taking place in Niumi. The *mansa* might claim one of every ten items exchanged, so caravans of several hundred slaves descending the river's north bank for sale in Juffure or Albreda would bring the *mansa* several times more revenue than he received in annual customs or tolls from trading vessels.

There were other customary sources of wealth related to trade. By traditional rights, vessels running aground off Niumi's shores became state property. In one instance in 1754, English merchants paid Niumi's *mansa* sixty-four gallons of rum just for the privilege of *attempting* to refloat their own grounded vessel. In another, in 1732, the *mansa* berated company officials on James Island for giving aid to a private trading vessel in danger of running aground. He had his eye on the cargo.[29]

Some of Niumi's rulers were masters at ransom and extortion. Well informed of conditions in the foreign enclaves, they would take advantage of European isolation or weakness. In 1708, when the James Island garrison staged an unsuc-cessful mutiny, Niumi's *falifo* sent word from Juffure to the island that the *mansa*'s canoeborne forces would attack and pillage the weakened factory unless given sizable gifts. Rulers became adept at playing French and English interests against one another, too. In 1752, English agent James Skinner lamented that Niumi's *mansa* "comes 2–3 times each month to the Fort & demands spirits &c, which we always give him expecting he would turn the French out of the river, according to his promise. Instead he told the French at Albreda of his plan & likewise got more from them." When Skinner refused to entertain the *mansa*'s entourage on his next visit, the ruler kidnapped an Englishman living in Juffure and charged the English five kegs of rum for ransom.[30]

Ruling elites of Senegambian states regularly mounted war parties to raid neighboring villages or even some in their own states, capturing persons working in fields or fleeing from a village and enslaving them. They called such activity "horse-running"; it was the combined sport and productive work of the ruling strata.[31] Such raiding satisfied the desires of the elites to demonstrate their warrior capabilities and brought yet more wealth to the state's rulers through ransom, sale, or increased production. Perhaps because of their steadier revenues from external trade, however, Niumi's ruling lineages did not do much marauding and raiding, especially of their own villagers. Only when a *mansa* lost control of difficult warrior elements in his entourage would internal raiding take place. Admittedly vague oral and written evidence suggests that, on occasion after the mid-eighteenth century, common villagers, including Euro-Africans and Europeans engaged in commerce, suffered increasingly from the depredations of Niumi's warriors acting beyond the *mansa*'s control. Such activity partly explains the virtual disappearance of Niumi's Euro-African population by 1800; the almost continual revolutionary activity of its dependent territories through the first half of the nineteenth century; and, when combined with the increasing availability of firearms, growing British power, and other economic and social factors, the violent rebellions of the mid-nineteenth century that weakened Niumi's ruling elite.[32]

A Wider Material and Intellectual World

Through its connection to the Atlantic trade, Niumi gained more direct and regular access to a larger material and intellectual world. Back through the years, with their connection to the coastal trading area of Senegambia and upper Guinea, persons in Niumi tapped into exchange of regional products—kola nuts, cloth, foodstuffs, cowhides, and slaves, for instance—and through indirect trade from across the Sahara they acquired products and ideas from a world as far away as the Mediter-ranean and Middle East—horses, leather goods, metalware, figs, dates, and an acquaintance with Islam and some of the material and intellectual accouterments of the religion. But in its manifestations in the Gambia River, the Atlantic trade put Niumi's population in touch with a material and intellectual world that stretched beyond what they had known. By the seventeenth century, men and women in Niumi were habitual consumers of products from all around the Atlantic and from central and East Asia. Furthermore, although they were not always as receptive to foreign ideas as to foreign products, mostly because they neither wished nor needed to be, they were becoming increasingly familiar with the ideas of people across large bodies of water and vast expanses of land.

Niumi's Changing Material World

Discussion of the material goods people in Niumi received in exchange for local and regional commodities, including slaves, leads one to put to rest forever the "gewgaw myth." Stanley B. Alpern explains that practical cloth and metal goods tended to dominate European imports into West Africa during the Atlantic trade, but that "the range of commodities was so broad that inbound European ships eventually came to resemble . . . 'floating supermarkets.'" Curtin lists a typical sample of goods the Royal African Company exchanged for 180 slaves in the Gambia River in 1740 and 1741: it includes twenty-five different items—five varieties of cloth; five of beads or other decorative items; four of metal or metalware; two each of firearms, gunpowder, and lead; spirits, silver coins, cowrie shells, salt, and paper.[33]

Generalizations about Gambian imports through the seventeenth and eighteenth centuries show changes in African preferences and suggest corresponding changes in ways of life. Items of apparel and personal decoration made up almost half of all imports, with preferences shifting from beads to cloth. Metals and metalware constituted another third, iron bars being more important in the seventeenth century and silver becoming more so in the eighteenth. Weapons made up from 10 to 25 percent of imports—swords through the seventeenth century and firearms, increasingly, in the eighteenth. Holding steady were imports of spirits, with tobacco entering the picture toward the end. Throughout the period, African demand was the primary determinant of what European shippers brought to trade, just as European demand for gold, slaves, hides, or beeswax led Africans to produce those commodities.

Items of apparel and decoration remained the greatest import into the Gambia throughout the years of the Atlantic trade and beyond. (Even today one cannot walk down major streets in The Gambia's capital or visit markets in Niumi villages without noticing imported cloth, clothing, and items of adornment for sale.) Dress and personal decoration were the major way many West Africans displayed their wealth or indicated their social status. Clothing, jewelry, and beads served this function and the Atlantic trade supplied all three. Waist girdles were one of the most popular adornments for persons of both sexes. Gambians had access to beads before commencement of the Atlantic trade, but the multicolored glass beads from Austria, France, Germany, and Holland, along with crystal, pearls, coral, and semiprecious stones from distant parts of the globe, brought new possibilities in personal decoration. Most of the beads, purchased by the ton in Venice or Amsterdam, were inexpensive to Europeans, and for some the markup in the Gambia was considerable. But Alpern argues, "the vital measure of personal ornaments is surely the pleasure they give, the charms they set off, not their cost of production. To call cheap but pretty beads rubbish is to see them through the eyes of a Western sophisticate, not those of an African consumer." Furthermore, not all glass beads were inexpensive for Europeans and some—the carnelians that came from Bombay and became especially popular in the Gambian trade, for example—along with Mediterranean coral and crystal, were not cheap at all.[34]

Cloth was a different story. Residents of Niumi had access to good cotton cloth from the savanna lands east of the Gambia. People there had grown cotton since Muslim traders had brought the cloth and seeds across the Sahara from North Africa in the first millennium, and they spun cotton thread and wove sturdy cloth. There had long been a steady trade of cotton cloth east and west across West Africa's savannas. As early as the eleventh century Muslim travelers noticed cotton cloth in use as currency along the Senegal River, and English trader Richard Jobson early in the seventeenth century reported that cloth in the Gambia River was "the staple commodity to pitch the price upon, to value other things by." The excellent indigo-dyeing techniques used between the Senegambian Atlantic coast and the upper Niger River gave merchants there an advantage over cloth traders from elsewhere.[35] When Europeans began importing beads, they, too, fit into the currency structure, so that eventually cloth (or in some cases silver coins) served as the large units of currency and beads were the equivalent of small change.[36] Cotton producers inland from the Gambia were eager to exchange cloth for the salt they needed from Niumi's Atlantic coast. Through the 1600s, little European cloth interested consumers in Niumi—they did not like the designs of the European material, it was more expensive, and it did not hold up under local laundry methods—though Europeans did find profit in buying African cloth in the upper Gambia and trading it along the Atlantic coast for foodstuffs or slaves. In the 1680s, when beads and semiprecious stones made up about 40 percent of European imports in the river, textiles constituted only one-tenth as much. But as English and French traders got easier access to the finely woven, brightly colored Indian textiles that were passing through Liverpool or Marseilles, and as some of the Indian imports gained elite status among West African consumers, the Europeans began to import cloth that appealed to Gambian consumers.[37] Northern European producers also imitated Indian cottons (though most Africans continued to prefer the real thing), and they made increasingly fine woolens and linens and such useful items of clothing as kerchiefs, hats, and caps. Thus, cloth and clothing imports rose steadily after the seventeenth century as beads and semiprecious stones declined in relative terms.

All of this enabled people in Niumi to adorn themselves more colorfully, more fully, more comfortably than before. With increasing frequency, wealthier people dressed up with more clothing, wearing linens and woolens on top of cotton garments, and wrapped themselves in more layers on chilly dry-season nights. Brightly colored wraps covered the heads of prominent women in public; men wore long gowns with wraps and more hats and caps; cotton sheets covered things appropriately kept from sight—corpses at funerals, brides at weddings, the future *mansa* in an inauguration ceremony. In the Muslim enclaves, religious men had an easier time dressing like their North African models, in long, loose-fitting gowns.

The importing of great quantities of personal decorations and cloth had a social effect that went beyond the aspect of wearing one's wealth. A major use of cloth currency was in social exchange: men who were inclined to marry needed cloth to provide to the family of the prospective bride. This compensated the woman's family for its loss of a productive member—the amount was related to the economic, social, or political position of the bride's family—and it symbolized the mutual obligations each family had to its in-laws. Cloth, and to a lesser extent items of personal adornment, all easily stored items that retained their value, became standard payments for bride wealth. The more and better cloth and beads one had, the more wives one could marry from larger and stronger families from a wider region. And the more marriage ties one had with such families, the more one had influential and prosperous outsiders on whom to rely in times of need—famine, especially, or physical threat. In time, male members of the wealthiest and most influential families in Niumi came to have dozens or scores of wives, often women from wealthy and powerful lineages around the lower Gambia. Likewise, women from Niumi married prominent men from a wide area. These interfamilial ties were the essence of security in the lower Gambia, and the Atlantic trade increasingly provided the wealth and goods for Niumi's prosperous families to create and maintain such relationships. Records of Royal African Company gift giving in the first half of the eighteenth century contain evidence of the connections of Niumi's prominent lineages—African and Euro-African—and of those with lineages in other states throughout the region. They suggest, as well, the obligations families had to their in-laws, responding to tragedies, attending funerals, or sending men to fight in neighboring wars—obligations, incidentally, in which the English and French trading in the river were involved as well.[38] The political and social stability of the lower Gambia and a greater region of Senegambia was based on the mutuality of interests of the region's leading lineages.

Metals and metalware also made up a significant portion of Niumi's imports from Atlantic trade. "Without iron and alcohol one cannot live there, much less trade," wrote Abbé Demanet after a visit to Niumi in 1764. Niumi had blacksmiths, but they worked iron rather than produced it. Long before Europeans arrived in the river, Niumi obtained iron from West Africa's interior and local blacksmiths turned it into useful products: farm implements, weapons, utensils, chains, gongs, and other things. By the seventeenth century, however, so much iron was entering the lower Gambia via the Atlantic that the "bar," based on a standardized piece of flat wrought iron common in the lower Rhine and early brought to West Africa by the Dutch, became the standard unit of currency for Gambia trading. Iron imported from the Atlantic partially replaced imports from the eastern hinterland, and this iron continued to make up one-third or more of Gambian imports through the seventeenth century. Then iron imports declined steadily, replaced partly by silver and metalware in the 1730s. By the end of the century, metals and metalware (not counting cutlery and weapons) were an insignificant part of the trade. The ability to obtain high-quality, inexpensive iron was good for Niumi's blacksmiths, farmers, and soldiers. Moreover, as more metalware in the form of copper basins, brass pans, and pewterware entered the region and made their way into the lives of wealthier people in Niumi's villages, the women's art of pot making declined.[39]

Weapons were important elements of European trade into the Gambia River until recent times. Swords and cutlasses were major imports into the eighteenth century; firearms and gunpowder grew slowly in volume throughout the period. Metal swords and spears were the weapons of choice of Niumi's horsemen; use of firearms in warfare was slow in coming. Before the nineteenth century, Africans around the lower Gambia seldom used guns to fight with because they were slow to load, inaccurate, undependable, and cumbersome. They used firearms, instead, for hunting, for keeping predatory animals from crops, for noise making at celebrations, for ceremonial functions and saluting arriving vessels, and as symbols of royal prestige and power (for in most instances only the ruling lineages could afford to keep guns in significant numbers).[40] So before 1800, firearms affected Niumi's population in surprising ways: through controlling dangerous and predatory animals and thus enhancing crop production, and providing another way for the ruling lineages to display their wealth and status—as a form of conspicuous consumption.

Spirits, normally brandy or rum, were another commodity in steady demand in Niumi. European traders had to include rum or brandy as part of the *mansa*'s annual custom (in 1726 he received half his customs in twenty gallons of rum); ships entering the Gambia had to give gifts of spirits in Juffure; and, generally speaking, some form of "cordial water" oiled the wheels of commerce throughout the region. "Without brandy there is no trade," wrote the chief factor at James Fort to the Royal African Company in 1680. Over the last quarter of the eighteenth century, as British and French traders had their attentions drawn to revolutionary and military matters in other colonies or at home, American traders worked the Gambia trade and brought copious quantities of rum. The ruling lineages were the greatest consumers of brandy and rum, not only because they were the wealthiest, but because part of the worshiping ceremonies of the traditional religion involved libations for the spirits (and the practitioners) and because the lifestyle of young male lineage members involved dangerous feats on horseback and unpredictable behavior in public, all of which alcohol enhanced. The availability of strong spirits played a role in what seems to have been the growing militancy, and predatory nature, of Niumi's rulers and their entourages. By the mid-eighteenth century the warrior groups surrounding the *mansa* were making life hard for European traders; by the early nineteenth century, they were making it hard for their own subjects. Only the Muslim lineages in the state and those unable to afford a draft of "bumbo" now and then remained outside Niumi's culture of alcohol.[41]

Finally, Niumi obtained from the Atlantic trade small, but not insignificant, amounts of paper. Literate Muslims in Niumi's society used the paper largely for the manufacture of charms containing writings from the Qur'an. Its continuing importance is an indicator of the persistence of Niumi's Muslim enclaves. Once those enclaves began to expand and more people began converting to Islam in the mid-nineteenth century, requirements for paper would increase.

Niumi's Changing Social and Intellectual World

Niumi's main riverside villages—Juffure, Albreda, and Sika—were quite the cosmopolitan places in the first half of the eighteenth century. A visitor would see several villages inhabited partly by black Christians bearing Portuguese surnames and dressed in long gowns with crucifixes around their necks. Living nearby would be matriarchal women of considerable influence, wealthy in their own right, rather than their husband's, from their prominent positions in regional trade. None of this would be typical of West African societies inland and any distance from the Atlantic; yet, Niumi's society still had a number of elements similar to those in such grand states Mali and Kaabu. These included a strong, at times parasitic, group of rulers who identified more closely with distant lineages of their elite class than with the lower-class elements in Niumi, and a body of apolitical Muslims, some living detached from others but growing in influence because of their importance in trade and the reliance of others on the Muslims' work with supernatural forces. These characteristics existed because Niumi's society, while based on the traditional Mandinka model, changed over the long time of dealing with persons and institutions involved in Atlantic and Sudanic trading and broadened social structures to include new elements that were useful for the functioning of the cross-cultural trade.

Luso-Africans

The two centuries of Niumi's history under study were a time of steady Luso-African rise among the state's commercial elite, followed by a relatively rapid decline.[42] Filling a niche in the waterborne trade by connecting settlements near the Atlantic with merchants bringing goods from beyond the Gambia's headwaters, these offspring of Portuguese traders and African women grew in importance through the middle of the seventeenth century and beyond. When northern Europeans became firmly established in the river in the 1660s, Luso-Africans were the dominant middlemen in the trade between the Atlantic and the head of navigation. The first ledger of the British outpost on James Island, begun in January 1664, lists thirty-one different persons with Portuguese surnames trading for, or with goods of, the Royal Adventurers. Some amassed considerable wealth and had ties through marriage to ruling lineages of the Gambian states. In the 1730s, enough Luso-Africans resided in Sika, east of Juffure, that a priest from the Cape Verde Islands visited there twice each year to administer the sacraments.[43]

A number of the prominent mulatto traders were women. At the start of the eighteenth century one of the most influential persons in the lower Gambia was a daughter of Niumi's *mansa*, who had been married to several Luso-African traders and who, through her father's rights, had inherited their property when they died. "Signora Belinguere," she was called by the director of the Compagnie de Sénégal, who met her in Juffure in 1700. She was literate in French, Portuguese, and English; resided in a square "Portuguese house" with white walls and a vestibule; had a network of sources that provided her with commercial intelligence; and could secure credit for nonaffiliated traders. According to another Frenchman, she also was "the reef upon which many whites of several nations have foundered."[44] English records from the 1730s list several "señoras" as prominent persons in Niumi's trade, and a generation later one Señora Llena, who lived in Juffure, owned a number of slaves whom she hired to work on European vessels as linguists and boatmen. Llena was married to Haly Sonko, brother to Niumi's next *mansa*, and he interceded on her behalf when her economic interests brought her into conflict with Niumi's ruling elite.[45]

Not all of Niumi's mixed Euro-Africans were wealthy entrepreneurs, however. Many of them were *gromettas*—auxiliary boatmen, interpreters, and other sorts of commercial and cultural intermediaries. In the mid-seventeenth century, the English Royal Adventurers employed "Lopeez the Grometta" and hired "Dom do Aldea" to tend their cattle. In 1729, five of the seven Royal African Company linguists and messengers had Portuguese surnames. Five years later the company hired Philip Gomez, Emanuel Vos, and Barnaby Lopez to man provision "factories" at various locations in Niumi.[46] And some of Niumi's Luso-Africans were slaves. Royal African Company accounts from the 1730s contain references to António Gomez, a "Castle Slave," who ran errands for the company, and Superanca Vas, who had "belonged to" Robert Plunkett, governor of the James Island establishment. One Luso-African, Diogo Gomes, was in the special category of slaves of the ruling lineages. Indeed, Gomes was the head slave of *Mansa* Alimaranta Sonko in the 1720s. During Sonko's reign, Gomes carried on trade on his master's behalf, and he continued a prosperous commerce of his own after Sonko died in 1725. A decade after Sonko's death, the English were still dealing with Gomes, whom they identified as "the late King of Niumi's head slave."[47]

Neither prosperity nor ubiquity in the river's commercial milieu was characteristic of the Luso-Africans for good, however. Niumi's Luso-African population declined steadily after the middle of the eighteenth century. The cultural hybrids had been able to sustain themselves and, in some cases, to prosper by performing commercial functions beyond the inclinations of others. But as French and British interests in the river began to compete and English factors at James Fort determined to send their own traders up the river to obtain more commodities at better prices, they undercut and gradually displaced the Luso-Africans. Muslim merchants in Niumi may have been hurt by the same actions, but they had their work with the supernatural to fall back on for their primary livelihood. Luso-African Christians did not come from so much of a magical/supernatural tradition—or at least one that incorporated the making of protective charms that fit so well into traditional African practices. Niumi's rulers hurt the Luso-Africans, too, with their insistence on customary rights of inheritance from foreigners dying on Niumi soil—and regardless of where they were born, the Luso-Africans remained foreign in this regard—or of all persons tied to the ruling lineages in relationships of dependence. As the latter half of the eighteenth century wore on, some Luso-Africans melded into Niumi's African population and disappeared from the record; some drifted off to areas of more promising trade south of the Gambia. By the late 1750s, Portuguese names no longer appear in the English ledgers. Those who remained on Niumi soil into the 1760s and beyond clung to relationships with French traders in Albreda. A French clergyman noted in 1764 that Niumi's "Portuguese Christians" were something of a sad lot, having not seen a priest in twenty years. By the end of the century there no longer was a noticeable Luso-African presence in Niumi, unless, of course, one counts the cultural remains of square houses with white walls, pirogues carrying the trade goods, and a trade language of the region with many words rooted in Portuguese.[48]

Muslims

While Niumi's Luso-African population was moving toward its demise, Muslims in the state were holding their own. Like their counterparts throughout central parts of Eurasia and down the East African coast, followers of Islam along the lower Gambia River benefited from their association with the material goods of trade, the supernatural elements of their beliefs, and their own accommodationist leanings that enabled them to fit pre-Islamic beliefs and objects of worship and veneration into manifestations of the Islamic faith. As more wealth came into Niumi through growing commerce, Muslim lineages prospered, either through their own trading or through remuneration for their protection and divination. A good part of their wealth was in slaves, which were vital to both facets of their work. With slave labor growing crops to sustain the family, men of the lineage could travel for trading or study through the early years of their lives and then settle down to practice their "Muslim works."[49] European observers voiced contempt for the religion of "the Mohammedans," so they failed to recognize the level of scholarship and learning that clerics achieved. In the eyes of others, however, such men were part of a body of scholars and mystics who were advancing Muslim religious thought throughout the realm of Islamic civilization. Learned Muslims in Niumi in the eighteenth century may not have been making the pilgrimage to Mecca, but they were involved in traveling widely to attend schools of Islamic scholarship and mysticism. Some Niumi marabouts carried the title of *Fodé*, an indication that they had mastered some of the most advanced religious texts.

Eighteenth-century Niumi was thus a society with a visible and valuable Muslim presence. Records from James Island in the 1730s, listing gifts rendered in hopes of facilitating English trade, bear evidence of Muslims' importance in that commerce. The Royal African Company's largesse went to "Oil for the Mahometans," to the "Great Mohamedan priest of Sika, on having lost his slippers," and to the "great priest's son that is with the King." The same records show that Niumi's rulers and prominent traders retained Muslim clerics to work as advisors and protectors: Company payments go to "Seca Scaroe, Bushreen [marabout] of Niumi," to "Bram Bojan to go to the great Priests to get their opinion for the best place for the new King of Niumi to make his town," and to "the Bishreen attendants of Sr. Antonio Vas." The Sonko royal lineage of Berending had a Muslim lineage permanently attached as clients. Elders of the Fati lineage of Aljamdu say they built their settlement in the last quarter of the seventeenth century a few miles from Berending at the request of *Mansa* Jenung Wuleng Sonko so they could be near enough to "work for him."[50] And the Tall lineage of Juffure, who provided the *falifo* of Niumi, was not only a Muslim but, by the 1760s, a recognized cleric.[51]

Ideas of militant Islamic revival that were spreading through the Muslim world, or even influences from movements of religious reform and revolution that had taken place not far north and east of the lower Gambia from late in the seventeenth century, apparently had not spread among Muslims in Niumi.[52] Niumi's commercial and clerical lineages went about their trading, scholarship, and supernatural work in the same pacific way, to their benefit and those among whom they lived and worked. These lineages would be well placed in the middle of the nineteenth century, when reformist movements against non-Muslim or partially Muslim rulers were spreading across Senegambia, to take up the banner of reform and lead a movement against Niumi's ruling lineages.

The Soninke

By the mid-nineteenth century, more people in Niumi would consider their rulers in need of reform. Niumi's ruling lineages were typical of those throughout Africa's western savannas: They considered themselves privileged, lived off the produce of their slaves and the nonroyal families in their states and off the trade that passed through their territories, had minimal constraints on their behavior, and did what they needed to maintain their elite status. This may have been the case from the time of consolidation of Niumi's ruling groups in the sixteenth century. The predatory *nyancho* elite of Kaabu, from whence came several of the ruling lineages in Niumi, was the reputed model for aristocratic privilege and uncontrolled, despotic behavior. There is no reason to believe they were not this way from the start. It may be that Senegambian rulers became more oppressive after the ending of Atlantic slave trading, but evidence does not exist to support the claim. The ruling groups of West Africa's savanna states never were simply benevolent protectors. Such was not the nature of statehood at the place and time.

Still, over the eighteenth century changes were happening among ruling elites. Across West Africa's grasslands, ruling groups were beginning to identify more with others in their class and less with peasants in their ethnic or political units. Eventually, ruling lineages of most of the Senegambian states were related to one another, sometimes indirectly, through marriage. They formed a tightly knit group—a surclass of restricted membership that transcended political boundaries—connecting across a wide area those elite lineages with interest in common political and social goals. As such, they formed a kind of "interlocking directorate" of the states. Sometimes they disagreed and quarreled over trading rights or inheritance; sometimes their disagreements resulted in fighting between individual states or among groups of states; but none of their fighting was totally destructive. Like family feuds, these quarrels ended short of serious damage because, although living in separate states, they shared the interests of an expanded family. Solidarity and stability remained uppermost in their minds. So long as they controlled the fighting resources of the region—in soldiers on horseback, canoeborne forces, and iron-tipped weapons—and practiced a form of collective security, calling on powerful related lineages in other states when threatened, no one from outside or below could mount an effective challenge to their supremacy and control.[53]

Among Mande speakers, members of the ruling elite came to be known as *soninke*. Formed partly in reaction to the spreading acceptance of elements of Islamic culture, the *soninke* identity included possession of political authority, glorification of the attributes of the horseback warrior, worship of the traditional pre-Islamic spirits, showy manifestation of wealth in dress and material goods, and consumption of alcohol with attendant unpredictable behavior. *Soninke* tended to keep aloof, preferring to marry persons of their class from other states than local persons from lower classes.[54] Increasingly, rulers stuck with rulers, warriors stuck with warriors, and the more numerous peasants, artisans, and slaves in their midst could fare as they wished, so long as they supported the ruling strata.[55] If that support was not forthcoming and especially if it was being diverted elsewhere—toward Muslim mystics, for example, or toward the acquisition of wealth by lineages of the lower classes—rulers were positioned to take what they wished in a fashion that peasants, traders, and clerics would consider oppressive. In time, the lower classes would seek ways to end their oppression.[56]

The Changing Nature of Dependence

Still other changes in the eighteenth century had ominous portent for people on all levels of Niumi society. Curtin renders a judgment about Senegambia during the century following 1740 that bears on the depth and nature of the region's dependence on the world market. Over this period, he writes, the region's "foreign trade increased enormously because Senegambia sold more to Europe at higher prices. But the returns in the form of imports may not have been those best calculated to increase Senegambia's own productive capacity."[57] He arranges Senegambian imports from the Atlantic trade into three groups—raw materials (iron and silver), consumer goods (brass and copper ware, pewter, textiles, beads and semiprecious stones, and paper), and nonproductive goods (arms and powder, spirits, and tobacco)—and notes that the importing of raw materials dwindled to almost nothing over the eighteenth century while that of consumer and nonproductive goods rose steadily. Had the region brought in more raw materials for productive use and fewer consumer and nonproductive goods, he believes, it might have created "a greater capability of further growth." As it was, the region generally, and Niumi specifically, became more and more dependent on items its wealthy ruling strata enjoyed and made use of for social and political purposes, but not items that enabled them to become productive over the long term. For these consumer goods and nonproductive items, they exported slaves, gold, and raw materials that others around the Atlantic basin used in productive ways.

This may not have been the only way in which Niumi's dependence was growing. Scraps of evidence suggest that by late in the period of Atlantic slaving, people living in Niumi had grown dependent on the Atlantic economic complex for items critical to their survival. This was not always the case. For a part of the sixteenth century, Niumi's rulers were dependent on foreign traders for horses, and from early in the state's participation in the Atlantic trade, its larger population had become reliant on imported iron for tools and weapons, and imported cloth for clothing and symbolic wealth. Yet, approaching the middle of the eighteenth century, Niumi remained largely self-sufficient in foodstuffs and even at times an exporter of grain. The Royal African Company regularly bought "country corn" from the *mansa* and others in Niumi for the garrison on James Island, and from late in the seventeenth century the company stationed agents in certain Niumi villages to buy provisions for the island and waiting ships. Niumi growers were selling grain to English agents as late as the 1740s.[58] As long as Niumi produced enough millet, rice, and maize to feed its population, it could withstand fluctuations in demand and periodic disruptions of the Atlantic trade.

But a period of about a dozen years after the mid-1740s that was disastrous for agriculture across Senegambia ushered in a period of change for Niumi. The result of drought and swarms of crop-devouring locusts, the crop failures, followed by regular recurrences, altered Niumi's agricultural self-sufficiency and, at least for a time, turned it into an importer of foodstuffs from different ecological zones to the east and south. No records from James Fort after 1741 refer to purchases of grain in Niumi. From the 1740s the English began having to look to the river's south bank and farther upriver for grain. More important, within a generation of that time Niumi itself was importing foodstuffs, exchanging salt or merchandise it received through Atlantic trading for grain. Interesting letters out of James Fort from the 1760s and 1770s suggest how the English could get the upper hand with Niumi's *mansa* and stop having to "pay as much in liquor as we get in water." They call for acquiring armed sloops to cut off Niumi's canoes "from the higher parts of the River, from whence they draw their chief supply of Corn."[59] The English factors never got their armed vessels, and they abandoned James Fort for good only four years after the last of these letters was written in 1775. But that those in charge recognized Niumi's vulnerability in its dependence on grain imports shows that by the last third of the eighteenth century, the state had a different, more dependent relationship with the trade of the Atlantic and its Senegambian hinterland. Some of the wealth the state was getting from the Atlantic trade was passing on elsewhere so people in Niumi could have enough to eat. This was dependence of a different nature—dependence on trade for an essential commodity rather than a desirable one or a luxury good. From that time on, such dependence would be a recurring theme in Niumi's history, and soon there would be an even greater world economy on which to depend.

Part III
THE COLONIAL PERIOD
1816–1965

Kolimanka Manneh was Niumi's *mansa* from 1815 to 1823. When he began his reign, European ships entering the Gambia still had to come near Niumi's Atlantic shoreline and fire a multigun salute to the *mansa*, a cannonade that Manneh would order returned from his village of Bunyadu, six miles in from Barra Point. The vessels then had to sail twenty-five miles upriver to Juffure, where masters had to pay customs and take on local boatmen and translators before proceeding to trade. When in 1816 the English wanted to reestablish an outpost in the Gambia to stop slaving and encourage legitimate trade, they ended up selecting Banjul Island, connected to the river's south bank, rather than their old post on James Island. Part of their reasoning was that Manneh, whose armed vessels patrolled the surrounding waters, would not take lightly to losing his customs payments on slaving vessels. They wanted distance between their new outpost and Niumi's *mansa*. Even from Banjul (which they named Bathurst), five miles across the river and claimed by another Gambian ruler, the English paid Manneh an annual custom for allowing them to settle in the river. He was indeed one of the last Niumi rulers to exercise power far outside the confines of the state.

At the time of Gambian independence from sixty-eight years of formal British rule and nearly a century and a half of British control, on February 18, 1965, forty-three-year-old Jerre Manneh was Kolimanka's nearest descendent, his great-great-great-grandson. Manneh lived in Bunyadu, as did his royal ancestor, but in less stately circumstances. He had gone to school through Standard Four (grade eight), but had been yanked—almost literally—out of his village to serve during World War II. His limited education helped him land a spot with the signal corps and thus not to be sent to Burma with the majority of the Gambia Regiment. Following the war, he worked as a telephone linesman around Bathurst, but in the 1950s he returned to Bunyadu and tried to enter politics, running for the newly created seat in the Gambian Parliament for his home district, Lower Niumi. Twice he was defeated. So as most Gambian adult men of the twentieth century, Manneh took up peanut farming, and he worked the hard-packed red soil around Bunyadu for the next thirty-five years. His compound on the edge of Bunyadu was not large by local standards. Villagers regarded him as a hard worker, good and wise, but his influence did not extend far beyond the compound.

The fall from power of the Manneh lineage, as evident in a comparison of the lives of these two men, is only one personal manifestation of a broad range of changes that came to the lives of everyone living in Niumi between the time of the British establishment of Bathurst in 1816 and the achievement of Gambian independence in 1965—an era one can consider an elongated colonial period in Niumi's, and Gambia's, history. Reasons behind the changes are many, but overriding elements include early encounters with the more powerful, industrializing core nations of western Europe, followed by full incorporation on the periphery of a world system that was restructuring, broadening, and strengthening to include much more of the globe. In 1826, only three years after Kolimanka Manneh's death, Niumi's new *mansa* ceded to the British control of the state's riverbank and any right to collect customs or tolls on passing river traffic; by 1850 the Niumi state was greatly weakened and most Niumi villagers were becoming involved in producing peanuts for export to the world system's core countries so they could pay for imports from the same regions; in 1897, when most people in Niumi were struggling to produce peanuts and stay ahead of debts incurred to buy imported food, Niumi's dealings with the British government and the world economy were institutionalized in a formal, colonial relationship; and in 1965, Niumi became part of a newly independent country, The Republic of The Gambia, whose common citizens were dependent on an exchange relationship—still peanuts for foodstuffs and other necessary commodities—that was the basis of the country's economy and its political stability. This long colonial period set the stage for life after independence, meaning that since 1965, Niumi residents, and Gambians generally, have found it difficult to move individual props, let alone rearrange the entire stage.

5

A TIME OF TRANSITION IN NIUMI

1816–1897

I account for this disparity to the terrible enfield rifle. I saw no less than three men inside the stockade fall before one discharge, so thick were the warriors they never moved after. I would not allow the soldiers to bayonet the bodies of such brave foes.
— Col. George A.K. d'Arcy, 1866, after storming a Niumi village and finding 350 dead, no wounded, out of a force of 800[1]

Owing to the failure of the ground-nut crop from want of sufficient rain and the destruction of their food crops by locusts, the natives began to feel the pinch of famine early in the year. Their position was made worse from the fact that the merchants, who in former years had given out credits of rice, to tide the people over the rains, decided to discontinue the practice. Already the people had begun to hunt in the forests for roots and berries, and to pawn and sell their clothing, many being reduced to wearing rice-bags as their sole covering.
— Annual Report (Gambia Colony), North Bank Province, 1901[2]

Historians who concern themselves with expansion of the world economy, dependence, and related matters do not agree on when different parts of Africa became dependent on the world market or, using Wallerstein's terminology, became fully incorporated into the modern world system. It was natural to look at the colonial period in the first half of the twentieth century as the time when European nations established a formal, superior-subordinate relationship with their African colonies. Yet, a quarter century ago some began to consider the roots of dependency and underdevelopment in the dealings Africans had with European shippers in the seventeenth- and eighteenth-century Atlantic slave trade.[3] Still others, Wallerstein perhaps foremost among them, believe much of Africa went through a "process of incorporation" between 1750 and 1900, when the capitalist world economy needed "new areas of low-cost *production*, as part of the general expansion of its level of economic activity and rate of accumulation."[4] Examination of Niumi's history supports this last belief more than the others. As noted in Chapter 4, one wonders if, in their reliance on European imports to exchange for foodstuffs in the last third of the eighteenth century, Niumi residents were not then moving toward a new form of dependence on the growing world market. But in terms of clearly becoming one of the areas of low-cost production for the expanding world economy, Niumi made the change between 1835 and 1850. This change was related to the industrialization of Western Europe. In Niumi it resulted in great social and political upheaval that brought about a changing of old ways and, by 1900, the demise of the state. The nineteenth century is, thus, a true turning point for Niumi's history.

Following a French sacking of the fort on James Island in 1779, the English abandoned the outpost, leaving the Gambia River with no seat of British authority for the next thirty-seven years. The French supported a tiny group of traders at Albreda until 1804 and then left as well. During this time, when the British and French were experiencing revolution abroad and at home, followed by wars that involved most of Europe, independent traders remained busy in the Gambia: English, French, and American merchants, as before, came to the river for slaves, hides, beeswax, ivory, and small amounts of gold. The British Parliament's outlawing of the slave trade after 1807 did not slow traffic on the river. Then, in 1816, largely to bring about closing of the Gambia to slavers, the British reestablished a formal presence in the river, not on James Island but on a sand spit called Banjul Island, nearer the river's mouth. Over the period between its abandonment of James Island and its establishment on Banjul, Britain experienced the early phase of the Industrial Revolution. This is largely why, in terms of power, confidence, intent, and ability to do as it wished on foreign shores, it was a different group with whom rulers and traders in Niumi had to deal after 1816. Fuller territorial acquisition was not a British goal and would not be for another two-thirds of a century, but commercial control was. Already it was clear to some in Britain that Europe's poorly paid industrial labor force would not consume all that manufacturers were producing. Africans and Asians could help fill the consumption gap. What was necessary for this to happen was the elimination of obstacles to trade, so that merchants armed with inexpensive British manufactures could extend the market beyond rulers and traders to the foreign masses.

So, fairly quickly, using gunboat diplomacy, the British set out different terms for commercial relations with Niumi. Moreover, as the leading state of the industrializing West, Great Britain would grow ever stronger in relation to Niumi, a typical polity that was not industrializing and increasingly outside the core of the world economy. The small Gambian state would soon fit into a niche in the world system as a supplier of raw materials—in Niumi's case it would be peanuts—and a consumer of manufactured goods. By the end of the century, Niumi would be so economically and politically weak, and so dependent on its relationship to the world economy, that it would forfeit its sovereignty to Great Britain's colonial juggernaut with little fanfare and almost no effective opposition.

Over the same period of British absence from the Gambia, on either side of the turn of the nineteenth century, events were taking place in the Islamic world that would have equally lasting effects on the people of Niumi. For centuries, Muslims in West Africa had been pragmatic merchants, intent on finding accommodation with the rulers and village heads among whom they traveled and lived. They demanded little of their hosts and, when individuals in Niumi converted, accepted a form of worship that included pre-Islamic rites and practices. But reform efforts that had been alive in the Islamic world since late medieval times began to appear in West Africa, first in a religious hotbed along the middle Senegal River as early as the seventeenth century and then in several locations across West Africa's savannas at the beginning of the nineteenth. Seemingly content with their mutually beneficial modus vivendi with the state's *soninke* rulers into the 1770s, Niumi's Muslims nevertheless were aware of successful reformist jihads in West Africa, some not far away. The growing desire to purify the Islamic faith, to move from accommodationist religious practice to one where Islamic law governed the behavior of all residents of the state, would spread to serious Muslims around the lower Gambia and make Niumi ripe for religious reform at the very time when other social, political, and economic changes were sweeping into the state, making it harder and harder for the traditional ruling lineages to maintain control. Thus, the world outside, from greater distances away, would make itself felt with increasing strength in Niumi, in old ways and new ones.

Revolutionary Change in the West

Global issues were critical for the beginning of Western Europe's Industrial Revolution.[5] Worldwide population growth after the seventeenth century, partly the result of the dissemination of American food crops, created more laborers for industrial production, more consumers, and more producers of raw materials. Encounters with new plants, animals, people, and stars in voyages around the globe helped set sixteenth- and seventeenth-century European minds to revolutionary thinking about science. The growing global commerce on which western Europeans were thriving brought in necessary capital and raw materials as it connected them to vast markets. Some of this wealth helped seventeenth-century monarchs turn old sovereignties into more powerful nation-states. Capital, management, labor, government policies that favored risking capital, and entrepreneurs participating in the world economy came together in Great Britain after the middle of the eighteenth century to begin a process of industrialization. In its simplest essence, this involved harnessing new forms of energy to machines that produced more, and less expensive, goods in factories.[6] The factories were the places of production; from them soon radiated transportation networks that connected to the world's resources and a global market. This process of change was so dramatic that it is called a revolution—the first real change in the way humans tapped energy and produced goods since the agricultural revolution 10,000 years earlier. Practical invention of new machines to spin and weave cotton was symbolic of Britain's Industrial Revolution in the early nineteenth century.

Perspective 6   **Burungai Sonko**

In stories told about Niumi's past, the state's *mansa* from 1823 to 1833, Burungai Jeriandi Sonko, is a scoundrel. As the tales go, Sonko usurped the seat of power from the chosen mansa, a close relative, first by threatening to expose the intended as an adulterer (after an episode of what one might call entrapment) and then by threatening to blow up everyone at the installation ceremony with a pile of gunpowder if they did not name him as the next ruler. While perhaps extreme, such intrigue was not different from what others before him had done to gain political authority. People today remember Sonko's evil exploits partly because he had the misfortune of serving as Niumi's *mansa* at the time when Great Britain decided to use its burgeoning power to break Niumi's lock on river traffic. The British pressed Sonko into ceding them Niumi's entire riverbank for a mile inland, offering him paltry quarterly payments in return for the land and rights to exact tolls on shipping that had long belonged to Niumi's rulers. As he weighed the offer, Sonko had to stare out onto the nearby river at a heavily armed British man-of-war and the first steam-fighting vessel ever to churn up West African waters, both with big guns trained on his village of Essau. Then, when Sonko organized a force to oust a British garrison from a new fort on Barra Point, in sight of Essau, he faced troops from various corners of Britain's Atlantic empire, French forces on land and sea, and mounted soldiers from African states on two sides whom the British lured into the fray with promises of payment and spoils. By a final treaty in 1832, Sonko and his headmen had to declare "their sorrow for the outrages they have committed" in "an unjust and cruel war" against the British, and had to confirm their loss of sovereignty over the state's riverbank. After Sonko's pivotal reign—he died within a year of signing the treaty—Niumi's royal lineages began a steady slide toward oblivion. In the face of growing British power to enforce their will and Muslim reformers' inclination and ability to stand against the armies of the state, the royal lineages saw their position steadily weaken. After the 1850s, only the ironic support of the same British who had begun the decline kept the *mansa* in charge of state government, and by the end of the century the collapse of the Niumi state in the face of formal British takeover went almost unnoticed. Thus, it was simply being the mansa at the beginning of the end rather than his methods of gaining power that left Sonko unpopular in the minds of the state's oral traditionists.

As a result of these changes, the Britain of the 1820s already was dramatically different from the country half a century earlier—in wealth, productive capacity, military capacity, commercial inclination, and attitude. Other countries in Western Europe and North America—France, the United States, Germany (after its unification in 1871)—industrialized in England's wake, competing to apply science to production, work with new and stronger metals, discover new sources of energy, and perfect mass production. The same spirit of invention that automated textile production by the 1780s provided the railroad and steamship for rapid world transportation on land and sea by the 1830s and brought firearm technology from the flintlock musket to the breech-loading rifle and machine gun by the 1880s. The Industrial Revolution was the major factor in the rise of the West to worldwide economic and political dominance in the twentieth century.

Accompanying the early phase of the Industrial Revolution in Western Europe were new thoughts about old human issues. Lumped together, we refer to the body of fresh ideas entering the realm of Western social and political thought after the middle of the eighteenth century as the Enlightenment. Through application of scientific method to consideration of society, government, and economy, European thinkers began to question such previously accepted institutions as slavery, divine-right monarchy, and mercantilism. By the end of the eighteenth century, intellectual forces were in motion in Western Europe and North America that eventually would end the slave trade and slavery, give greater consideration to fundamental rights for humans, make steady efforts toward broader participation in government, and open the marketplace to all without government interference.

Thus, in addition to forces and products of industrialization, it was political and social results of the broad new liberal ideology that enhanced European power in the nineteenth century. Political change at home enabled European states to tap more fully the resources of their populations and to extend their control of trade in foreign areas; then an intensification of national rivalries brought the industrial European nations into intense economic and political competition around the world. The French Revolution unleashed the forces and ideas of Europe's growing middle class, especially the credo of liberalism, which provided the basis for governmentally ensured freedoms to act, trade, and prosper. It also brought forth an ideology of nationalism that united people of one country across classes and enabled them to mobilize their growing populations in efforts considered of national importance. Through the middle of the nineteenth century, under policies of laissez-faire economics, such national competition was largely a private affair around the arena of world trade. But in the second half of the century, as England, France, Germany, and the United States continued industrializing at an ever-greater pace, the nations began to recognize that national competition might require the force of government intervention. A series of economic depressions after 1870, created by overproduction of Western industries, led Europeans to believe their long-term economic well-being might require a return to rigid mercantile principles. What followed were efforts on the part of European nations to peg out areas of the non-industrial world as preserved markets for the future and sources of raw materials needed for industry. The result, by the last two decades of the nineteenth century, was a rush of the strongest and wealthiest nations at the core of the world economy to incorporate territory in Africa and Asia into formal empire.

The desire for markets and tropical products was only one reason for Western Europe's "scramble for Africa" between 1880 and 1900. All are related to the Industrial Revolution. Medical advances, especially the identification of the malaria suppressant quinine, enabled Europeans to live longer in the tropical environment—long enough for soldiers with superior weapons to conquer and officials with bureaucratic formalities to administer; advances in the technology of firearms and new methods of producing inexpensive steel, from which the weapons were made, gave Europeans novel advantage over the less-well-armed Africans; and faster steamships and new telegraph lines enabled European governments to manage affairs better around the world.[7] Such industrial and technological advancement gave Europeans a sense of superiority over others that was utterly out of touch with any sense of the past, yet that did not matter. And because northern Europeans were light skinned and Africans and Asians dark, the former ascribed their perceived superiority to "race." In a corruption of Charles Darwin's ideas of evolution, Western intellectuals by the 1890s were interpreting recent global events as a struggle among humans for social supremacy that whites were winning and darker peoples were losing because of the latter's lack of fitness to survive. If Africans were to avoid social regression and perhaps ultimate extinction, "Social Darwinists" argued, Europeans had to take them over and "civilize" them. It was a burden, poet Rudyard Kipling would inform the English-speaking world, to bring along these "new-caught, sullen peoples, half devil and half child," but one that whites had to bear.[8] This fit well with arguments missionaries were making for government assistance in efforts to save black souls. And industrialists realized that "civilized" Africans living more like Europeans would want more of the goods European industries turned out and might be able more efficiently and inexpensively to produce raw materials the Western industries required. The new circumstances of the West's industrial existence, with the ideology that was evolving that combined Christianity, philanthropy, and self-aggrandizement, all fit neatly into a rationale for taking political control of territories around the world where previously Europeans had traded freely with Africans, Asians, and Americans. Niumi would be only one very small place in Africa, and Africa just one of several great landmasses lying mostly south of the Tropic of Cancer, that would be affected by these changes in Western Europe and the world economic system it dominated.

Islam's Militant Strain

Central parts of the Muslim world experienced political decline in the seventeenth and eighteenth centuries. The once-mighty Ottoman, Safavid, and Mogul empires of Central Asia either were gone or declining by 1800. Muslims around the world could look around and see Europeans not only steadily gaining an upper hand in world trade, but also physically encroaching on Muslim territory. Napoleon's foray into Egypt between 1798 and 1801 exposed the weakness of the Ottomans and made Muslims wonder if they had strayed too far from the Path or, indeed, if the path they were on was leading in the proper direction. Steady Western incursions in age-old Muslim lands from southeastern Europe to southern India—at first through trade and related technological and cultural exchange—heightened Muslims' search for a proper response. As early as the mid-eighteenth century, followers of Abd al-Wahhab on the Arabian Peninsula attempted to revive Islam by a return to its purer practice. By the nineteenth century similar purifying reform movements were springing up around the Islamic world, from Sumatra and India to the Caucasus and lower Nile. Islamic revolutions that swept across West Africa's grasslands in the nineteenth century thus fit into a broad pattern of reformist movements in Islamic history.

But the more one knows about the spread of Islam in West Africa, the more one recognizes that the fit with the reform efforts across the Muslim world is not tight—that a strain of militancy, probably not unique but not shared widely, existed among some West African Muslims for a long time in the past and that West Africa's Islamic revolutionary leaders, while worldly enough to know of, and be affected by, the currents of reform existing elsewhere, were social revolutionaries with political ends as well as religious reformers. Some scholars trace a continuity in Islamic militancy in West Africa back to the Almoravid movement, an eleventh-century Berber effort at reform in the western Sahara.[9] After the Almoravid decline, a group of Berber scholars, the Zawāyā, kept the tradition of Islamic purity and learning alive in western-Sahara religious centers, and these scholars were important in passing along their ideas to a group that originated in the Futa Toro region of the Senegal River valley, the Torodbe. Not so much an ethnic or lineage grouping as a body whose members held similar deep beliefs and shared ascetic ways, the Torodbe were, in John Ralph Willis's words, "slaves or descendants of slaves from a broad spectrum of Sudanic society. Any believer willing to disdain the despised crafts and embrace a sedentary existence which espoused the cultivation of Islamic learning" could enter the fold. It was not kinship, ethnicity, or territorial ownership that held them together, but the brotherhood of Islam.[10] From the Senegal valley, Torodbe scholars took their ideas of religious purity (and perhaps a sense of a heritage of militant reformism) and spread out around West Africa, some all the way across the drier savannas to northern Nigeria, some along the middle Niger and upper Senegal, and some southward toward the lower Gambia. If Jahanka lineages kept alive Islamic scholarship and magico-spiritual works between the middle Gambia and Senegal, it was Torodbe clerics who did the same in the states between Futa Toro and the lower Gambia, and pacifism was not dyed so deeply in their cotton cloaks as it was for the Jahanka.

Zawāyā and Torodbe clerics began showing their militant side late in the seventeenth century. What vexed them was not so much that rulers of the states in which they were residing were not Muslims—quite a few were, of sorts—but that Islamic religious practices in the states were heavily mixed with traditional rites and that the rulers were a long way from enforcing the Sharîa, the Islamic law that Muhammad dictated for people living in the realm of Islam.[11] In most cases the reformers followed proper form by first attempting to foster change through peaceful means (jihad of the tongue and hands) and then purifying themselves (jihad of the heart) before resorting to religious war (jihad of the sword). The Mauritanian cleric Nāsir al-Dīn may rightfully be regarded as the source of much of the subsequent Islamic militancy around Senegambia and beyond. In the 1660s, he began preaching conversion and reform, and he sent missionaries to move and spread the word among peoples south of the Senegal River. This *toubenan* reform movement, as the French on the Senegal knew it, gained popular support among persons in the Wolof states and further afield. Nāsir al-Dīn's political uprising against traditional rulers in Futa Toro and Jolof in the 1670s did not last long after his death in 1674, but a militant jihad soon broke out in Bondu, farther up the Senegal in the 1690s, and then in the highland area of Futa Jalon to the south. The states formed from these efforts quickly moved away from reform and became similar to the old secular polities, but the *toubenan* spirit never cleared from the air south of the Senegal.[12]

In the middle of the eighteenth century the West African leader of the Islamic Qadiriyya brotherhood began espousing reform and his ideas spread widely from a center north of Timbuktu. A second jihad in Futa Toro was short lived, but in the early part of the nineteenth century, Torodbe reformers led movements to purify Islamic societies on a larger scale and with greater success: Usuman dan Fodio, a local Qadiriyya leader, led a successful jihad in the Hausa states of northern Nigeria in the first decade of the century, creating the Caliphate of Sokoto that would last into the twentieth century, and soon afterward, Ahmadu Lobbo overcame non-Muslim rulers along the middle Niger and formed the fundamentalist Caliphate of Hamdullahi. News of such activity reverberated around West Africa's Muslim world, especially among clerics who were disaffected with their own rulers.

Thus, Niumi was on the edge of an area long buffeted by currents of Islamic reform. Muslim lineages in the state, relatives of some of the oldest and strongest Torodbe reformers in Senegambia, carried the idea of jihad in their intellectual baggage. They would be good candidates to pick up the prescribed effort to purify the faith when it entered the region with a handful of individual reformers in the decades after 1850.[13] In this vein, they would make a prolonged effort to unseat Niumi's non-Muslim *soninke* lineages and would leave in their wake a weakened state unable to mount any kind of effective resistance to British takeover in the last decade of the century.

Weakening of the Niumi State

It was not the decline or eventual halt of Atlantic slaving that brought about a crisis for Niumi's ruling elite. Slave exports via the river remained on a relatively steady, high plateau through the first two-thirds of the eighteenth century, averaging between 1,000 and 1,500 per year. The trade fell to about 800 per year in the 1770s, to 300 per year in the 1780s and 1790s, and then to 150 per year in the first decade of the nineteenth century.[14] It came to a halt soon after 1816. But Niumi's ruling families and their entourages received their wealth not from the capture and sale of slaves so much as from the tolls they charged passing commerce—*any* commerce.

So it is important to recognize that as the slave trade was declining over the half century after 1770, other trade (termed "legitimate" trade by the English anti-slave-trade forces) was taking up the slack and its purveyors continued to provide Niumi's rulers revenue from tolls on shipping. Hides, beeswax, ivory, and gold—all were in demand internationally and all could be obtained in the Gambia for fair, albeit rising, prices. Niumi's rulers taxed the movement of such trade across its boundaries and continued to charge tolls, duties, and fees to shippers plying the legitimate trade as it had done for those coming to the river primarily for slaves.[15]

What seems most to have brought about the start of a long decline of Niumi's ruling class and served as a trigger for the start of sweeping political, social, and economic change in the region was not the waning slave trade, but the new attitude Britishers brought with them when they returned to the Gambia following the Napoleonic wars. Always before, trade in the river was on African terms. British garrisons on James Island since 1660 were so dependent on the good graces of residents of Niumi for food, water, and cultural mediation to facilitate trade that it could not have been otherwise. Customs that traders in the river had respected for a century or more brought Niumi's ruling lineages the tolls and fees that enabled them to maintain their sizable retinues and their elite lifestyles. But the British who resettled in the Gambia in 1816 were a different bunch, separated from the previous group by a long generation that had seen the effects of early industrial technology and two decades of warfare. These men commanded greater power relative to Niumi, held different attitudes about trade and about who was in charge, and in a broad sense tended to recognize a greater cultural, social, and technological distance between themselves and the Africans among whom they came to reside.[16] This would not bode well for the toll collectors residing along the lower river's north bank.

As an act of war against their French enemies in 1800, the British had taken Gorée Island, and for fifteen years English, Africans, Anglo-Africans, Franco-Africans, Luso-Africans, and others conducted coastal trading from that rocky Atlantic outpost nestled just below Cape Verde. When they returned the island to France a year after the Treaty of Vienna in 1815, the British resettled the Goréean community on Banjul Island, eight miles up the Gambia from the river's entrance into the Atlantic at Cape St. Mary's. The low, sandy island had no regular inhabitants. For some years prior to its British occupation, women from Niumi had made residences there during the rainy season for growing rice and cotton.[17] The British named the island Bathurst after the British Colonial Secretary, the Earl of Bathurst. The transplanted merchants believed there was sufficient trade in the river to justify expenditures on the new outpost, but the British government had another reason for Bathurst's existence. In a climate of growing humanitarianism, Parliament had outlawed the slave trade in 1808, but most people familiar with the trade knew that legislation alone would not halt the centuries-old traffic. Big guns at the Bathurst settlement would be a major step toward stemming illegal slaving in the Gambia, by this time carried on mostly by Americans in vessels under the Spanish flag.

Perspective 7   **Niumi and the Settlement of Bathurst**

From a modern perspective, Britain's decision to locate its principal Gambian city and port on the *south* side of the river was one of the most damaging acts imaginable for the subsequent history of Niumi. Not only did all trade soon come to focus on Bathurst, but also almost all colonial and postcolonial investment in development occurred there. Today, Banjul (the former Bathurst) and Kombo-St. Mary's (the adjacent region on the river's south bank) are far and away the most populous, prosperous, developed sectors of The Republic of The Gambia. The country's major medical, educational, banking, and commercial institutions are located there. Along paved streets and roads residents obtain safe water from spigots under the illumination of streetlights. A forty-minute ferry ride across the river, Niumi is a different world. It has two paved roads, electricity only in a handful of spots, minimal sanitary facilities, one major (since 1988) and two minor health centers and a couple of dispensaries staffed by technicians, and no banks. Before 1995 it had no secondary school. People in Niumi have to cross the river to do business, an effort that can take half a day in travel. It was not that way two centuries ago, but the focus of power and wealth switched sides of the river, away from Niumi, over several decades after the British established their commercial, strategic, and colonial headquarters on Banjul Island. Nothing in Niumi has been the same since.

Standing between the Bathurst merchants and commercial profit, however, was the centuries-old custom of shippers paying tolls and excises to the traditional master of the river's trade: Niumi's *mansa*. The small British expedition that reconnoitered in 1815, prior to resettling the Gorée traders, was in no position to dictate new terms. The expedition's leader, Captain Alexander Grant, was careful to assure *Mansa* Kolimanka Manneh that he could continue to collect the same tolls. (Grant did explain that vessels conducting slaving in the river would be seized without payment.) So, for a brief time, masters of vessels continued to order salutes fired to the *mansa* and then sail up to Juffure to pay their dues to the state's *falifo*. After June 1817, however, it became apparent that the Bathurst merchants were not ones to follow old ways. Because of vague charges of "misconduct on the part of the king and his people," Grant advised captains entering the river to pay but half of Niumi's ordinary duties and fees. Early in 1820, when shipmasters complained of the time it was taking to visit Juffure for customs payments (one vessel having to lay by for ten days as someone went to the royal village to fetch the absent *falifo*), Grant began having the Bathurst customs officer collect the *mansa*'s due and deliver it to him. Such an arrangement continued until July 1822, when, at the behest of Bathurst traders, administrator Charles MacCarthy simply began paying values considered roughly equal to Niumi's tolls out of revenue accumulating from

Bathurst's own import duties. Within half a dozen years it was apparent that old relationships in the river no longer held. Soon the British would begin pressing their new superiority in the relationship. Once they did, gunboat diplomacy, rather than careful negotiation, would characterize their actions, and it would remain that way for the next half century.[18]

Their experience during Bathurst's early years showed the British what they needed to do. Their outpost rested on shifty ground both in a literal sense—Banjul being a sandbar backed by swamps and mangroves—and a fiscal one. Costs of maintaining the settlement came from import duties worth in the neighborhood of £40,000 in the 1820s, but Niumi's customary tolls added to the expenses of shippers, who passed them along to the Bathurst merchants. The latter grew increasingly disturbed. Then, when Manneh sensed he was not receiving his due, he made bellicose gestures that threatened the poorly garrisoned British settlement. "The King has frequently crossed over and levied contributions on the Merchants," reads one retrospective critique of Grant's years in charge, "and one very disgraceful transaction took place. . . . The King . . . went to Government House and told the Commandant that he would take the place and burn his house if he did not give him what he wanted, and I am sorry to say that he succeeded in intimidating the Commandant."[19]

To exasperate the British further, at the same time they settled Bathurst, the French had reestablished themselves at Albreda, twenty-five miles upriver on Niumi's riverbank. Bathurst merchants suspected that French goods were entering the river duty-free, giving their rivals commercial advantage. A way for the British to act toward solving all of these problems and to gain firmer command of shipping and thus clamp down more strongly on the slave trade was to take control of the strategic riverbank across from Bathurst—territory that had been Niumi's since before Europeans knew there was a Gambia River. Ceding its riverbank and control of shipping was not something Niumi's rulers would do lightly.[20]

In 1823, Kolimanka Manneh died. As on most occasions when political authority in the state moved from one lineage and village to another, there was a period of disruption. The British took the occasion to press Niumi to cede its riverbank. Once installed, the new *mansa*, Burungai Sonko, refused such a request, recognizing that giving up territory along the Gambia would be tantamount to committing strategic, financial, and political suicide. Sensing advantage in a show of force, the British brought the HMS *Maidstone*, one of the cruisers of the British African Squadron patrolling the coast for illegal slaving, and the *African*, the first British steam vessel in African waters. Each ship was armed to a degree never before witnessed in Gambian circles. Under this pressure, a British offer of quarterly payments of 400 Spanish dollars (about £87) in exchange for cession of a strip of Niumi's riverbank a mile wide and "the sole right to the navigation of the River Gambia with all claims and demands for customs or dues of whatever sort to which they have been entitled and have received from time immemorial" (excepting whatever tolls Niumi's rulers wished to charge French vessels visiting Albreda) did not appear to be such a bad deal. On June 9, 1826, Sonko signed the treaty. It was symbolic of the new power relationship with the British and the new commercial position in which Niumi found itself with the end of a demand for slaves for the Atlantic trade. Although Niumi's rulers could not have realized it at the time, it was symbolic also of the beginning of the decline of Niumi's sovereignty and of a way of life for its ruling groups that had enabled them to live as elites for several centuries. Thereafter, change would come with increasing speed, and for the *soninke*—the old ruling class—the change would not be for the better.

If the traders and administrators in Bathurst thought that Niumi's rulers were going to sign away their livelihood with nothing more than foot dragging, the next half-dozen years proved how wrong they could be. As effects of the new treaty—especially of the loss of their traditional shipping customs—became evident, a general malaise settled among Niumi's ruling families. When the British almost immediately began construction of a fort, Fort Bullen, on Barra Point in the Ceded Mile (the term used for the territory along Niumi's riverbank), followed by erection of a battery of guns in the fort and stationing there of a garrison of thirty troops from a force sent to the Gambia from Sierra Leone, Sonko and his entourage made known their displeasure. One British official in 1827 labeled Sonko "an insane drunkard, who has always been troublesome, and can only be restrained by fear."[21] Reports circulated around Bathurst in 1829 that the *mansa* was "sorry he ever ceded any part of his territory," and early in 1830 his men seized part of the cargo of a British coasting vessel that had run aground at the river's mouth, as was his traditional right. Sonko preferred losing half of his annual payments from the British to returning the cargo. Thereafter Niumi's ruler was "frequently troublesome" to the Bathurst merchants.[22]

Events came to a head in 1831, triggered by arrogant aggression abetted by cultural ignorance on the part of Bathurst's settlers.[23] An English agricultural society wanted to establish a colony of pensioners and liberated slaves on Dog Island, off a point of land on the Ceded Mile, to experiment with the growing of hemp. They did not realize that Dog Island was where residents of one of Niumi's seven royal villages, Sitanunku, harbored their most precious fetishes and animist spirits. No one was to reside there, let alone foreigners. Within a matter of weeks, Sitanunku villagers had run off the Dog Island settlers and Niumi's *mansa* had closed all paths of trade and stopped canoes from going to Bathurst with supplies. Bathurst authorities reinforced the garrison at Fort Bullen. On August 22 and 23, a large force from Sonko's village, Essau, burned a British settlement of discharged soldiers outside the fort's walls, engaged the fort's garrison, and forced it to flee for safety across the river. The British reacted quickly, intent on showing Niumi's ruling lineages just how far reaching were their resources. They organized a blockade of Niumi's coastline to cut the state's supplies of food and munitions, sent an influential African trader to the states surrounding Niumi to arrange for its isolation by land (and to persuade one of the states to threaten attack on Niumi's eastern border, forcing Sonko to send some of his force to the other side of the state), called for more troops from Britain's colony in Sierra Leone, and asked the French on Gorée for assistance. Eager to protect the interests of the traders at Albreda, France sent a warship to bombard Essau and harass the Niumi soldiers there over ten days. The governor of Senegal followed by sending eight officers and forty-five men to bolster the British force.

On November 11, a well-armed unit under British command—451 officers and men, backed by the heavy cannon on two armed colonial vessels—assaulted Barra Point and retook Fort Bullen from a Niumi force that the Bathurst colony's lieutenant governor, George Rendall, believed "could not have been less than 2000." Six days later the combined British and French force marched on Essau and engaged the Niumi army in a five-hour fight that ended in a standoff. Eleven in the colonial force were killed and fifty-seven wounded. Niumi might have experienced greater casualties. The colonials kept up a daily fire on Essau for the next month, and it was wearing. On December 19, the *mansa* of Kombo, the state on the south side of the river, went to Bathurst and, speaking for Niumi's ruler, asked the British for peace. He suggested that the people of Niumi were "so reduced as to consent to any conditions." Rendall assessed the situation at the end of January 1832: "The people of [Niumi] have suffered so severely from the strict blockade kept upon their coast, and by the kings of Salum and Baddibu who closed their communications on the landside that I am induced to hope they will be very quiet for some time to come."[24]

The formal result of the "Barra War" for Niumi was a humiliating treaty, signed on January 5, 1832, by Sonko and seventeen other Niumi officials, the provisions of which abridged the sovereignty of the state. Those from the Niumi side, the treaty reads, "having publicly declared their sorrow, for the outrages they have committed, and given their solemn promise never to offend again," had to deliver hostages from each royal lineage for their "good faith," ratify again the 1826 treaty ceding a mile of the state's riverbank, agree to seek the consent of the lieutenant governor of Bathurst before selecting a new *mansa*, indemnify residents of Barra Point and Dog Island for losses sustained, turn over all pieces of ordinance in Essau, and promise "to hold peace and friendship with the subjects of His Majesty the King of Great Britain for ever."[25] After at least three centuries of maintaining Niumi's sovereignty in the face of warfare, slave raiding, and threats from within and without, the state's ruling lineages had met their match.

New Systems of Production and Exchange: The Peanut Revolution

A year before Niumi soldiers attacked Fort Bullen, in 1830, British traders had sent a few baskets of locally grown peanuts to the British Institute for Tropical Agriculture in the West Indies. For some time, they had been looking for primary products in world demand that they could obtain along the banks of the Gambia in exchange for the consumer goods being manufactured in Western Europe in ever-greater quantity. This time they found one.

The Portuguese had brought peanuts to West Africa from Brazil as early as the sixteenth century, but farmers in Niumi never paid them special attention—nor did anyone else along the Gambia River for a long time.[26] Over the centuries, peanuts had become one more of a host of crops grown for local consumption, mainly as a hedge against failure of the grains. When people were *really* hungry, they would eat peanuts. Ruling elites had slaves feed the tops of the plants to their horses and some believed this made the mounts stronger and likely to live longer.

But peanuts in the Gambia would have their day. Through the first third of the nineteenth century, demand grew steadily in Europe for vegetable fats and oils that could be used in candles, cooking oils, lubricants, and, particularly, soap—it was a time when people around the Western world were becoming aware of the relationship of personal hygiene to good health. A popular tropical oil in use for soap production since the latter part of the eighteenth century was palm oil, obtained along the forested coasts of lower Guinea. French cooks had begun using peanut oil as a cheaper substitute for olive oil and soon there were experiments with its use in soap manufacture. Four years after the initial British investigation of Gambian peanuts, 213 baskets of the product left the Gambia and ended up at Forster and Smith, the London firm that was to become Britain's leading peanut importer. Forster and Smith had experience in the West African trade as importers of palm oil, rice, beeswax, and mahogany. In 1835 the firm built a mill in London to crush peanuts and render their oil, and the demand for peanuts was under way.

Other factors relating to the world market aided the rise of Gambian peanut production for export in Niumi. In Europe in the 1830s, factory workers and common laborers made paltry wages, so there were not masses of people with disposable money for the purchase of industry's large and growing output. This was especially true for Britain's leading industry: textiles. Industrialists saw African consumers as candidates to fill the consumption gap. To entice a broader range of Africans to consume European goods, British and French traders offered liberal credit to almost anyone, including many who previously had been outside the commercial network in the Gambia River. Large numbers of people with fewer means and less influence in Niumi found it possible to obtain imported goods for trading. Once peanuts proved to be a major item in demand, common peasants had a way to pay their debts and obtain still more inexpensive European manufactures that they increasingly desired. After the 1830s, a broader segment of Niumi's population became involved in the market, eventually acquiring more on credit and paying their debts with peanuts.

For a time, Gambian peanut exports grew with unprecedented speed. A market for Gambian peanuts blossomed in the United States after 1835, and soon three-quarters of the Gambian peanut crop was crossing the Atlantic and ending up for sale in New York and New England, at fruit markets and newsstands, at circuses and shows. A restrictive American tariff in 1842 all but stopped such imports momentarily, and then they fluctuated wildly. France then stepped in as the major buyer of Gambian peanuts, and with the exception of lean years caused by revolution and war, it would remain such for a long time. The initial reason for French interest was tied to French consumers not liking the yellow, palm-oil-based soaps. Once Marseilles soap makers found they could make a blue-marble soap with peanut oil as a major ingredient, the rush for the small legume was on. Marseilles imported one ton of peanuts in 1841, 205 tons in 1845, 5,500 in 1854.[27] As demand grew, farmers along the Gambia responded. By the 1850s the sons of men who never had exported a nut twenty years earlier were exporting over 10,000 tons of peanuts a year with a value in some years of over £130,000; for their grandsons, by the end of the century, it was 30,000 tons at £200,000.[28] Providing additional incentive were falling prices of European manufactured goods, the result of increases in efficiency of production and transportation. Between 1817 and 1850 the price of British textiles sold in the Gambia River dropped by 75 percent, prompting Niumi's growers of cotton and weavers to buy imported cloth with profits from peanut sales rather than produce their own. With world prices for peanuts holding firm in spite of the increased African production, entering the market for a number of years was simply smart economics.[29]

Like other regions of coast-wise Senegambia, Niumi quickly became one of large-scale peanut exporting. Its male farmers made the transition to export production over a short time and remained the state's major peanut producers thereafter. They did so, argues economist Jan Hogendorn, largely because of particular circumstances of the time and place. Such farmers had surplus land and wanted a variety of reasonably priced European products at the time the world market beckoned. They were able to clear additional land, interplant peanuts with food crops, and produce nuts for export while for a long time continuing to grow sufficient food for consumption.[30] The continuing existence of slavery in the region played a role, too. By the 1840s captives from regional wars, who once might have been marched toward the coast for sale and shipment across the Atlantic, could be taken to such places of export production as Niumi and sold there. Slave laborers were critical to Niumi's peanut production; numbers of slaves grew there through the middle and late nineteenth century.

Beginning in the 1840s, another phenomenon added to Niumi's peanut exports and became an important part of seasonal life and the workings of the state's peanut-based economy: "strange farming." This involved people from elsewhere migrating to Niumi before the beginning of the rainy season, taking up temporary residence in a village, making a peanut crop, selling it, and returning home with cash or goods.[31] The roots of strange farming extend back even earlier, to the eighteenth century, when the Atlantic slave trade was at its height. Dealers who marched slave caravans to Juffure in the dry winter months for sale there to Europeans might encounter low demand, and thus low prices, on arrival. An option to selling cheaply was to rent land and put the slaves to work growing a crop, which they would sell once harvested and then hope that prices for slaves were better. It is possible that at the same time small handfuls of farmers from the region of the upper Senegal and Gambia rivers moved toward the Gambia's mouth for a season of farming nearer points of exchange with European merchants. These early strange farmers sold their crop for trade goods and then marched inland with them and became traveling merchants over the dry season.[32]

Once Niumi's farmers began growing peanuts for cash, the land along the lower river lured people from as far away as modern Guinea and Mali, intent on bettering their social and economic positions at home in ways that required wealth. Some young men went strange farming for one or several seasons to acquire the bride price for marriage. Aware of traditional requirements to share wealth with needy kinsmen, they recognized the benefits of improving one's personal economic position away from family demands. Niumi had the advantage of having farming land near the river (meaning low transportation costs) and a relatively light population. The prospective strange farmer would come to a Niumi village between late April and early June and inform the village head that he wanted to make a crop with the coming rains. The village head either would assume the role of the individual's landlord or would designate another to serve in that position. In either case, the village head collected a custom payment from the stranger, a portion of which went to Niumi's *mansa*. The landlord would provide a dwelling for the stranger, see to it that he had sufficient food for the farming season, designate a plot of land for the stranger to farm, and make sure the stranger had tools and seed. The stranger would be required to work for three or four days of every week in his landlord's fields, and he would give the landlord one-tenth or a little more of the peanuts he produced.[33] The stranger would be gone soon after the sale of his crop, but one strange farmer might return to the same village several years running if the experience was profitable. In this way, the land of Niumi produced more peanuts than its regular, small population could grow.

The merchant populations at Bathurst and Albreda and British officials up and down Africa's west coast encouraged the migration of distant farmers or anything else that would increase peanut production and trade. Supplying peanuts for the European market was a worthy engagement for Gambian merchants, but every bit as important were issues related to colonial revenue. Bathurst and other coastal outposts were proving expensive. The troops, gunboats, colonial steamers, constables, and administrators cost money that British taxpayers did not want to pay. The key to having funds for such settlements was a bustling commerce. British port authorities at Bathurst levied duties on goods imported; as the quantity of imports rose to exchange for peanuts, so did Bathurst revenues. Then, in 1863, as indigenous warfare threatened trade and production up and down the river, bringing Bathurst merchants to press for expensive military operations to bring order, the British administrator in Bathurst imposed an export tax on peanuts.[34] It was not a large tax, but one that brought in greater revenue as peanut production climbed toward the century's end. Its historical importance was great, however, for taxes on peanut exports would become an important part of Gambian revenues from that time on, through the period of formal British control of its Gambia colony and through the early decades of independence.

There were more reasons for common folk to grow peanuts. Always a supplementary crop for the peasant, the peanut had been of minor significance and thus outside the realm of taxation by ruling elites. Niumi's rulers might get a tenth of a peasant's millet crop, but if they took anything of the peanuts that common farmers grew, it was only the plants' tops for fodder, which farmers did not want anyway. Now, with demand for peanuts at the waterside expanding, peasants could grow peanuts and trade them to European buyers and thus, seemingly for the first time, gain access to a source of wealth all their own. With such a resource, they soon were able to acquire commodities that previously only the ruling elites could afford—metalware and cloth, decorative items and luxury goods, and especially weapons, in this case firearms and gunpowder. These last items turned out to be of particular importance, for such weapons would enable the peasantry at first to resist their frequently oppressive *soninke* rulers, and then, as peanut exports and firearm imports continued to mount, to rise and attempt to overthrow them for good. This seems to be what happened in Niumi over the half century following 1830, when the region experienced one of its most disruptive periods ever: a time of far-reaching political, social, and economic change, the era of the Soninke-Marabout Wars.[35]

The Soninke-Marabout Wars

Before the nineteenth century, Muslim elements in Niumi were apolitical and peaceful. They were distinct minorities among Niumi's common villagers, who held strong ties to the soil and their ancestors, and who honored and placated the spirits of both. The pragmatic Muslims accepted traditional African elements in their religious practices. They could perform divination and supernatural work for non-Muslim rulers and live in a land ruled by infidels because they held to a pacifism that counseled removal from affairs of state and accommodation where necessary or practical. Such was the case for Muslims living across much of West Africa before the eighteenth century.

But militant Islam with roots extending deep in West African history began to affect Niumi around the middle of the nineteenth century. The human catalyst for Muslim-led uprisings along the Gambia was a member of a Futa Toro lineage, *Shaykh* Umar Tal. Umar may have been a typical, itinerant Torodbe cleric through his early life, but on a pilgrimage to Mecca in 1830, he was made West African head of a new Islamic brotherhood, the Tijaniyya, which through its ritual and enhanced mysticism held greater appeal for common people. When Umar returned, he was not just another Muslim pilgrim and mystic. He also was a scholar of considerable repute, and he burned with the reformist fire that previous Torodbe clerics had kindled in Futa Toro. After two decades of traveling and teaching, Umar launched a jihad around the headwaters of the Senegal and then marched north and eastward, overcoming non-Muslim rulers across large chunks of territory. Before his death in 1864, his empire extended to Timbuktu and covered thousands of square miles of West Africa's grasslands.[36]

Niumi's connection with *Shaykh* Umar and its ties to Islamic reform were through

Photo 5   **A descendant of a *Soninke* fighting man, dressed for battle as his ancestors did during the Soninke-Marabout Wars. Note protective amulets worn on the body.**

a Torodbe cleric residing in the state of Baddibu, immediately east of Niumi. His name was Maba Diakhou.[37] Maba's father had moved to Baddibu from Futa Toro around the beginning of the nineteenth century and established a Qur'anic school there. As was typical, Maba studied away from home through early adulthood. In 1850, not long after he had returned to live and teach in Baddibu, *Shaykh* Umar visited him, acquainted him with the Tijaniyya, and blew on the embers of Islamic revival that already might have been glowing within Maba.

The glow probably existed because the lower Gambian states were prime targets for reform. By mid-century the *soninke* rulers had become weak and ineffective. Like Niumi's rulers, most had difficulty controlling the warriors in their midst. *Soninke* drank excessively, took what they wanted from peasants, flaunted their non-Islamic worship of spirits, and lived off the rest of the population at a time when the rest no longer needed the protection the *soninke* offered. *Mansa* Demba Sonko of Niumi, whom the British described soon after he gained the position in 1834 as "very well disposed and sensible, anxious for peace," did not wear well. Twenty years later, British administrator Luke Smythe O'Connor described Sonko as "a man of unwieldy frame and indolent habits . . . much changed in appearance, depressed, attended by few adherents, and in reality holding a shadow of power in his dominions."[38] Sonko had turned increasingly to mercenaries to prop up his authority and some of them were out of control. They rustled cattle, plundered traders, and harassed Muslims in their enclave villages. When Jokadu rose in 1853 in the same quest for independence from Niumi it had been attempting for the better part of a century, Sonko employed a Serahuli warlord, Ansumana Jaju, to put down the rebellion, giving Jaju one of his daughters in marriage and three of his sons as warriors in the transaction. Then Jaju would not leave. Instead, he and his mercenaries did as they pleased. O'Connor believed they "had almost unlimited sway" and were the "main cause of aggressions" in Niumi.[39]

What is more, the recent rise of peanut exporting gave Niumi's peasants the means to fight their oppressors. Income from the sale of peanuts went mostly to the growers and merchants who transported the nuts to the riverside. With the new income they acquired firearms, which the British and French were bringing in enormous quantities, and with the weapons they took on their oppressive rulers.[40] Through the 1840s and 1850s, Niumi had to use more of its resources to keep dependent areas in check. By 1860, reform and rebellion were ripe along the entire lower Gambia's northern bank, and Maba was well placed geographically, spiritually, and militarily to lead the movement.

Maba led a successful jihad against the *soninke* rulers of Baddibu in 1861, and this encouraged Muslims in Niumi. In April 1862, after nearly three decades in power, Demba Sonko died in Berending. In the disorder that followed, 700 Niumi Muslims rose and stormed Jokadu, forcing its Niumi-backed *soninke* ruler to shave his head (signifying capitulation to Islam). They then called on Maba for help in a war against Niumi's ruling lineages. Maba sent his brother, Abdu, with a large force, and together the Muslims swept across Niumi. Through early May they burned *soninke* villages and had their way. At Berending they burned the town and exhumed and desecrated Sonko's corpse. Then they pushed on toward Essau, where the state's war leader, the *suma*, had drawn the remaining *soninke* force behind a stockade for a final stand.

In dire straits, the *suma* appealed to the British. As fate would have it, the administrator of the small colony, George A.K. d'Arcy, had formed a low opinion of Muslims during service in India as a colonel with the Third West Indian Regiment.

Perspective 8   **Kelefa**

Across a large area from Senegal to Guinea, the most popular tale sung and told by griots is the epic of Kelefa Sanneh. Its popularity is due partly to the music—a strapping good tune—but also to Kelefa's symbolic significance as the last of the great *soninke* warriors.

Kelefa was a member of a royal lineage in a state south of the Gambia. By young adulthood he had a reputation as one of the fiercest warriors alive. On horseback, with spear, he would take on anybody and fight for any noble cause. His contempt for death was legendary. When Niumi's *Mansa* Demba Sonko faced rebellion in Jokadu, he sought help from various *soninke* warriors, and as Jokadu's success mounted, Sonko turned to Kelefa. In spite of warnings of doom from seers, the brave Kelefa rode to Niumi to join the battle. He was leading Niumi's royal forces toward victory, riding and using his spear with great effect, when he met his symbolic fate. A soldier of Jokadu, who had paid a Muslim diviner to bless a bullet for his gun, climbed a tree with his weapon and just as Kelefa was raising his spear to thrust it at another Jokadu fighter, the gunman fired and hit Kelefa in the chest. Fighting from a distance with a firearm, rather than face-to-face, was the height of cowardice in the eyes of the *soninke*, but that no longer mattered. The tide of battle turned in Jokadu's favor, Kelefa left the field and eventually died in Juffure, and the glory days of the *soninke* warriors were numbered. Hearing the story of the death of the greatest of these warriors, at the hands of a Muslim-inspired gunman who was hiding in a tree, reminds Gambians of the end of soninke rule in the Gambian states and the demise of an elite lifestyle that had existed for several centuries.

He considered Gambian Muslims "crafty, ambitious and sensual, besides being given to slave labour and dealing." His opinion of Niumi's ruling lineages and their retainers was not a great deal better—they were "warlike drones"; yet d'Arcy rationalized that, at least, "from this wild unthinking people the kings had been hitherto elected," and he seemed intent on keeping it that way. So with Niumi's *soninke* under siege, d'Arcy sent members of the Gambia Militia to beef up West Indian Regiment troops at Fort Bullen, on Barra Point, where several hundred *soninke* women and children sought protection. One six-pound field piece, two howitzers, and two rocket guns pointed out from the fort over Essau's stockade at the Muslim lines, 1,000 yards to the east. Inside the stockade, the melodramatic d'Arcy could see the *soninke* army, "all dressed in the death-colour, yellow, and sounding their fetish bell," readying a "desperate stand."[41]

The big British guns deterred the Muslims for the time, but they could not dampen the spirit of the Muslim leaders. At a meeting convened at Albreda between representatives of the Muslims and the state's ruling lineages, d'Arcy made known his displeasure at the Muslim actions and forced a cease-fire and Muslim recognition of a new *soninke mansa* for Niumi. But the reformist urge among Muslims was strong and the next decade witnessed repeated attempts to overthrow the *mansa*, forcing British authorities to use more troops and gunboats to prop up the weak ruling lineages. On one occasion, in 1866, d'Arcy led 140 West Indian troops and 100 members of the Gambia Militia on an expedition to burn and drive Muslims out of four of Niumi's river villages. At Tubab Kolong, which d'Arcy considered the Muslims' main "fetish and maiden fortress," a British man-of-war bombarded the village and then a colonial force stormed it, leaving 350 dead among the Muslim force of 800.[42] A year later, Muslims sacked the *mansa*'s village, Bakindiki, killing the ruler and driving stragglers south toward the river, and in the early 1870s, Maba's successor in Baddibu was rebuilding stockades in the Muslim villages and threatening once more to attack the ruling lineages. Under such circumstances, the rulers rounded up their people, herds, and possessions and headed for Barra Point and English protection at Fort Bullen. This enabled them to continue installing a nominal *mansa* through the last decades of the century, though his authority and control never again approached what it had been a few generations earlier.[43] By the 1880s, Niumi's population was mostly Muslim and just waiting for the moment when the old ruling lineages would give up the ghost.

Formal British Takeover

The ruling lineages never recovered from these wars. A *mansa* of the Niumi state continued to receive an annual subsidy from the British and to levy tolls on cattle passing through Niumi to the markets in Banjul; slaves and retainers continued to work the royal fields and keep a few horses alive for pomp and ceremony. But by the last quarter of the nineteenth century, Niumi's rulers were powerless in the face of British will.

Ironically, it was not the British who would hasten the process of ending the Niumi state. By the 1870s Niumi was so much a part of a wider world that political events taking place on other continents could have serious implications for its population. Between July 1870 and January 1871, Prussia humiliated the French Army and in the ensuing peace treaty took portions of French territory for the new German state. Barely a year later France joined the rest of Western Europe in experiencing an economic slump that involved a fall of consumption, a glut of manufactured goods, industrial slowdowns, and fears of a sharp downward economic spiral. French planners began thinking that state expenditure on railroads, roads, and canals might pull the nation's economy out of the slump, and such expenditures overseas, particularly as they might tie into a quest for empire in North and West Africa, would bring the army to conquer people over vast amounts of territory and thus help the French military regain its lost prestige. Wise economists also seem to have realized that once persons in the newly acquired empire began consuming French-made products, it would be a further step toward solidifying an outlet for French industrial production and a hedge against future slumps. So France began construction of a railroad between Dakar and Bamako on the upper Niger in 1879 and proclaimed protectorates over ports along the West African coast in 1882. These were the years when Henry Morton Stanley was busy working to "open up" the lower Congo River for Belgian King Leopold II, events that brought unease to the competitive, industrialized European nations. German fears following the economic downturn and a perceived need to counter British occupation of Egypt in 1882 prompted Otto von Bismarck to announce German protectorates over territories in West and Southwest Africa, and then the European "Scramble for Africa" was on. Most Western nations met in Berlin over the winter of 1884–1885 to rationalize and justify the takeover of Africa that was under way. Within a decade, one or another European state would lay claim to almost the entire continent.[44]

With so much territorial acquisition going on—with gold discovered and pioneer columns forging northward out of South Africa, with Leopold II staking a personal claim to central African territory that was fifty times the size of his native Belgium, with the French Foreign Legion chasing resisters around the Niger's headwaters and Britain's Royal Niger Company consolidating the palm oil territories along the lower Niger under British protection—Gambia, its trade, and its affairs raised little interest in European colonial circles. For a time in the 1870s, French and British officials discussed an exchange, the British leaving the Gambia River to the French in exchange for a few French possessions that would allow Britain uninterrupted control farther down the coast. But protest by British traders in Gambia to members of Parliament helped nix such a trade. Then, as France gained the territory surrounding the Gambia, the two countries negotiated bilaterally to determine who might claim what. Representatives met in Paris in 1889 and agreed to delineate boundaries giving the British control along about 200 miles of the river. It took another fifteen years for a succession of joint surveying teams to set the exact boundaries—a series of straight lines and arcs that limited British territory to an area seldom more than ten miles in from either bank.

So it was that with the shake of hands, the scoring of a long straight line on a map, the shouts and waves of surveyors, and the pounding of boundary stakes in 1891, the greater part of what once had been the Niumi state got separated from a lesser part that included the salt-producing islands north of Jinak. The former became British territory, the latter, French.[45] No force in Niumi was strong enough even to hassle the survey team, let alone resist the extension of British authority. By the 1890s most residents were caught up in the monotonous annual cycle of the peanut. Their concerns were more with rains, locusts, and market prices than with who claimed the land that was the key to their livelihood. Following the suicide of *Mansa* Wali Jammeh in 1883—an act symbolic of the frustration and humiliation felt by Niumi's once-proud rulers—Maranta Sonko of Essau assumed what was left of political authority in the state. In April 1893 the Gambia's British administrator agreed not to "interfere with any homage, deference, or respect" that Sonko was accustomed to receive and to continue paying him £110 annually in return for cession of all Niumi territory between the Ceded Mile and the new boundary with Senegal to the

---

Perspective 9   **A Fanciful Tale About Gambia's Borders**

As anyone looking at an accurate map of The Gambia can see, someone took care in designating the country's boundaries. Straight lines make up most of the border of the western third of the country, and then carefully scribed arcs, smoother than the Gambia's twists and bends, follow the river eastward to set off the rest of the country from surrounding Senegal. A French-British boundary commission worked this out and surveyors set the lines, scribed the arcs, and placed the markers. Records of the commission's work exist in public archives and historian Harry A. Gailey described in *A History of the Gambia* (1965) how the borders were set.

None of this matters, however, when better tales come along and one has, as described by Craig Emms and Linda Barnett in the *Bradt Travel Guide for The Gambia* (2001): "It is said that the borders of The Gambia were set by a British gunboat that sailed the length of the river. The gunboat was supposed to have fired its gun both north and south, and the border was placed where the shells landed." This is the version of history taught in Gambian schools, written in books on Gambian history by local authors, and told by taxi drivers to their riders when conversation allows. Gambians want to believe such a tale because it holds symbolic truth: gunboats symbolized British power at the end of the nineteenth century and British agents relied on that power to negotiate with the French, in meetings no Gambian attended, for dividing the territory. Though eventually a surveying team used instruments to delineate the boundaries, their placing was arbitrary in Africans' eyes, with no more logic than (and based on the same symbolic power as) firing shells over the heads of Gambians and then connecting the spots where the shells landed.

Emms and Barnett conclude their paragraph on boundaries: "However this is probably just a fanciful tale as there is no historical evidence to support it." This statement earns them a spot in Clio's heaven.

---

north. Sonko also had to agree to collect no tolls and pledge loyalty and obedience to the colonial government. Indicative of how much the British had Sonko in their pocket was his request, in February 1896, for British protection. Parties met and negotiated a treaty to that end in January 1897. The British administrator named Sonko Niumi's first "Head Chief," and until his death in 1910, he would represent the colonial government in what used to be the Niumi state.

A Deepening Dependence

Through the second half of the nineteenth century, more and more men in Niumi became involved in peanut production. Even those who had other primary occupations—blacksmiths, leatherworkers, bards, clerics, traders, even one-time royal cavalrymen—planted a peanut crop so they could obtain cash to buy com-

Perspective 10   **The Death of *Mansa* Wali**

On January 12, 1881, Niumi's *Mansa* Wali Jammeh showed up on horseback, with an entourage of forty men, to see the British-appointed police constable, Nbye Buss, in Berwick Town on the British-controlled Ceded Mile of Niumi's territory. Jammeh was seeking one of his wives, who had run away and was residing with Buss's wife. When Buss refused to turn over the runaway, Jammeh pointed a gun at him; Buss fended off the weapon with his sword, but as he was doing so, the gun discharged, killing an onlooker. Because the incident took place on territory that was nominally British, Gambia's administrator, Gilbert A. Carter, called for an inquiry and a coroner's jury found Jammeh guilty of "willful murder." The administrator issued a warrant for Jammeh's arrest, but instructed police not to enforce it so long as the *mansa* remained in the part of his territory that was outside British control.

On June 9, 1883, however, when in spite of dire warnings he visited Bathurst, Jammeh was apprehended and sent to jail. He apparently had anticipated the events: He left directions for the care of his children and snuck a penknife into the cell under one of his loose garments. On the evening of June 11, the *mansa* used the knife to sever the arteries in his neck and cut a deep gash in his abdomen. He lay back on the bed in the cell and quietly bled to death.

"The deceased appears to have been exceedingly unpopular among his subjects," reports Carter, "which fact was strikingly evidenced by the whole of his male followers deserting him. [T]hree of his wives and as many children alone remained to see to the disposal of the body which eventually was buried at the expense of the colony."

Gambians continue to tell stories about the death of *Mansa* Wali, but their version differs from the official one in British records. *Mansa* Wali was murdered while being held in the Bathurst jail, Gambians say. ("Do suicide victims slit their own throats *and* stab themselves in the abdomen?" they ask.) He was a popular leader in the eyes of Gambians, who believe the British concocted the suicide story to cover up his murder.

G.T. Carter to the Administrator-in-Chief of Sierra Leone, Bathurst, June 14, 1883, CO 1/68. Francis Pinkett to Earl of Derby, Sierra Leone, June 30, 1883, CO 87/120.

modities, often with clear ends in mind: accumulation for marriage, acquisition of some newly designated necessity, conspicuous consumption to heighten status, or a host of others unique to the individual. Young students at the growing number of Qur'anic schools grew peanuts for their teachers; slaves of wealthier lineages, or, increasingly, some not-so-wealthy lineages, spent much of their time growing, harvesting, winnowing, or hauling peanuts. Just after the century's end, Niumi's first colonial commissioner, J.H. Ozanne, estimated that "practically the whole of the male population is engaged in ground-nut production eight months of the year."[46] Such had been the case for several decades.

What also had been the case was the steady decline in the ability of people in Niumi to grow enough grain to feed themselves—something they were having difficulty doing even before men were devoting more of their labor to producing peanuts—and the related importing of rice from distant markets, with merchants providing the rice on credit. Precisely when this change to increasing dependency on the merchants and the expanding world market occurred is difficult to determine, but the late 1850s seems to have been a critical time. Food was certainly scarce in earlier times: As noted, in the mid-eighteenth century, Niumi's residents needed to import grain from the Gambian hinterland to carry them through the hungry season until their own millet or rice was harvested. A century later the situation was worse. Gambian administrator O'Connor wrote in 1857 that "natives until the present year have cultivated enough grain for their own subsistence, but an alarming scarcity of foodstuffs have [sic] this year struck considerable parts of the river." Rice imports were valued at £6,007 that year, £19,351 the next, and £28,208 in 1859. The era of reliance on food imports from the world market was apparently underway.[47]

The nature of peanut farming was part of the problem. Unlike most other cash crops that Africans turned to in the nineteenth century—palm oil, cocoa, coffee, rubber—the peanut is grown in the same season and parallel to food crops. With the limited labor supply along the Gambia River, when men began growing peanuts it meant they grew less millet, sorghum, or rice. At the end of the harvest they would have less grain, but more goods or cash (cloth and silver coins remained current) to use in exchange. They could obtain imported grain to substitute for the decrease of production. Worldwide technological conditions were right at the time, too, to allow for such importing from much farther away than before. The tentacles of world shipping were stronger and reaching farther: larger and faster vessels were finding it profitable to carry bulkier items over longer distances. Fast-sailing vessels and steamers could bring rice from Asia, Europe, or the Americas to the Gambia River, where merchants were eager to sell the rice to peanut growers.

A problem of timing made a simple cash-for-rice transaction impossible, however. People in Niumi needed rice at a time of year when they lacked cash. At the end of the harvest season, around the end of the calendar year, they had food to eat and, once they sold their peanuts, cash, which enabled them to purchase commodities they desired during the "trade season," between December and April. By the time the summer "hungry season" set in, when food from the harvest was running low, cash was in short supply as well. But merchants eagerly advanced family heads enough rice to get them through until the next harvest, with payment, at interest rates that eventually approached 100 percent, coming half a year later, when they sold their next year's peanut crop. In this way, in the 1860s and 1870s, people of Niumi got bound up in what Kenneth Swindell calls "webs of indebtedness." The local merchants who bought their peanuts and sold them guns, cotton goods, spirits, or tobacco connected them to the European firms, which served as

Perspective 11 **Women's Changing Roles**

Some of the changes that altered life in nineteenth-century Niumi had effects on women that were not necessarily beneficial. Prior to the move to peanut exporting in the mid-nineteenth century, it seems there were no absolute gender divisions of labor in Niumi. Men and women worked at growing the same crops: millet, sorghum, rice, and, in kitchen gardens, an assortment of vegetables. Both contributed to the household food supply. Once peanut exporting took hold, however, men became the sole producers of peanuts, planting the cash crop instead of some of the food crops they normally grew. Women worked to make up the food shortage through more extensive growing of rice. By the century's end men had ceased growing rice altogether; it became "women's crop," and even taboo for a man to set foot in a rice field. (During times of upheaval, men would accompany women walking to and working in rice fields for protection, and in normal times they would carry rice back from the fields, but they would not touch growing rice or do any work in the fields.) As controllers of the household's cash-crop revenues, the men increased their power within the family at women's expense. Men fulfilled their obligations for household food supplies by purchasing imported rice. If household members needed other things, it was to the men they turned for the purchase.

Thereafter, nearly all colonial policies designed to promote agriculture focused on the peanut, man's cash crop. Introductions of higher-yielding seeds, improved tools, fertilizers, and improved marketing increased men's incomes and power in the household. In spite of growing dependence on rice imports, little was done to improve women's ability to grow more and better rice until the mid-twentieth century. Only recently, after studies revealed women's importance to household food production (and after peanut exports had fallen significantly), have development projects focused on women's work.

The spread of Islam after the mid-nineteenth century may have led to increased male control and female subordination, though that is difficult to determine with certainty. Muslim men typically exert control over their wives and daughters. What is not clear is whether men exerted such control in Niumi prior to Islam's growth there. A reasonable premise is that they did not—to the same extent.

Jennie Dey, "Gambian Women: Unequal Partners in Rice Development Projects," *Journal of Development Studies* 17 (1981): 114–115; Swindell and Jeng, *Migrants, Credit and Climate*, 91–92, 234.

the ultimate creditors. By the end of the century, Ozanne would be calling favorable attention to the merchants: "[They] have come to the assistance of the Natives by supplying whole towns with rice at 16/- a bag (90 pounds each) delivered at the traders' wharves, payment to be made with groundnuts next season." Such indebtedness locked Niumi's farmers into the world market in what would turn out to be a hard and fast connection. By the late-nineteenth century, people in Niumi were dependent not only on the natural elements and the world market price of peanuts, but on the world price of rice, costs of transportation across the seas, and rates of interest they might be charged.[48]

Of course, such dependence did not have to result in hardship. After all, some modern Arab states are entirely dependent on exporting petroleum and importing almost everything they consume, and their standards of living are among the highest in the world. In a year when the local peanut crop was strong, world market prices for peanuts were high, and the price of rice was low, people in Niumi could get along fairly well: there would be enough to eat, men could acquire wealth for marriages, people could dress well and even accumulate a stack of cloth or a bag of coins. But in Niumi these circumstances did not often prevail, and it would not take long for the downside of the dependent situation to rear its ugly head. Falling peanut prices related to the worldwide depression of 1873 led Niumi's farmers to join others in calling for a *tong*, a refusal to sell until prices rose. In the late 1880s another downturn in prices resulted in another *tong* and refusal to repay debts, prompting merchants to suspend trade. It was a situation that would go from threats and tension to harmful action. Ozanne described the situation in the first year of the twentieth century: "Owing to the failure of the ground-nut crop from want of sufficient rain and the destruction of their food crops by locusts, the natives in the Protectorate began to feel the pinch of famine early in the year. Their position was made worse from the fact that the merchants, who in former years had given out credits of rice, etc., to tide the people over the rains, at the close of which the first corn is ripe for gathering, decided to discontinue the practice. Already the people had begun to hunt in the forests for roots and berries, and to pawn and sell their clothing, many being reduced to wearing rice-bags as their sole covering."[49]

Rice bags for clothes and roots and berries for dinner would become commonplace. During the first half of the twentieth century, which was the heart of British colonial rule in the Gambia, a series of world events—wars and economic depressions, mainly—on top of their position on the periphery of the now-globe-encompassing world system would keep people in Niumi from gaining much from the political economy managed by their new British rulers.

6

NIUMI AS PART OF THE GAMBIA COLONY AND PROTECTORATE

1897–1965

*Get out of your rut or get under. Progress called for all over the
world. We are backward and bushmen too much. Work. Keep
yourselves, feed yourselves, improve yourselves!*
—Advice to Niumi farmers from Emilius Hopkinson, commissioner,
North Bank Province, 1921[1]

[I]n this bad year a little hunger must be expected and borne with.
—Hopkinson, 1929[2]

Maranta Sonko is a sad figure in Niumi's history. In the only photograph of him,
seated with twenty-seven other colonial chiefs at their initial meeting with Gambia's
British governors in Bathurst in 1897, he stares at the camera without a hint of
expression on his narrow, angular face. His hair is thin and short, his beard gray,
his eyes tired. From the looks on the chiefs' faces, it is clear that neither the photograph nor the meeting was their idea. The last in the line of Niumi's rulers that
stretched back half a millennium, Sonko became *mansa* following his predeces-
sor's suicide in 1883 and found the position empty of almost all traditional power
and authority. He was surrounded by Muslims, vessels that carried salt toward the
upper river paid no tolls, and slaves who once tended horses for his state's cavalry
now busied themselves growing peanuts. There were only half a dozen horses left
in the territory, anyway. He had reason to be sad.

In 1893 Sonko signed a treaty with Gambia's British administrator, giving up
rights to collect tolls and taxes and pledging his loyalty and obedience to Her
Majesty's Government in England in exchange for a £110 annual payment. Four
years later, he signed a second document placing Niumi under British protection
and limiting the annual payment to £83/6/8.[3] It was then that the colonial government named him Niumi's first "head chief" and brought him across the river for
the chiefs' meeting.

Sonko never took to his new position. In 1902 the government divided Niumi
into two administrative districts, leaving Sonko as chief of only "Lower Niumi,"
not half the region his ancestors ruled in former days. But it mattered little to the
old man. The commissioner admonished Sonko for inactivity, after which records

Photo 6 **The main street of Maranta Sonko's village, Essau, as it looked in 2009.**

show he got "a good deal smarter," but soon he withdrew again from colonial affairs, leaving chief's duties to his son. The younger man grew into the situation in ways his father could not. Official reports bear evidence of the old chief's decline: in 1903 his influence was "nil"; in 1905 he was "getting infirm—and very deaf"; in 1908 a visitor noted that "he seldom moves from his yard"; and the commissioner's report of 1911 reads simply: "Maranta Sonko died during the rainy season of last year."

Soon after his death, the commissioner convinced residents of Sonko's village, Essau to tear down the village and relocate it half a mile to the southeast, on higher ground. The old place was a "miserable site . . . on the edge of a mangrove swamp infested by tse tse," the commissioner argued. Now they all would be better off.[4]

In contrast to Sonko was J.H. Ozanne, the first British commissioner for Gambia's North Bank Province, which included Niumi. In the photograph with Sonko and the other chiefs, Ozanne is dressed in a white tunic over black pants. From underneath a white helmet, he glares sternly at the camera's lens with a look of confidence. It was a tall order Ozanne had faced in 1893 when he hopped over the boat's side, waded through a few inches of water, and set foot on Niumi's sandy soil. He was the administrator who was to establish British authority, and with it bring peace, order, prosperity, and the "benefits of civilization" to people living along a strip

144

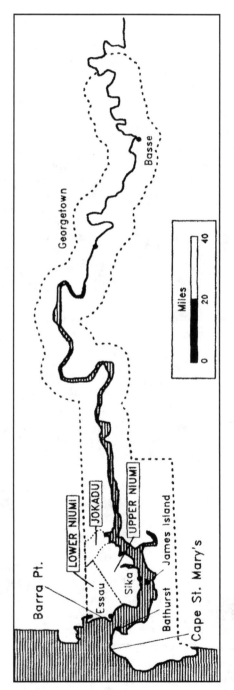

Map 8   **Colonial Gambia**

of wooded savanna 150 miles long and 10 or 12 miles wide—land that contained no roads, only walking trails and horse paths connecting villages, and people who had been engaged in social upheaval and civil war for two-thirds of a century. He should have felt overwhelmed.

But it appears he did not, and his smug countenance speaks of the confidence in Africa's new rulers that was the result of their coming from the industrialized West. Several centuries of involvement at the center of world-spanning commercial capitalism and a century and a quarter with steam-spouting, steel-producing, railroad-building, risk-taking, mass-producing, sometimes mind-boggling industrial capitalism had affected Europeans. Blind confidence was a personal manifestation.

With confidence so widely shared among people in the strongest nations of the Western world, it must have been shocking for many, then, to find that the first half of the twentieth century was a period of mixed fortunes for the world they dominated, including repeated episodes of political crisis and difficult economic times. By 1900 most of the world was divided into nation-states or colonies subordinate to powerful nation-states, and integrated into a vast economic network in which people residing in the individual nations participated unequally. This is Wallerstein's modern world system, resting not so much on political control by colonial rulers as on the economic relationships—especially the unequal division of labor—in the still-spreading capitalist economy: people in the industrialized nations produced manufactured goods (and financed production, controlled transportation and communication, and managed vast military power) while those outside the industrial zone worked to subsist and produce raw materials as they consumed some of the industrial production. At the heart of relationships among the powerful Western nations was intense competition, sometimes benign but often rabid, which would play a major role in bringing about two world wars and a long economic depression in the first half of the twentieth century, all of which set back the world economy and all those involved in it. In the end, after the second of the world wars, a movement toward colonial independence would come alive among many around the world. People living in Niumi, in Britain's Gambia Colony and Protectorate, would be caught up in all of these activities.

Had he known what was on the horizon, Ozanne might have allowed himself momentary pause, for there was more to make his task daunting. Somehow, amid the trading and competing and warring that would be going on around the world, while the European colonies in Africa and Asia were bringing economic benefit to their mother countries, at a minimum by leveling out the spikes and dips in international trade, the European authorities were supposed to "develop" their colonies—to find ways to improve the lives of persons living there. It was a tall order, and Ozanne was at the beginning of what was to be a long process of change through a difficult period. Perhaps he could have accomplished more under different circumstances. As it was, he contracted blackwater fever and died not quite a decade after he had taken on the task.

The Unsettled Twentieth-Century World

As with modern political, intellectual, and social history, for economic history and study of the modern world economy, there is something pivotal about the beginning of World War I. Before the war, Europeans were imposing colonial order on Africa and people long outside the world economy were being drawn into it. At the same time, Japan and China were moving toward greater participation in the global economy and world affairs. Western forecasters as late as 1912 or 1913 could reasonably conclude that the economy was in sound shape and that people at the center of industrial production and world trade would have smooth sailing for some time to come. With a long run of decent commodity prices, some believed, the colonial world also could move toward a stronger economic position that would eventually result in better lives for its millions of people. World War I turned the lights out on that vision and set the world on a long course of political and economic instability.[5]

Although the war began in central Europe in August 1914 and involved initially the most powerful nations of the industrialized European world, it did not take long for people in Europe's colonies to realize that this was an event of global proportions. In various parts of European empires, young men were placed under arms and shipped to participate in the fighting. Over 1 million African soldiers fought in campaigns in Africa or Europe, and still more African men, women, and children were convinced or coerced to serve as carriers for one or the other armies. Over 150,000 Africans lost their lives in the war effort.[6] In parts of Africa, people would begin asking why. Intellectual currents emerged from the war that would affect the world's colonized people, too. For Western nations the war was a colossal effort, a war to end all wars, people said, and to ensure that it was, various changes were necessary in the way nations conducted their affairs. American President Woodrow Wilson brought to the peace table his famous Fourteen Points, among which was the idea of "self-determination"—that "peoples" have the right to determine who governs them. Neither Wilson nor leaders of the European colonizing powers believed this doctrine need apply to African and Asian "peoples" under colonial authority, but in establishing a League of Nations Mandates Commission to deal with the colonies Germany and the Ottoman Empire lost in the war, taking them on as "a sacred trust to civilization" and looking to points in the future (however distant for most African colonies) when the colonies might be able to handle their own affairs, the peace settlement brought to the fore the notion of colonial independence. The war hurt European prestige among colonized people, too, and began to erode the psychological dominance colonizers held in the early decades of the twentieth century. Combining these elements, one can see the roots of a movement to end colonial rule and grant colonies their independence that would blossom after World War II, a quarter century later.

Of equal importance, World War I disrupted the world economy. A good portion of world production focused on the war effort; patterns of trade changed; wartime inflation appeared and spread; and at war's end the once-dominant nations of Western Europe found themselves in debt to the United States, whose economy was largely self-sufficient and whose interests in colonial Africa and Asia were minimal. What in the wartime economy hurt colonial people most was the opening and steady widening of a gap between export prices in Europe and import prices in the colonies. Large import and export firms found it a time for enormous profits, while European governments, caught up in the war effort and clinging to the free-trade mentality of the previous century, failed to take preventive action. The terms of trade for producers of raw materials and importers of manufactured goods continued their decline into the 1920s. The gap narrowed only slightly at the end of that decade and then widened again with the onset of the worldwide depression of the 1930s. Thus, many colonized people experienced depression and worsening standards of living for the better part of a generation before the onset of the so-called Great Depression. For many African colonies, in economic terms the period between 1914 and 1945 was simply one long, bad time.[7]

The Great Depression of the 1930s made the previous era seem bountiful by comparison. Triggered by a sudden collapse of the stock market in the United States and subsequent retrenchment in the American economy, the Great Depression showed how thoroughly integrated into a global economy were most of the world's people. The economic downturn dragged nearly everyone into a downward economic spiral. Within four years of the October 1929 stock market crash, world trade dropped by almost two-thirds and industrial production by one-third. Demand diminished for most raw materials, so prices for primary products fell and remained low. The effect of these depression years on Africans was uneven; mild recoveries occurred in some places in the middle and late 1930s. Still, it would remain for World War II, and the productive efforts of the major countries involved, to jar the world out of its worst economic crisis. Of course, other ramifications of the war would not be positive.

Economic matters were not the sole reason why the most powerful nations in the world squared off after 1939—one never can discount Hitler's notions of racism and geopolitics, nor his psychosis—but Japan had a position at the core of world economics in mind when it fought to create its "East Asian co-prosperity sphere"— its own world system, or subsystem, one might argue—and the worldwide political economy was at the center of thinking in the major warring nations. Japan's rapid takeover of much of the Pacific Rim by early 1942 showed the European world how important colonial production was to its economic and material well-being and its ability to wage war. Raw materials and foodstuffs that once flowed in from Java or Cambodia now had to be obtained elsewhere, and it was this rapid rise in demand for primary products that stimulated the economies of colonies from India to West Africa. For many colonial producers the war meant boom times, though a sudden European urge to manage colonial economies more closely, coupled with rising prices of imported goods and the inability to acquire many products long imported, partially deadened the boom.

This war involved fighting on a grander scale than ever before by many more people. Hundreds of thousands of troops from British and French colonies in Africa and Asia fought for the Allies against Nazi forces in Europe and North Africa or Japanese forces in East Asia. Recruits from British West Africa ended up as part of the 81st or 82nd Division of the West African Frontier Force and spent much of the war in the campaign to reclaim Burma from the Japanese.

For most of Africa and much of Asia, World War II was important in its role of moving the colonial world more rapidly toward independence. It is true that World War I cracked the facade of European invincibility and introduced the right of self-determination. It is true, too, that educated Africans had picked up on the Pan-Africanist spirit in the Americas in the 1920s and 1930s and already were agitating for improved conditions in the colonies before the war began. But all of this would have been slow in coming had it not been for the impetus provided by World War II. Many war-related events raised colonial peoples' expectations. British Prime Minister Winston Churchill and American President Franklin D. Roosevelt met on a cruiser off Newfoundland in 1941 and signed an agreement on war aims, the Atlantic Charter. One of the aims was for "the right of all peoples to choose the form of government under which they will live," an item that Churchill did not consider applicable to all peoples in Britain's colonies (barking in November, 1942, "I have not become the King's First Minister in order to preside over the liquidation of the British Empire"),[8] but one that colonized people the world over saw applying to themselves. Then, the millions of African and Asian soldiers who had served outside their colonies came home with a fresh outlook. They had witnessed the vulnerability of Europeans—many had killed some, in fact; they had seen how differently others lived and even had fraternized with women and men who recognized them as friendly forces and treated them accordingly; they had learned languages and new skills; and they had risked their lives for their rulers with expectations of concessions leading toward living conditions that were materially and emotionally more satisfying in return. But it was not to happen with the speed they had envisioned.

The postwar economic position of the colonial powers stifled such desires. Europe needed to rebuild and Europeans, naturally focusing on their own hardships during the war years, were starved for everything from clothing to automobile tires, so the products of postwar manufacturers, consumer goods especially, went to purchasers at home rather than to those abroad. Furthermore, England owed massive amounts of money to the United States, had almost nothing America wanted, and was dangerously low on sterling. In dire need of dollars, the British government initiated tight policies at home and with the colonies that prevented importing American goods, which were about the only goods available. Colonial subjects, who had gone without for as long as anyone, were rightfully annoyed. Many, including ex-soldiers, had more money than ever before, yet they could not buy—not even the fine cloth they needed to pay the bride price for a long-delayed marriage. Disaffection with such things economic brought about agitation to alter things political—a movement that led persons in Britain's colonies to look for leadership in those more political aware. Such individuals were among the earliest products of an overseas education and were influenced by the milder-speaking nationalists of a generation before.

After the war, Britain was under growing international pressure to develop its colonies and provide them the basis for independence. The United States and the Soviet Union, emerging from the war as the world's great powers and beginning a competition for allies that would turn into a long Cold War, recognized the popularity of their anticolonial positions. With its massive industrial production and need for raw materials, America was moving toward becoming an advocate of free trade—the antithesis of colonial economic relationships. The *idea* of decolonization did not cause Great Britain's newly victorious Labour party problems, but the timing did. In the end, colonial people took care of that. India already had exacted a British pledge of independence during the war and the United Nations trusteeships (the lineal descendants of the League of Nations mandates) in the Middle East were moving rapidly toward independence soon after. It was in this postwar milieu that Kwame Nkrumah of Britain's Gold Coast colony in West Africa stepped forward and speeded up the independence movement for all sub-Saharan Africa. Relying on ideas garnered from schooling in America and London and methods of political organization acquired from left-wing associates through those years, Nkrumah organized Africans to push the British into rapid movement. Once Britain committed itself to independence for one of its colonies—Ghana (the former Gold Coast) in 1957—the others were not long to follow.

Little Gambia was dragged along toward independence in the rush. Gambian development lagged, fewer Gambians were educated, political development and constitutional reforms were slower; still, on February 18, 1965, Britain gave up its ties to its oldest African possession and the Republic of The Gambia was born. The existence of Gambia as an independent nation would have been to the absolute surprise of all those involved in establishing colonial rule there two-thirds of a century earlier.

Establishment of Colonial Rule

The year 1893 is not when Great Britain began to administer a Gambia colony. Since the foundation of Bathurst in 1816 it had done so, and over time a handful of land outside of Bathurst was added to the colony—the area between Bathurst and Cape St. Mary's, Niumi's Ceded Mile, McCarthy Island 190 miles upriver, and other bits and pieces. This amalgam constituted the Gambia Colony that for most of the nineteenth century was administered from Britain's more important possession to the south, Sierra Leone. But 1893, four years after its agreement with France, is when Britain added to the tiny colony and accepted administrative responsibility for lands on either side of the river for 220 miles inland. All of this territory was not equal in British eyes, however. Bathurst and Kombo-St. Mary's, some thirty square miles where virtually all expatriate government officials and traders resided, remained *colony*; all the rest, over 4,000 square miles, populated almost entirely by Africans, was *protectorate*—to be governed separately, brought along more slowly (as was considered necessary given its less advanced state), and generally treated as a weak stepsister to the area around Bathurst. Niumi, though in sight from the capital across the river, was part of the protectorate.[9]

Any notion that British authorities were feeling their way blindly through the 1890s in search of policy for governing some of their recently acquired African territories is wrong.[10] The British were old hands at administering foreign possessions; they had perfected the practice of ruling through indigenous political systems in India—"indirect rule," they called it—and never doubted its necessity in Africa. In fact, the British Colonial Office had a number of strict policies that its officials on the ground knew well. The most important—literally the bottom line—was that the colony's budget must balance. British taxpayers had no desire to be paying to administer—let alone to develop—some far-flung corner of the empire, so revenues taken in by the colonial government had to equal or exceed expenditures. Since revenues were normally thin, colonial administration had to be done on the cheap, and development would be a luxury beyond the reach of many colonies in most years and for a long time. This alone dictated indirect rule: fewer British officials meant fewer European-size paychecks. The policy worked where state structures had existed, and Niumi was one such place.

Gambia had an advantage over a number of other African colonies in that already it had a way of generating revenue. Many adult Gambians were involved in growing peanuts for export, for which they received the equivalent of cash. With their cash they were eager to buy imported goods. From Bathurst's beginning, the government levied duties on imports, and since 1866, it had been charging an export tax on peanuts. The government, trading firms, and private traders passed all of these taxes along to the producer and consumer, so Gambian peanut growers received considerably less for their peanuts than they sold for in Europe or America and paid more for their cloth or sugar or rice or matches than sellers got for the same items in England, Cuba, India, or Burma.

Such ways and means of raising revenue were part of established policy, and that was good for the new colonial administration. Immediately upon commencing formal control of colony and protectorate in 1893, the government enhanced its intake with two ordinances, one establishing licensing fees for traders (thereby ending the practice of African rulers or village heads charging traders fees to operate in their territory) and the other placing a tax on strange farmers (rendering to the government fees that the farmers previously paid to heads of villages in which they resided). Then in 1895 the government enacted the Protectorate Yard Tax Ordinance, the linchpin of its economic policy. Simply put, it required the head of each compound or "yard," the extended-family divisions of villages, to pay a tax, initially one shilling for every dwelling in the yard. The tax was not onerous, possibly less so than traditional payments people had to render when a *mansa* headed the state, but the method of paying and obtaining payment were different and difficult. Niumi's *mansa* had collected in kind—a portion of whatever families produced, usually grain, sometimes livestock, metal weapons or tools from blacksmiths, and so forth. But the new rulers wanted specie—cash—rather than produce or the cloth that served as a currency, and that would require changes. Ozanne informed Sonko, who passed along the word to village heads, that the way to obtain the cash for the Yard Tax was to grow peanuts and sell them to French traders during the next trade season. So common farmers and their families and retainers, students of Muslim clerics, visiting strange farmers, and slaves of the more prominent families grew peanuts, some of which, at least, found their way to French buyers who paid in the five-franc pieces that Gambians called "dollars." Before long, English buyers started paying in cash, too, using the same French currency, mostly, and little by little money began circulating. Ozanne was happy to report only minimal difficulties in collecting the Yard Tax the first year it was due.[11] All of this had the effect the British wanted: getting more Gambians to produce peanuts for the world market so they could consume imported goods. Ozanne wrote in 1899: "Since the introduction of direct taxation, the area of cultivation under groundnuts increases considerably every year, whilst that under corn, cotton and indigo is decreasing proportionately, as the natives now even more than in the past prefer to grow groundnuts for which they can get cash to pay the taxes and then as has been the practise buy other things."[12]

Simply establishing an apparatus to collect this tax was not easy, and that was but one of a number of difficult tasks that faced the colony's first administrators. Gambia's elongated shape made it an administrator's nightmare, and since the British were perpetually concerned about costs, they necessarily were thin on the ground. A governor (with an initial budget totaling less than £25,000), two traveling commissioners (Ozanne for the river's north bank and F.C. Sitwell for the south bank), and one battalion of the West India Regiment made up the advanced guard of British authority. Ozanne's initial encounters with men and women in Niumi were sometimes awkward but hardly hostile. A later administrator recalled: "The natives did not appear to resent the presence of the Commissioners in the country but looked upon them apparently with amusement, a frequent remark on their part being, 'Whatever are those monkeys walking the country for?'"[13]

Once the monkeys took away village heads' traditional revenues and then imposed a Yard Tax, some of the amusement turned to resistance. Maranta Sonko joined ten other chiefs in 1897 in informing the government that "they were all too poor to bear taxation," and over the next two years family heads in Niumi balked at paying. Early budget figures belie commissioners' pronouncements that they were collecting tax without difficulty, but most forms of passive resistance disappeared early in the new century when the government showed what backed up its authority.

The incident that prompted the new government's first show of force was a tragic event in 1900 in a village along the river's south bank. Commissioner Sitwell and seven members of his entourage were ambushed and killed while investigating a land dispute between neighboring villages. In response, a large and well-armed expeditionary force—with units of the King's African Rifles brought in from British East Africa to join companies of the West India Regiment from Sierra Leone for the occasion—marched on the villages in January 1901 and either executed or captured and deported as many of the perpetrators as it could turn up. The force then marched up and down the rest of the protectorate. In a village just a few miles from Niumi, where a village head had talked threateningly to Ozanne, the force marched in with weapons ashoulder, collared village leaders and made them beg forgiveness, levied a fine that required residents to give up their cattle, rounded up all firearms (mostly old flintlocks), and left with a warning devoid of all subtlety about future relations. Word of the incident got around fast. Ozanne noted: "The presence of so large a body of men has had a most wholesome effect, the Protectorate resuming its normal peaceful condition in a very short time."[14]

Common people in Niumi encountered the new government in a variety of other ways. Many answered a summons by a village head and found themselves escorting the commissioner on treks, carrying what seemed an inordinate amount of goods for one man, or clearing roads. Roads, indeed, proved an obsession with commissioners, and this may have been rightly so in their eyes, for until villages were reachable by government authorities, they could hardly be expected to contribute to the colonial economy or the government that economy supported. Another factor was that roads were readily measurable, their conditions easily monitored, and as such they became yardsticks for measuring colonial "progress." At one time or another, nearly every Niumi chief felt the hot breath of colonial authority on his neck because of a weakened causeway, a washed-out bridge, or a road rendered otherwise impassable by the rains. Chiefs had to provide labor to construct and maintain the roads. This did not sit well with the young, who ended up doing most of the work.[15]

People in Niumi might also encounter colonial rule through the new legal system the British established, but the difference from former legal constraints was neither great nor always apparent. As part of their indirect-rule theory, and out of sheer necessity, the colony's government quickly passed an ordinance recognizing customary laws and procedures that were "not repugnant to natural justice nor incompatible with any ordinance of the Colony." New courts headed by the chief administered such laws as they pertained to petty civil and criminal cases. Families arguing over land, persons seeking damages from an offending party, or individuals accused of arson or theft were likely to wind up before respected elders of the "Native Court," much as would have happened before.[16]

Social change was subtler. H. Lloyd Pryce, the commissioner who replaced Ozanne, reported in 1906 on how society in Niumi and neighboring Baddibu was changing: "The family system among the Mandingos is still very strong, but there are signs of its eventually breaking down. The young men are moving about more, going from place to place instead of hardly ever leaving their own towns

---

Perspective 12   **Forced Labor**

Though less up-front about it than the French, British colonial authorities forced their African subjects to work for them. A 1905 ordinance made Gambian chiefs and village heads responsible for maintaining roads, bridges, wells, and boundary markers, and for picking up rubbish and otherwise looking after the public good. There even was a competition with awards given to the chiefs whose districts had the best roads, and woe be to the chief in whose district a bridge washed out or a pile of trash caught a commissioner's attention. British reports fail to note how the chiefs got the work done: they tapped the young men's age groups that traditionally performed services for the good of the community, the elderly, or the infirm. When these groups did such work in the past, they received something in return: payment toward one of their number accumulating bridewealth for marriage, for instance, or the slaughter of a cow for a feast. With the new regime no such payment was involved. British officials in the early years of their rule traveled without automobiles and needed their gear toted. North Bank Commissioner Dr. Emilius Hopkinson entered in his diary in 1923: "Sent the loads with a change of carriers to Jurunku and went myself in a big canoe with ten paddlers to go by water to the same place." The porters and paddlers were local "recruits." Five years later, when the West African Frontier Force needed "60–70 carriers per day" for a two-week exercise in Niumi, commissioners, chiefs, and village heads got young men to do the work. Residents of Niumi disliked what they referred to as "carrying heavy loads" as much as any other aspect of colonial rule. Although the position of "badge messenger," the lowest level of colonial authority with duties ranging from carrying messages to arresting petty thieves, carried with it no salary, there was never an absence of volunteers for the position because it brought "exemption from porterage." Long after colonial rule was over, Niumi resident Lamin Sowe, reflecting on British rule, said: "They came to the village and just rounded us up and made us go off and clear the road or carry loads on our heads." When asked if he ever was paid for such work, Sowe let out a mighty, snorting laugh.

Monthly Diary, North Bank Province, 1913, CO 87/194. Lamin Sowe, Interview in Berending, Lower Niumi District, The Gambia, March 16, 1996.

---

and villages as formerly. They visit Bathurst and ports in French territory and get wider ideas thus becoming inclined to resist parental authority, and to forego that blind obedience the young rendered to the aged for years in the Gambia."[17]

Still, the change that some in Niumi feared most was the end of slavery. Niumi's population might have known nothing about the Berlin Conference and the European pledge, as partial justification for imposing authority on Africans, to stamp out slavery and the slave trade, but they had no doubt about British intentions in that regard. For the most influential element in Niumi, this was serious. Slavery, or conditions of dependency that approximated slavery, were important to Niumi's economy and society. Ozanne noted that virtually every lineage head had one or more slaves who had to work for the lineage between sunup and mid-afternoon, five days a week. The remainder of the time was theirs to grow their own crops. Ozanne found some living with their masters "more as a friend than as a slave," but such was rarely the case for women, who simply worked hard. Seldom did masters free slaves and their chances of running away were almost nil. Niumi's Muslim clerical families held large numbers of slaves who worked the ground as their masters went about "Muslim business," and some of the Muslim teachers kept students in a position of dependency that was close to slavery. Slaves were so important to production in Niumi that, according to Ozanne, "proclaiming freedom would paralyze all trade and cultivation." He predicted that slavery would not end without a struggle because, as one slave owner admitted, "they are our hands and feet."[18]

As it turned out, the master's fears were unfounded, at least for the short run. Not wanting to render the already difficult situation chaotic (and, of course, fearing the blow that paralysis of trade and cultivation would level on the colonial Treasury), Gambia Administrator R.B. Llewelyn, while outlawing slave *trading* in 1894, allowed slavery to continue on condition that masters not mistreat their slaves and that the slaves be freed on the master's death.[19] Slavery in Niumi thus died a slow death, and the effects such change would bring to society were gradual. By the end of the second decade of the twentieth century, there were no longer many individuals who, in any legal sense, were bound to others in conditions of servitude. Memories of slavery, and of who were slaves in previous generations, lingered much longer.

One important change that occurred in relation to the end of slavery was in how people accumulated wealth. For hundreds of years the ruling families and other prominent lineages of farmers, clerics, artisans, and traders invested a portion of their wealth in horses or slaves. But by the last years of the 1890s, conditions had so changed that it was no longer necessary for ruling lineages to buy horses and it was not possible to buy slaves. "Now there are no slaves and they keep no more 'war boys,'" wrote Ozanne in 1896, "so they don't need horses." In five years, the price of "native ponies" dropped by 75 percent. Men who had wealth began investing it in cattle, and to a lesser extent sheep and goats, the price of which rose accordingly. Moreover, because Mandinka were farmers, those who owned cattle welcomed into the region Fulbe pastoralists, who tended the herds for a portion of the produce. As the herds grew, more milk and milk products entered people's diets, and the manure from cows tethered in fallow fields improved fertility and reduced the necessity of moving villages to find fertile farmlands. By 1907, there were "practically no horses" in Lower Niumi District and "very few horses" in Upper Niumi—a telling commentary on the end of a way of life. Colonial agents

Perspective 13   **Sexism: A Prejudice Across Cultures**

Niumi's colonial governors, mostly upper class Englishmen, had almost nothing in common with Africans in the Gambia protectorate and little occasion to interact with them. When they did, there were few bases of common understanding. Once in a while, though, something turned up. On one occasion this involved their outlook on women.

During their service in Gambia, governors were expected to make tours of the protectorate, partly to oversee the commissioners' work, but also to keep in touch with "the natives," to learn what was going on in the portion of the territory that supported the colony, to look at crops, listen to complaints, make speeches, and show authority. George C. Denton, Gambia's governor from 1901 to 1911, made a number of "tours of the provinces," and toward the end he became more familiar, and more relaxed, with the men he encountered.

In April 1910, on a tour of Upper Niumi, he met in Sika with the chief and headmen of eighteen villages. Seated in a circle, the African men listened to the governor's pronouncements and then had an opportunity to ask questions. At the end of the session, one of the chief's questions elicited cross-cultural male bonding. Denton's report reads: "Again the Head Chief prompted by some old Kebas [respected elders] asked me if I would give them a Prison in which to shut up their wives who were very 'puzzling.' I told him that it was not only in Niumi that the ladies were 'puzzling'; it was the same all the world over and was one of their many charms, and I certainly could not give him a prison in which to shut them up for such a reason. After a little thought and consideration, they grasped the point of what I had said and went off into fits of laughter, a thing they very rarely do at a meeting."

Denton to Secretary of State, Bathurst, May 1, 1910, CO 87/183.

believed all of this an improvement, and in some ways it was. But the fact that wealth tied up in cattle could be wiped out by disease, and that the great coming together of people and animals of the world was introducing new diseases to mammals in West Africa, meant that regularly, through the first half of the twentieth century, lineages would see a good portion of their wealth disappear with the onset of a "cow killing." As with most elements of change, for the people going through it, this was a mixed bag.[20]

The World of Peanuts

For every year of the last century, the typical resident of Niumi, male or female, old or young, directly and indirectly, teetered along a delicate annual life-balance, set in course each June by a decision about how much land to plant in peanuts and how

Photo 7   **A peanut farmer uses a short-handled hoe to clear and prepare a field in Lower Niumi.**

much to plant in food crops. After a little experience the decision is a rational one, and families are able to get by with the results of the choice—in some years. The problem that arises comes from the variables: weather and pests on the one hand, and fluctuations of market prices for peanuts and imported commodities on the other. People in Niumi are dependent on each; every year, the difference between general well-being and starvation and misery rests on these factors.

Like farmers everywhere, those in Niumi had always been at the mercy of the rains, wild animals, insects, and crop diseases. When too little or too much rain fell, when warthogs and baboons rampaged, or when swarms of locusts descended, people knew they would be in for a long hungry season. By the twentieth century, the less-obvious force of the world market became a factor as important as rainfall and crop-devouring animals. Governor Denton took note of the situation in 1903:

> With regard to the general condition of affairs in the Protectorate the Ground-nut crop is a very large one and I hope that the export will reach 40,000 Tons. Unfortunately the crops in other countries are also large and in consequence the price has fallen very low. . . . If the price in the European Markets goes up there will, perhaps, be a rush later on in the season but this is very doubtful. Several Natives have said to me, "What is the good of our growing more nuts than the merchants can buy?" It is very difficult to answer this question satisfactorily as, except in a very few instances, it is almost impossible to make them grasp that the Gambia Crop has very little effect on the European Nut Market.[21]

The European nut market was a fickle one, indeed. People in Niumi faced that reality soon after they began exporting peanuts. In 1852 Gambian farmers sold 10,908 tons of peanuts worth £153,098. The next year they increased peanut production to 11,226 tons, but the crop brought 12 percent less, £135,404. In 1854, the size of the export crop was 9,162 tons, 15 percent below the 1852 level, but was worth 30 percent less than the 1852 crop, £109,846. Later years hammered home the theme more dramatically: peanut prices bobbed up and down like a pirogue on the Atlantic, with various world events causing major waves. Rises in the 1880s related to the growing popularity of margarine and entry of Germany and the Low Countries in the trade were offset by drops caused by global economic retrenchment in the first half of the 1890s. Invention of the hydrogenization process that made it easier to convert peanut oil into fats boosted European demand and resulted in a run of good prices after 1910. In response, in 1914 Gambians exported 66,885 tons of peanuts worth £650,461. Then World War I turned the global market upside down. Buoyed by the previous year's success and blessed by steady rainfall, Gambian farmers in 1915 turned out their biggest crop yet, half again as large as in 1914. But France, where Gambians had been selling three-quarters of their peanuts, stopped buying. Germany had invaded northeastern France, where much of the oil rendering was done, the war siphoned off French industrial laborers, and oil extraction was a lower priority in the war economy. The result was that the price of peanuts dropped by £2 to £4 a ton. The Gambian crop eventually sold, but for only £400,435, two-thirds the value of 1914's much smaller crop. Something besides rain, wild animals, and insects was affecting how much Niumi's farmers were gaining from their hard work. Of course, trading people living along the Gambia River, no greenhorns in international commerce, were used to price fluctuations for slaves, hides, beeswax, gold, and the commodities that they demanded from foreign importers. But now, reasons for the rising and falling prices were less obvious. What was clear was that a bountiful peanut crop did not always bring bountiful income.[22]

The colonial government was mindful of the consequences of the planting decision and had no desire to see people in Niumi experience hunger. Yet in most years the government lent its heavy weight to the peanut side of the balance—simply because Gambians had to grow peanuts for the colony's fiscal health. Taxes (paid with cash from peanut exports), export duties (on peanuts), and import duties (on items purchased with cash from selling peanuts) paid for colonial administration and, in theory, were eventually going to support projects that would improve the lives of the colonial subjects. Thus, commissioners made sure chiefs and village heads recognized the importance of planting peanuts, even if it meant growing less food. Rice imports could make up the difference.

For this reason, it was important to colonial officials to regularize and gain control of the importing of rice and the extension of credit. Too often farmers in Niumi and the rest of the protectorate were adhering to locally proclaimed *tongs* (refusals to sell peanuts), and merchants, stung by such action and the resulting

---

Perspective 14   **Debt-Peonage on Both Sides of the Atlantic**

The lives of persons in Niumi paralleled those of several million persons of African descent—some probably related to them through common ancestors—living in the American South in the first half of the twentieth century. Dependence was key to both their circumstances. The poor, southern, rural, African American family, not long out of slavery in the latter nineteenth century, had no money and no land. To make a crop the farmer had to strike a deal with a landowner, allowing the family to live on and work a plot through the growing season and then, once the crop was harvested, to pay the landowner with a share of the crop. To feed his family, the farmer also had to negotiate with a merchant to provide food on credit, to be paid after harvest and the crop's sale. Once the landowner took half the crop and then the farmer sold his portion, he often did not have enough cash to pay off the merchant and almost never enough to provide for his family through the next growing season without having to borrow again. It was a life in perpetual debt, at the mercy of the elements and such human- and economic-related matters as the honesty of southern whites or the price of cotton on the world market.

At the same time, farmers in Niumi were in a similar situation. Along the Gambia River villagers were not dependent on someone else for land, but as farmers there began growing more peanuts to sell, in place of millet or rice to eat, they began to need to purchase rice. If harvests were poor or peanut prices low, the farmers would not have enough cash to buy sufficient rice in January to last until the fall harvest. So traders, initially, and then the colonial government, advanced them rice, and later seednuts and fertilizer, on credit, payable when they sold their peanuts. Often they were unable to obtain enough money from sale of the next year's harvest to repay what they had borrowed the previous year. As with their counterparts in the American South, debt became their way of life. Unlike American sharecroppers, whose exploitative system withered away with the mechanization of cotton production after World War II, however, the situation of continuing debt did not end in Niumi. Half a century after that war, household heads in Niumi found themselves, still six months before the harvest, already running short on food. Soon they would be heading out to "find some rice," seeking an advance so they could make it through until the next "trade season" and vain hopes of better times.

---

unpaid loans, were denying credit. So when, early in the twentieth century, such a holdup and refusal took place, the government stepped in and distributed 4,000 bags of rice on credit. By 1906, the number of government-distributed bags more than doubled, and it issued on credit 500 tons of seednuts as well. It became normal procedure for village headmen to sign, in the presence of the commissioner, to be responsible for collection of their villagers' "rice debt." From then on, government and traders would be in the same position, depending on the year, of being the peanut farmers' creditors. Even when merchants made the loans, the government pressed for repayment.

Government officials were not fond of the growing dependence and indebtedness, nor of the government role in it all, but they did not have workable ideas about how to change the situation. Governors seemed forever lamenting the situation and railing at commissioners, who lectured chiefs, who spoke to village heads, who passed the word along to farmers about ensuring a sufficient planting of food crops.[23] But most of them knew that family work units were planting close to capacity, so growing more millet would mean growing fewer peanuts, which no one seemed to want. "For over twenty years the natives have been urged to grow groundnuts for export to the exclusion of foodstuffs," wrote a feisty new director of agriculture for the Gambia in 1930, "and this policy has placed them entirely in the hands of merchants who pay them what they like for the local produce raised and charge them what they like for the necessary food."[24] Almost everyone involved recognized that it was a bad deal.

The ones who suffered from the bad deal were the farming families, who regularly experienced hunger, or lived in poverty, or both. As years of the twentieth century turned into decades, the situation worsened. Fairly good peanut prices after 1915, topped by record-high prices in 1920, prompted people in Niumi to borrow more heavily than ever from traders at the beginning of the 1921 growing season. For their part, the merchants eyed the bonanza and extended credit to all comers. Then came drought and locusts, followed by a dramatic drop in peanut prices related to a worldwide postwar depression. Niumi's farmers could not approach paying their debts that year. Commissioners had to intercede between farmers and traders and work out a schedule for debt repayment. Many would end up paying small amounts at the end of every year through the rest of the 1920s.[25]

Making these bad matters worse was a Gambian economic crisis in 1921 caused by a government decision to demonetize the French five-franc piece. Back in 1843, when the peanut trade was getting under way, British authorities recognized the silver five-franc piece as legal tender in the Gambia, fixing the exchange rate at the awkward amount of three shillings and ten pence half penny. Gambians liked the coin: it had heft, could be made into attractive jewelry, and held up well when buried for saving. It eventually made up much of the colony's circulating money supply. But World War I upset exchange rates and brought a much lower rate for the five-franc piece worldwide than the Gambia was offering. The British Treasury, its hands full with wartime matters, was slow to react to this discrepancy, so banks in Bathurst spent a long time paying 1.75 times the world rate for the piece. From all over, the coins flowed into Gambia at an alarming rate. In the face of a monetary crisis, British officials decided, in January 1922, to buy all the outstanding five-franc pieces and remove them from circulation. The effort cost over £400,000 and melting the silver coins gained back only half the sum. Although British decisions alone had caused the problem, it was the Gambian Treasury that had to pay; it did so by borrowing £178,000 from the West African Currency Board.[26]

The only way the colony had of repaying the loan was with money from peanuts. In November 1921, six weeks before the franc buy-up began, the Gambia's government more than doubled the export duty on peanuts, from 6/8d. to £1.5 per ton. Although the governor announced that additional revenues from the increased duty would be "earmarked for development works," officials knew that for the next nine years extra revenues would end up going to the Currency Board.[27] Most people in Niumi knew nothing of the monetary crisis, the loan, or the repayment. What they realized through the 1920s was that they were raising more peanuts and receiving less cash.

In fact, neither nature nor man seemed to be smiling on Niumi between the wars. Between 1923 and 1925, insufficient rains, locust attacks, and visits of a "cow killer," contagious peripneumonia (itself the result of growing contacts animals in Niumi had with cattle from a wider world), made life difficult. So did the ungoverned hand of shippers and traders. By the 1920s the buying and shipping of peanuts from West Africa to Europe involved the worst sort of collusion, monopoly, and price fixing. The largest shipping lines doing business with West Africa—England's Elder Dempster, Germany's Woermann Line, and Holland's West African Line—formed a shipping conference in which, rather than compete with one another, they divided the market among themselves and set inordinately high rates. Merchants in West Africa subtracted the high shipping charges from the price they paid growers for their crop and added them to prices they charged for imports. Moreover, the largest trading company in British West Africa, the African and Eastern Trading Corporation, merged in May 1929 with the second largest, the Niger Company, to form the United African Company (UAC), a firm doing eight times more business than its nearest competitor. The UAC undercut independent buyers and sellers and drove them out of business; then, once enough competition was eliminated, it raised prices on the goods it imported and lowered prices it paid for exports.[28] During World War II a disinterested commentator included among Gambia's shortcomings, "A commercial life . . . dominated by one firm, the U.A.C.; a firm which . . . has . . . no obligations to the Colony bar the payment of a lowish rate of Income Tax [and shows a] high-handed disregard . . . for the interests of the natives. . . . In theory there is competition in the Gambia, but in practice I always felt that the U.A.C. could make on its retail sales of imported goods, pretty-well what profit it wished."[29]

In spite of the ill effects of monopoly and collusion, it appeared that Gambian economic skies might be brightening by the end of the 1920s, when personal and government debts were repaid. The onset of the Great Depression proved otherwise. World commodity prices fell in 1930, rallied slightly in the middle of the decade, and then fell again. The price for peanuts dropped so low in 1930 that the governor advised Niumi's farmers to eat their peanuts rather than sell them. Gambia's government quickly scaled down spending, putting to rest plans for temporary increases for education, among other things, and raised existing import duties and levied new ones, meaning Niumi's population had to pay more for what they purchased.

Rapidly developed austerity programs meant that the government stopped advancing seednuts and food. Then, as peanut prices remained low, Great Britain felt it necessary to take action to support British industry. With unemployment in England at unprecedented high levels, the Colonial Office in 1932 instituted "Imperial Preferences" throughout the empire, a program that enabled colonial governments to place tariffs on non-British imports, to the advantage of more expensive goods made in England, thus raising prices again in Gambia.[30]

What hurt people in Niumi most was a 1934 Importation of Textiles (Quotas) Bill, which limited the amount of non-British textiles the colony could import. Recent flooding of the world textile market by manufacturers in Japan, where labor was cheap and currency recently devalued, prompted the action. In rationalizing the action, Gambia's governor, H.R. Palmer, showed that he recognized the disastrous effects the resulting rising cloth prices would have:

> Increased protection is . . . necessary today to enable [Britain] to meet the debts which she incurred in preserving the liberties of the world . . . . We aim at a return to the happy condition of former days, but until exchanges have been stabilized, until the barriers which other nations have erected can be lowered by negotiation, until prosperity and rising prices return to an impoverished world, until trade revives, some measures must be taken to preserve for the Empire the markets which her enterprise has created and defended. If those measures involve some hardship to Africans, as indeed they do, that hardship is nothing compared with the burdens borne by British citizens in the British Isles.[31]

If they remained unaware of the fact before, the depression years of the 1930s showed Niumi's farmers once again that the size of the local peanut crop did not necessarily relate to the amount of cash in their pockets after harvest or the amount of food they would have through the hungry season. It convinced them, too, how much they were at the mercy of unseen forces, visualized in the figure of the local trader. "The beginning of the wet season is already bringing the customary purchase of foodstuffs on credit at excessive rates of interest and the pledging of next year's groundnut crop,"[32] reads a 1937 North Bank Province quarterly report. The previous year's report was more specific: "There seems to be flourishing a credit trade in rice which is sold at enormous rates of interest against the security of the coming groundnut crop: the usual profit is 100% and this is so generally recognized that even constant warning that such a rate of interest would be unenforceable in a Court of law, if made the subject of a civil action, will not, it is feared, produce the proper number of refusals to meet the creditors' demands."[33]

Economic prospects would brighten for many during the years of World War II, but the basic situation of dependence on a world market for peanut prices and imported goods would not go away in the waning years of colonial rule. Notes from Niumi in the 1950s read, "short on food during the rains . . . 821 bags of rice issued on credit . . . traders are confident enough to give out a considerable amount of goods on credit during the growing season."[34] By then, it was an old story.

Development

Deepening dependence on the fickle world market was a downside of colonial rule, but there was supposed to be a corresponding upside: development. When European colonial powers took over African colonies in the last decades of the nineteenth century, development was not high on their agenda. They spoke loftily for the times about ending slave trading, opening Africa to commercial opportunity, and bringing the "light of civilization" to backward peoples. Perhaps this latter included something akin to development, but that was not clear. No European nation had sketched out plainly how it proposed to go about improving the lives of the residents of their colonies over the coming generations. Historian Roland Oliver writes: "The European powers had not partitioned the continent with a view to securing early gains through its rapid development. They had done so as an insurance against the future of growing protectionism, and their main concern was that the annual premiums should be kept low."[35]

One way to keep the annual premiums low was to stand firm on the policy that colonies be self-sufficient, each paying for its own administration and improvement projects with its own revenues. But this policy did not preclude development and social welfare in Great Britain's Gambia colony. Contrary to a commonly held notion that the tiny colony was forever an economic liability, Gambia in most years had revenues sufficient for reasonable levels of administration *and* development. Harry A. Gailey shows that the Gambia colony had always been self-supporting, that it was more prosperous than Sierra Leone when the two were attached administratively, and that over the years immediately following World War I it was second only to the Gold Coast in total imports and exports per capita among Britain's West African colonies.[36] So why was there not more improvement in living conditions for Gambians? The answer is different for different periods, up through the middle of the twentieth century.

Special circumstances involving Great Britain, France, and the Gambia rendered the small colony far less likely than others to be the site of efforts at improvement through the first three decades of British control, or even longer. Colonial Gambia was surrounded by French territory—it was almost literally a knife in the side of French Senegal—and it was in a larger region where French commercial interests were overwhelmingly predominant. Since 1866, the French regularly had made initiatives to work out a trade with Britain of spheres of influence, with the possibility of Britain exchanging Gambia for some French-controlled areas of the West African coast farther south where British traders were more active. Such an exchange might have taken place had not British commercial interests in the Gambia pressed Parliament to oppose it. Ideas of exchange were alive in the minds of officials in both countries into the 1890s, and the notion did not die when Britain and France demarcated the colonial boundaries for a final time in 1904. Through the first two decades of the twentieth century, the British Colonial Office was never entirely certain that over the long haul the Gambia would remain in British hands. Thus, it was reluctant to spend money on improvements for the colony or its population that might one day end up benefiting France or French subjects.[37]

Not long after British officials began to accept that Gambia was not going to be traded—a fact that never sunk in completely, but was recognized generally by the time of World War I—notions of colonial development were blowing in the wind. The 1922 publication of Lord Lugard's tract on colonial design, *The Dual Mandate in British Tropical Africa*, set protecting and advancing colonial peoples, along with developing Africa economically for the benefit of the world, as essential duties of colonial rulers. Thus, residents of Niumi might rightfully have expected steady, significant improvement in their lives, in health and education, for instance, through the 1920s and 1930s. That such improvements barely occurred was due largely to British fiscal policies as they applied to Gambia.

One conservative policy that continually pumped the brake on development had to do with the size of reserves in Gambia's Treasury. In only eleven years, between 1899 and 1940, a period that saw grand fluctuations in world prices, too much and too little rainfall, plagues of locusts and plant diseases, and spending related to world wars, did the colony's expenditures exceed its revenues. On this basis, the colonial Treasury gradually built up a sizable reserve—£107,000 by 1912 and a whopping £328,657 by 1920, the latter figure being twice as much as the colony spent that year.[38] Gambia's governors followed guidelines from the conservative Colonial Office and made sure there was plenty for budgetary emergencies. When an emergency did arrive—as in the demonetization crisis of the 1920s—the government borrowed, tightened the budget, and used current revenues. Funds held in reserve remained to accumulate. Perhaps it was a factor that they were invested in British government securities.

With such policies, government efforts to make life better for Niumi villagers remained few and of little significance. Records from the first and second decades of the twentieth century show yeomanlike work on the part of commissioners to vaccinate people against smallpox and cattle against rinderpest. But most of what the British regarded as "development works" consisted of constructing and maintaining roads, bridges, causeways, and the like that would tie Niumi's farmers more directly and efficiently to the Gambia River, which was their access to the world market. Priorities were clear from the beginning: when French colonial authorities in 1904 began charging duty on peanuts that Niumi's farmers were conveying to Bathurst via streams that ran through Senegal, Gambia's governor offered Lower Niumi's chief £100 if he would organize the digging of a long channel to give the boatmen access to the sea in Gambia territory. That same year the government spent nothing on medical care or education in Niumi.[39]

Outside of the vaccinations performed by the commissioners and an occasional visit of a medical officer on tour, people in Niumi received no formal medical treatment through the first three decades of the twentieth century (though one cannot help noticing such government expenditures as the £1,100 in 1921 for construction of new tennis courts at the Bathurst Sports Club, where European agents of mercantile firms got exercise).[40] In 1931, the untrained wife of North Bank Commissioner R.W. Macklin, with the assistance of a former Boy Scout who had a first-aid merit badge and training in first aid from the Protectorate Medical Officer, traveled with her husband throughout the province and did her best to minister to those with wounds and infections. Not until 1951 would the government open a health center for Niumi residents in Essau, and even then the center received only weekly visits of a "Health Sister," a dispenser, and two community attendants.[41]

Of course, the vaccinations were welcome and new roads and bridges beneficial—people did their dry-season traveling among villages more easily than ever—but within a generation, most adults in Niumi recognized that the most important development matter was education, the key to advancement in the new colonial world. Thus, nothing frustrated them more than their inability to get even the basics of the English language taught to children on Niumi soil. The fact was that no one in the Gambia was getting much education—it was one of the colonial government's most glaring and, in the end, telling failures. Government records show education's low priority. Minutes from the Gambia Legislative Council for November 22, 1929, read: "The Honourable L.C. Ogden said that in past years it had always been contended that the Colony could not afford both the main things which it needed, *i.e.*, Education and Agriculture. It had previously been decided that Agriculture should take the first place."[42]

The cheap way to educate colonial subjects was to allow missionaries to do it, and the colonial government was all for that. Roman Catholics, Methodists, Anglicans, and Muslims had schools in Gambia, but, aside from the latter, which instructed most students only in the Qur'an and elementary Arabic, the Christian schools served a tiny number of select people, almost all of whom resided around the capital. The colony's first governor labeled the educational situation "a lamentable condition, and injurious at once to the best interests of the people and the government," but injurious it would remain. In 1900, the government granted £416 to the Christian and Muslim schools, and twenty-five years later, when the colonial budget was nearly £275,000, it designated only £3,460 to education.[43] In 1923 Gambia's governor, Sir C.H. Armitage, opened a school intended for the sons of protectorate chiefs at Georgetown, halfway upriver. It was here that a number of influential Gambians of the post–World War II period received their primary education. Aside from a Wesleyan elementary school at Georgetown and a Catholic mission school at the far end of the colony, there was nothing more outside of Bathurst.

Boys and girls in Niumi had nowhere to turn. In the spring of 1932, St. Mary's Catholic Church opened a mission station and school in Essau, but it lasted barely a year.[44] It would be another seventeen years, in October 1950, before the government finally would see fit to open a school, again in Essau, and it would not be educating students effectively for another decade. A 1953 report of the school called it "the worst in the Protectorate," and included such damning remarks as "girls used as teachers' servants . . . children should not be allowed to use razor blades for handwork . . . discipline is appalling . . . useless teachers . . . all writing is poor."

A 1961 review of the school that by then had 163 pupils, 50 of them girls, found improvement.[45]

Six miles up the road lay Berending, with Bunyadu a mile away, and both of these former royal villages smarted over the privileges Essau received because its Sonko family provided Lower Niumi's chiefs. So when Essau got a school, Berending's elders took action. With fifty Berending children needing schooling, they decided in 1955 to build their own school, and they did so and arranged for a teacher before requesting permission from Gambia's board of education. Government had little choice but to sanction the impressive initiative, especially since the Berending school was going to pay its own way, and in March 1956 the school opened with thirty-eight students. They met in a low, mud-brick building with a thatched roof; the main classroom was forty feet long and fourteen feet wide; half a dozen students sat around desks designed for two that villagers had constructed out of old packing cases; and the latrine consisted of three boreholes. The initial students, all in one grade, got instruction in the Qur'an as well as in arithmetic, English, and Mandinka. The quality was low. "The teacher talks far too loudly and children must not be struck," reads a 1957 inspection report; "the standard of writing is appalling and the books are disgracefully untidy." In 1959 the school met in a UAC store while new buildings were constructed. After that, with a new teacher and advanced grades, the situation improved.[46]

Still, there was no secondary school in Niumi. Those who qualified for the government secondary school in Bathurst and who could afford the fees could seldom come up with the additional cost of room and board in the capital. Not until 1995 would a new government see fit to construct a secondary school in Essau, a handsome gray block building, where Niumi's youth could continue their education on their own soil.

As it was, education was a barometer for colonial development in Gambia. War, demonetization, depression, and another war—all made colonial officials jumpy about spending money that would not lead in a short time to enhancing revenues. When empirewide initiatives for development came along, as they did in 1929 and 1940, Gambia gained little, and the largest postwar development efforts were pointed toward making Bathurst a cleaner and healthier place to live and grand economic initiatives. Between 1948 and 1952, Britain lost over £1 million on a failed scheme to raise chickens outside Bathurst and produce eggs for the English market—this before Niumi had an elementary school.[47]

A Quiet Broadening and Deepening of Islam

For West Africa as a whole, the colonial period was the time of Islam's greatest expansion. The number of West African Muslims doubled in the first half-century of colonial rule, gaining the religion more adherents in those fifty years than in the previous thousand.[48] Such was not the case in Niumi, however. By the time of the colonial takeover, most Niumi residents accepted Islam and considered themselves Muslims. The most important period for the religion's spread in the state had been the middle of the nineteenth century, when the wave of Islamic reform, abetted by the social and economic change that accompanied peanut production, swept through, slowed only by British interference. But by the century's end British officials were less antagonistic toward Islam; in fact, they recognized ways it could benefit colonial government and their subjects in the protectorate, and they established policies that had the effect of encouraging the religion. Thus, the colonial period stands more as a time of consolidating gains and increasing the depth of knowledge of Islam in Niumi.

If Gambian administrator d'Arcy in the 1860s looked upon Niumi's Muslims as "crafty, ambitious, and sensual," his counterparts at the end of the century were much more favorably disposed toward the devout, austere men in long robes who conducted prayers in Niumi's villages. The reason for the change of attitude in the late nineteenth century was the widespread acceptance in Western intellectual circles of ideas about human progress set down initially by Auguste Comte. In league with some of the popular social Darwinists of later years, Comte argued that monotheism was the highest stage of religious development, far above the "fetishism" of traditional Africans and others. "Muslim propaganda is a step towards civilisation in West Africa," reads a 1910 French account that summarized the opinion of European colonial authorities generally, "and it is universally recognised that the Muslim peoples of these regions are superior to those who had remained fetishist, in social organisation, intellectual culture, commerce, industry, well being, style of life, and education."[49] Practical considerations lent weight to colonial governments' protection and encouragement of Islam. Throughout the Gambia protectorate, where the British had to establish and enforce the law despite being painfully understaffed, the existence of Maliki law and a body of Muslim legalists who studied and knew the law made administration easier. That Niumi's chiefs enforced Islamic law lent stature to the religion in general and to the learned men who knew the law in particular.

Continuing to be instrumental in popular acceptance of Islam in Niumi were old and new religious brotherhoods that had unique prayer rituals and emphasized different interpretations of Allah's will. The most important of these continued to be the Tijaniyya, which MaBa had championed: most of Niumi's learned Muslims and most of its Qur'anic schools had identified with the Tijaniyya since the nineteenth century. Moreover, not far north of Niumi was the home ground of Ibrahim Niass (1900–1975), who started a reformed branch of the Tijaniyya that gained broad acceptance. The Niass family was a lineage of Tijaniyya scholars respected among Niumi's population at the beginning of the twentieth century. In the late 1920s, Ibrahim broke from the family and established his own center of Tijaniyya practice near Kaolack, Senegal, thirty miles north of Gambian Niumi. In his reformed doctrine, he emphasized spirituality and mysticism, and wisely eschewed militant activities, instead focusing on personal purity—jihad of the heart. Niass named himself "Saviour of the Age," and following a successful pilgrimage to Mecca in

Photo 8   **The mosque in Medina Bafuloto (Kerr Cherno), Upper Niumi.**

1937, perhaps with some sense of ordination by the caliph of the Tijaniyya in Fez, Morocco, he began sending representatives across West Africa to gain followers. Ardent Muslims in Niumi were among those who made the pilgrimage to Niass's mosque near Kaolack, where he could personally initiate them into the reformed brotherhood. Niass popularized Islam through use of such modern devices as the radio to spread Qur'anic knowledge and encouragement of active participation by women and children. The existence of other, altogether new brotherhoods—the Muridiyya, for example, which glorified hard work as a means of gaining spirituality—in the hotbed of Islamic reform in nearby Senegal added to interest in the faith through the colonial years.[50]

A change that occurred in the first half of the twentieth century that helped Muslim teachers and healers do their work and gain in popularity was the growing ease of travel. No one ever moved too far from their homes in the rainy season, needing to remain close to crops and caring less to venture down puddled tracks amid the malaria-carrying mosquitoes that abounded. But in the dry season, between November and April, persons with things to sell—regular merchants, women with rice or vegetables, or Muslim diviners—looked to move from village to village in search of customers. Such travel had always been slow and dangerous: slow because it normally was on foot, perhaps leading a donkey or with human carriers, and dangerous if warfare was going on, brigands were lurking, or predatory animals stalked the wooded shoulders of paths. Colonial rule helped speed travel and make it safe. During the 1920s, motor trucks appeared in Niumi, first to carry peanuts to market and then to haul people and goods around. Through the 1930s, Niumi's roads were widened to support the motor traffic. Moreover, the *pax colonia* was a reality. The ending of warfare and the seasonal raiding and marauding of precolonial times, the rounding up and bringing to justice of bandits and thieves, the ending of toll charges in individual villages and states, and the killing of dangerous animals—all of which occurred soon after colonial authority was established— made short- and long-distance travel cheaper and safer. This helped the itinerant Muslim diviner move about and do his work, but, more importantly, it allowed persons from a broader area to travel to villages where Muslim scholars conducted schools, healed, and sold protections. By the 1930s Niumi was dotted by villages that were magnets for young men who wanted to learn to read Arabic and advance their knowledge of the Qur'an. Jinak, Aljamdu, Tubab Kolong, Medina Bafuloto, and Sika were villages that gained reputations for the learning, scholarship, and magical works that took place there in the hands of noteworthy clerics.[51]

Perhaps it was primarily Niumi's location near the leading Senegambian re- formers, from MaBa to Niass, which made it something of a regional center of Islamic learning and magic. By the mid-twentieth century, it was a place where noted Muslim lineages conducted schools; students came to reside from a broad hinterland to learn Arabic and know the Qur'an; and Muslim mystics divined, practiced healing, and made charms to bring good or ward off evil. Much of this activity is not evident in the records of colonial commissioners, who developed a modus vivendi with prominent Muslim scholars. Apparently government officials did not want to know too much about activities taking place in the major Muslim towns during the colonial period. This may have been because Muslims clung to forms of dependence not far removed from slavery, compounded by the fact that Muslim teachers took in students and made them work almost as if slaves in return for their board and spiritual guidance. But just below the more accessible veneer of chiefs, traders, and farmers, a greater Muslim subculture existed in Niumi through the years of the high tide of colonial rule.

The village of Aljamdu, several miles south of the old royal villages of Berend- ing and Bunyadu, is an example of a center of Islamic scholarship and mysticism that thrived in the colonial period. Muslims settled Aljamdu late in the eighteenth century, at the request of the *mansa* residing in Berending, who wanted the best protective charms for the royal lineage and assistance for Niumi's forces at war. But as the Niumi state weakened through the middle of the nineteenth century, the marabouts of Aljamdu took the side of MaBa against their sometimes-oppressive rulers. When British intervention thwarted their efforts and propped up the ruling lineages, Aljamdu's Muslim leaders stoically accepted the failure to create an Is- lamic state and went about their business in other ways. They opened schools and gained reputations as among the best scholars, teachers, and workers of magic in the lower Gambia. Families sent sons to Aljamdu to study the Qur'an; the Muslim

Photo 9   **A Muslim trader near his stall in a weekly market in Upper Niumi.**

leaders worked the young pupils hard through the farming season to produce peanuts. Aljamdu's mystics also made protective charms, and the village became a place to visit for healing and divining. Students from outside Niumi, who were especially gifted and promising young Muslims, stayed in Aljamdu or moved there, built families, and eventually participated in the business of schooling and mysticism that was the village's trademark. All was not harmonious among the various Muslim lineages that lived in Aljamdu; they sometimes competed for primacy in the workings of the schools and mystic practices. Disputes among competitors occasionally reached a level that brought attention: a commissioner's Quarterly Report of September 1939 notes: "Once again Upper Niumi District's numerous Mohammadan teachers have had a dispute over the appointment of an *Almami* [religious leader] at Aljamdu and unseemly brawling took place on two occasions in the mosque."[52] Such struggles suggest the importance of positions of authority among Aljamdu's Muslims and lead one to assume that with Islamic leadership went relative wealth and prestige.

One aspect of the broadening and deepening of Islam in Niumi was not entirely positive: the more devout persons became in their belief, the more conservative and accepting of their fate they tended to be. By the mid-twentieth century, the intense desire for change and the militant approach to bringing about such change that was evident in the likes of nineteenth-century reformers were vague memories from the past. Niumi's widely respected Islamic scholars and teachers of the colonial era and after are quiet, austere, judicious in speech and action, and not inclined toward politics. These were qualities the colonial government appreciated—it all fit with the more positive attitude toward Islam as being appropriate for residents of the Gambia Protectorate.

Naturally, the growing respect of the most scholarly of Muslim clerics and most devout of believers meant that their ways and attitudes spread among increasing numbers of Niumi's population. One who could not attain prestige through acquisition of wealth might be able to do so through strength of beliefs and depth of devotion to Allah. The difficulty of this position is that when one becomes less able to recognize the human hand in one's misfortune, one becomes less inclined to take action to improve life on earth. This seems to be a problem in contemporary Niumi, where hardships relating to insufficient food, poor medical care, poor education, and lack of government concern for people's welfare are written off to "Allah's will." It is life after death that will be more rewarding.

Niumi in a World at War

As in most places around the world, the periods of the twentieth century when villagers in Niumi experienced the most sweeping and rapid changes were those when the world was at war. For about a decade following 1914, and for the same time or longer after 1939, people throughout Europe's African colonies came closer than ever before to realizing the extent to which they were involved in a world stretching far beyond their villages, their administrative districts, their colonies, or their regions of the continent. New experience opened wider the eyes of Niumi residents.

World War I

Official word of the outbreak of World War I came to Niumi at a district meeting in November 1914. In the shorthand of his diary, Commissioner Pryce notes: "Explained position of affairs in Europe, all much interested, and proclaimed their loyalty. Warned all to be careful over their food, no waste to be allowed anywhere." But people in Niumi did not need Pryce to let them know something was afoot overseas. France had begun drafting Senegalese men soon after the war's outbreak, and large numbers of them fled south into British-ruled Niumi to avoid call-up. They brought word of the European war from the French perspective. Niumi's farmers put the Senegalese to work pulling peanuts.[53]

War-related problems came to Niumi in a rush. By 1914 persons all around the protectorate were dependent on imported rice. In theory they bought rice only when one or another of their food crops failed, but in practice the crops failed frequently enough, or farmers (with considerable encouragement from traders and seemingly quieter nods from colonial officials) simply opted to plant more peanuts for export and less foodstuffs to eat, so that imported rice had become a staple of their diets and their preferred grain. Rice imports came to Gambia mainly in British ships, but British exporters got much of their rice from Germans in Hamburg, who had cornered a good portion of the East Asian market. German firms had been quietly making a concerted effort to capture more of the West African trade, acquiring some goods from abroad and manufacturing for export what one Gambian official called "cheap, attractive articles of fair quality." By 1914 Gambia was getting over half its rice from Germany, along with some of the other commodities people wanted: cotton goods, spirits, hardware, beads, shoes, hats, and perfume. With the outbreak of war, Germany ceased being a source for Gambian imports, and soon German U-boats were doing their best to sink merchant ships leaving British and French ports for any destination. British firms were able to find rice from other sources, but not always enough, and prices for most imported commodities soared because of the war. "The behavior of the natives during a very trying and anxious time," writes Pryce in the middle of 1915, "has been all that could be desired. The low prices paid for the nuts after many excellent seasons, combined with the difficulty at times of obtaining essentials (these frequently at higher prices) from the traders, caused naturally a certain amount of discontent, but nowhere was there the least sign of disloyalty. . . . In all the Mohammedan mosques throughout the Province, prayers are offered daily for the success of the British forces, and for a speedy and successful termination of the War."[54]

There may have been no outward sign of disloyalty and daily prayers may have sounded for the Allied powers, but Niumi's young men lacked enthusiasm to participate in the largely European affair. As the war turned to stalemate and consumed manpower and resources, Great Britain joined France and Germany in deciding to use colonial forces to assist in the war effort. For the Gambia, this meant recruiting for the Gambia Company of the West African Frontier Force (WAFF). The WAFF was an organization of troops from each of Great Britain's West African colonies; Gambia got its own company in 1902. Fitted out in khaki shorts and shirt, red vest, fez, and chocolate brown tunic, the unit was to drill and stand ready to serve imperial needs.[55] Beefed up with fresh recruits, the Gambia Company trained outside of Bathurst and on April 15, 1917, shipped off to German East Africa, where it would participate in the war, largely against Africans fighting for Germany.[56] As casualties mounted, authorities in London recognized the need "to replace wastage," so called for 250 new Gambian recruits. The colonial government was able to sign up fifty in Bathurst "from the large number of labourers and drifters, mostly from the Protectorate, who are numerous toward that period of the dry season," but getting the other 200 from such districts as Niumi was not so easy. "Under European leaders the Mandingos make good and reliable soldiers," reads a retrospective military report from 1923, "but they do not enlist very readily."[57]

Asked to round up twenty-five men in a month's time, Pryce went recruiting across Niumi with a vengeance, only to be disappointed and frustrated in his failure. Meetings in the clerical villages, where people prayed noisily for British victory, turned up no eagerness for military service. "People here evidently require to be fetched," writes an angry Pryce. One reluctant Niumi man on whom Pryce was leaning to enlist told the commissioner, "Since you white men have come and taken us over we have come to look on ourselves as women. Now all of a sudden you ask us to be soldiers and we find we are supposed to be men after all." Another Gambian commissioner noted that by 1917 most Gambians just wanted the war "finished quickly before as they put it, 'the whole world is spoilt.'"[58]

Pryce recognized the difficult spot chiefs would be in if made to force people to enlist. Still, he thought the forceful approach the only way to get recruits, especially at the start of the planting season when men wanted to remain and get their crops in the ground. In the end, his "constant hammering" on Niumi's chiefs and village heads turned up twenty recruits, but they came from among the lame and the halt: many were rejected for medical reasons.[59]

On top of local problems related to the wartime restrictions on world markets and fighting the war, people in Niumi faced other issues of more pressing concern. When smallpox broke out in three riverside villages before the end of 1914, the colonial government could not get serum for vaccination. It isolated the villages and hoped for the best. Then, in the rainy season of 1917, one of the "cow killers," this one probably rinderpest, swept into Niumi from Senegal, its first appearance since the 1870s, and decimated the large herds of the wealthiest families. Pryce estimated that between 75 percent and 95 percent of the cattle in Niumi died before the year was out. Because lineages kept a good part of their wealth in cattle, the disease wiped out family fortunes. One of the many long-term results of the epidemic was its effect on agriculture, for cow manure was the only fertilizer farmers had for their food crops. Pryce notes that the people accepted the loss "with their usual equanimity."[60]

Nondomesticated animals, on the other hand, had a field day. To forestall smuggling of guns and gunpowder following the outbreak of war, the colonial government prohibited their importation and sale. Before long, hunting and animal control came to a standstill. There had not been an elephant in Gambia since 1906, but the number of lions increased, packs of hyenas grew in size, and the animals grew bolder. Through the war years, Niumi villagers had serenades of roaring and cackling through many nights, and it was common knowledge that one had to keep a lamp burning atop a grave for a full week after burial to keep hyenas from digging it up.[61]

Yet the war-related event that most devastated Niumi's population was the great influenza pandemic of 1918. In global terms World War I involved a great coming together of previously separated people. As they mingled, they spread diseases that long had been confined to more isolated regions or spread more slowly. One of these diseases was a new strain of influenza that passed among people of the world after the war's end. The result of a mutation of the H1N1 virus, which may have appeared first in the United States in the spring of 1918, the influenza spread with unheard of speed and horrible effects. Between one in five and one in three of the world's 1.8 billion people contracted the disease over a two-year period. Estimates of the death toll range from 20 million to 100 million.

The influenza arrived in Freetown, Sierra Leone, a major coaling station for British and Commonwealth vessels traveling the African coast, on August 15, 1918, when the HMS *Mantua* put into port with 200 members of its crew suffering from the disease. Laborers loading coal rapidly acquired the disease—twelve days after the *Mantua*'s arrival, 500 of 600 dockworkers were too sick to work—and spread it among the colony's population. From then on, crews of every vessel stopping at Freetown were at risk and their vessels became carriers.[62]

Gambia dodged the influenza bullet for a year, but when the SS *Prah* from Sierra Leone arrived in Bathurst with an infected passenger in August 1919, its time had come. Influenza rushed through the colonial capital, forcing the closing of mercantile offices and bringing government operations to a standstill. Within a month 322 of Bathurst's 8,000 people had died. The acting governor reported that for three weeks "funerals were passing the bungalows at a rate of fifteen a day." A posting of guards at docks and the only bridge leading out of Bathurst to enforce a quarantine did not work. The flu crossed over to Niumi within a matter of days and, according to the commissioner, "raged in the district."[63]

If there were good and bad times for people to get sick in Niumi, late summer was a bad one. Because of the shortage of food and the prevalence of malaria-carrying mosquitoes toward the end of the rains, it was an unhealthy time under any circumstances, and it was a period when all hands were needed to keep farms free of weeds and predators. The influenza nearly brought farming in Niumi to a halt, especially because, unlike other strains of the virus, it was most fatal on young adults, those normally capable of doing most of the work in the fields. "Weeding and clearing came to a complete stand-still for a considerable time in August and September," reads the district's 1919 Annual Report; "people who were not suffering themselves from the epidemic, and there were but few, having to look after and attend as best they could to those who were ill, farms were neglected and had to take their chances, the result being that all crops suffered considerably." Weeds took over, forcing owners to abandon farms. A British visitor found "whole villages of 300 to 400 families wiped out, the houses having fallen in on the unburied dead, and the jungle having crept in within two months, obliterating whole settlements." The timing of the epidemic was bad, too, because postwar prices for peanuts were high and a bumper crop would have meant relative prosperity. Across the North Bank Province, 1,600 persons died in one year from influenza.

World War II

World War II had other kinds of effects, and residents of Niumi felt the war earlier and more strongly than many others in the colony. From the moment the commissioner called in Niumi's chiefs and told them of the war's outbreak, the colonial government applied itself to controlling the people's dispositions and sentiments.

"The intricacies of European politics are, of course, beyond the comprehension of the majority of Protectorate natives," reads a North Bank Province Intelligence Report of August 31, 1939, "but steps have been and are being taken to ensure the correct direction of their sympathies."[64] Niumi's residents thus were treated to the riverside arrival of a "show boat" with catchy music and films with anti-German messages, and bards from Niumi attended a "*griot* competition" in Bathurst where, according to a London-based propaganda agent, competitors were primed "with rude things to sing about Vichy and the Germans, and the opposite about the British Empire."[65]

Niumi's location, across from Bathurst and astride the major road leading north into Senegal, was a major reason why its people felt the effects of war so strongly. The commencement of war turned the once sleepy colonial capital into a bustling entrepôt for Allied efforts. In the late 1930s the British ran residents out of their homes in one end of Bathurst, converted it into a seaplane base, and constructed storage facilities for fuel and supplies. From then on, it seemed that construction projects occurred regularly between Bathurst and the Atlantic as the region grew into an important communications and storage point for the Royal Air Force and Royal Navy, a major BOAC staging base, and after the United States entered the war, a passage point for American flyers on their way to campaigns in the Middle East and Mediterranean. The pull of laborers to the capital to construct the new facilities drew Niumi's young men. A 1941 intelligence report notes "a steady flow in the direction of Bathurst of anyone with anything to sell or with spare time after farming and hopes for a job," and as the war progressed, the movement became steadier: "How frequently the younger men in this Province go to and from Bathurst," the commissioner commented. "After returning for planting and weeding, many went to find work—and buy food. Now they are coming back to dig nuts, and shortly will be wending their way again to Bathurst."[66]

Finding work to buy food became critical for Niumi residents as Bathurst pulled in foodstuffs from the lower third of the colony to feed its workmen, foreign servicemen, and expatriate civilians. A colonywide "Dig for Victory" campaign to get men and women to grow more food crops, so they would have to import less, met with mild success. For some the Bathurst market provided a grand opportunity. A 1941 intelligence report notes: "Ready employment and good wages, as well as the market for fruit and garden produce, has to some extent offset in the people's economy the rise of all prices." Yet, for others without sufficient foresight, effects of the war could hasten starvation. Elimination of a number of markets around the world where importing firms had long obtained products for Gambian consumption compounded colonywide food and commodity shortages. Gambians had grown dependent on rice from Burma, for example. In December 1941, when Japan entered the war and effectively cut off Europe from many Asian markets, Gambia had outstanding orders for 1,400 tons of Burmese rice. As early as 1940 Niumi's chiefs forbade removal of food from their districts without permission, but the decree was largely unenforceable because of the high prices paid in Bathurst.

The colonial government had to find ways to provision the capital and importing food from Niumi was one of the easiest. To compensate for the drain on Niumi's food, the government brought in and sold cracked wheat from the United States, but people did not take to it and there never was enough. A Provincial Bulletin of August 15, 1944, reports people buying leftover seednuts to eat and laments, "there has certainly been hunger in the bigger Mandinka towns." Rationing of foodstuffs and other items went into effect in 1942.[67]

Niumi felt the war's effects, too, because of its border with Vichy-controlled Senegal. Senegal's government regarded British Gambia as actively hostile (and vice versa), and Niumi lay astride the logical invasion route of soldiers coming south from Dakar. As early as 1940, a battalion of the WAFF crossed the river to patrol Niumi's roads and paths, and the British began mounting espionage and counterespionage activities along Niumi's border.[68] As 1941 progressed and Allied fortunes in the war looked bleak, war-related activities picked up considerably in Niumi. By June the government had erected a coastal battery on Barra Point, inside the remains of Fort Bullen, to ward off Axis planes.[69]

Recruitment for the Frontier Force reached Niumi as the gun battery was being set in place. The colonial government put together recruiting parties, accompanied by a noisy band that marched from village to village and offered rousing speeches.[70] Chiefs put the conscriptive bite on young men and Lorimer notes in evident exaggeration, "it was every where good naturedly accepted."[71] Good-naturedly or not, by April 700 men had stepped, or had been pushed, forward from the larger North Bank Province, and Lorimer reckoned that "after the farming season a further 250 recruits could be similarly obtained." Five percent of Niumi's male population had enlisted or been conscripted by the middle of 1941. Two years later, the War Office began sending West African troops to Burma, "where their porter and jungle capacity would be invaluable."[72]

Local troops were shipping out, but Niumi's border with Senegal still needed protection. The government met this need in two ways. In mid-1941 it authorized formation of two platoons, sixty men, of a "Home Guard," officially named the Gambia Local Defence Volunteers. These were men who knew the region and thus would be able to act as guides, guards, gatherers of intelligence, and, if necessary, saboteurs. If Gambia faced an assault from Senegal, they would then become guerrillas, harassing the enemy and delaying their advance. Commissioner Lorimer joined the force himself, and through two years in the middle of the war, men of the Home Guard met, drilled, and passed along what information they had of French activities across the border.[73]

In truth, the Home Guard was something of a ragtag band of quasi-soldiers. There was forever difficulty finding boots for them, let alone the puttees their dress requirements called for, and finally the government purchased locally made sandals to outfit them. It was hardly a force to stop an advancing line of trained soldiers as might come south from Senegal. So, before the end of 1941, the government decided to station permanently, in a new camp on the edge of Essau (appropriately

Perspective 15 **A Surprise Wartime Visitor**

World War II brought air traffic to Gambia, so people in Niumi probably paid scant attention to the Pan American *Dixie Clipper*, a tri-motor seaplane, that flew in low on the evening of January 14, 1943, touched down in the river, and taxied close to Bathurst. Had they known who was inside the plane, they might have taken more interest: it was U.S. president Franklin D. Roosevelt.

Roosevelt was on his way to Casablanca, Morocco, to meet with British prime minister Winston Churchill. The two Allied leaders needed to plan strategy for the war, which was lately taking a positive turn. In 1943 an American president did not simply board a plane in Washington and fly to Morocco. Roosevelt and his entourage took a train to Miami, Florida; boarded the seaplane for hops to Trinidad and Brazil; and then flew across the Atlantic to the nearest safe port, which was Bathurst. From there, after a night on an American cruiser in the river, they motored through Bathurst and out to Gambia's airstrip, where they boarded an Air Corps C-54 transport for the final leg into Casablanca.

Roosevelt never set foot in Niumi, but he saw it. The "tireless landscape watcher" (as an aide described him) flew over and boated alongside Niumi's shoreline. On the return stopover in Gambia, the president and aide Harry Hopkins toured wharf towns on a tug, Roosevelt observing while Hopkins trolled for fish. What lingered in the president's mind were images from his drives through Bathurst, which a trip official described as an "incredibly squalid, disease ridden town."

His Gambian venture was Roosevelt's first direct experience with the colonial world and he was shocked. In Casablanca he told his son Elliott, "I must tell Churchill what I found about his British Gambia . . . Dirt. Disease. Very high mortality rate . . . Life expectancy . . . Twenty-six years. Those people are treated worse than the livestock. Their cattle live longer!" Elliott remembers it being that night when he first heard his father speak about a "United Nations . . . bringing education, raising the standards of living, improving the health conditions of all the backward, depressed colonial areas of the world." It was a formative time in Roosevelt's thinking on the U.N.'s role in pushing for colonial development and independence. On the personal level, the president would not stop nagging Churchill about "that hell-hole of yours called Bathurst," which brought the prime minister to press the Colonial Office to begin cleanup and development projects.

Donald Wright, "That Hell-Hole of Yours," *American Heritage* 46 (1995): 47–58.

camouflaged to look from the air like an African village), an organized battalion of the Frontier Force. This necessitated construction of the campsite as well as a supply depot at Barra Point, the labor performed by Niumi men. Such activity brought vehicle traffic that made Niumi's roads, according to Lorimer, "well-nigh impassable." To supervise necessary road rebuilding and repairing, beyond what chiefs could accomplish, the British brought in and stationed near Berending a company of Nigeria Pioneers.[74]

Allied victories in North Africa in 1942 removed the threat from Vichy-controlled Senegal, but did not lessen the unpredictable effects of the war on Niumi. Problems related to food shortage in Bathurst would not go away. When meat grew scarce in the capital in 1941, the Gambian government allowed herdsmen from Senegal to bring their cattle down a "free lane" through Niumi to Barra Point, so the animals could be transported across for slaughter. This seemingly benign act brought hardship because the herdsmen carried smallpox and caused an epidemic in one Niumi village. Also, the foreign cattle once more brought the dreaded rinderpest and more local cattle died. Government efforts to rid Gambia of these killers of humans and animals had nearly succeeded before the war.[75]

In addition, typical wartime clashes occurred between soldiers and civilians. Through 1942 a normal amount of testiness existed: young Berending men did not like soldiers congregating near the village pool where girls and young women did laundry. There had been minor incidents and one serious one, a rape. Most men were uneasy, too, because of the colonial governor's October 1942 decree making "every British subject and British protected person . . . age 18–55, and ordinarily a resident of Gambia . . . liable to combatant service . . . either in or beyond Gambia." Even if not tabbed for combat duty, Gambians could be called to perform any work or personal service the governor deemed necessary in connection with the colony's defense.[76] The simmering pot boiled over in January 1943, when a group of soldiers decided to attend a Berending dance. A procession of drummers was advancing through the crowd and the soldiers were asked to make way. Apparently, they did not make way sufficient for "juju drummer" Demba Sonko, who shoved a battalion sergeant, swore at him loudly, and, ripping off his shirt, challenged the soldier to a fight. Before the incident was quieted, villagers had brandished machetes and soldiers had fetched rifles. Although ordered back to their base, the soldiers made loud threats to burn Berending to the ground. Sonko's harsh sentence of six months in jail and then banishment from Niumi was not enough to satisfy the soldiers, while it further angered villagers.[77]

Yet, the significance of most of this paled in relation to effects residents of Niumi felt indirectly because of the damage the war did to international trade. As the middle of the twentieth century approached, Gambians were more than ever dependent on an exchange relationship with the larger world, exporting peanuts and purchasing imported foodstuffs and manufactured goods. The war-related threat to merchant shipping and emphasis on production of war materiel over consumer goods cut international trade. People felt the effects in every Niumi village. With 5 percent of its most robust young men off fighting for the Allies, crop production was reduced and the Bathurst market pulled in locally grown fruits and vegetables, so villagers had to purchase food from somewhere else. What made this all especially frustrating was that, because of the construction work, soldiers' pay, and increased demand for the foodstuffs they were selling, Niumi villagers had far more cash in their hands than ever before. But now there was nothing to buy. Lorimer labeled 1941–1942 "the worst trade season for years," noting that "cloth is almost unobtainable and food very scarce in the towns." The absence of sugar, cigarettes, and cloth were, in Lorimer's estimation, "bad for morale." Gambia's governor expressed "great concern . . . that, at a time when financial opportunity is provided for a general raising of the standard of life for the African, the imports necessary to achieve this aim should be in such short supply."[78] Colonial officials would lament the shortage of trade goods long after the war's end.

Lorimer seemed to have a sense of the range and depth of effects the war was having on Africans in his district. Applying what he knew about Niumi's residents to all Gambians, he wrote in 1943:

> "[E]vents of the past year have provided an immense 'opening of the eyes' to European methods and 'civilisation.' The Gambian has received much enlightenment and some rude shocks. But he is an intelligent citizen with a good deal of hard common-sense and I think that the events of the period have done incomparably more good than harm. They have, especially, made him conscious of the advantages of proper education and a higher standard of nutrition and housing— all this due to contact with the Army—and this consciousness should provide the spur to the successful carrying out of the various development schemes now planned, to the lasting benefit of the people."[79]

The commissioner was at least partly right: soldiers from Niumi had their eyes opened to other ways of life; were more conscious of the benefits education, better nutrition, and better housing could provide themselves and their families; and expected rapid improvement in their lives that development would bring. What Lorimer failed to foresee was what might be the result if such improvement did not arrive with anticipated speed.

Postwar Malaise

For a while, Niumi's men fighting for the Allies overseas kept things astir back home. The North Bank Province (it was renamed a division in December 1944) provided more soldiers than any other province, and nearly all of those posted outside Gambia sent part of their paychecks home. Whenever Lorimer distributed drafts from the troops to their families, he noted a run on such cloth that existed in local shops. "Soldiers on leave and discharged heroes return to very well dressed wives," he commented wryly.[80] All was not good news coming from the overseas Gambia Battalion, however. By the rainy season of 1944, the reality of the worst that war could bring began to filter in. Lorimer refused to allow the announcer on the colony's river steamer to read publicly a two-page list of those from the province who had been killed or wounded in Burma, but on October 12 some partially disabled members of the battalion came home. Thereafter, a steady stream of men, most wounded or otherwise traumatized by the war, returned to Niumi's villages. The stories they told of fighting halfway around the world might have enchanted some, but they frightened and angered others. The largest group of survivors returned from Burma in January 1946. Of course, this did not include the 288 Gambians who died in Burma.[81]

Those coming home to Niumi after the war were different men, returning to altered circumstances. Gambia's governor received a "warning of a confidential nature" from his counterpart in the Gold Coast: Such men, the warning reads, "have had much time on their hands and have devoted it to improving their educational and technical qualifications and to discussing their future civil lives. In the opinion of their officers these men will expect on their return to find opportunities and facilities for employing with profit in civil life such skill and knowledge as they have acquired."[82]

Moreover, although they complained of their treatment in service to the British Empire, Niumi's men in the Frontier Force were paid as common soldiers and had managed to accumulate savings, most through Post Office Savings Bank accounts. Once home, they had money to spend. Many used part of what they accumulated to marry—certainly, for some, into families they never would have had the means to enter before. Others used their money to buy traders' licenses in hopes of entering into the world of buying and selling, and thus competing with foreign merchants on their soil, but they were frustrated. Since early in the war, Gambia had been having trouble obtaining cloth, the commodity villagers wanted most. Such phrases as "extremely bad news about cotton goods" pepper reports of Gambia's colonial secretary throughout the war years and beyond.[83] Then, a localized economic depression hit the lower Gambia when war activities around Bathurst fell off with the conflict's end. By early 1946, the British had shut down the military bases in Niumi and the electric lighting plant on Barra Point that provided them power. Suddenly, nights in Essau and Berending were pitch-black again. At about the same time, American and British military personnel returned home, and military and civilian operations in Bathurst's vicinity closed or were cut back dramatically. There was an exodus from the capital on an unheard-of scale. Women in Niumi, who had developed a profitable tomato-growing business during the war, suddenly lost their market. Prices for vegetables spiraled downward; the artificial, war-related economy was over; and Niumi's men and women quickly faced an economy similar to the one they had lived with in 1938—growing peanuts for export and food crops for local consumption; importing rice, kola nuts, cotton cloth, and such small items as soap, matches, and cigarettes; and not much else.[84] And things got steadily worse. By 1947 officials in and out of British government were facing the reality of a markedly different world for the United Kingdom and the British Empire than existed before the war. Great Britain had huge war debts, was facing the loss of American assistance, and, perhaps most devastating of all, no longer was making money from overseas investments. "Any inability to hold our own in world markets," warned the colonial secretary in a July 9, 1949, telegram to Gambia's governor, "must deprive us of essential supplies and our standards of life will suffer."[85] "Our," in this case, referred to British citizens. Of immediate importance was Britain's lack of dollars to pay for goods it needed to import, brought about by its lack of exports. In August 1947 the home government asked the colonies to bite the economic bullet by reducing imports—especially of petroleum products, automobiles, textiles, and appliances—and to increase colonial production of exports that could be sold for hard currency. For Gambians, that meant growing still more peanuts, but at the same time they were not to import most of the items they wanted to buy with the cash they had or would receive.[86] Naturally, the returned servicemen were angry, and so were a number of others who had accumulated money in the war economy and now wanted to consume items they never before could purchase. The educated and politically aware among them recognized that Marshall Plan dollars to rebuild war-torn Europe did not alter the larger British economic position. Such money seldom trickled down to the colonial level.

The servicemen were demoralized as they demobilized. Of the 4,000 Gambians released from duty by March 1947, 2,500 returned to homes in the protectorate several hundred of them to Niumi. Although the Gambia had an Employment of Ex-Servicemen Ordinance, it applied in reality only to those resettling around Bathurst, and without jobs the government's good intentions came to naught even there. Between December and April, veterans could gain low-level employment loading peanuts—just the kind of work few of them wanted.[87] Those with skills might find work in the civil service, but most veterans from Niumi, some missing a limb or limping from wounds, returned home and planted a peanut crop when the next season's rains fell. The war was over and the narrowness of life's options settled once again onto those in the farming villages.

Toward Independence

Because educated Africans living in and around the colonial capital dominated Gambian politics, and because almost everyone in mid-twentieth-century Niumi was poor and uneducated, its villagers did not get involved in political activity and the movement for independence from British rule until the very end of the colonial period. Over the objections of their conservative chiefs, they were dragged into political participation only after independence was in the wind.

As with many others in colonial Gambia, people in Niumi got an introduction to modern politics through the activities of one Edward Francis Small. Small was the leading edge in Gambia of a political movement that had been more active in Britain's other West African colonies for a slightly longer time.[88] He was Bathurst born in 1891, the son of tailor John W. Small and his mistress, Annie Eliza Thomas, an immigrant from Sierra Leone; his education was at home and then, on government scholarships, at Wesleyan schools in Bathurst and Freetown;

and his early work was in the civil service, as a postal clerk in Freetown and with the Public Works Department in Bathurst, and as a clerk with the Bathurst trading firm of Maurel and Prom. He left the latter post to train as a Wesleyan minister, and in 1917 the Wesleyans sent him upriver, to Ballanghar, center of a regional peanut trade, for missionary work. Once there, he seemed to pay as much attention to the economic plight of his congregation as he did to their spiritual well-being, quickly growing disillusioned with what he perceived as the exploitation of the illiterate peanut farmers by Bathurst-based traders and with the acquiescence of church leaders in the situation. In this fashion, he irritated both church and government. In February 1918 the commissioner of the province wrote to Gambia's Governor, "I do not consider that Small is a fit person to be at an out station such as Ballanghar. . . . [H]e lacks judgement, courtesy and self control, and I should be obliged if you would inform the Head of the Wesleyan Church at Bathurst that his removal from here is absolutely essential."[89] That alone would have gotten Small removed, but a fistfight with James Walker, a local representative of the Bathurst Trading Company, ostensibly over Small's ringing of church bells late at night, hastened the process.

In 1918 Small got involved with the National Congress for British West Africa (NCBWA), an organization consisting of educated Africans in Nigeria, the Gold Coast, Sierra Leone, and Gambia, who were working to gain greater influence for themselves and their educated peers in the governance of their colonies. The organization's leaders placed Small in charge of Gambia's local committee, and, as such, he was the colony's delegate to the 1920 NCBWA meeting in Accra on the Gold Coast and one the next year in London. A 1921 NCBWA mass meeting in Bathurst, attended by several hundred, got the attention of Gambia's colonial government and prompted commissioners to agree in their 1922 conference not to allow any NCBWA member to "tamper with chiefs."[90]

Small had made earlier, abortive efforts at starting a newspaper, *The Gambian Outlook and Senegambian Reporter*, but following his 1920 trip to England he recommended publication of the journal that would occupy part of his time for a number of years. The remainder of the 1920s saw him passing to and fro between Dakar, London, and Bathurst, organizing an NCBWA meeting in Bathurst in 1925–1926, seeking money for an ambitious Gambian railroad scheme, and keeping barely a step ahead of creditors. He did not endear himself to Gambian authorities when he organized a Bathurst laborers' strike in 1929, nor did he calm any fears by reprinting in *The Gambian Outlook* anti-imperialism articles by the likes of John Reed and George Padmore or by attending the European Congress of Working Peasants in Berlin. Colonial authorities speculated on Small's membership in the Communist party.

Back in Gambia in June 1930, Small focused his energies on a cooperative marketing scheme, the Gambia Farmers' Union, which had been on his mind since his days in Ballanghar. His new focus was prompted by a continuing awareness that Gambian peanut growers received only a fraction of the price European firms paid for the peanuts and by the depression-related 40 percent fall in peanut prices between December 1929 and February 1930.[91] Small wanted to have Gambia's peanut growers market their own peanuts and thereby cut out the expatriate middlemen and shipping lines that overcharged. By so doing, he believed, the Union could "give Gambian farmers the full benefit of European nut prices, and by bettering the farmers financially to stimulate them to greater output, which should tend to benefit the whole country."[92] A tireless worker, Small wrote to a long list of bankers, shippers, and buyers to arrange credit and transportation of the Union's guaranteed output of peanuts.

Later in 1930, two agents of Small's Gambia Farmers' Union crossed the river from Bathurst and went among Niumi's villages, asking farmers to join the union at the cost of a shilling, and sought out the chiefs of Upper and Lower Niumi to see if they would call a district meeting so he could inform farmers about the union. Under the influence of buyers and shippers in Bathurst, who saw Small as a "self-appointed champion of non-existing grievances felt by an imaginary body of citizens,"[93] the colonial government had forewarned each chief, so neither joined nor called a meeting. Only the headman of Berending, a village with a reputation for doing things its own way, paid his shilling and signed up.[94] Two years later, Small was still at it, informing the North Bank commissioner of his intention to travel about Niumi "to organize delivery of a cargo of nuts by the Gambia Farmer's Co-operative Marketing Board, for which credit of £10,000 has been opened in the Bank of British West Africa in Bathurst."[95] The commissioner did all he could to prevent Small and his message from reaching Niumi's farmers.

None of these schemes benefited anyone in Niumi in the short run, but they eventually played a role in improving peanut-buying practices and establishing farmers' cooperatives. Small himself was a harbinger of the more active and better organized Gambia politicians in the post–World War II era. Nationalist movements in the Gold Coast and Nigeria moved Great Britain after 1945 to grant those colonies more liberal constitutions as steps toward becoming independent, and this, in turn, brought new constitutions and political parties to the less politically developed colonies of Sierra Leone and Gambia. Gambia's 1947 constitution allowed for taxpayers living around Bathurst to elect a representative to the colony's legislative council, a seat Small won with the organizational help of his Bathurst Trade Union. In 1951, when the number of elected representatives grew to three, the first Gambian political party appeared, the Gambia Democratic Party, and the three leaders of the party won the seats.

Throughout the 1950s, as more parties formed, Gambian politics tended to be personalist in nature and to reflect the interests of Africans living in and near the capital. Trade unions and a militant youth movement, the Gambia's Young People's Association, were the best-organized groups and thus the centers of political activity.[96] Of course, this meant that all those residing in such protectorate areas as Niumi—all together amounting to nearly 85 percent of Gambia's population—were ignored. Thus, when the protectorate-born, Wesleyan-educated, Glasgow-trained veterinary doctor David Jawara formed the Protectorate People's Party (PPP) in 1959 for the 1960 elections and made one of the party's major themes overcoming the long neglect of the protectorate in favor of the colony, he garnered nearly 40 percent of Niumi's vote. Two years later, when Great Britain authorized full internal self-government with a constitution that allowed the protectorate twenty-five of thirty-six seats in the House of Representatives, 81 percent of Niumi's votes went to the PPP. Residents of Niumi believed they had a government in power that would champion their interests; they looked ahead to independence three years later with optimism.[97]

The optimism was unwarranted, partly, at least, because political independence would not alter Niumi's position on the periphery of the world economy. Niumi residents would have agreed, no doubt, with Gailey's assessment on the eve of Gambian independence "that the new state will enter this world with only minimal facilities provided by the seventy year colonial administration of Great Britain."[98] They knew better than anyone that within the boundaries of old Niumi, at the beginning of 1965, there were two elementary schools, one dispensary, one paved road, and no trained physicians. They realized, too, that none of this mattered much, for any services or amenities that cost money were practically out of everyone's reach. But it was not simply the authority of commissioners, ordinances, and courts that kept people in Niumi in poverty. Regardless of the source of the authority—and of the authority itself—Niumi's residents remained producers of a primary product wanted by the industrialized core nations, and consumers of manufactured goods the industries produced. There was no visible alternative to continuing in this position.

Through the postwar years the same efforts in search of revenue to run the government and provide for development continued. Following the failed egg project, attempts to find exploitable minerals or petroleum proved futile. Still, there was optimism. After the Korean War, the world economy jumped ahead and there was a decade of prosperity. Prices for primary products held firm or advanced, the world's industrial nations produced goods cheaply, and Gambians at the time of their independence joined others in believing that prosperity was just around the corner. As almost everywhere else in Africa, The Gambia entered the world as a sovereign state with its citizens mindful of what had come before, but hopeful nonetheless.

Part IV
THE POSTCOLONIAL PERIOD

Independence or In Dependence?
1965–2009

Everybody knows the fight was fixed
The poor stay poor, the rich get rich
That's how it goes
Everybody knows
—Leonard Cohen and Sharon Robinson, "Everybody Knows," 1988

We have met the enemy and he is us.
—Pogo (Walt Kelly), 1971

Every Gambian of sufficient age remembers the coming of the country's independence on February 18, 1965. For some, it was the experience of a lifetime, generating feelings of optimism and bringing joy to their hearts. The positive outlook was based on simple facts: for sixty-eight years a British colonial government had managed Gambia's economy with the fiscal soundness of the mother country, rather than improvement of the lives of its Gambian subjects, foremost on its agenda. Now the colonial hobble would be untied, Gambians would be making economic decisions themselves, to benefit themselves, and development would necessarily follow. The most starry eyed envisioned progress pouring down on the small country like water from a cloudburst signaling the start of seasonal rains. Some grinned (and held tight) as they bounced along the country's washboard roads in the back of rattling vehicles, thinking, "Not much longer will I have to endure this." Others dreamed of schools and health centers in every good-size village. There even was talk of bridging the Gambia River, not upriver where the crossing is a few hundred yards, but between Banjul and Niumi, a distance at its most narrow of three miles, tying together the two halves of the country and bringing development equally to Niumi and the river's north bank. Those thinking in less grandiose terms pondered merely a life with enough to eat, a fair market for goods produced, and reasonable possibilities for timely marriage, production of a family, and caring for elders. For nearly everyone in the world's newest country on February 18, 1965, these were the headiest of times.

For good reason, the Independence Day celebrations on February 18, 2009, were far more subdued than in 1965, and seemingly scripted. Gambian President Yahyah A.J.J. Jammeh gave a speech championing peace and stability, soldiers passed in review, National Assembly members pontificated, singing groups performed and students dutifully paraded. Otherwise, had Gambians not gotten the day off from work or school, they would have spent it like most other days: preoccupied with the hard times of everyday life. The rains had been bountiful in 2008, but somehow this did not translate into farmers having more cash from selling crops. The Gambian dalasi, which had been tied to the British pound and thus worth about $2.60 in 1965, had fallen steadily through the last third of the twentieth century. By Independence Day in 2009, one dalasi was worth about four cents. The price of gasoline, which the government ceased subsidizing in 2002, went up 100 percent by early 2003 and continued its steady rise. If the global recession of 2008–2009 was not affecting Gambians as much as people living in other places, it was mainly because Gambians had so little to lose. Always telling of the country's circumstance is its listing in the latest (in this case, 2007–2008) UNDP Human Development Index: 155 out of 177 nations (below Zimbabwe and Haiti), or the same organization's statement that 59 percent of Gambians live in absolute poverty—that is, on less than one dollar per person per day. One could honestly repeat in 2009 what government critic Halifa Sallah said on the country's Independence Day in 2003: "[W]e are yet to address the problem of a growing population living in abject poverty."[1]

But on February 18, 2009, an additional problem faced Gambians that was not part of the Independence Day scene in 1965, not even visible on the farthest horizon. This was oppression by its own, corrupt government under the direction of (however oxymoronic the phrase) an elected tyrant. Jammeh had gained power in a coup in 1994 and, after a new constitution followed by an election in 1996 and a few years noted more for promising words than positive action, Jammeh steadily enriched himself and his cronies as he ignored the rule of law and rode roughshod over citizens' rights. No longer was there a press free to criticize the president's Independence-Day remarks nor an environment where one could feel safe in one's home, government security forces having arrested, illegally detained, tortured, burned out, and even (as alleged but never fully investigated) murdered Gambians considered oppositional to Jammeh and his political party, the APRC. For anyone not flaunting the party's flag and bright-green colors, The Gambia, in 2009, was not a place to feel secure.

Why this is the case—why the optimism at independence has been so thoroughly dashed and why the outlook for the future looks so dim, in so many ways, to so many living today in Niumi (and The Gambia generally)—is the question that underlies this book's last section. When using the world-systems model as an aid to understanding Niumi's history, one is tempted to think of it as more appropriate for the past than the present. Reasonable people can disagree over when people living along the Gambia River became fully involved on the system's periphery, but by the middle of the nineteenth century, by which time men in Niumi were producing peanuts to exchange for food, cloth, guns and gunpowder, and other real and perceived necessities, while women were growing what food they could as they managed domestic affairs, it seems evident that persons living throughout the region were locked in a system of production and exchange they could not easily escape. It was a system that drew them away from producing life's necessities and kept them from accumulating wealth. Great Britain's formal takeover of the Gambia colony in the 1890s, giving it still greater control over political and economic decisions, solidified Gambians' dependent situation. Much of the investment that went into colonial Gambia during the sixty years of British rule went toward advancing the dependent relationship that rested on importing and exporting: Banjul's port was one of colonial West Africa's best, river traffic moved goods efficiently from the far end of the colony to the port, and eventually roads followed the same pattern so that exports could move most easily toward the Atlantic and imports could reach the colony's eastern end. It was the classic pattern of colonial dependency, with the mother country at the distant core, in control of operations, and the colony on the periphery, its residents having little choice but to follow the only pattern laid out for their survival.

But Edward Small and others like him fought to gain independence so Gambians could make their own economic and political decisions, did they not? And while one recognizes that it would take several years following independence to affect major structural changes that would lead toward altering Gambia's dependent relationship to the system of world trade, one would expect that to happen in due time, would one not? And with the recent era of increasing globalization supposedly bringing greater freedom to the marketplace so that those involved could pursue more initiatives that would serve them best over the short and long term, would one expect elected leaders to continue with policies keeping the country's citizens tied to a system that requires production for a world market that pays poorly for what they produce and consumption from a world market that charges dearly for the imports they deem necessities? And with globalization's ability to spread modern ideas about governance, and with The Gambia entering the world as a republic, would one expect its elected leaders to wax megalomaniacal and tyrannical?

These questions, of course, are rhetorical. One imagines a scenario at independence of The Gambia steadily weaning itself from such complete dependence on exporting and importing, developing an infrastructure to facilitate local production for a regional market, becoming self-sufficient in most foods and some other necessities, and gaining international acclaim for being one of the few African nations whose government champions human rights and respect for the rule of law. So what went wrong? And is globalization likely to bring any improvement?

7

INDEPENDENT NIUMI IN THE FIRST REPUBLIC OF THE GAMBIA

1965–1994

The more things change, the more they remain the same.
—Alphonse Karr, Les Guêpes, January 1849

Don't forget who taught us how to drive.
—Bakary Sidibe, tiring of complaints about
Gambian drivers, September 1974

Gambian independence, on February 18, 1965, was a time for countrywide celebration. At villages up and down the river, people slaughtered large animals, prepared feasts, and danced into the night. The grandest celebrations were in the capital. Bathurst was packed with visiting dignitaries, the duke and duchess of Kent the most easily recognized. Because Niumi was just across the river, large numbers of its residents put on their best clothes and boated over to see or participate in drama festivals, wrestling matches, or drumming and dancing contests. A Berending youth group was featured, performing traditional dancing in Bathurst's Box Bar Stadium. Many from Niumi were in the crowd at MacCarthy Square on the night of February 17 when, as midnight approached, the Union Jack came down and Gambia's red, green, and blue flag inched up the flagpole. The fireworks that followed lit faces full of contentment. It might be a rocky road ahead, but Gambians would now be driving their own vehicle.[1]

It took only a short time for people to feel a letdown after experiencing all the independence hoopla. Three days following the event, walking down one of Bathurst's now-empty streets, the few remaining decorations cluttering the sidewalk or flapping in the Sunday morning breeze, a Gambian told a friend, "You know? It's as if nothing had really happened. Everything's the same as it was."[2]

The speaker could have been any one of the several thousand Niumi residents. They had a new government, all their own, but most other aspects of their lives were about the same and not likely to change.

Global Realities of the Mid-Twentieth Century

The world that Niumi's residents were celebrating entering as part of an independent nation was one that neither their ancestors at the beginning of the century nor their colonial commissioners fifty years later could have dreamed of. And since the time

190

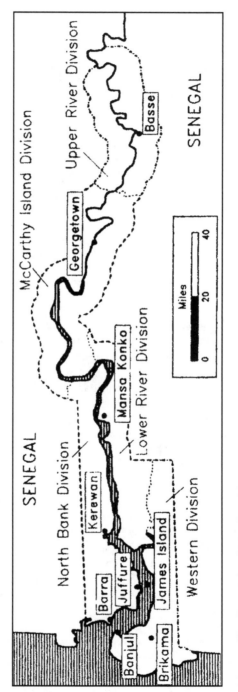

Map 9 **The Republic of The Gambia**

of African independence, the pace and scope of change have been so rapid and broad that few leaders of the continent's new nations have been able to grasp the consequences of that change and plan adequately for the future.

A major phenomenon of world history since 1965 has been the reinvigoration of globalization, the old process that now involves the integration of people all around the world into a global network wherein changes in one place affect people in every place. A factor in getting globalization moving again was the desire of the world's strongest nations to broaden the openness of world trade, thus allowing them to take full advantage of their positions in the center of the world economy. This was coupled with advances in technology that began reaching many aspects of human living, directly or indirectly, and built on themselves so that technological change started coming faster, and affecting more people, every year.[3]

The stage for increased globalization had been set by the end of World War II. The Soviet Union and the United States emerged as the strongest nations in the world—politically, economically, and militarily. In its own way, each tried to institutionalize its position of power around the globe. The Soviet Union spent mightily on industrialization and military strength at the expense of its people's future social and environmental improvement, and used that strength to support and control allies in selected spots around the globe. The United States recognized its need for markets for the goods it was producing (which amounted to 65 percent of the world's output in 1945). It also was mindful of the damage national protectionism had done to world trade during the depression years of the 1930s, and saw the need for international economic institutions that would work to restore trade disrupted by the war and then allow for management of the world economy to the country's long-term advantage. It was in this context that representatives of forty-four nations met in July 1944, in Bretton Woods, New Hampshire, and eventually reached an accord that would result in the establishment of the International Bank for Reconstruction and Development (the World Bank) and the International Monetary Fund (IMF). More negotiations in 1947 brought twenty-three countries to sign the General Agreement on Tariffs and Trade (GATT).[4] The World Bank and the IMF lent money, provided by member nations—over half from the United States at first, but more in recent years from Western Europe, Japan, and oil-rich nations—to countries to assist in reconstruction and development "by facilitating the investment of capital for productive purposes [and] to promote private foreign investment by means of guarantees or participation in loans [and] to supplement private investment by providing, on suitable conditions, finance for productive purposes."[5] For the first decade or more, most of these loans went to rebuild the economies of war-ravaged Western Europe. Then more of the money went to developing nations. Loans and technical assistance from these institutions were funneled to nations open to capitalist development, often for such projects as improvement of port facilities that would promote importing and exporting, and usually came with stipulations. These often involved abolishing import controls, freezing wages, limiting government expenditure, and removing price controls—measures that would turn out to be favorable, over the long run, for nations that imported raw materials and exported manufactured goods. GATT was not a lending institution but an agreement among signatories to hold meetings (called "rounds") for the purpose of keeping tariffs low and equally applied, to establish a code of conduct for international trading, and to resolve trade disputes. Viewed together, the World Bank, the IMF, and GATT served as powerful forces for restoring world trade after fifteen years of depression and war and then of making sure that the global market would remain free and open.

Much of the technological change was the result of the prolonged period of hot and cold war. Western military-instigated advances in communications, transportation, and information management brought people into closer and faster contact. The world economy became even more thoroughly integrated, increasingly dependent on, and responsive to, world-market conditions. These new technologies were most efficient when involved with large-scale production. Corporations expanded to increase the scope of their control. With worldwide operations, newly forming multinational corporations could take advantage of cheap labor, easy access to raw materials, and expanding markets no matter where each existed.

The rapidly growing world economy did not immediately bode ill for the less-advantaged nations. For the third quarter of the twentieth century, as the rebuilding of the war-torn world, followed by military spending associated with the Cold War and conflicts in Korea and Vietnam, created demand and stimulated production, world output tripled. The price of petroleum that fueled world transportation and some electrical production remained artificially low, while most basic commodity prices held firm or rose. Consequently, even those on the periphery of the system found their lives improving (as measured by gross domestic product per capita), not as rapidly as in the core areas, but improving in real terms nonetheless.

Among the core nations, the catchword through the 1960s and 1970s was "growth." As consumers of world resources and producers of goods to be sold around the globe, these nations sought more and greater markets, especially on the system's periphery, where improved and more widely disseminated medical technology was bringing an unprecedented rise in population. Increased resource production in the peripheral nations, the result in part of grants and loans, would provide people more money with which to consume—if there was a general openness of the market. And grants and loans were useful carrots to reward countries for political allegiance in the era of Cold War competition.

Some of this fit nicely with the philosophies of peripheral nations, where emphasis was on development. While a handful of nations allied themselves with the Soviet bloc and pursued socialist development policies that encouraged slow building from the bottom to improve more equally the lives of most of the nations' peoples, more countries saw the practicality of accepting the inequalities and working with the capitalist world system that was in place. These countries recognized the need for money to develop; saw that their major means of getting money was through exporting the lone resource, or the small group of resources they had been exporting; wanted access to the material goods the core nations could supply; and thus established policies that made for openness of trade and stimulated greater resource production. Early forms of development in these countries tended to focus on port construction, bridge building, and road improvements rather than expansion of health facilities or schools, the thinking being that improved infrastructure would bring greater trade and more money, which could then be tapped for better medical care or improved education. In this fashion, through the 1960s and into the 1970s, with such notable exceptions as Cuba, Tanzania, and Guinea, most poor nations worked with a consortium of public and private institutions in and around the core nations to tie themselves more thoroughly to the world economy and build up their national wealth as the first step toward development. If foreign banks and multinational corporations were involved in a peripheral nation's economy more deeply than its citizens might wish, well, so be it in this necessary stage toward general betterment. Thus went the common thinking.

Technology enhanced the fiscal position of many of these developing countries with advances in agriculture related to a "Green Revolution." With mechanization and new kinds of tools, agricultural-exporting nations could increase their acreage under cultivation, and with new seeds developed through hybridization and new chemicals for weed control and fertilizers, they could improve crop yields. Perhaps the poorer peasant families could not afford the best seeds and fertilizers, but larger producers could, and export production shot up. Through the 1960s and beyond, the economic outlook on the periphery was brightening. Some thought the optimism of the independence period was not misplaced.

Naturally, those in charge of governments in poor countries were impatient to experience the benefits of development. If better lives were to be led, they believed, if personal wealth was to grow, if the number and quality of material possessions were to increase, if more advanced schooling and access to health care were to be available, let it be now rather than later—at least for some. The "some" most often turned out to be themselves—government bureaucrats, loyal political allies, and wealthy private citizens, who often were involved in business that the government approved. This being the case, an important route toward social and material advancement was through the civil service. Government ranks swelled with educated and partially educated friends, allies, and kin of higher officials. Of course, so did the government payroll.

It would take just a few years of the middle-1970s to burst the bubble of satisfaction for core and periphery nations alike. In retrospect, one can see the unhealthiness of relationships in the world economy of, say, 1970—of global dependence on petroleum, the price of which remained artificially low; of core dependence on exports to the world's growing numbers of poor people; of peripheral reliance on monocrop agriculture and dependence on imports for basic needs. But it was the combination punch of prolonged drought conditions and drastic measures of the major oil-producing nations to raise oil prices that made many realize that dependence on the world economy had its pitfalls.

In this age of growing awareness of the effects of human actions on the environment, debates over the causes of drought in Africa can be heated. What cannot be
disputed is the record of reduced rainfall. The period between 1950 and 1967 was
one of above-average rainfall for West Africa's sahel, but as if someone turned a
giant spigot, in twenty-seven of the next thirty years rainfall in the sahel nations
was below average, seriously so in the early 1970s, most of the 1980s, and the first
half of the 1990s. In Banjul, where the best records are kept, twenty more inches
of rain fell per year, on average, between 1950 and 1966 than between 1967 and
1985. Gradually over this period, Niumi's once-forested and grassy landscape
became more and more like the sahel. Villagers began seeing desert foxes and
desert snakes along the Gambia River's north bank. A problem of special gravity
for farmers involved reduction of rainfall in August, when crops were at a critical
stage of flowering and grain filling. When this happened, the results were disastrous.
Richard A. Schroeder lists "sharp reductions in food production, devastatingly
high mortality rates in livestock herds, deforestation and denudation of landscapes,
massive relocation of rural populations, and the outbreak of disease epidemics that
contributed to hundreds of thousands of human deaths," as conditions produced
by such prolonged drougt.[6]

If this were not enough, the Organization of Petroleum Exporting Countries
(OPEC) shocked the world with an oil embargo that ended up raising the price of
crude oil by 380 percent between 1973 and 1975. The cost of oil was the trigger
for rapid inflation of most of the world's currencies, and as inflation rates soared,
the volume and value of world trade spiraled downward. The Green Revolution
was not beneficial in some world economic matters. While it resulted in much
greater staple crop production and thus more food for growing populations, for
many commodities it meant that supply outstripped demand, thus lowering world
prices. From the late 1970s, nations that balanced their budgets with revenues from
the sale of cocoa, cotton, coffee, peanuts, palm oil, or coconut oil found greater
need for money (to purchase petroleum products and other imports), yet had less
of it because of their reduced revenues from exports. To fill the budget gap, such
countries sought increased aid, and sometimes they got it: so long as Cold War
powers were vying for allies, strategically important poor nations, at least, could
obtain aid to fill in budget deficits. Once the Cold War began winding down in
the 1980s, however, neither Soviet supporters nor Western nations were as eager
to prop up poor countries with foreign aid. The countries thus turned to increased
borrowing, something they had been doing to a lesser extent through the 1960s and
1970s. The amount of debt poorer countries owed to wealthier ones rose quickly;
the proportions were staggering: from $50 billion in 1970 to $400 billion in 1980
to over $1 trillion in 1990.[7]

By the mid-1980s, conditions in the world economy were not improving for
the poorer nations. The gap between rich and poor seemed to be widening as the
public debt of the poor nations continuing growing. Here and there, governments
toppled, replaced by military rulers or governments of questionable popularity and

stability. Many countries tottered along the brink of default on their loans. With the global economic outlook dimming for poorer nations, and with growing concern over default in the world's wealthier nations, where economic well-being relied partly on interest from loans and profits from global sales, the major international lending agencies took action: before approving new loans that poorer nations now needed desperately, sometimes simply to pay the interest on their existing debt, the World Bank, IMF, and cooperative private banks began insisting that the developing nations' governments agree to alter the structure of their economies. Such "structural adjustment" often included curbs on government spending, reduction of the size of the civil service, devaluation of currencies, and ending of price supports for imports (including foodstuffs). Into the 1990s, some poor countries that took these prescribed measures began recovering from the most immediate of their economic problems, at least in the short term, but it was often at the expense of their popular support. With fewer jobs, higher prices, fewer public services at greater expense, and a general deterioration of the quality of life, people questioned their governments and looked askance at the system that kept them hungry, unhealthy, and impoverished. It was not a situation that bred stability.[8]

Around the developing world in the 1980s and early 1990s, governments struggled, teetered, and toppled. Some, like Mexico, were important enough to their neighbors and the world economic system to be bailed out by rich nations. Others, like Liberia, were economically and strategically insignificant, so were allowed to collapse. Through it all, few thought much about The Gambia. It was full of "smiling, happy people," the tourist brochures read, and it had a reputation for being one of Africa's small number of working democracies.

New Rulers, Old Rules

As revelers returned from across the river, and as the hubbub of independence celebrations died down in Essau, Berending, Aljamdu, and Sika, Niumi's villagers took stock in those early months of 1965 and believed their lives to be on a good course. It was not just that their colonial rulers of sixty-eight years were gone and that fellow countrymen were now running the country: the party in power, the People's Progressive Party (PPP) of Prime Minister Jawara, had its origins in the plight of Gambia's long-neglected rural areas, where development paled in relation to the advances experienced in Bathurst. Jawara presented himself as a reserved man of modest means and needs, making it easy for his rural constituents, who resented the urban elite, to consider him "one of us." Jawara played up this image whenever possible, reminding villagers how he had spent years in the 1950s traveling the colony's back roads as a "cow doctor." "There is not a cow in the Gambia that does not know me personally," he would announce at campaign stops.[9] Close to home, Essau's Alhaji Mang Foday Sonko—Maranta Sonko's great grandson—had won a seat in Gambia's Parliament. People in Niumi expected the government, the party, the prime minister, and their new government representative to look after them.

They anticipated prosperity in good years and a fair shake even when crops and prices might not be so favorable.

They got neither. For a few years the optimism prevailed. The new government was of the practical school that thought one must build on what one did best. For The Gambia, this was growing peanuts, which still made up 90 percent of the country's exports. "An amazingly simple answer to this country's crushing economic problem is now being put forward here," reported an observer at independence. "It is just to grow more groundnuts. . . . [I]nstead of chasing difficult alternatives, why not make the most of what nature favors? . . . [I]f the annual crop was something like 100,000 instead of 70,000 tons this economy could look very different. [I]t may be that the country's main economic problem is not that its only export is groundnuts but that there are not enough groundnuts to export."[10]

It seemed a reasonable argument. Only the world market stood as a hurdle. "I can say with confidence," said Gambian Finance Minister Sherif Sisay in 1966, "that this country could, in the foreseeable future, balance its recurrent budget with a modest surplus available for development expenditure, if it could rely upon the world price of groundnuts remaining at the levels prevailing during the past season."[11] These were arguments that Niumi's farming families could understand and do something about. Crops grew well through 1967—in fact, The Gambia exported more peanuts that year than ever before—and the government-set price of 140 dalasies per ton was not bad. Most Niumi farmers did not know that the government agency that marketed the peanuts, the Gambia Produce Marketing Board, sold the crop for 307 dalasies per ton, meaning that they had received 46 percent of the actual export price.

But then the first of a series of drought years came along. It was unfortunate that the drought arrived at the time when Great Britain was reducing subsidies to the Gambian government, as had been scheduled during negotiations for independence, prompting Gambia's officials to seek ways to enhance annual revenues. With such private buyers as the UAC and the Compagnie Française de l'Afrique Occiden-tale recently excluded from peanut marketing, the government had an easier time still in bringing in more revenue: it merely had to pay the peanut growers a small proportion of the export price. So, in 1968, for the first drought-reduced crop, the marketing board again paid growers 140 dalasies per ton, even though the price it received had gone up to 372 dalasies per ton—rendering Niumi's farmers just 38 percent of the crop's export price. And over the next fifteen years they received a steadily smaller proportion—29 percent of the export price in 1974, 23 percent in 1984.[12] Retrospective criticisms of the Gambian government's first twenty years were sharp: "On the average, between 1964/65 and 1984/85, the peasants were robbed of 60 per cent of the international price of groundnuts!" wrote a commentator in *West Africa*. "For 20 years the Jawara government 'officially' took, free of charge, three of every five bags, leaving the peasant with a gross of two. With deductions for subsistence credit, fertiliser, seed, etc., the peasant would end up with a net one bag out of five."[13]

Photo 10 **Sign preparing citizens for participation in the electoral process, Essau, Lower Niumi.**

Adding to the difficulty was the growing need to import rice, and its cost. Gambians had not been able to produce enough food for their population for a long time, but as the population grew more rapidly after the middle of the twentieth century (meaning a larger proportion of the population would be under a productive age), as agricultural production focused on peanuts, and as more people moved to urban areas and found alternatives to farming, the need for food imports grew. Through the first half of the 1960s, The Gambia was importing between 9,000 and 10,000 tons of rice each year—at a time when the escalating warfare in rice-producing regions of Southeast Asia cut production and led to a rise in the world price. The Gambia's government controlled and subsidized the price of rice to keep it low—largely to mollify the city people, who did not grow any food for themselves and thus had to buy whatever they consumed—but by planting time in 1968, just when Niumi's villagers were running low on food and needing to buy rice, the rising world price forced the government to raise The Gambia's controlled price. It was a bad year for peanuts and homegrown food because of the drought, and it turned out to be a bad year to need rice.[14] Outwardly, the situation in The Gambia continued to look promising. Through the 1960s the country experienced an annual growth rate of 4.5 percent, against a population increase of 2.6 percent. Annual per capita income for 1968 rose to $260, an all-time high. World peanut prices went up steadily through the mid-1970s, and so even with the persistent drought cutting into crop yields, the government could boast large exchange reserves and almost no foreign debt, circumstances rare indeed for developing countries of the time.[15] Government planners must have been concerned by the rise in petroleum costs in 1974, the related rise in the costs of many other imports, and the dip in peanut prices that occurred in the mid-1970s, but not so much that it did not launch its First Development Plan in 1975, an economic directive driven partly by government officials' political concerns and partly by their self-interest.[16] The PPP was comfortable with its support from the likes of Niumi folk; they were part of its traditional, rural political base that the party could count on. But party leaders worried about urban groups in and around Banjul (the new name given Bathurst in 1973, which is the old name for the sandy island the city rested on). They recognized that an economic plan to benefit urban dwellers that did not appear to ignore "the provinces" entirely could enhance their grip on political control, adding urban support to complement their solid rural backing. Such a plan, too, would provide resources for their personal economic benefit, for they were now mostly urban dwellers and policies that favored bureaucrats and businessmen living in Banjul or its residential communities favored them. The new plan created several new, urban-based state agencies (that could be filled through patronage appointments); doubled the size of the civil service and increased public investment, largely in urban enterprises, over six years; and provided tax breaks and loan guarantees for urban-based businesses. What business were they fostering? It turned out that with import duties considerably lower than those of surrounding countries, Gambian businessmen could import foreign-produced goods and then reexport them to merchants in Senegal, Mauritania, Mali, Guinea-Bissau, even Upper Volta, where higher tariffs were in place to stimulate manufacturing. The reexport trade became an increasingly important element in Gambia's economy. From the mid-1970s, a major way for people with any money to have it grow was to get involved in trade and transport: buying and selling goods and moving them, or moving the people seeking them, around the country and across borders.

As was typical, the plan was financed not by taxes on the trade, for such might slow the reexport business and would certainly irritate urban merchants, but by government profits from the marketing of peanuts that farmers grew in Niumi and other rural areas. Gambia's government was "taking from the poor rural areas to enrich a selected few in the urban areas," wrote a commentator in *West Africa*.[17] Those few squeaky wheels in Niumi, who recognized that profits from their hard work were going to benefit businessmen and bureaucrats across the river, got a few squirts of government grease: a new road here, a grade added to a school there, and perhaps an opportunity to open a branch of a Banjul-based business enterprise in the local community.

Around 1980, The Gambia's peanut-based economy began to wither like the plants in the drought-plagued fields. In addition to the lack of rainfall, parasite infestation and labor shortages in rural areas—the latter resulting from young men heading off for perceived opportunities in Banjul—cut peanut production. At the same time, the world-market price for peanuts plummeted. The marketing board kept a huge reserve so it could cope with such fluctuations, but it was staffed largely by political patrons who were not particularly clairvoyant (and, it turns out, had a hand in the cash drawer), and then the Gambian government drew off 40 million dalasies of the reserve to cover its own budget deficits. By 1984 the marketing board had no reserve and owed the Central Bank 110 million dalasies. A year later, Gambian peanut production was 45 percent lower than in 1976.[18] With its usual source of revenue collapsing, but not wanting to alter its urban-friendly policies, the government sought grants from Western donors and loans from commercial banks. To entice either one, they trumpeted Gambia's open economy, its stable position as one of Africa's few working democracies, and its status—with peace existing all around and no standing army—as the "Switzerland of Africa." It was a package few lenders could resist. In 1981 the World Bank declared The Gambia a worthy place for investment, noting that "the economic policies of the government, including producer prices, have been quite satisfactory . . . [and] the poor growth record of the 1970s was almost exclusively attributable to unfavorable weather conditions."[19] Even after an abortive coup in 1981 that left 1,000 dead and necessitated Senegal's army remaining on hand to keep order, short-, medium-, and long-term loans were available. So between 1980 and 1985, as even the world's wealthiest nations were fighting inflation and worrying about cash flows and payment balances, The Gambia's government borrowed heavily so many of its citizens, particularly supporters of Jawara and his party, could live beyond their means. By 1985 The Gambia owed the World Bank, the IMF, and private commercial banks in various core nations a sum equal to 114 percent of the little country's annual gross domestic product (GDP). It had fallen behind paying the interest on these loans, too; its debt-service arrears—simply the interest on its loans that was *overdue*—amounted to almost two-thirds of the 1985 GDP. Yet, oddly, as more of the money for the civil service and urban development came from foreign borrowing, most Gambians seemed to ignore its source. Like some slowly advancing disease, foreign debt came to be recognized as a problem only after its consequences threatened national death.[20]

Under the circumstances such a threat was not long in coming. By 1985, as if smacked rudely in the face with, and completely surprised by, Gambia's economic problems, foreign donors and lenders began refusing to provide further money. Food and fuel shortages began to appear, even around the capital, where at times electricity was off as much as it was on, and there were times when the government had foreign exchange in reserve to pay for only two weeks of imports. In August 1985, a sobered government introduced an economic recovery program in line with structural adjustment requirements set out by the IMF. No one doubted that officials from the lending institutions had whispered loudly in the government's ear.

The new program drastically cut government spending (forcing layoff of 20 percent of the government workforce), allowed the national currency to depreciate 120 percent in six months (thereby raising prices of imports), and took measures to raise government revenues (hiking utility and transportation prices, cracking down on customs fraud). This was mostly difficult news for poor villagers in Niumi, but it was at least partially offset by another portion of the policy on which the IMF insisted: raising the price paid to farmers for their peanuts 50 percent *above* the world price, which required a government subsidy equal to 8 percent of the country's GDP. It was an effort to return peanut exports to their previously important role in the country's economy.[21]

The reform program worked, at least at first: inflation fell to an annual rate below 10 percent, trade deficits fell, the government paid its debt arrears, foreign currency reserves grew, and over four years the annual per capita income in The Gambia grew by 4.9 percent. Foreign donors and lenders smiled and reopened their coffers. By 1990, The Gambia was again a developing country recommended for investment. But for people in Niumi the results of the program were mixed. The immediate rise in payments for peanuts, abetted by a return to near-normal rainfall for two years, meant that its farming families had more disposable income. Annual per capita incomes went up 12 percent in three years in rural Gambia. A temporary dip in the world price of rice even helped many get through the hungry season. The benefits for farmers were not long lasting, however. After three years of subsidies and higher prices for peanuts, the government began cutting the subsidies until they were gone altogether by 1990. In that year Gambians exported 130,000 tons of peanuts; then the falling prices and another series of years of low rainfall brought a dramatic drop—to 75 tons in 1991 and 65 tons in 1994. In the latter year, agricultural production made up only about one-quarter of The Gambia's GDP, and peanut exports were just over 10 percent of export earnings.[22] By the 1990s, the peanut was at risk of losing its position at the center of the Gambian economy, a position it had held for 150 years. Older men in Niumi must have scratched their heads, patted their empty stomachs, and wondered what was happening to the life they had always known, tied into the cycle of the peanut.

A temporary alternative to peanut farming for some Niumi residents, which also was related to effects of the structural-adjustment program, had to do with the re-export trade that passed through the region. Measures intended to liberalize trade and enhance the "outward orientation" of The Gambia's economy brought further lowering of import duties. This meant that Gambians could import foreign goods at prices cheaper still than nearly all the neighboring countries. Thus, even more than before, Gambian merchants imported foreign products for rapid sale across the nearby international borders. Following the 1990 breakup of the Senegambian Confederation, an attempted amalgam of the economies of Senegal and The Gambia in the wake of the 1981 abortive coup, Senegal took action to stop the cross-border trade, but official checks at customs stations merely brought increased smuggling. It was impossible for Senegal to patrol its nearly 500-mile-long border with The Gambia. Between 1991 and 1994, reexporting activity accounted for 85 percent of The Gambia's merchandise exports and made up 20 percent of government revenue. Because one of the major routes to Senegal was through Niumi, up the road that connected the Barra ferry to the border north of Fass, large quantities of goods moved across the river from Banjul and passed northward. Senegalese traders came to Barra to obtain merchandise, too, so the market at Barra expanded considerably. Up and down the bustling road, wherever cars and trucks might stop, traders set up shop and serviced the traffic with food, drink, kola nuts, batteries, cigarettes, and matches.

Then, suddenly, the bottom dropped out of the reexport market. In 1993, a French franc crisis in the European monetary system caused panic in European and related African currency markets. After further tightening control of the Gambian border, Senegal devalued its currency, the CFA franc, by 50 percent in January 1994, thus making Gambian exports more expensive in Senegal and neighboring countries. By the end of the year, the harsh reality of these actions was apparent. Gambia's reexport trade had fallen by 66 percent from the year before. The Gambia's government would have to look for different sources of revenue to make up for the export losses, and some people in Niumi, who had been enjoying economic activities ancillary to the reexport trade, packed up their little shops and enamelware basins and went home.[23] Where to turn next? Quite a number of Niumi residents were not too sure.

A Chance Encounter With World History and a Boost for Tourism: Alex Haley and *Roots*

Niumi never made it onto many African maps, let alone world ones. Its name, and any of the others it went by, almost never were read or spoken outside the small area around the lower Gambia where people knew of its existence. But one village in Niumi, Juffure, the old commercial center down on the southern riverbank where state officials used to collect the *mansa*'s tolls from passing river traffic, gained worldwide attention almost overnight in 1976, several years after an African American, Alex Haley, visited the village, interviewed one of its elderly residents, and told the world in his book, *Roots: The Saga of an American Family*, that he had discovered his African kin. Occurring at a time when tourism was picking up in The Gambia anyway, this began an experience with European and American tourists in Niumi that has had an effect on the way some of its population lives.

Tourism's roots in The Gambia were shallow in the mid-1970s, when *Roots* appeared. At independence, the country had only two hotels, both in Bathurst, a city not a lot more inviting in 1965 than it had been a few decades earlier, when visitors described it variously as an "open sore," "one of the worst tropical slums in Africa," or, in one unnecessarily graphic commentary, "a water-logged sponge, floating in a sea of its own excreta."[24] The 1960s was a time in northern Europe, however, when a growing holiday crowd had money to spend and was feeling the need to flee the short, sunless days of winter and sniff the tropical breeze.

Such breezes have always blown steadily, hot and dry, between November and April, along The Gambia's unspoiled Atlantic beaches, and over the winter of 1965, a Swedish company, Vingressor/Club 33, took advantage of the country's proximity to Europe—it is a six-hour flight today from London to Banjul—by bringing 300 tourists to enjoy the weather. Thereafter, word about The Gambia spread across Europe's snow belt. These tourists brought money with them, of course, and this caught the eye of officials in a Gambian government chronically in need of foreign exchange, so the die was cast for officially sanctioned tourist growth. The government in 1970 designated a Tourism Development Area along the country's Atlantic coast south of the Gambia River; hotels began to appear; Vingressor met competition from other tourist agencies; and growing numbers of Scandinavians, British, Germans, and Dutch began appearing in the country (sometimes insufficiently clad, in the eyes of Gambia's conservative Muslim population): nearly 3,000 of them by 1971 and over 20,000 by 1974.[25]

Hardly a one of these tourists ventured across the river and into Niumi before word got out about Haley's interview and its supposed consequences for his historical and genealogical investigations. The man he interviewed was Keba Fofana, a less-than-successful member of one of Juffure's old maraboutic lineages, whom Haley claimed to be a *griot*—a fact that made a number of Juffure villagers laugh and several of Gambia's egotistical *griots* angry. Haley was a writer, who was seeking an angle for a book on his family's history in America. Convinced that he had found the angle in Fofana, in Juffure, in The Gambia, Haley wrote *Roots*, which tied the region into the history of peoples of African descent across the Atlantic. The book was an instant success from its publication in 1976: Doubleday sold 1.5 million copies in one year and the book went into translation in several dozen languages. A subsequent serialization of *Roots* for television played for more American viewers than any program that preceded it and eventually aired around the world. All of this focused world attention on the Gambia River's place in an important segment of global history and connected Juffure to popular intellectual currents.[26]

The basic story behind Haley and *Roots* is straightforward.[27] The author said he remembered stories his elderly relatives told around the Tennessee home of his youth: of a family genealogy that went back to an African ancestor they called "Kin-tay" and of words in an African language handed down over the generations. With the help of a Gambian acquaintance and advice from a few academics, he identified his ancestors as speakers of Mandinka and likely residents of the Gambia River. In the mid-1960s Haley traveled to Bathurst, where he told his story to several Gambians, including government officials who were not blind to what the story could do for tourism. These men promised to seek an oral traditionist who could help Haley with his quest, and they found one—Fofana in Juffure, a nice old fellow, who was willing to tell an appropriate story at an appropriate time for appropriate remuneration. Haley returned to The Gambia, hired an entourage of fourteen people, rented a launch and several vehicles, and visited Juffure, where Fofana told him what he wanted to hear about his ancestor, Kunta Kinte: as Haley would write in *Roots*, the young man "had been kidnapped into slavery not far from his village, chopping wood, to make himself a drum."[28] Haley had located a record of a ship that sailed from the Gambia River to Annapolis, Maryland, in 1767, so he dated the episode to that year. This provided him the makings of the story line for *Roots*, which he describes as "a novelized amalgam of what I *know* took place together with what my researching led me to plausibly *feel* took place."[29] The book won a Pulitzer Prize in a category of literature created for *Roots*: "Faction"—a story based on fact, but with fictional dialogue.

What *Roots* did for Juffure was to make it a tourist Mecca for Americans primarily, who want to visit an ancestral home of African Americans, but for others, as well. In good years as many as 10,000 tourists have traveled by boat, or by automobile following the ferry ride, to the village of 500 people. Some Juffure villagers eyed the bonanza. Haley returned several times and made promises for a new mosque, scholarships for foreign study for village youth, and (according to varying accounts) a beach hotel, a trade school, farming tools, and advanced machinery. Television crews, reporters from Western newspapers, and sundry writers and students were frequent visitors to Juffure, too. By the early 1980s, aware of the dilapidated state of village housing, residents had constructed a replica of the village as it might have looked in the eighteenth century, with round mud dwellings and thatched roofs (as opposed to the existing rectangular mud buildings with roofs of corrugated metal).[30] Eventually they added a market catering to tourists, selling masks, statues, drums, and carvings. The Gambian government stationed a policeman in Juffure to keep order and limit tourist visits to three days per week, but such limitations were easy to get around.[31]

Though it has not added Niumi or an accurate portrayal of the region's history to anyone's ken, *Roots* changed life in Juffure. Some elements of the change are positive. The village gained an elementary school that it never had before, and Albreda, next door where the boats land, has a secondary school. Juffure has its own diesel generator to power a water pump and to provide occasional electricity for night lighting and cold drinks for tourists. The road that autos take south from Bunyadu down along Niumi's southern riverbank, connecting Juffure and a dozen other villages to the country's main east-west thoroughfare that leads from the Barra ferry, is better than it was in 1976, but not remarkably so. More wealth exists in the village. Visiting tourists pay a 15 *dalasi* per person tax, which pays a dozen Juffure boys to act as tour guides and pays a stipend to the village head. Other people carve and sculpt and weave and turn out masks and statues for the new craft market, and there are hawkers of sandwiches and drinks as well as some jobs in a new restaurant at the riverside that sells Gambian specialties plus "chicken and chips." Some tourists spend freely and occasionally a visitor will "adopt" a young Juffure resident and send the family a regular check or agree to pay the child's school fees.

But all of what *Roots* brought is not so clearly beneficial. Juffure residents are bitter because so many of the author's promises were never fulfilled. The mosque never amounted to anything more than plans and 200 bricks for a foundation. Haley's death in 1992 meant that the promised largesse would never reach Juffure. Still,

Photo 11   **Marker at the beginning of the "Roots Heritage Trail" in Juffure, Upper Niumi.**

some villagers have come to believe that the world owes them something for their residence in Haley's supposed ancestral home. They live off tourist money, so they get it where they can, pressuring, cajoling, or begging as they deem necessary.[32] One is tempted to consider that they are doing what persons in Juffure had done long into the past: taxing the trade for what it will bear. One of the consequences of such activity is that, just as Haley provided a distorted depiction of life in a precolonial West African village and state, residents of Juffure are giving Western

Perspective 16   **Alex Haley and Niumi's History**

The late Alex Haley was a professional writer, not a professional historian. Although he wrote of "years of intensive research in fifty-odd libraries, archives, and other repositories on three continents" (*Roots*, 584), he took liberties with historical fact in *Roots*. Respected historians have described the inaccuracies of many of his portrayals, and a professional historian and certified genealogist located documentation disproving all of his pre–Civil War genealogy.

Haley's portrayal of eighteenth-century life in Niumi has little basis in fact. The state is hardly mentioned, its *mansa* a shadowy figure some distance away whose "personal agents" supplied slaves to white traders in the river (49). The Juffure in *Roots* is a stereotypic African village, "four days from the nearest place on the Kambi Bolongo [Gambia River] where slaves were sold" (47). Few Juffure residents in *Roots* have ever seen a white man, and when a band of whites and their accomplices overcome Kinte and take him to a waiting ship, the Africans are powerless to respond. The adolescent Kinte is a proto warrior with dreams of visiting the Mali Empire as he guards the family peanut fields.

In reality, Juffure was the point of contact where Africans, Euro-Africans, and Europeans representing segments of an economic system spanning half the globe met to carry on the exchange of slaves, cloth, iron, and other commodities in agreed-upon fashion. The village was in sight of James Island, where for a century English traders had maintained a garrison, and next to Albreda, where lived French and Franco-African traders. And members of the Kinte lineage were not warriors, but traders. If a branch of the family lived in Juffure in the 1760s, it was involved in the exchange of slaves and other commodities with Europeans. For that matter, it was Europeans, rather than Africans, who at the time were most vulnerable. Had any European kidnapped an African on Niumi soil, the *mansa* would have exacted retribution that threatened the continuing existence of a European presence in the river.

Alex Haley was a warm, delightful raconteur, and *Roots* was an important phenomenon in raising interest in African American history and the African Diaspora. What remains difficult is that so much of the book and television series continue to be regarded as having a basis in fact. Their portrayals enforce old stereotypes and distort much relating to this important segment of world, African, and African American history.

Gary B. Mills and Elizabeth Shown Mills, "Roots and the New 'Faction': A Legitimate Tool for Clio?" *Virginia Magazine of History and Biography* 89 (1981): 3–26.

Philip Nobile, "Uncovering Roots," *Village Voice*, February 17–23, 1993, 31–38.

tourists a distorted sense of life in a contemporary West African village. The *real* Africa they see in Juffure is almost as different from the typical West African agricultural village as Haley's portrayal of eighteenth-century Juffure is from the former center of Gambia River slave trading.

Modernization?

For thirty years following independence, a variety of environmental and ecological, demographic, social, political, technological, and economic changes—some local and regional, some global—affected the way people lived in the land that once was the old Niumi state. Most observers believed that, as in much of the rest of the world, change came faster than ever before.

Unfortunately, one of the things that did not change much under the Jawara government, which now is termed Gambia's First Republic, was the poverty in which nearly all Niumi residents lived. Relevant figures for 1993 are saddening: The mean annual income of persons living in Niumi in that year was just over the equivalent of $200; only 17 percent of the population had income of more than $300 and only 3 percent over $500. People spent more than these amounts—on average about $600 throughout the year, meaning their income was supplemented by something else, usually money sent home by relatives living abroad. But this was $600 for *everything*: housing, upkeep, clothing, food, transportation, medical care, school fees—everything. On average, Niumi residents throughout 1993 spent $1.60 on medical care (less than they spent on candles), $2.00 on rent and dwelling repairs, $7.00 on bus/taxi and ferry fares, $3.00 on school-related expenses, and $20.00 on clothing and shoes. They spent $90 on food, nearly one-quarter of which was for rice and other grains.[33]

Because the great majority of Niumi residents have forever gained their subsistence and occupied themselves most fully by growing foods to eat and crops to sell, what happens with farming may be the most important factor in their lives.[34] For this reason, the regional drought that has afflicted West Africa's sahel and savannas with little relief since 1967—and it is now known to be by far the worst drought of the twentieth century and seemingly one of the worst for such a sustained period in centuries—has been devastating. Niumi's farmers believe that before 1968, the rainy season had more reliable rains that lasted a month or six weeks longer than now. Of course, the drought has reduced crop yields and rendered some swamplands unusable for rice production, meaning in a world of steady prices, cash-crop farmers have had less cash and subsistence farmers have had less food. But it has not even been a world of steady prices: the government's economic recovery program, based in part on devaluation of the dalasi, was supposed to help rural dwellers by bringing higher prices for their cash crops. This did not happen for long, however, because of a coincidental, dramatic drop in world commodity prices. Yet, imported items cost more.[35]

If drought and prices were not enough of a problem, the absence of the most dynamic segment of its labor force added to rural Niumi's woes. Many young adults were simply leaving—going off to one or another urban area. Their reasons for going were tied largely to the forces of "modernization." More Niumi youth than ever were getting some education. By the mid-1990s over one-quarter of the elementary-age children and 15 percent of secondary-age children were in school. This was good for the literacy rate,[36] but not for rural development. After having four or five years of schooling, and gaining acquaintance with other ways of life in other places, young men looked upon the small rural village of Niumi, where one can barely scratch out an existence on the farm, as the last place they wanted to end up. So they were leaving for the city. The Gambia's annual rate of urbanization grew to 8 percent; it became one of the most urbanized countries in sub-Saharan Africa. Some from Niumi went simply to Barra or Essau, nearer ferry access to Banjul, and where there were better prospects for employment and a lot more going on. Others took up with relatives across the river around greater Banjul, where one-third of the country's population already resided and where nearly all of its economic opportunity existed. In 1993, 10,000 persons living in Banjul and its nearby dormitory communities were migrants from Niumi. Most were young adults. All of this altered the demographic nature of Niumi's villages, which generally were in decline. Populations of many were shrinking, and nearly all the shrinkage was in the number of people of productive age, especially working males. (Virtually every village had fewer people of prime productive age, many more children, and more men and women beyond the prime working age.) This meant that in spite of the rapidly growing population, farm labor was in short supply.[37] Thus, the drought, the recovery program, deteriorating terms of trade, and an absence of a workforce commensurate in size to the population combined to deal Niumi's farming villages a near-mortal blow.

In altering farming practices to cope with the changing conditions, Niumi's farmers exacerbated their problems. Their response to declining yields related to the drought was to plant more fields more often. The growing tendency to plant the same plot year after year, even in the face of long-held knowledge that the land needs a long fallow period for restoration of fertility, was "leading to impoverishment of soils around villages," writes Kathleen M. Baker, and "storing up trouble for the future."[38] Fertilizer that could restore much of the soil's fertility was not in heavy use because of its cost. It was even prohibitively expensive for most of Niumi's farmers to rent cattle for nighttime tethering in fields to provide dung.

There turned out to be few viable responses to Niumi's chronic labor shortage. For nearly all of its existence, Niumi has had a small population. Since the peanut boom of the mid-nineteenth century, strange farmers filled in during the rainy season, migrating to Niumi to make a crop and then returning home. By the 1990s, however, this had become a thing of the past. Strange farmers stopped venturing into Niumi during the hard years of the 1980s. The unprofitability of farming, coupled with the possibility of finding more lucrative work in urban areas, put an almost complete halt to agricultural labor migration.[39] So who were the primary workers in Niumi's fields by the mid-1990s? They were the remaining village men of working age, men beyond the normal age for farming, boys younger than once considered appropriate for farm work, and, especially, women.

Women were having a particularly rough go of it. Some men found it possible to act in response to the decline of soil fertility by using ox-plows to plant larger fields with less labor, switching their energies to growing drought- and animal-resistant cassava or planting fruit trees. Mangos, which bear fruit after five years, turned out to be especially popular. A small number of men, recognizing the importance of women's contribution to household food supplies from their rice fields, looked after children. But none took up food preparation or helped with the production of rice. Conversely, women in Niumi tended to shy away from machines—looking on such as in man's domain—and their rice farming, often on small plots that trapped rainwater during the summer and early fall, did not lend itself to mechanization. Niumi's women, who were important providers for their families, still did virtually all of their farming by hand, bending at the waist to work in the rice. Development projects financed by the Peoples Republic of China, Taiwan, the World Bank, the United States, and Great Britain, even some aimed specifically at improving rural women's lot, did not have beneficial results. "It seems this project is just like the Chinese one when we suffered before," said one Gambian woman on learning of another foreign-sponsored effort.[40]

By the mid-1970s, drought had so reduced food production and so devastated livestock herds that Gambians in rural areas were having to resort to desperate measures—migration to cities or change in existing agricultural and herding practices, for instance—to ward off starvation. Even with food-aid assistance from international donors, hunger was an element of life that nearly every adult villager had to deal with. In places, the drought conditions meant there was not sufficient rainfall to counteract the intrusion of salt into the women's low-lying rice fields. Faced with dwindling food resources and unable to grow their traditional subsistence crop, women began turning to vegetable gardening, not simply the "kitchen gardening" long done in the rainy season to supplement the family diet, but dry-season, hand-irrigated, commodity production in communal gardens, many of them located on no-longer-productive rice fields on the outskirts of villages.

At the time rural Gambian women were taking this initiative, in the mid-1970s, the United Nations declared an International Decade for Women, which brought aid agencies to adopt "Women in Development" (WID) strategies for increasing food production and fostering rural development in the world's poorest countries. Gambian women tapped into funding from these agencies to pay for well-digging, fencing, tools, and seeds, and within a few years there were productive gardens around many Niumi villages. Women gardeners found they could not only add vegetables to the meals they prepared—turning in a healthy direction the typical Gambian diet of rice, small portions of meat or fish, and oil—but also sell vegetables in village and regional markets and thus have cash at their disposal.

The gardens were a promising aspect of women's lives, but the gardens required

Photo 12   **Women drawing water at a large garden in rural Gambia.**

especially hard work. To grow vegetables throughout the long dry season, the plants had to be watered twice per day, morning and evening. The water came from wells that might be as close as fifty feet or as far away as 500 feet. The women garden-ers had to draw up the water, hand over hand; fill as large a receptacle as they could carry; tote the receptacle atop their heads to their garden plots; fill watering cans; and then water the plants. It all showed remarkable enterprise through hard times, but it still meant having to work laboriously while remaining responsible for childrearing, food preparation, and other household duties without prospect of assistance or relief.[41]

Of course, there were some changes for the better. Part of the reason the popula-tion began to grow at such an astonishing clip, doubling between 1975 and 1995, was related to greater longevity and lower rates of child mortality. Life expectancy at birth was about forty-two years in 1990, up from thirty-two in 1960, and the mortality rate of children under five was 241 per thousand, down from 375 per thousand in 1960.[42] Access to more modern health and maternity care was greater in Niumi in the early 1990s than ever before. In 1988, amid considerable fanfare, President Jawara laid the foundation stone for a £300,000 health center in Essau, funded by a grant from the British Overseas Development Administration. That, an officially designated Minor Health Center in Kuntair, and a dispensary at Medina Bafuloto served the entire Niumi population before 1994.[43]

Greater access to education and improved health care were the most promising aspects of people's lives in Niumi approaching the mid-1990s. But otherwise, the outlook was dim. In 1994 nearly one-third of Gambian imports consisted of food. As the country's trade fell off, it became necessary for the government to cut the annual budget by 23 percent, with some of the cuts coming in health care and education. Even before this the UNDP, which publishes a Human Development Index based on longevity, knowledge, and living standards, had The Gambia ranked second from the last, 159 out of the world's 160 nations.[44] This ranking included the 30 percent of the country's population living around the capital city, where longevity, knowledge, and living standards were each considerably higher than in Niumi. Few believed that the widespread change that had come to the region since independence had improved people's lives.

The country's president was the focus of dissatisfaction, naturally enough, and this grew after his electoral victory in 1992, when the lively Gambian press began reporting on government corruption. High officials in Jawara's government had been raking off funds from the Gambia Cooperative Union, which marketed peanuts. (Relating the breadth of corruption in the government to Jawara's old boast of all the country's cows knowing him personally, one Gambian remarked, "If there are cows in Gambia who know Jawara personally, they are very rich cows.") Though evidence did not show conclusively that the president had enriched himself at state expense, news articles noted that Jawara had been collecting ridiculously large per diems while vacationing for long periods in Europe—something that did not fit at all with his "one of us" image among underfed Gambians in rural communities. On top of these matters, resentment bubbled up through the civil service and the army, especially over tardy paychecks.

Niumi farmer Jerre Manneh was like many others at the time who found himself in the unlikely position of looking back favorably on colonial days: "No one wants to be ruled by someone else," he said, "but things were cheap before independence and people were not so hungry . . . We had thirty years of nothing . . . Corruption [under Jawara] was everywhere . . . President, ministers, MPs, all of them . . . took our money."[45]

From Manneh's front porch to similar vantage points at the far end of the country, and from office workers' cubicles to market stalls and military mess halls in and around the capital, people were unhappy in the spring of 1994. As rice became more expensive, as salaries of bureaucrats were being paid weeks late, and as prospects for better circumstances seemed as dim as they had ever been, people's patience with the government of the PPP under Jawara, the only government the republic had known since 1965, was growing thinner by the day.

8

NIUMI IN THE RECENT WAVE OF GLOBALIZATION

The Second Republic, 1994–2009

Globalization reduces poverty, but not everywhere.
—The World Bank, 2002

No coup d'état or elections can remove me.
—His Excellency President Sheikh
Professor Alhaji Dr. Yahya Jammeh, 2006

On the morning of July 22, 1994, people living in Niumi got out of bed, prayed, ate their porridge, went to the fields or to the shop, cooked and cleaned, and went about their business as they would on any other hot, humid, rainy-season day. But this was not any ordinary day: before it was over, they had a new national government. Beginning around daybreak on the 22nd, four junior officers in The Gambia National Army organized a coup d'état that, within a matter of hours and without spilling any blood, gave them control of the country's governing apparatus. Assuming power was the Armed Forces Provisional Ruling Council, headed by the highest-ranking of the four coup planners, a twenty-nine-year-old high-school graduate named Yahya Jammeh.

Coups are always anathema to stable nations, but this one, in a country considered one of Africa's few working democracies and coming on the heels of two decades that saw sixty countries take steps toward more representative government, brought particularly stern criticism. The people most affected, Gambia's citizens, were less critical, and some were almost euphoric.[1] The two decades of drought had been wearing on Gambia's population, disgust with the Jawara government was widespread, and the young officers now in charge were making promising statements about ending corruption, providing opportunities for youth, and promoting rural development. People asked: could life under a new government, whatever its genesis, be any worse?

Fifteen years after the coup, in 2009, a quieted and sobered Gambian population had its answer: life, indeed, could be worse. Under international pressure, The Gambia returned to an elected government under a new constitution in 1996, but Jammeh steadily assumed greater power and used it to keep himself and his party in control. With a security apparatus that acted with impunity and a president who increasingly showed disregard for the constitution, the rule of law, and human rights, The Gambia moved toward becoming a police state, with Jammeh as its dictator. Citizens were rounded up for no clear reason, detained for long periods, and tortured; protesting students were shot and killed; gays were threatened with beheading; and journalists were harassed, detained, and eventually held for long periods under trumped-up charges, with one "disappearing" and another murdered, leading to a stifling of the once-free press. Meanwhile, Jammeh was amassing great wealth, flashing a résumé that listed bogus awards, and astonishing the world's medical community with a claim that among the several diseases he could cure was HIV/AIDS. Some interpreted his actions as signs of megalomania; others saw them as evidence of mental derangement.[2]

All this was taking place against a backdrop of a recent wave of globalization that, according to theorists, was supposed to spread prosperity to the developing world and thwart the very kind of oppression that Gambians were suffering. But after fifteen years of The Gambia's so-called Second Republic, the only part of globalization that appeared promising to many residents of Niumi was their enhanced ability to leave the country. Every week, men and women paid to board leaky boats that crept out of a Niumi creek to begin a dangerous journey toward a European promised land. If a boat reached its destination, the refugees would try to sneak in, find housing, and locate menial jobs that would allow them to buy food and, in time, send money home to their struggling families.

Jammeh's tyrannical rule tests the idea that globalization and global influences are the most important factors determining how people live in a very small place in Africa. As the Gambian dalasi loses value against other world currencies and the price of imported rice and gasoline continues an upward climb, police with automatic rifles threaten riders in bush taxis at road checks and armed soldiers storm into homes and whisk people away for interrogation, illegal detention, or even such archaic practices as witchcraft exorcism. After considering the circumstances of their lives in 2009, people living in Niumi are hard-pressed to answer which has a bigger effect on their lives: the global or the local.

Globalization's Newest Wave

"Globalization has happened before, but not like this," wrote a team of World Bank economic experts in 2002.[3] "Not like this" referred to the speed and extent of global economic and social integration over the previous dozen years. Globalization was a slow-moving train through most of the twentieth century, but it became a high-speed express in the late 1980s, and even the global recession of 2008–2009 does not seem to be slowing it appreciably.

The event that may have had the greatest long-term effect on the lives of people living on earth at the end of the twentieth century occurred in 1989 in Berlin. In November of that year, thousands of people forced open crossing points of the Berlin Wall and then demolished the concrete monstrosity that for thirty-four years had separated the two Germanies and, in a larger sense, the West from regions of

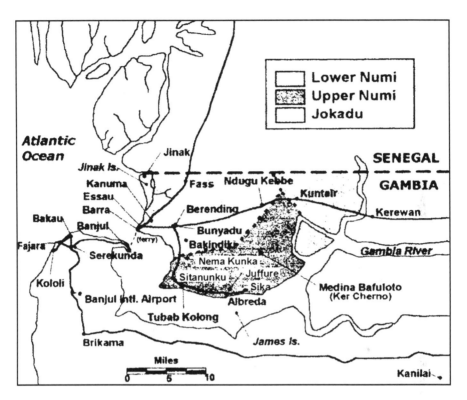

Map 10 **Niumi, 2010**

the world under Soviet influence. The wall's destruction did not begin the collapse of Soviet communism and the ending of the Cold War—both had been under way for some time—but the wall's demolition serves as a symbol for the opening of the world following nearly half a century of its artificial division. The economic reform that swept over China in the 1990s further reduced barriers separating people and nations.

Building strength in the 1980s and readying its further spread with the Cold War's end was the economic system of the world outside the wall: capitalism. As communist and socialist systems were weakening prior to the wall's dismantling, capitalism was gaining vigor and direction through policies being implemented in the world's wealthiest nations and carried out by international organizations. British prime minister Margaret Thatcher and U.S. president Ronald Reagan ushered in the new policies, leading away from the Keynesian model of economics, popular since the Great Depression, wherein government directed and helped finance the economy, and back toward the model of Adam Smith, champion of natural forces acting freely in an unfettered market. Already in place to help spread these policies were the World Bank and the International Monetary Fund (IMF), each financed by Western capital and controlled by individuals aligned with Western governments. The 1980s thus saw these organizations become blatant pushers of free-market ideology, insisting on economic liberalization in existing capitalist countries and opening markets in those falling away from Soviet influence. Helping to implement these changes was an institutional framework to promote free trade and curtail national protectionism in the form of the General Agreement on Tariffs and Trade (GATT), replaced in 1994 by the World Trade Organization (WTO), which had more members and broader authority to oversee trade negotiations. Regional agreements among nations to join their economies—as in the European Union (EU), the North American Free-Trade Agreement (NAFTA), and the Economic Community of West African States (ECOWAS)—worked to open trade even more. All these changes amounted to a powerful force in a world system ripe for restructuring with the Cold War's demise. The result through the 1980s and early 1990s was the steady integration of national and regional economies. More and more people began to recognize and speak in terms of "economic globalization."[4]

What helped speed along this new wave of economic integration was the revolution in information storage and retrieval—the computer, based on fast-working, tiny microchips—and telecommunications—based on fiber optics, satellites, the Internet, and portable tools for access. These innovations not only increased the speed by which actors in the world economy could gather information and make decisions, but also the number of people who could be involved and the scope of their involvement.

The international lending institutions served as a catalyst for the spread of globalization by stepping up their insistence that countries needing economic aid take specific actions to qualify for new loans or tempting debt-reduction programs. As before, these actions typically included such measures as balancing budgets, making currencies convertible, keeping inflation low, weeding out corruption, and reducing the size and scope of government by ending public ownership of utilities, industries, banks, and telecommunications systems. A fundamental idea behind these requirements was that countries meeting them would be open to foreign investors looking to place the huge amounts of capital they controlled. Indeed, one of the major characteristics of the new wave of globalization was that large amounts of capital moved into and out of nations with ease and speed. This was because the same computer and telecommunications technology that was enabling persons in one country to communicate almost instantly with persons in another also was allowing investors to compare economic conditions of one country with another, minute by minute, and, if the conditions were more favorable in one, to move their investments in a flash.

If big global investors moved money into a country or if a multinational corporation decided a country was a prime site for manufacturing or for a service center, then that country experienced economic growth. Conversely, if investors considered a country too big a risk and withdrew investments or if a multinational corporation decided to build its factory someplace else where profits promised to be less elusive, then the country losing the investments or never getting the factory faced hard times. This is what happened, on a growing scale, over the 1990s and for the first years of the twenty-first century.[5]

No one disputes that globalization improved the living circumstances of many, especially in such rapidly developing "new globalizers" as Brazil, China, India, and Mexico. But countries holding the bottom billion of the world's people, concentrated in Africa and Central Asia, have missed the chance of globalization-enhanced development. People in these countries "coexist with the twenty-first century," writes Paul Collier, former director of Development Research at the World Bank, "but their reality is the fourteenth century. . . . Even during the 1990s, in retrospect the golden decade . . . , incomes in this group declined by 5 percent." As most people in most countries are enjoying longer lives, better health, higher incomes, and greater opportunities for schooling, "much of the rest of the developing world . . . is becoming marginalized."[6]

The leaders of the World Bank, the IMF, and the WTO cling to a free-trade dogma that is unproven as a remedy for extreme poverty. These agencies' realm is defined by statistics and long-range forecasts; they are staffed by smart economists, trained at the best Western institutions and with experience in government and private trade; and they champion measures they profess are likely, under favorable circumstances, to lead countries—especially those with resources, capital, and infrastructure—toward economic growth, which they regard as the engine of development. But rather than help the world's poorest nations, the prescriptions these organizations offer have, over the years, benefited the capital-rich countries that provide them their leadership and financial backing. The global economic designers express a belief that by making the prescribed economic and political changes, the developing nations will be helping themselves as well as stimulating the world economy, while at the same time brightening the prospects of those in core nations who have capital to invest. Not everyone has agreed. Since the late 1990s, protests over World Bank, IMF, and WTO activities have regularly disrupted the organizations' meetings on several continents.[7]

Of course, economics is not the only manifestation of globalization that has brought change to the world. For some time now, people have simply been moving around the earth with greater ease and less expense than ever before. Many are more willing to relocate because they can easily and cheaply keep in touch with family and loved ones back home—through telephone (including the free service Skype), e-mail, texting, and tweeting. Once established in a foreign country, where even a job at minimum wage may provide ten or twenty times what a person might make back home, it is now easy and inexpensive to send money to the most distant spots on the globe—by wire transfer, by courier, or, more recently, by informal trust networks among fellow nationals. Sometimes a person most helps the family by leaving, finding employment overseas, and sending home a monthly stipend.

On top of these realities, globalization is speeding up social and cultural change.

The computer, the cell phone, and the Internet have brought many more people in closer and faster touch with one another, and their ways of thinking and doing are changing as a result.

What all these changes mean for life in Niumi, and whether or not globalization's effects on people living there are, on the whole, positive or negative, are matters of dispute. As this book attempts to show, for centuries people living in that small region along the Gambia River have been changing as a result of their relationships to a widening world. It argues, too, that the place of Niumi in larger economic systems has been a critical factor—often *the* critical factor—in determining how people in the region lived. If the newest wave of globalization results in keeping Niumi on the periphery, dependent on impersonal market forces, its residents incapable of competing with people and institutions in the wealthier nations, then one would have to conclude that globalization is not for Niumi's poor, which is just about everyone living there.

Soldier to Statesman to Tyrant

Once word spread around Niumi about what had happened across the river on July 22, 1994—that a group of junior officers of The Gambia's army had ousted the only president the country had ever elected and was handling government business by caveat of a military council—people were cautiously hopeful. After the new government had arrested corrupt officials of the former government, built a new secondary school in Essau, put resources into agriculture, and built a paved road across Niumi, people were happier with their leaders than they had been in a long time. But once growth slowed in the world economy and Gambians began feeling the effects, once corruption stormed back into government ranks, once the newly elected president began spending great sums on a fleet of expensive cars for himself and his ministers and on his palatial residence while civil servants were not being paid on time, and especially once the president began gathering great power in his office, violating the country's new constitution and tearing away at citizens' human and civil rights, Niumi residents began realizing they were not just experiencing more of the same, but were under the oppressive yoke of a tyrant. Now, however, they were afraid to say so.

By all accounts, the 1994 coup was almost spontaneous, planned only the night before. The plotters' grievances were military in nature—they were angry with Nigerian officers who held senior positions in The Gambia National Army—and they shared with the public a growing resentment of the corrupt and out-of-touch Jawara regime. Aided by a planned training exercise with U.S. Marines that allowed them access to army weapons and vehicles, the soldiers rushed to take over the national airport, the radio station, and the State House. Jawara and his family were hustled off to an American LST, which was on hand for the exercises, and the soldiers detained senior government officials. By late afternoon, Radio Gambia was announcing that the Armed Forces Provisional Ruling Council was in charge with the virtually unknown Yahya Jammeh at its head.[8]

The Gambians' stoic acceptance of the coup can be attributed to the beaten-down state of the country's population, mired in poverty and lacking any real hope for better lives, on top of their dissatisfaction with their existing government. Underscored by a quarter-century of drought, the period since independence had seen other long-poor and once-colonized nations surge ahead while The Gambia remained near the bottom (ranked 166 out of 173 nations in the 1994 UN Human Development Index) in all comparative measures. Vacationing in the United Kingdom on the Gambian people's tab, Jawara seemed neither to know what to do nor to care.[9]

The response of Western nations looking to solidify existing democracies and establish new ones was hardly stoic. The United States suspended all aid to The Gambia, the British Foreign and Commonwealth Office advised tourists to stay away, and a host of nongovernmental agencies and charities packed up and left. Because tourism by this time had become a vital part of the Gambian economy, the country suffered through several years of canceled reservations, hotel closings, layoffs, and consequent budget pinches. Aid from a handful of Islamic countries was important in sustaining The Gambia through these rough times.[10]

Eventually, in the face of international pressure, the ruling council oversaw a modification of the country's 1970 constitution, which the public ratified in August 1996, and soon afterward held elections. Recently retired from the army (after rapid promotion to colonel), Jammeh was elected the first president of the new Second Republic, and his new party, the Alliance for Patriotic Reorientation and Construction (APRC), gained a majority of the seats in the National Assembly. The government's major opponents were in jail during this period, journalists were not free to speak their minds, and individuals who opposed the APRC were threatened and knocked around, so only the most partisan government supporters claimed that the elections were fair. But continuing international pressure pushed Jammeh to release some of his potential opponents from detention, relax some of the press restrictions, and allow opposition political parties to form prior to new elections. That he permitted these parties to organize only a few months before a scheduled voting in 2001 prompted the major opposition party to boycott the elections, thus helping return Jammeh to the presidency and giving him an enormous APRC majority in the National Assembly.[11]

If not the first step, this election was the biggest one along the road toward tyranny. From this time on, the government and the ruling party were indistinguishable, and as head of both, Jammeh increasingly controlled all. He would make a decision on an issue and then the National Assembly would take whatever action the president directed. Debate on legislation of national importance soon became limited to the reasoned voice of one or two opposition assembly members, with APRC members not bothering to respond, followed by an overwhelming vote as the party leader had directed. The president also began firing ministers, chiefs, and justices with impunity, that latter in violation of constitutional prohibitions, so the only judges who remained were persons eager to do his bidding.[12]

Photo 13 **"In Jammeh We Trust": Painting on a building in the center of a Niumi village.**

Ironically, about the only things constraining the new Gambian government were guidelines set out by the IMF and World Bank. In 1996 these institutions, in an effort to ensure "that no poor country faces a debt burden it cannot manage," created a Heavily Indebted Poor Countries (HIPC) initiative.[13] With 31.6 percent of its annual expenditures going to service its $450 million debt, The Gambia was the very kind of country this program was designed for. The initiative promised to reduce The Gambia's debt by one-fifth once it reached a prescribed "completion point," which required privatizing state enterprises, halting subsidization of commodities, and levying fewer and lower duties on imports (lowering the maximum tariff from 90 percent to 18 percent). To make up for lost revenue while continuing to have money for another HIPC requirement and improved social services, the government had to raise taxes paid by its already impoverished people. This was much to ask any leader of a very poor country, let alone one intent on becoming personally wealthy as quickly as possible.

And feather his nest Jammeh did, steadily, persistently, inexorably. As Gambians struggled to find food to meet minimum human requirements, funds poured into Jammeh's home town of Kanilai, a once-tiny and insignificant village located on the southern border with Senegal, sixty-five miles southwest of Banjul, turning it into one of the only rural Gambian villages to have electricity, street lighting, paved roads, and running water—not to mention its own zoo and game preserve, wrestling arena, bakery, and luxury hotel with swimming pool. Friends and cronies of Jammeh lived well; most others continued to struggle.[14] Beyond the president's rhetoric (and not counting Kanilai), there is scant evidence that Jammeh ever intended to do much to improve the working and living conditions of people living in rural areas like Niumi.

For a time, much of the criticism of Jammeh focused on his lack of social graces, his blatant efforts to gain support (such as, on campaign trips, giving money to school principals to throw parties for students or simply tossing money to children as he passed by), and such out-and-out foolish schemes as building the zoo in Kanilai.[15] It took longer for Gambians to recognize that the president had no idea how to proceed toward improving the national economy. In the 2002–2003 growing season, when insufficient rains caused pathetic harvests—peanut production was off 47 percent from the previous year, swamp rice down 74 percent, coarse grain down 31 percent, and the quality of all nuts and grains so low that none could be used for seeds—Jammeh persisted in blaming the laziness and idleness of Gambian men and their propensity to engage in soccer matches when they should be growing crops. He even banned the popular rainy-season soccer games—something, a few critics fruitlessly pointed out, he had no constitutional or legal right to do—so that young men would concentrate on farming. He insisted for a while that Gambians focus on subsistence crops so the country could achieve food self-sufficiency. Then, in an abrupt turn, he told the National Assembly in March 2003 that "the current policy is to shift away from subsistence agriculture to a more dynamic, commercially oriented production aimed at making farming a viable business undertaking."[16] Less than a year later, in a speech to all Gambians, the president announced discovery of oil in Gambian waters and very likely on land, offering the "potential of turning the smallest country into the richest country on earth." Five years after that, in 2009, BBC News reported that in spite of Jammeh's desire to give The Gambia a "new future" based on petroleum exporting, "the country has yet to strike crude oil."[17]

In the meantime, as he gained greater power, the president seemed to feel threat-

---

Perspective 17   **Shades of Colonial Days in the Second Republic**

Under colonial rúle, farmers in Niumi got blamed for being lazy when they had bad harvests: "Get out of your rut or get under!" shouted the commissioner after a poor crop yield in 1920. Colonial officials also regularly required villages to provide workers for uncompensated labor on colonial projects: road building, well digging, rubbish removal, or the much-hated porterage. Both actions raised people's ire. Now, however, long after Gambia has become independent, are Gambians equally angry when the independent nation's government says and does similar things?

In 2003, following meager rains and a poor harvest, President Jammeh blamed the low yields on the laziness of Gambian men generally and the propensity of young Gambian men specifically to sit idly in urban streets when they should be out working in the fields. "Go back to the land!" he told Gambian youth repeatedly. A few years later, managing scores of large farms around the country given to him by chiefs, who gain and keep their positions by pleasing him, Jammeh called on villages to send workers to weed and harvest the farms' crops. Pressure to heed the call came through village heads and local political functionaries. "When they say to work, everyone has to go," said a resident of one Niumi village. "You have to have a really good excuse to get out it." To transport workers from villages to the fields (as well as to transport harvested produce from the farms), Jammeh uses government vehicles. These are not public or communal farms: the president considers them his own. Profit from the sale of the produce comes to him and he donates all or part of it—the lack of any public accounting makes it impossible to determine much about the foundation's finances—to the Jammeh Foundation for Peace, from whose coffers he doles out grants to villages that support him politically so they can purchase vehicles and tools or dig wells and build fences.

Ironically, farmers in Niumi during colonial times were freer to voice complaints about their government than they are now. Villagers today know they are best off saying little. When summoned to work, most simply cast their eyes downward, climb onto the government truck, and spend the day toiling in the president's fields, just as their great-grandparents did when the colonial commissioner insisted.

---

ened by anyone opposing him or his government. State security forces, the National Intelligence Agency in particular, did his bidding, and the violence they inflicted on Gambians knew no precedent in the country's history. In 2000, when young people gathered to protest an alleged torture-death of one fellow student and an alleged rape of another, security forces fired into the crowd, killing fourteen students and a journalist. Since then, the record of illegal detentions, disappearances, murders, harassment, and arrests for trumped-up crimes has grown to frightening propor-

Photo 14 **The *Kanilai*, carrying passengers and vehicles from Barra to Banjul.**

tions. "Fear now reigns in Gambia," Amnesty International's Tania Bernath wrote in November 2008, "where any person considered to be a perceived enemy of the government is at risk of being arrested, tortured and even killed."[18]

In such an atmosphere, and with Jammeh controlling all branches of government, state radio and television, and even the (inappropriately named) Independent Election Commission and handing out tractors and farm implements to villages he considers sufficiently supportive while denying favors to others, elections hold little meaning. In 2006, nearly half of Gambia's registered voters did not bother to vote. The president repeatedly and audaciously pledges to bury "six feet under" anyone who opposes him and vows to remain in office for the next forty years: "elections and coup d'états cannot remove me from power," he says openly.[19]

Through all of Jammeh's enhancement of his wealth and power, people in Niumi are glad, perhaps for the first time, that a wide river separates them from the seat of national government. They trudge to their farms and gardens, scour the countryside for firewood, and otherwise go about their lives. As they watch and listen, trying to figure out which government-recommended agricultural pursuit might serve them best, how many dalasi they will need to travel to the regional market, or from whom they can borrow enough to pay this year's tax or the doubled fee to sell vegetables in the market, Niumi villagers are aware of one thing about globalization: so far, it is not making their lives any better, and, if it somehow is related to government actions, it might be playing a big role in making them worse.

Is Globalization Good for the World's Poor? Niumi as a Case Study

The Economy

Anyone visiting a collection of people in The Gambia today sees a remarkable range of enterprise. Around the populated capital region exists a buzz of activity. Women fruit sellers beckon like sirens from their stalls, the smells of meat-and-oil sandwiches fill the air, the bread-delivery man rides by with fifty loaves tied to his bicycle, taxi drivers beep and wave to gain the attention of potential riders, and young men (and, at night, women) sidle up and begin conversations, hoping they can find a service to provide. Life is quieter in rural villages, but the same level of enterprise is there. Knots of people mill around village shops, which can take on the look of a foxhole with a shopkeeper on guard duty behind fifty-kilogram bags of rice. *Lumolu* (regional markets) rotate among villages, and on a market day people come from all over to buy and sell food, livestock, cloth and clothing, hides, batteries, animal parts for making jujus—you name it. There are even stalls for auto repair. Behind compounds and outside villages Gambians have devised ingenious modes of production: on the east side of Medina Bafuloto, one man has cobbled together a device to saw boards out of tree trunks using a truck's diesel engine and metal arms, levers, belts, and pulleys welded and connected with who knows what, the saw cutting to the millimeter and the lumber cured and sold or made into furniture. But in most considerations of the Gambian economy, such operations exist below the line of sight. Profit margins in many are thinner than people from more developed countries can comprehend.

The standard view that Gambia's Gross Domestic Product (GDP) has three main parts—peanut production, reexporting, and services (largely tourism)—is now not entirely true. The Gambian government is no longer forthcoming about such matters, but from other sources—some of which, admittedly, are as reliable as holding up a wet finger in the wind—one gets a sense that the economic times are changing. To different degrees, all parts of the change affect men and women in Niumi, and all are tied into a much wider world.

Peanuts remain important in Niumi, but for a number of reasons not nearly as important as they once were. In a pattern that harks back to early colonial times, men in Niumi grow peanuts in order to obtain cash to pay taxes and buy imported rice. These days, they need money also for such modern necessities as flashlight batteries, transportation to (and gifts for) a cousin's naming ceremony, scratch cards for the cell phone, and payment of children's school fees. For most men, growing peanuts has long been the only way to produce something to sell.

Of late, the global market for peanuts has seemed stacked against this very kind of enterprise. The market has weakened because of reductions in peanut use due to allergies; fears of aflatoxin, a cancer-causing chemical produced by molds that can develop in peanuts; and most recently fears of salmonella in processing plants. Another problem for Gambian growers in particular is quality. The cocktail-peanut market is a big one, but Gambian peanuts are too small for such use. Adding to the problem is that the largest market for peanuts in the world, the United States, remains largely closed. Recent reforms in a Depression-era quota system of tariffs and price supports have been counterbalanced by agreements in NAFTA that opened the U.S. market to Canadian brands of peanut butter and Mexican raw peanuts.[20]

Not all the blame for declining peanut production in Niumi falls on global circumstances, however. For Gambian farmers, drought and a growing population are twin barrels of a gun aimed at their basic, cash-producing enterprise. As Niumi's population grows, villagers need more cropland. One way to get it is to cut trees and clear more fields, a process that changes Niumi's landscape and contributes further to the reduction of rainfall. Another way is to reduce the length of time fields are left fallow, from twenty years to three or four, relying on fertilizer to replace the soil's nutrients. Growing peanuts presently requires expensive chemical fertilizer. Gambia's government subsidized fertilizer imports before the 1980s, but this did not help farmers much because traders bought the fertilizer in The Gambia and sold it at profit across the border in Senegal, where there were no government subsidies. When the economic recovery program put an end to subsidies, fertilizer became almost prohibitively expensive, especially since the farmers needed it in July and August, when they were at their poorest and their families at their hungriest.[21]

Making matters worse were frustrations related to the Gambian government's apparent ambivalence over peanut marketing. For the first twenty years of independence, the government played a major role in price setting and marketing; then, under forced structural adjustment, it exited the arena, calling economic liberalization "the life belt of both food and cash crop production." In 1996, with peanut revenues and food production declining, the Jammeh-led government complained that "privatization, credit and interest rates of liberalization, and removal of subsidies [are] impacting negatively on the agricultural sector," and in 1998 it seized the assets of the largest peanut-marketing firm in The Gambia, owned by a Swiss firm, Alimenta, with an eye toward once again managing the process.[22] This was not to the liking of the institutions of international finance that were holding out the carrot of debt reduction, however, so the government had to pay Alimenta for its hasty action. Since then, government-run marketing of peanuts has been, in a word, disastrous. For half a dozen years the government purchased peanuts on credit and forced growers to wait, sometimes until the next harvest season was approaching, to redeem their chits. Many farmers had to remove their children from school until they could get the money from their peanuts. After watching peanut exports dwindle and feeling "the hot breath of farmers," the government ended buying on credit in 2008. Private buyers in the field, however, lacked cash and were unable to secure loans from either the government or wary bankers, so peanut buying ground to a halt. Lacking options, some farmers in Niumi loaded up their peanuts and hauled them across the border to sell in Senegal. Their only alternative was to let the nuts rot.[23]

For his part—and his part is big, since he personally took over the Ministry of

Agriculture in 2008—President Jammeh uses the peanut issue as a tool to garner political support. He promises free seed nuts and fertilizers to farmers living in villages that support him in elections and, when not threatening young Gambian men that they must go "back to the land" and hack out a peanut crop, offers tax concessions to "wealthy citizens" willing to engage in large-scale agricultural production.[24] Niumi's farmers, who are neither wealthy nor able to grow anything on a large scale, find such actions confusing and hurtful.

Trying to remain hopeful, persons inside and outside the government found optimism in commercial prospects after the U.S. ambassador to The Gambia, Jackson McDonald, announced in February 2003 the inclusion of The Gambia under the terms of the African Growth and Opportunity Act (AGOA), American legislation enacted in 2000 "to stimulate economic development in Africa and to integrate African economies more fully into the global economy."[25] Thirty-seven sub-Saharan African countries are now included under this act, which offers duty-free importing into the United States of approximately 7,000 products. To continue inclusion under AGOA, African nations need to make "satisfactory progress" toward the typical IMF and World Bank economic goals: move toward a market-based economy, eliminate trade and investment barriers, combat corruption, protect workers' rights, and advance policies to reduce poverty. (Gambia's bid advanced rapidly after 2002, when it nabbed and handed over to the United States a suspected terrorist.) But for The Gambia, inclusion in AGOA never amounted to much. The act turned out to benefit only half a dozen African countries, mainly through oil exports. None of the exports on the long AGOA list are produced in The Gambia, and the AGOA information site reads, "little scope seems to exist for any rapid expansion of [Gambian] exports to the US."[26]

In recent years, especially as the peanut trade has declined, most Gambian exports have been reexports, mostly basic consumer goods. Though difficult to track and not charted in official statistics, the reexport trade, according to estimates, has contributed in some years to as much as one-third of The Gambia's GDP. Men and women in Niumi remain positioned to take advantage of this commerce with several weekly *lumolu*, the popular regional markets, occurring within a few miles of the Senegalese border and with the road from Barra north to Senegal, toward Dakar's market of 2.5 million people, entirely reconstructed in 2009.

When the reexport trade is thriving, there is an unmistakable bustle in Niumi's markets and along the road northward, but this is not always the case. A government plan in 1999 to monitor imports more closely in order to raise customs revenues brought a 22.5 percent drop in Banjul port traffic in one month and disrupted the reexport trade for half a year, until the close scrutiny ceased. Rocky relations with Senegal do not help. Receiving Gambian reexports does not please Senegal's government, since the trade undermines its effort to build local industry and cuts its customs revenues, so from time to time it clamps down at border crossings and delays movement of goods. People in Niumi are thus ill-advised to count on a thriving reexport trade. A UNDP-sponsored study in 2008 calls the future of this trade "cloudy" because of efforts at "tariff harmonization, crackdowns on unofficial trade, and efforts of other countries to increase their share of intra-regional trade."[27]

Some Niumi residents join other Gambians in hoping that an expanding tourism industry can be the engine for the region's economic improvement. In 2007–2008 nearly 140,000 tourists came to The Gambia, mainly from the United Kingdom, Germany, The Netherlands, and Scandinavia. Tourists bring a lot of money and spend it freely—in 2008, tourism accounted for nearly 18 percent of Gambia's GDP, surpassing peanut exports as the country's biggest earner of foreign exchange—but the majority of tourists come on package tours paid for in Europe, where the money stays. One in seven jobs in The Gambia is in the tourist sector, and these jobs pay better than most others.[28]

Only a handful more tourists come to Niumi than came ten years ago. In 1996, suffering from the drop in the tourist trade following world reactions to the military takeover, Gambia's Ministry of Tourism and Culture created a "Roots Heritage Festival," a several-weeks-long series of events in June (near the start of the rains, when tourists do not ordinarily visit) to commemorate Alex Haley's saga, *Roots*, and highlight Gambian history and culture. The ministry saw to the tidying up of James Island, constructed a silver statue near Juffure's wharf that calls attention to the plight of slaves shipped from there, and built a small slave-trade museum nearby. Initially, more tours brought sightseers to Niumi's southern riverside, but the heightened interest did not last. The Roots Festival quickly became more of a celebration of Gambian culture in the capital area (and Kanilai), with parades, music, wrestling matches, dancing, displays of artwork, and nighttime masquerades. Those tourists who actually ventured to Juffure did not spend much time or money there, not even after construction of a small hotel overlooking the river west of Juffure in 2006. U.S. Peace Corps volunteer Brooke Oppenheimer, who lived right behind Juffure during the festival period of 2002, seldom saw a tourist. "They go from the boat to the *alkalo*'s [village head's], then to the Kintes' [the family from which Haley claimed descent], then back to the boat," she said. "It barely takes half an hour. They leave a little money with the Kintes and maybe buy a soft drink; then they're gone." In fact, some of the visits did more harm than good. One government-trained tourist guide told a group visiting James Island in 1998 to keep a keen eye on the ground for beads, suggesting that such relics from the slave-trade era made nice souvenirs. The Gambian law that prohibits removal of objects from such sites is openly ignored.[29]

This incident points toward one of the many dilemmas facing the Gambian government in relation to tourism. It wants to protect the country's rich natural heritage—Gambia has exceptional habitats for wildlife as well as pristine beaches, natural waterways, and wetlands—while at the same time expanding tourism and thereby adding hard currency to its meager holdings and providing jobs for local residents. But the two goals seem mutually exclusive. So far, the government has dealt with the dilemma by passing some of the world's most admirable wildlife-protection laws and creating several national parks and protected areas, but then, as with so much else, failing to enforce the laws or do what is necessary to protect the parks. Niumi National Park is the best example. Created by the government a decade ago, the park consists of nineteen square miles that include Jinak Island, at Niumi's western edge, and adjacent mainland. The park's resident caretaker and park booster, Jibril Camara, is quick to list the rules protecting the park's habitat and wildlife: no cutting of trees, no killing of animals, no kindling of fires, and only carefully regulated fishing. But on a ride through the park (over a road of deep sand gouged by deeper ruts), one sees Africans hacking down trees and burning brush. A man apprehended after slaughtering a dolphin off Jinak Island was allowed to take the dolphin's carcass and proceed on his way when he pleaded ignorance of the law and promised not to do it again. And Japanese trawlers take massive loads of fish from the rich Atlantic waters off Jinak. Residents of the Niumi village of Kanuma, whose ancestors owned the land that makes up the mainland portion of the park, do not recognize the government's claim. Kanuma elder Buba Sonko says, "There is no park. No such thing exists. That land belongs to Kanuma. We grow crops there, we graze cattle there, we fish those waters, just as we always have. Some government officials have been coming here to discuss the park idea with us. We said, 'No, the land is ours and we do not want a park here,' so they left. We continue to till the land and use it as we see fit."[30]

Caretaker Camara shares the government's desire to develop land in the park for tourism. "There is nothing else to do here," he says. "Our youth are just sitting around." He knows what the government knows: that Jinak's Atlantic beaches may be the most valuable property in the country and the next place to catch the eye of developers. Jinak Island, thought of as a magical place, is twelve miles long and only two miles across at its widest, a strip of sandy beach, mangroves, trees, and scrub that is separated from the mainland by a tidal creek. It is in sight from The Gambia's heavily populated capital and some of its tourist hotels, but it is not easy to reach and is lightly populated. Therein lies its appeal (or some of its appeal—see Perspective 18): it is a naturalist's heaven with great swarms of migratory birds, hares, fowls, warthogs, Nile monitors, even leopards, and it has eight miles of some of Africa's nicest and least-spoiled beaches, where one can stand staring out into the waters and see nothing living in any direction besides cavorting dolphins. Visitors there experience "the feeling of being castaways on some pleasant tropical island." This is just what globetrotting tourists crave, so it will probably not be long before developers with capital buy the beachfront and begin building hotels.[31]

Camara and the government part company over who will benefit most from such enterprise, however. The government considers this beach part of its Tourism Development Area, the zone in which it can sell land to persons capable of developing it for "appropriate use." The park caretaker disagrees, saying that the government placed the island in a protected area but then gave it back to the people of Jinak, so that anyone wanting to develop the Atlantic beach will need to get

Perspective 18   **The Treasure of Treasure Island, or, Do You Believe in Magic?**

Jinak Island—also known as Paradise Island, Treasure Island, and Magic Island—has no roads and is hard to reach. One gets there overland along an unmarked track that ends at a hundred-yard-wide tidal creek crossed only by leaky dugouts paddled by nine-year-olds. Pirogues from Banjul travel there, but their safety record is spotty and passengers arrive wringing wet. Once on the island, however, the absence of noise, the miles of unpopulated sandy beach, and the Gambian sunshine make it a paradise.

The island's magical qualities are largely spiritual. Even before the arrival of Islam, Jinak possessed powerful spirits, and then marabouts set up practice there, making it the place to go for prayers, predictions, protections, and efforts to make the future turn out the way one wants. Jinak marabouts are expensive, but they are effective, so people make the difficult venture when in need of that line of work.

And Jinak holds treasure: "From time immemorial," says one person, "the island has been a place where *cannabis* has grown." The plant, from which is derived marijuana, grows across West Africa, but it grows *really well* on Jinak. The island's residents claim that it grows wild, but somehow the crop grows even through the dry season and in straight rows. Also, something besides two tourists a day and the run of people seeking protective charms supports the island's 2,000 residents. "Cannabis is one of the country's leading cash crops," claims one person, "and it makes up half the farms on Jinak."

The island's crop is not cultivated primarily for its hemp. Shops disguised as clothing stores are little cannabis-processing operations. The pot is taken across the river for sale to Europeans in the coastal resorts, but also to Gambian villages, where older men use it to help them endure the day's fieldwork and younger men sit smoking it, drinking strong Chinese tea, and listening to reggae.

The Gambia has laws prohibiting possession, use, or sale of marijuana, with fines and jail sentences for violators. How is the crop grown so openly on Jinak? The answer is that Jinak has magic that Gambians believe in. "Bad things happen to anyone causing the island's residents trouble," says one person. Proof occurred in 2000 when two police officers found cannabis growing there and made arrests. Within a month, both were jobless. Most residents believe the officers should have known better; some add that the incident shows the government's involvement in the drug trade. Rumors abound: government does not arrest drug dealers because it is involved in the trade; government officials are bribed; packages arrive at Banjul Airport addressed to "high government officials"; Nigerians coordinate Gambian drug trafficking. All one knows for sure is that, down many a Gambian street and walkway, smoke is in the air.

People who spoke about this topic asked not to be identified.

permission from Jinak's elders to do so and to pay them for development rights. Of course, much needs to happen before any development occurs: arrangement of an easier way to reach Jinak, investment in generators, and a system to provide water. But once such things are in place, tourism is likely to do more to alter the western edge of Niumi than seventy years of British colonialism did. And maybe it could begin an upward spiral of economic growth in Niumi that would lead toward sustainable development.[32]

Sustainable Development?

If Niumi's transportation system were considered a barometer for development, a cursory glance at it might suggest that everything was moving along according to some grand IMF plan. The ferry service that connects the region to The Gambia's capital is a noticeable measure. The Gambia Ports Authority currently uses three boats of nearly the same size, all of decent speed, to make the trip back and forth between Barra and Banjul. One of them is the *Kanilai*, named for the president's home village. Commissioned in 2005 and similar in configuration to its immediate predecessors,[33] the *Kanilai* makes the four-mile crossing in thirty to forty-five minutes, which is a matter of pride among riders. Travel between Niumi and the capital is thus much better—faster and easier—than it has ever been. So is waiting for the boat: the government in 2009 commissioned a new terminal in Barra with a seating capacity of 300. These improvements can only aid in the growth of trade and tourism.[34]

The government introduced greater safety measures in the river crossing, too, in part due to the tragedy of the Senegalese ferry *Joola* in September 2002. The *Joola* was carrying over three times as many passengers as authorized, had few passenger names or addresses, and had life preservers for only a fraction of those on board. As it passed twenty miles off Gambia's Atlantic coast on its way from Dakar to Ziguinchor in southern Senegal, the boat capsized in a storm, killing more than 1,800 people, with some of the bodies washing up on Gambia's Atlantic beaches. So, now, all vehicles that get onto the Banjul-Barra ferry are to be weighed so that the boat's capacity is not exceeded, all passengers are to write their names and addresses on a manifest before boarding, and each boat is limited to 400 passengers—still a lot given the vessel's size. As memory of the *Joola* disaster fades, however, passengers and ferry staff ignore the rules. The cost of the crossing remains low: five dalasi, a little more than twenty cents. The privately operated pirogues that compete with the government ferries remain under close scrutiny, heightened even more since an overloaded pirogue capsized on Valentine's Day, 2002, killing several dozen people. Each passenger of these long, motorized canoes now must wear a life vest during the crossing, and the numbers of passengers are limited.

Niumi also has another impressive new road. Everyone marveled when in 1997 a smooth, two-lane, blacktop highway opened between Essau and Kerewan, thirty-eight miles eastward. A gift of the government of Taiwan, the road was eventually

Photo 15 **Signs of health initiatives in Essau, Lower Niumi.**

extended to the eastern end of the country. And in 2009, the road connecting Barra with Essau and then heading north to Amdalaye on the Senegalese border was rebuilt. Vehicles in decent repair make good time on these roads as long as drivers remain vigilant for the cattle, donkeys, dogs, sheep, goats, monkeys, and children that wander into the road. With the improved ferry service and roads, Gambians wanting to go very far upcountry now cross the river at Banjul and head eastward along the north-bank road.

These advances in transportation reflect similar improvements in education and health. The military officers who took over in 1994 proclaimed their new regime the government of youth and promised to emphasize education. One of the first edifices constructed under the new regime (after the raising of a massive victory arch in Banjul that only the president is permitted to pass under) was a new senior secondary school in Essau, the first to exist anywhere on the river's north bank. In recent years, senior secondary schools have also been opened in Albreda, Medina Bafuloto, Berending, and Kuntair. With the government's initiatives and assistance from international organizations, figures on school attendance across the country have improved. On any given day of the school year, 60 percent of the children of the appropriate age are attending primary school and 40 percent secondary school, and by 2007 three-quarters of children of the appropriate age were completing a primary education.[35] The Gambia's secretary of state for education announced that the country, by late 2002, had nearly achieved one of the president's goals: having a basic school within walking distance of every child of appropriate age. Some of the schools around the country's capital are good institutions with exceptional, professional teachers. And the University of The Gambia, a physically decentralized institution that grew out of a St. John's University (Nova Scotia) extension, offers high-school graduates a chance to further their education without leaving the country, as was necessary before. Young women and men from Niumi were in the first graduating class at the university in 2003.

Health care also has spread in Niumi. Essau has a large, government-run health center and Kuntair and Medina Bafuloto have smaller ones; Ndugu Kebbe and Nema Kunku have health facilities run by nongovernmental organizations (NGOs). The health centers send teams to visit villages for regular "trekking clinic" hours, providing prenatal and maternity care, elementary diagnosis, and basic treatment. People needing more extensive care, laboratory work, or hospitalization still need to cross the river to Banjul, where the Royal Victoria Hospital has been upgraded in recent years. There are more physicians in Niumi, too, thanks to a post-1998 influx of Cuban doctors, who neither complain about rural postings nor expect high salaries. In addition, there have been effective vaccination campaigns in Niumi against polio, efforts to provide more safe drinking water, and steady educational campaigns about HIV/AIDS, keeping the infection rate low (0.9 percent of persons age 15 to 49) in comparison to many sub-Saharan African countries.[36]

But in terms of development, it this is about it. A glance inside any Niumi classroom or a conversation with a parent of a sick child reveals how far there is to go. Even traveling can be difficult once off the main roads. Once-decent laterite roads appear never to have been graded or maintained. Cars end up finding their own way around washed-out sections, carving new roads through the bush with everyday use. The vehicles themselves are nearly all autos, vans, and trucks driven several hundred thousand miles in a European country before being shipped to The Gambia. Nearly all leak fluids and have wires sticking out of dashboards, springs poking up through seats, doors that do not close, or windows either permanently up or down. If one refused to ride in a vehicle with bald tires, one would not travel by auto in Niumi.

If statistics relative to education are moving in a positive direction, a glance behind the numbers reveals a sacrifice of quality for quantity that seems partly related to government efforts to meet statistical goals so debt reduction will kick in. There simply are not enough schools, classrooms, or desks to provide regular education to Gambian children, so the school day is divided into halves with students attending either mornings or afternoons, not both, and often sitting two to a desk in classrooms that lack books and materials. In spite of government intentions (and misleading proclamations), many students have to walk as far as six miles each way to attend school, causing them to arrive late and leave early. Throughout the day during school terms, Niumi's roads and paths are dotted with children in dusty school uniforms, walking seemingly endlessly.

Photo 16 **A cell-phone tower rises on the outskirts of a village in Upper Niumi.**

Once at school, students in Niumi classrooms are not apt to encounter qualified teachers. Around the country's capital, 99 percent of teachers have credentials; in rural areas, most do not. When necessary, the government simply appoints new instructors, usually people who recently left school and need work. The new appointees are posted to rural schools, where, the hope is, they will pick up teaching skills as they work.[37] Even when new teachers have been trained, normally at Gambia College in a two-year program beyond high school, most are woefully ineffective. The reason is that teaching is not what most of them want to do. "Who would aspire to be a teacher here?" asks former Niumi teacher Oppenheimer:

> The pay is horrible. Those with anything on the ball know they can make more money in business or communications. And new teachers know they will be posted to the provinces, where they will be miles from their families, electricity, music, contact with the world. Almost none of them really want to teach in the first place. What they want is to get out of the country. With a degree and some teaching experience they know they'll have a better chance of getting a visa. So they get the qualifications. Then, when they get sent to a distant village, they simply run away and never come back. We call it "RATS": the Run-Away-Teacher Syndrome.[38]

In addition to appointing men and women who never finished secondary school, the Gambian government has opened teaching to foreigners. Most of these are young men from such English-speaking, problem-ridden West African nations as Liberia, Sierra Leone, or Nigeria, who see teaching as a stepping-stone to something better. Few of them have any stake in the communities where they teach or real interest in the children in their classrooms.

Among the many problems with education in Niumi is the perpetuation of old social customs and teaching methods. Curricula contain lessons supporting gender bias, and many teachers openly display their belief that male students are superior to female students. The typical Niumi teacher also comes from a system of education that long believed that sparing the rod spoiled the child, and that mentality still exists. Some observers read progress in the replacement of stout blows to the head and shoulders with lesser raps on the hands.[39]

Students from Niumi who attend the new university are experiencing problems of a different sort. Books coming from outside The Gambia have always been expensive, but the declining dalasi has made their acquisition all but impossible. The university's library is stocked primarily with out-of-print textbooks. The History Students Association collects books as it can and has its own library in a supportive professor's office, but these have a way of vanishing. More important for some individuals is the university's failure to offer required classes. Several students who graduated in 2003 had to petition to graduate without core requirements because the classes had not been offered in the students' last two years. Finding qualified faculty to teach courses is another problem. Many Gambians with appropriate qualifications prefer to take positions outside the country, where the pay is much higher and teachers encounter fewer problems with everything from research materials and computer access to steady electricity and working bathrooms. President Jammeh, chancellor of the university ex officio, has compounded the problem by bringing politics into the institution. Faculty who speak in support of him and his policies advance; those who do not stagnate, or worse. In 2009 he fired the highly qualified senior lecturer and former head of the Faculty of Humanities and Social Sciences, Dr. Boro Suso, because Suso was a member of an opposition political party.[40]

As with education, statistics showing improving health care mask a difficult reality. The great majority of Niumi's population does not seek treatment for health disorders, yet patients overwhelm its few clinics. Prenatal care is minimal—one woman, eight months pregnant and weeding vigorously in her garden, is unaware of prenatal vitamins—and the stay in a health center for a "normal birth" under a midwife's care is ninety minutes. It is not surprising that Gambia's infant mortality rate remains 82 per 1,000 live births. Eight of ten pregnant Gambian women are anemic, and in a 2001 study in an area east of Niumi, 70 percent of women interviewed had at least one reproductive disorder.[41] During the structural adjustment of the 1980s, Gambia's government began emphasizing "cost recovery in the provision of health services," a bureaucratic euphemism for "charging for health care," so people lacking money turned to natural healers or went without care altogether. Cuban doctors work in Niumi, but their numbers are declining. In 2003 The Gambia had fewer than one physician per 10,000 people (compared to 26 per 10,000 in the United States). In assessing progress toward its Millennium Development Goals, the UNDP lists The Gambia as "Off Track" in "eradicating extreme poverty and hunger" and "reducing child mortality."[42]

Society and Culture

Not everything in Niumi these days is as it appears. Near a large mosque in a village known for Islamic education and spiritual works stands an old man in a long robe, heelless slippers on his feet and a knit cap covering his shaved head. He is staring at his hands, which hold a string of beads. You have seen it before: he is reciting the respectful names for Allah, one as each bead passes through his fingers and slides down the string. But wait. You walk closer, see the beads are not moving, and realize this is not a religious exercise. The man's focus is on his cell phone, cupped securely in his hands that hold the beads. He is texting.

Today, communication by cell phone is all over Niumi. Phones ring in surprising places—in the *gellie-gellies* that bounce along dirt roads connecting rural villages, in school classrooms, in market stalls where women in colorful wraps sell golf-ball-size dabs of peanut butter, even in remote vegetable gardens—and as everywhere, they go off with an assortment of electronic melodies. One Muslim official has posted a sign on the outer wall of the mosque, asking those entering to turn off their phones. The frequent ringing, he says, disturbs prayers.

Photo 17 **Girls and boys taking a mid-day break with their teachers beneath a mango tree at a school in Upper Niumi.**

Across Niumi, one sees the effects of globalization in technology and culture. The most distant village in the district has at least one television aerial sticking up from a housetop. Schoolboys congregate in these places to keep track of the fortunes of their favorite Premier Soccer League teams; women (and often their husbands, children, and grandchildren, if truth be known) come together in the evenings to view the latest imported serial drama; and people watch television, in addition to listening to the radio, to get world news. (Fewer bother to tune in for local news, it having become less informational and more a vehicle for government propaganda.) Schools have received donated computers and their students crave access to the Internet.[43] Just about anywhere in the territory, young people identify themselves by their preferences in sports teams (Manchester United is currently big) and music (the Senegalese Youssou Ndour remaining popular).

But not everything in Niumi is bending to change from outside. Families re-main strong, and women and men alike continue their society's age-old desire to have many children, though there is evidence that the barrage of information from international organizations showing overpopulation at the root of many of their problems is sinking in: the fertility rate is down from 6.0 births per woman in 1990 to 4.8 in 2006.[44] To get the clearest view of life in Niumi in its modern form, one needs to focus on the areas where the anchors of old ways are being tugged at by waves of the wider world that wash continually across Niumi residents, especially the young.

One element of Niumi society that seems fastened in deep sediment involves the extended kinship system. People in Niumi do not consider themselves individuals so much as members of large, caring families. Traveling anywhere in the country with a resident is slow going because the person is forever stopping to greet and talk to cousins, brothers, mothers (often more than one), sisters, aunts, uncles, and more cousins. Mothers' sisters often are regarded as mothers themselves, "aunties" can be individuals who are not truly related, but who have come to live with the family, and uncles can be the closest relatives of all. Obligations of care, shown through such little things as taking time to talk or such big things as sharing what little wealth one possesses, appear to be borne willingly. That Niumi family structures seem as strong as ever is all the more amazing given that, in the rapidly globalizing world, young people are leaving family and village in search of greater opportunities and different lifestyles, sometimes moving far away for long periods. It is in spite of separation that hearts rest with the family. Individual efforts most often tend to the betterment of the family group.

The difficult situation of young people is evident on a walk through any Niumi village. Children are everywhere: preadolescents are the first to greet visitors on the village's edge, young boys kick up dust with their makeshift soccer games, younger children follow strangers like the tail of a comet, round-faced and runny-nosed toddlers surround adults as they sit in a compound, and only the rare woman from late teens to mid-thirties does not have an infant at her breast or strapped to her back, making not a peep but looking around with wide eyes. But except in a few places, there are no males older than fifteen. It is not that the older ones are shy or working in distant fields. They are simply gone, off to places where there is advanced education, an easier (and looser) lifestyle, less pressure, more (and more engaging) activity, and the chance to make money in ways other than farming. Now that young Gambians get information from school, radio, television, and conversation with older siblings and friends about the nature of modern life, farming is the one tradition they no longer cling to. "They look upon farm work as torture," Oppenheimer says. "Their parents punish them by making them work on the farm. It is the last thing they want to do. They all just want to leave and go to Kombo [the greater-Banjul urban area]. Their ultimate goal is to get out of The Gambia."[45]

The positive aspects of Gambian culture involving the strength of the extended family and the attitudes that surround it go hand-in-hand with widely held ideas about family size. Every man and woman of appropriate age in Niumi wants to have lots of children: the typical woman wants eight or ten and the typical man more in the range of twenty. When combined with the declining infant mortality rate, the result is a devastating population explosion. Anyone who has been to Niumi, gone away for a few years, and returned is stunned by the visible change in numbers of people: markets are teeming, roads are crowded, villages have grown together, trees have been felled to clear more fields and supply firewood, trash has multiplied. In a country where once there was considerable solitude, today one has to go a long way to be out of sight of another human being. Figures back up these impressions. While the population growth rates of much of the rest of the developing world, under the influence of information disseminated by international organizations, have dropped dramatically, those of the poorest countries in Africa have not fallen at the same rate, and The Gambia's growth rate remains at 2.6 percent (in contrast to the U.S. rate of 0.88 percent and the world rate of 1.2 percent). Over the last forty years, the country's population has increased from 315,000 to 1.8 million.[46] Part of this increase is due to immigration from other countries, but much of the increase is simply because women are having lots of children. While the total fertility rate of women worldwide has dropped dramatically, from 7.1 to 2.6 births per woman through her childbearing years between 1960 and 2000, for example, it has not fallen nearly so much in The Gambia, where now the average woman gives birth to five children. This is the case at a time when life expectancy is inching upward—it was 59 years at birth in 2006, up from 50 in 1990—so the result is more people. The Gambia's population density has gone from 122 people per square mile in 1969 to 425 in 2009, higher than that of Nigeria, West Africa's most populous nation. At its current rate of growth, The Gambia's population will double within just over three decades.[47]

There are serious reasons for concern over the size and speed of the country's population growth. A United Nations report points out what population scientists have known for some time about the effect of population on economic growth: "Since 1970, developing countries with lower fertility and slower population growth have seen higher productivity, more savings and more productive investment. They have registered faster economic growth."[48] And more important than economic growth are issues involving life's length and quality. At some political risk, Gambian vice president Isatou Njie Saidy regularly underscores the importance of curbing population growth. She points out that the country does not stand a chance of meeting its United Nations Millennium Development Goals, which include cutting poverty and hunger in half by 2015 and reducing maternal and child mortality, if it cannot slow its population growth.[49] The country cannot currently produce enough food to feed its people because the number of Gambians of unproductive age (1–15) is roughly the same size as the number of those 16–55, who are productive. Although Gambia's economy has grown, the growth cannot keep up with the population: the GDP has gone up 58 percent since 2000 while the GDP per capita has advanced only 14 percent.[50]

If these facts are so clear, why do women and men in Niumi want such large families? The answer has to do with the way life used to be. Before the middle of the twentieth century, nearly all sub-Saharan African societies faced one overwhelming problem: how to sustain their numbers. Under their former circumstances, when disease, drought, and pestilence kept life expectancy low, it was not development that people sought to sustain, but their very existence. This circumstance changed a few decades into the twentieth century, when such facets of globalization as the introduction of modern medicines to a wider world, better transportation systems to move food to those in need, and scientific improvement of food production techniques began to increase life expectancy and bring about steady population growth. But the thinking on childbearing that formed over the previous thousands of years has not changed with the altered circumstances. In addition, in a country that has practically no government-sponsored social security and no secure pension system, the young members of the family group will be responsible for caring for the elderly, and the more young family members there are, the more likely that several will survive to adulthood and, thus, the more secure will be an elder's life.

This thinking diverges with the factor of gender. People in Niumi expect members of the extended family to contribute to the good of the whole, and the more contributors the family can add, by having children, the more it will prosper over the long run. But in most people's eyes, male children contribute more than female, because once young women reach productive age, they marry and thereafter contribute to their spouse's extended family rather than to their father's. No bride price is large enough to compensate for an adult lifetime of labor. Male and female grandchildren of the late Niumi farmer Jerre Manneh agree that Manneh never enjoyed a comfortable standard of living in spite of his hard work and frugality because "ol' Pa did not have enough sons."[51] He had eight daughters, but they did not count so much. In fact, women in The Gambia generally do not count so much as men, and that assumption stands sentry against different ideas about women entering Niumi from the wider world.

Women's Roles

In recent years, women have become a central focus of development efforts around the world. "Gender equality and the empowerment of women" is one of the United Nations' eight Millennium Development Goals for achievement by 2015, and UN Secretary General Kofi Annan in 2003 called gender equality "critical to our ability to reach all the other [goals]."[52] The big international financial institutions that press developing countries for reform emphasize measures to improve women's lives; organizations fighting the spread of HIV point to the importance of women's having the knowledge, skills, and self-confidence they need to protect themselves; and population experts insist that educating women is the way to bring population growth under control. The most casual glance at Niumi in the first decade of the new millennium shows how much the weight of tradition burdens women from birth to death and how much their lives will have to change to meet these goals.

Across The Gambia, women have long been subservient to men. A girl is expected to help her mother during her youth, marry young, have lots of children, do all the cooking and caring for her extended family (unless she can share these chores with co-wives, whose presence must be tolerated), and find ways to earn

Perspective 19   **Advice for Niumi's Lovelorn: Appropriate for Whom?**

"How do I keep my spirit up?" asks Aina, who is "Discouraged in Dating," to the "Lovelines" column in the Gambian *Sunday Observer* on February 16, 2003. "I don't seem to be very good at this dating thing . . . Every time I fall for a guy, it turns bad, and the rejection is never from my side. The problem is I'm starting to think it's me . . . I hate feeling so down on myself. If I'm not happy with me, how am I supposed to ever be happy with someone else?"

"You are absolutely right," writes column editor Eric Orji in response. "Until you are happy with yourself, you can't be happy with anyone else." Orji tells Aina to write a "relationship resume," seeking patterns in her choices of men ("Do you keep picking men who can't commit?") and her behavior ("Ask yourself, 'What are the ways in which I'm not meeting a partner's needs?'"). "This assignment," he writes, "will help you realize your romantic strengths . . . and weaknesses."

Girls and young women in Niumi's villages regularly read this column. For them, newspapers are a link to a more modern world. A copy of the *Sunday Observer* costs five dalasi (about twenty-five cents), so it does not have a large paid circulation, but each copy is shared widely. Newspapers cross to Niumi on the ferries and go to the villages in the hands of riders of the *gellie-gellies.*

What must a young Niumi woman think when she reads about romantic love and dating? Love and romance are irrelevant to most Gambian marriages. Many fathers arrange marriages once their daughters reach fifteen or sixteen, and dating is not part of any social process they will experience. Furthermore, to be adult, female, and single is considered one of life's most unfortunate circumstances. Yet here are women writing about love, dating, commitment, even a "ten-year relationship without marriage," and here is an authoritative male columnist who does not find their problems extraordinary.

Might such "modern" influences be affecting the nature of relationships in Niumi? The concept of romantic love is evident in the profusion of Valentine's Day dances and published professions of love (both prose and poetry) that young people text to newspapers. Niumi youth seem increasingly to associate dating with sex: boys brag about their exploits, and girls fear admitting to having had sex, for their virginity at marriage is prized. Are there new standards, or do the old ways prevail? It must be a particularly confusing time for a girl to come of age in a Niumi village.

money on her own to buy things family members need until she reaches a status equivalent to "granny" in old age. The Gambian government is following sound international advice by encouraging female education, but a number of parents do not want to send their daughters to school. Some believe that giving women modern education erodes society's moral values; others argue that educating

Photo 18　**A young woman watering her vegetables in rural Niumi.**

women is investing in a benefit that ultimately will accrue to the family of the woman's husband. Niumi girls who attend school know that, no matter how much they achieve, their fathers may remove them from school to marry soon after they reach puberty. "Girls don't worry about doing well in school because they know they won't be able to continue," says Oppenheimer, an upper-basic (grades 4 to 6) teacher, so "they find a way to slide through."

One unfortunate way of sliding through is by going along with their teachers' demands for "extra work" outside the classroom. Oppenheimer has seen the worst of this practice: "Most upper-basic teachers have girlfriends among the students," she says. "I witnessed fights breaking out between male teachers over their student girlfriends. Four girls are pregnant in the local junior secondary school (grades 7 to 9). One took a concoction of roots to abort the fetus at seven months."[53]

Whether or not schooling is involved, at some point along the rocky path between infancy and adolescence, most girls growing up in Niumi must deal with a matter that has become controversial thanks to world opinion and the presence of international NGOs. The long-standing practice among certain Gambian groups of removing more or less of a woman's genitalia is termed "female circumcision" by those who consider it an integral element of their culture, "female genital mutilation" (FGM) by those who consider it a barbaric act that should be eradicated, and "female genital cutting" by those who hang onto the fleeting hope of remaining neutral in the argument.[54] There is no delicate way to describe what the procedure entails. It is far more dangerous and traumatic for girls than is the circumcision that boys experience regularly in various societies of the world. It once was performed on a group of girls between the ages of ten and fifteen by a specialist operating with a sharp knife, followed by coming-of-age rituals and a long seclusion. Over recent years the procedure has changed in light of pressures from the modern world and a spreading sense of global opposition. These days, younger girls are being circumcised, some in infancy, and without much of the ritual or any seclusion. The operation is performed away from medical clinics, and birth complications, maternal death, infertility, urinary incontinence, tetanus, and mental trauma are among the risks of the procedure. According to 2006 government data, 78 percent of Gambian girls undergo FGM, and in some rural areas the percentage reaches 90. More than nine of every ten Mandinka women in Niumi have experienced FGM, though the proportion of Wolof and Fula women is smaller.

It is not surprising that much of the world recognizes the brutality of FGM and condemns the practice. International organizations working specifically to stop FGM have had branches in The Gambia since the mid-1980s, and the issue is alive among Gambian women's groups. It did not take long for Alice Walker's 1993 film, *Warrior Marks*, which included interviews with Gambian women in its dramatic damning of FGM, to raise awareness in Niumi of global opinion, and the NGOs have received increased funding and have broadened their activities to rural areas. One group, Tostan, begun in The Gambia by a returned Peace Corps volunteer from Senegal, has been particularly effective. But many people in Niumi, women more than men (it being perceived as a woman's issue) and older women especially, ignore the pressure and cling stubbornly to the practice. The pressure on girls to be circumcised can be intense. "Society rejects you if you are not circumcised," says one twenty-six-year-old woman. "You will have difficulty finding a husband, you will not be welcome in meetings of women's groups—even when you come up to a group of women, they will stop talking among themselves until you leave." Some mothers refuse to have their daughters circumcised, only to have grandmothers and aunts intervene and see that the operation is carried out while the mother is away. One university woman, who wears stylish Western clothes and is popular among students who consider themselves "modern," says that she may have her daughters "circumcised" when the time comes. She opposes the practice in principal, she says, but pressures on her might be too great to resist.

Reasons why so many persist in such a brutal practice are not as simple as one might think. Some Gambians, seemingly as many women as men, say that FGM helps fit a woman for her prescribed role in society, which is to marry and bear children. Virgins and circumcised women are the most readily married; uncircumcised woman can be unwanted as marriage partners. Parents sometimes arrange marriages while their daughters are still children, and marriage often occurs soon after a woman passes through puberty. An unmarried adult woman has little identity. Once married, a woman's status is tied to her childbearing. Women who turn out to be infertile frequently are divorced for that reason, without question. Women who have few children tend to be respected less than women who have more.

Others claim they support continuing female circumcision for cleanliness (spiritual and physical) or for religious reasons. One woman told a reporter: "The prophet said Muslim males and females should be circumcised." Ylva Hernlund found in extensive interviews, however, that the reason stated most strongly by Gambians is "respect for tradition and conventional norms of behavior." One woman said, "We must do as tradition dictates. Some women have been paid to come and confuse us so that we will abandon what our ancestors have been practicing. Who are these people to raise their voice?" Regardless of the reasoning, Hernlund writes, those not circumcised are insulted as *solema*, which "means not only 'uncircumcised' but also rude, ignorant, immature, uncivilized, unclean—'someone who does not know herself.'"[55]

Ending FGM is a thorny issue for the Gambian government. In 1997, President Jammeh stated that the policy of his government was "to discourage such harmful practices," but party supporters forced him to reconsider. In January 1999, he defended the practice, stating, "FGM is part of our culture and we should not allow anyone to dictate to us how we should conduct ourselves." Referring to Gambians who were speaking publicly against FGM: he told a crowd, "There is no guarantee that after delivering their speeches they will return to their homes." As late as May 2009 Jammeh threatened to silence a Gambian Muslim leader who spoke against FGM, only to tell a reporter three weeks later that he backs a ban on FGM and supports the NGOs working toward that end, but that he is not ready to support passage of a law banning the practice.[56]

The government's ambivalence over FGM mirrors its work toward achieving gender equality and women's rights. Under its new constitution, women can vote and hold office. The country's vice president and a few assembly members are women. Efforts to get more women into school may hold promise. Under current policy, every child can attend basic school (through grade 6) without having to pay school fees (though there are costs for uniforms, materials, and examinations). A policy announced in 2002 requires boys and young men to continue to pay fees for secondary school, but girls need not pay. This has helped equalize gender in school attendance, but the task of broadening education to "empower women" is a big one. In 2007, only 41 percent of women aged 15 to 24 could read and write, versus 61 percent of men of that age.[57]

Lately, however, Gambian women may be taking some matters into their own hands. Mothers' clubs have been sprouting in villages across the country with the goal of improving girls' prospects for adult living. The members advocate for girls to go to school, they work to support the schools in their villages, and they participate in health groups, sharing information on reproductive health, disease prevention, and nutrition—all while learning to read and write themselves.[58]

At the root of the new women's activities—literally as well as figuratively—are initiatives in vegetable gardening. As noted, Niumi women have taken advantage of local circumstances and global initiatives to begin a new horticultural enterprise. "The garden boom," as anthropologist Richard A. Schroeder terms it, "marked the emergence of a new regime in gender/environment relations along the North Bank" of the Gambia River.[59] Women began spending long hours of the day at their gardens, prompting men to complain that their wives were neglecting their traditional roles, including looking after the husbands' needs. Men grumbled that the garden plots had become their wives' "second husbands." Ironically, because men through the drought years produced less food and had less cash from selling peanuts, women, who began to earn money of their own by selling vegetables, stepped in to lend money to their husbands (who then gave it back so their wives could buy food). In time, some women skipped their husbands altogether and used their cash directly to buy needed food, clothing, school supplies, and even some things for themselves. In an act of ironic defiance, women, too, began referring to the gardens, which provided for their needs in ways their spouses once did, as their "husbands."

Once fully involved in gardening, women developed new attitudes toward domestic relations. "Our husbands stopped buying soap, oil, rice," one woman said. "We provide all these things. Obviously our marriages would change. We do all this work while our husbands lie around home doing nothing. Whenever we return from gardening, we still have to do all the cooking, and all our husbands can say is, 'Isn't dinner ready yet?' And then they start to shout at us. Remember, this is after we have already spent the whole day at the garden working. . . . A husband who has nothing to give to his wife—if that wife gets something from her own labor, she will surely find it more difficult to listen to him."[60]

It was not so much men's unhappiness with the new circumstances at home, however, but new global directions in the channeling of development aid in the late 1980s and through the 1990s that threw up the biggest roadblock in the path of women gardeners. According to Schroeder, by the time the United Nations held its "Earth Summit" in Rio de Janeiro in 1992, where most of the world's nations agreed that environmental protection needed to be a part of development, "a sea change in the thinking of development officials was under way world-wide."[61] Aid agencies with development money replaced their focus on women by one on improving management of the environment. Gambian government officials, who themselves were becoming concerned over such environmental matters as beachfront erosion (because of its threat to tourist hotels on the Atlantic), loss of groundcover from bush fires, poor sanitary conditions in cities, and an alarming rate of deforestation, went along with the global focus on environmental protection. "In the long run, gardens don't matter," said a government spokesman, "if we don't do something to address the more fundamental problems of sustaining successful natural resources management in the region."[62]

In this milieu, the Gambian government collaborated with foreign donors to begin a forestry initiative, urging villagers to plant fruit trees and providing funds for fencing and wells for the trees. Men ended up planting the trees—mango, papaya, and cashew—and the spots they chose for planting were in the low-lying areas where women had gardens. The men assumed that the gardeners would happily water the saplings as they watered their vegetables. But it did not take the women long to realize that once the trees reached reasonable size, they blocked the sun from the vegetables and forced the women to move their plots to less favorable locations. So the women reacted in passive-aggressive, or sometimes purely aggressive, fashion. Some simply refused to water the trees; others voluntarily "pruned" the trees to the point where they had almost no foliage and died.

Eventually, men and women worked out the issue in a variety of ways. Some men moved their tree-growing operations to areas still close to the wells but far enough away so the grown trees would not cast shade on the women's vegetables. Some women moved their gardening operation farther away from the village, requiring a longer walk, but freeing them from having to water trees in addition to the vegetables. Tensions linger, however, over the broader social issues about men's and women's position in the household economy. Of particular interest here is that such gender-based tensions between a traditional patriarchal system of household management and new ideas about who provides for a family are similar to those occurring in other places across the modernizing world. A decade into the twenty-first century, they remain on the forefront of people's minds in Niumi.

Freedom, Dignity, and Human Rights

If the Republic of The Gambia was known globally for anything besides *Roots* during the nearly three decades of the First Republic, it was for its guarantee to its citizens of personal freedom and human rights. Through the 1970s and 1980s, when it became commonplace for African governments to thwart democracy, stifle criticism, and in many places force their populations to live in fear of raids on their homes, illegal detention, torture, and even death at the hands of the state, The Gambia stood out as a small nation where people could live freely, speak their minds, and vote in reasonably fair, multiparty elections. Arnold Hughes and David Perfect write that President Jawara's "personal commitment to human rights was far greater than almost all other African leaders and had a much wider impact than in The Gambia alone." Under Jawara, The Gambia played a pivotal role in writing, adopting, and bringing into force, in 1986, the Organization of African Unity's (OAU) African Charter on Human and People's Rights. In recognition of this role, the document became known officially as the "Banjul Charter," and in 1989 the OAU established the headquarters of the African Center for Democracy and Human Rights Studies in The Gambia.[63]

Given the situation in The Gambia in 2009, the country's impressive history in regard to democracy and human rights makes for a painful irony. In his fourteen years as the country's president, Jammeh has corrupted democratic practices, ignored the rule of law, and steadily eroded his countrymen's personal freedoms and basic rights as human beings. It is one of the saddest elements of the Gambian situation today. Knowledgeable citizens who watch the arrests and illegal detentions, hear the tales of torture, learn that their favorite journalist has "disappeared," and witness government forces invading their homes must look on the handsome, glass-and-block African Center for Democracy and Human Rights Studies building and wonder what its international sponsors are doing to help them. So far, the answer is very little.

For a time, people residing in Niumi's villages were able to avoid serious confrontation with government security forces. Some did so by joining the ruling APRC and thereby occasionally benefiting from the president's largesse, perhaps gaining use of a tractor or receiving free fertilizer. Others tried simply to keep their opinions to themselves, doing what they must to remain unnoticed and thus avoid trouble. Such activities kept the government wolf from the door of their private residences— at least until early 2009. That is when the witch-hunters came to Niumi.

It was a bright afternoon in early February when seventy-five-year-old Barra resident Ali Marr had his afternoon meal interrupted by a loud, large group of armed soldiers, policemen, and "Green Boys," the Red-Guard-like supporters of Gambia's ruling APRC Party, escorting a gaggle of "witch-hunters" wearing, as described by a friend, "big red clothes that have mirrors and jujus hanging all round their bodies." One of the soldiers told Marr that the witch-hunters would remove "evil things" that were "buried in his compound" while the soldiers would take him to a waiting bus. The soldier's announcement that all was done on orders of "H.E.," the common way of referring to His Excellency, the country's president, frightened Marr into cooperation. When he boarded the bus, he was surprised to find his frail, sickly elder brother Kolley Marr in one of the seats and in the others a number of other relatives and villagers from Barra and nearby Essau, mostly old people, many of them women. The group was driven to the ferry, taken across the river, and then conveyed to a compound in Kololi, fifteen miles east of Banjul (and, ironically, almost within earshot of the African Center for Democracy and Human Rights Studies).

Once in the compound, Marr's captors charged him with being a "wizard"— something he continually denied—and turned him over to the red-clad gang for "treatment." Over the next three days, he and the others were forced repeatedly to drink a foul-tasting concoction and to wash themselves with a smelly liquid. Many who did this lost control of their bladders and bowels, hallucinated, and voiced "crazy things," some falling unconscious. Virtually everyone under this treatment vomited repeatedly. Shortly after their release and return to Barra, Kolley Marr died and Ali developed chest pain and swelling legs. Two months after the experience, Ali still could not stand straight, walk more than a few steps, or swallow even soft rice. "I have lost my blood brother," he said, "and now am the breadwinner for the family. My health condition is deteriorating and it does not allow me to do anything, and [I] am just sitting at home."[64]

In spite of the obvious evidence, a cowed public was slow to accept the president's role in the witch-hunting. Heightening fears surrounding the matter was the March 8, 2009, arrest and ten-day detention of Halifa Sallah, among the most visible of Jammeh's opponents and one who was investigating and writing about the witch-hunts in the newspaper *Foroyaa*. Eventually, however, a kind of explanation was whispered from person to person: the president had suspected "witchcraft" in the recent death of an aunt and brought in the witch-hunters from Guinea to "cleanse" the country.[65]

Many in Niumi hope, perhaps vainly, that criticism of a watching world will help them regain the security of person and home that they remember from earlier times. Following the June 2009 arrests of seven veteran Gambian journalists (including a breast-feeding mother) for printing the self-evident statement that the government could not itself be absolved in the 2004 murder of respected journalist Deyda Hydara if it did not investigate the incident, Amnesty International joined other groups in organizing an international "Day of Action," asking "all members of civil society . . . to call on the Gambian government to uphold its people's basic rights and freedoms."[66] The Gambia is not a large enough blip on anyone's radar, however, to bring anything beyond strong rebukes (as from the U.S. State Department when six of the seven arrested journalists were convicted and sentenced in August 2009 to two years of hard labor in the notorious Mile Two Prison).[67] For now, people in Niumi avoid talking about politics or government. They respond politely to the heavily armed soldiers who man checkpoints along the roads leading from Barra and no longer bother to look at the self-censored newspapers. Privately, they agree strongly with the Gambian who told *New York Times* reporter Adam Nossiter, "Human rights is not here right now." Many doubt that it will return any time soon.[68]

Niumi in Diaspora

Globalization has made it simpler for men and women from Niumi to live somewhere else, outside the country, and has enhanced their desire to do so. No one really knows how many Gambian nationals live in Europe or North America since many go underground and reside in these places illegally, but rough estimates range between 80,000 and 100,000. Many "Diaspora Gambians," as they are called, are young adults, but not all; some are educated, but some have not completed primary school; some are studying or working abroad temporarily and fully intend to return to their native land, but some will never again set foot on African soil—entirely by design.

Globalization is at the heart of Gambians' desire—and ability—to get to Europe or North America. Information on the latest Hollywood release, the current rivalry in the English Premier Soccer League, or a text message from a cousin or friend

Perspective 20   **The Sad State of the Gambian Press**

Keeping track of what is happening in The Gambia in 2009 is not as easy
as it once was. The government controls Gambian radio and television,
so no one pays much attention to their laudatory news and features. Until
recently, it was left to a marvelous group of journalists, with roots running
back to E.F. Small's anticolonial *The Gambian Outlook and Senegambian
Reporter*, to report on government feasance and malfeasance in feisty
journals named *The Independent*, *Foroyaa* (Freedom), and *The Point*.
These newspapers found their way across the river on the ferries, entered
Niumi compounds as wrappings for bread, and were read and reread until
the print wore thin. Niumi's villagers thus maintained a critical awareness
of government activities that rendered them informed participants in the
country's political process.

That was then; now it is different. Though he proclaims (with an admittedly odd metaphor), "Criticism is my fertilizer," The Gambia's president
shows he will not tolerate expression of disagreement with his policies or
even an independent press seeking its own sources for reporting on government activities. The Media Foundation for West Africa (MFWA) in 2007
published a sixty-three-page dossier listing press-freedom abuses of the
Jammeh-led government since it took power in 1994. Escalating over recent
years and thought to be committed largely by Jammeh's undercover political
police, the National Intelligence Agency (NIA), these abuses include the
burning of journalists' houses and of the entire press of *The Independent*,
forcing it out of business; failure to investigate the 2004 murder of *The
Point's* co-publisher, the widely respected (and forever politely critical)
Deyda Hydara; and numerous illegal arrests and detentions without trial,
the most egregious involving *Daily Observer* reporter Chief Ebrima Manneh, who was held incommunicado by the NIA for eight months before
the government announced his "disappearance" and claimed he had never
been in its custody. More recently still, Pap Saine, Hydara's co-publisher
at *The Point*, was arrested and charged with publishing false information
for an article of four column inches on page 3 of the paper's January 30,
2009, edition, informing readers that an arrested Gambian diplomat had
been moved from police headquarters to jail. "Pap's mistake was in citing 'our sources,'" one knowledgeable person said. "Jammeh doesn't like
unnamed sources from within his government." Another person warned,
"Watch out for the NIA." The MFWA reports of "several journalists es-
caping into exile," while "those within are practicing self-censorship as a
means of protection."

"Arrested Gambian Diplomat Now at Mile 2," *The Point*, January 30, 2009; "ECOWAS
Court to Hear Journalist Manneh's Case," *Gambia News and Report Magazine*, June
26–July 2, 2007. Persons who spoke about this subject asked not to be identified.

attending a party in Houston or Seattle, Birmingham or Leeds, makes "going West" (their shorthand for traveling and living in one of the countries in Europe or North America) the ambition of many Gambian boys and girls. A twentieth-century revolution in transportation has enhanced their ability to do so. Today it takes a Gambian five hours to make the trip to Portugal that it took the survivors of Nuno Tristão's fatal voyage two months to travel in 1444. Planes fly most days of the week from Banjul to one or another European city and to Dakar in Senegal, where travelers make connections for flights to the United States. Few Gambians can afford the cost of intercontinental travel, but the growth of tourism has helped link Gambians with Europeans, or much more rarely Americans, who are willing to pay for a Gambian to visit their country. Gambians who can get money for air travel from their extended families can take advantage of American colleges and universities interested in adding "diversity" to their student bodies by enrolling persons from small African countries. Even short visits can turn into stays of long duration, legally or otherwise. Once Gambians settle overseas and get even menial jobs, they can begin saving to help bring over family members. In Western cities, Gambians lodge with their countrymen, sometimes several to a room, and are content to take jobs no others want. Many are remarkably enterprising, such as the Gambian in New York who sells Chinese-manufactured cloth bags on the street. After purchasing a gross of bags and finding he did not get what the seller promised, he took his case to Manhattan's small-claims court and got his money back.

Going West can pay off for all concerned. Some of the large compounds in the Tourism Development Area west of Banjul, near the Atlantic, are owned by persons born in Niumi or other remote parts of The Gambia who found a way to get to England or Germany or Sweden, stayed long enough to accumulate money, and eventually returned and bought property to house parents or siblings—and maybe uncles and aunts and their offspring to boot. One compound in Kololi, sprawling but not gaudy, is the home of about a dozen young persons, all born into a family in the Niumi village of Berending. One young man of the family, who dropped out of junior secondary school, had no desire to farm, and quickly grew tired of being a burden on the family, went to live with a relative across the river, near where the tourists roam. Personable and bright, he made friends with a visiting German, who agreed to sponsor his traveling to Hamburg. The young man stayed in Germany several years, saving all he could, before returning to The Gambia and buying the compound. Now, his youngest brothers and sisters, along with some cousins, nieces, and nephews, live in the compound so they can attend the better secondary schools around the capital, find work in the tourist industry or elsewhere, and enjoy a more modern setting than the one they left in a Niumi village. "I was just another hungry mouth to feed back home," says the man from Berending, who, like many other Gambians speaking about contemporary matters, wanted to remain anonymous for this interview, "but this way I not only do not draw from family resources, but I feed and house others and help them along their way. This was the best thing that could happen to me and to my family."

Among Niumi youth completing secondary school, the desire to go West can be so strong as to cause mental trauma. Young Gambians call this "the nerve syndrome" or, more simply, "the nerves." A man from Kuntair in his mid-twenties, Bala, tells of a friend who remained in Banjul after his "O-levels" (the equivalent of graduating from high school), working at a bank. "He believed he would be able to go West once he completed school," Bala said, "but opportunity was lacking. That's all he thought or talked about. When he got a call from another friend who had made it to London, it was just too much for him. They admitted him to RVH [Royal Victoria Hospital]. I visited him there; he stayed quite a while. It was the worst case of 'the nerves' I ever saw."[69]

The pressure on young Niumi residents to contribute to the family, especially after three decades of devastating drought, brings some to take desperate steps to get to Europe to seek work. Some go overland, remarkably enough, reaching Mali, where they hire guides to take them across the Sahara to Morocco, Tunisia, or Libya, and then go by boat to a country in southern Europe. Others pay to board a motorized pirogue in The Gambia and make the weeks-long trip northward, traveling mostly by night and hoping eventually to be able to sneak into Spain. The number of young Niumi residents who have perished on such a trip is greater than most villagers wish to admit. For his part, Gambia's president does nothing to deter the desperate young people from leaving, and he voices criticism of Spain for turning away the boaters when they are apprehended coming ashore.[70]

Over recent decades, communities of expatriate Gambians have formed in various European and North American cities. Several online newspapers and blogs keep individuals in touch with events in The Gambia and other matters of common interest. In the United States, Washington, DC, Seattle, Minneapolis/St. Paul, and New York have good-size Gambian communities, but the largest number of Gambians living outside their home country anywhere in the world is in Atlanta, Georgia. One member of this group estimates their number at 3,000. While the group includes computer engineers, construction workers, and taxi drivers, most hold jobs on a much lower level, providing care for the elderly or infirm or cleaning rooms in one or more of the city's many hotels.[71]

Atlanta Gambians hold a celebration every July 4, organized by the Atlanta Gambians Emergency Relief Association and the more politically oriented Save The Gambia Democracy Project. (They hold the celebration on America's Independence Day holiday rather than The Gambia's, which is February 18, because the latter is at a time judged by Gambians to be too cold in the United States for celebrating. Many, too, have time off work to celebrate on the Fourth of July. The date of the July 22, 1994, coup is a Gambian holiday at a more weather-appropriate time of year for Gambians in the United States, but rare is the diaspora Gambian willing to recognize this as a day to honor.) Expatriate Gambians from around the United States come to Atlanta to attend, and in 2009 a politician long opposed to the current Gambian government flew in from Banjul for the event. In addition to a soccer tournament, cultural events, and a Miss Gambia USA beauty pageant, the occasion is a time for music and dancing. At the 2009 event, the soundman and disc jockey was a man born and raised in a Lower Niumi village.

Diaspora Gambians are naturally concerned with the circumstances of their families and fellow nationals back home. Rapid, cheap communication allows them to keep in close touch, and electronic transfer enables them to send money home without concern for its being stolen in the mail. "Every Gambian in America," one expatriate Niumi resident said, "and I want to emphasize—*every Gambian in America*—sends money home." All across Niumi, it is remittances from abroad that make the difference between constant hunger and more comfortable living. "In Albreda, some families receive $1,000 a month from four or five children working overseas," says Peace Corps volunteer Peter O'Neall. Fellow volunteer Chris Honeycutt adds that in Aljamdu, "As you pass by, you can tell the compounds of the families that receive remittances: they have mud-block [rather than woven-reed] walls and better housing."[72] In another anonymous interview in 2007, a Gambian from a Niumi village attending college in the United States reported having saved enough from his university stipend to send money home so his mother could make the *hajj* to Mecca. His mother called in December from outside the Muslim holy city, telling him that she had run out of money, forcing him to borrow from a friend and wire her a few hundred dollars so she could complete the pilgrimage and return home. "She probably bought a few too many gifts for the children," he said laughing, a little painfully.

The concerns of Gambians overseas, however, extend beyond the daily welfare of the family back home. They care about difficulties their fellow nationals face in their struggle to live abroad and about prospects for their country's future. A few clicks on an Internet search engine turn up several dozen Gambian self-help organizations: the Seattle Gambians Association, for instance, and the Gambian Association of Minnesota, UK Gambians, Gambians in Finland Association, and even an Association of Basse Citizens Abroad (for those from a large, upriver Gambian town). Many of these groups work to provide emergency relief for fellow Gambians and, according to one group's mission statement, "to protect and preserve the heritage, culture, history, language, and strong family lifestyles of all of our members and families." Working with an organization called Books for Africa, the Gambian Association of Minnesota, in May 2009, sent 35,000 textbooks (grade 5 through university-level) valued at $165,000 to be distributed to selected Gambian schools.[73]

The growing tyranny of Jammeh and the APRC government has also prompted Gambians to form organizations working to publicize the country's political circumstances—which most people in the world know nothing of, let alone care about—and, in the end, to bring about change. Among these organizations are the Movement for Democracy and Development, based in New York, and the Save The Gambia Democracy Project, based in Atlanta. The latter tried—unsuccessfully, in the end—to unite opposition parties for the 2006 Gambian presidential election, and both are working with such international organizations as Amnesty International and Reporters Without Borders to publicize the loss of press and personal freedoms. As their names suggest, these are not revolutionary organizations; they seek to use the democratic process to unseat their country's despotic ruler. Some critics believe that such actions are futile when dealing with a dictator who rides roughshod over constitutional checks and vows he will remain in office, come what may, for the next forty years. Frustration is evident in the eyes of these groups' members as they pool their meager funds to support attempts to return their country to democracy and the rule of law.

While almost no diaspora Gambians support the president or his party, many of them do not participate in the political organizations or speak openly against the Gambian president. "Too many are afraid of reprisals against their families back home," one Gambian living in Atlanta said, "or afraid they will not be allowed to return to visit." Such fears are not imaginary. In March 2007, Fatou Jaw Manneh, a one-time reporter for the Gambian newspaper *The Independent* (which the Gambian government shut down in 2006) and a legal resident in the United States, was arrested by government security forces as she arrived at the Banjul International Airport, coming home to pay respects to her late father. Eventually charged with sedition, Manneh remained in the country for a year as her trial dragged on. Sixteen months after her arrest, she was found guilty and sentenced to serve four years in prison or to pay a fine of 250,000 dalasi ($12,000).[74]

Young men and women from Niumi who are studying overseas face the dilemma, upon completing their studies, whether or not to return home. If they do, they know they will never be able to earn one-tenth of what is considered a modest salary in one of the Western countries. They can support their extended families much better by working—legally or otherwise—overseas and sending money home. They know, too, that if they return they will need to stifle their thoughts on politics and swallow any criticisms they might have of their country's government. They will also face an existence without the ease of life in developed countries: the steady flow of electricity, the Internet connection (if only from a computer in the nearby public library), the modern appliances, the smoothly running cars and good roads, and the culture that is, for most of their countrymen and many others around the shrinking world, somehow contagious.

EPILOGUE

NIUMI, 2009: GLOBAL RECESSION, LOCAL OPPRESSION

Freedom's just another word for nothin' left to lose.
                                                    —Kris Kristofferson, 1969

The global recession, which became evident in the second half of 2008 and by 2009 was proving to be the world's worst economic downturn since the Great Depression, was the background for my most recent visit to Niumi. Triggered by a financial crisis in the United States, the recession had spread quickly to Europe and Asia. Among the results were a sharp drop in international trade and falling commodity prices. I wanted to see what effects this global economic situation was having on people in Niumi.

I knew, too, that to assess anything about life in The Gambia, I had to go there. Statistical data for the country are necessarily several years old—the 2008 UNDP Human Development Index is based on information from 2006—and imprecise. ("How does one figure Gambia's gross domestic product per capita," asks a Dutch businessman, "when one can only guess at the size of the country's population?") Moreover, most available statistics reflect conditions for the entire country, meaning they lump together the more developed capital region with the less developed, rural parts of the country, which include Niumi. Being there, looking and listening, is the only way to determine if, for example, people are getting enough to eat, school-age youngsters are actually attending school, or pregnant women are getting vitamins from the new well-baby clinic. A visit would also allow comparisons with previous visits in order to judge if the human condition is improving. So in January and February 2009, my wife, Doris, an experienced Gambia hand herself, and I went back to The Gambia.

Riding across the Gambia River on the Barra Ferry is a snap compared to the experiences of long ago. Crowds taking the ferry are larger, a reflection of the country's still rapidly rising population. The dingy terminals of old are gone, replaced by new, more efficient, and a little less dingy facilities with wharfs and docking apparatus that port workers adjust for the tide. As I approach the adjustable dock, I remember all the times strong, young Africans carried me piggyback over several yards of water when the boat's prow came up short of the pier.

Ferries now stick to more-or-less hourly schedules (*Inshallah*, Allah willing, Gambians would add) for the thirty- to forty-five-minute crossing. Commercial activity around the terminals is as great as ever, and passengers do not get a break

Photo 19   **Banjul Ferry Terminal: The gate is opened and the crowd rushes to board the Barra Ferry.**

from hawkers once on the boat. Clothing worn by passengers comes from all over the world. The young man wearing the brown, orange, and white Cleveland Browns home-jersey with "Edwards" and the large "17" on the back turns out not to know of Braylon Edwards, the Browns, or the National Football League. He does, however, want my e-mail address. Women dress in colorful wraps with head ties; many of them between puberty and middle age have dozing infants tied to their backs. One small girl, maybe three or four years old, has a doll tied to her in motherly fashion. Young men and women dress differently, some women in tight jeans and tops (the subject of criticism from older Muslim women) and some of the men would-be Rastafarians.

Outside the Barra terminal, between the ferry's gate and the car park, where money changers and sellers of provisions for further travels have long held sway in a maze of paths and walkways, budding restauranteurs have set up shops. These can be as little as a lone table with chairs inside a small, covered enclosure made of corrugated metal or old wooden packing materials. They bring the smells of grilling meat and some of the country's favorite rice dishes into the mix with the human odors that accompany crowds everywhere. Buyers learn after partaking that government efforts to enforce internationally accepted standards of hygiene for these public food sellers are not working to anyone's satisfaction.

Perspective 21   A Movable Feast: Transportation as Marketplace

Gambians seldom miss a chance for mercantile activity. All towns have market stalls, and vendors use ingenious ways of carrying wares so they can patrol streets for the occasional sale. Captive groups are particularly fair game. This makes the ferry crossing the Gambia River a hawker's delight. One ticket allows a vendor to ride back and forth all day, restocking at either terminal when running low. What do the vendors sell? Here is a list of items offered to passengers on a single passage between Barra and Banjul on Tuesday, February 17, 2009:

Food and Drink

Sandwiches, spicy meat and oil	Bananas	Bread, long loaves
Cookies, half a dozen varieties	Oranges, peeled	Gunpowder tea
Peanuts, shelled, with and without skins		
Coca-Cola lookalike and Fanta	Chewing gum	Cashews, raw or roasted
Flavored water in plastic bags	Doughnuts	Hard candies

Cloth and Clothing

T-shirts, NBA, NFL, Ohio State	Men's belts	Young girls' dresses
Cloth, woven, by the piece	Baby clothes	Flip-flops
Cloth, dyed, by the piece	Washcloths	Women's underwear

Health and Beauty Products

Hair products, combs, brushes	Vidal Cream	Petroleum jelly
"Colgate Herbal" toothpaste	Lip balm	Perfumes
"Menthol Plus" cough drops		

Dry Goods

Sim/scratch cards for cell phone	Portable radios	Flashlights
Watches, "Rolex," others	Magazines	Batteries
Unidentifiable items, boxed and not boxed		

Services

Shoe shine	Shoe repair

Charity

Blind persons, led by children	Elderly persons, led by children

Perspective 22   **Global Health Standards Meet Local Health Customs**

On Thursday, February 12, 2009, officials from Gambia's Department of State for Health made a spontaneous visit to Barra in Lower Niumi. At the urging of the World Health Organization and the UN Food and Agricultural Organization, the government had begun stressing public health and hygiene, giving them more attention in the basic school curriculum, passing a new antilittering law (with a list of eleven offences, including "urinating in the street"), holding workshops, and launching ad campaigns. President Jammeh designated one Saturday each month as "Operation Clean the Nation," when schools and businesses close from 9:00 a.m. to 1:00 p.m. and everyone is to gather trash and clean their compounds. The visit of the health officers to Barra was meant as a surprise inspection of food vendors and public toilets, but someone apparently tipped off the bread and meat sellers, who failed to show up for work that day.

The officials were disappointed after their inspection. They found one local restaurant owner placing fried fish on the ground next to "remnant food soaked in water." A grilled chicken vendor admitted he washes his chickens in the river, having no other option. The public toilets at the car park were "in a bad state," a local water shortage forcing the attendant to haul up river water for people to use in cleaning themselves. "Just in between the . . . toilet and a nearby, filthy gutter," observed a reporter, "food items were spread on the ground on sale to members of the public." The car park's "chef de garage" blamed dirty conditions there on the crowds, saying, "We can't [clean] when there are too many people around." An official in nearby Essau said highway construction was the cause of the water shortage, a problem, he assured inspectors, that "will soon be resolved."

These problems highlight the difficulty of instituting health standards acceptable to a global community in a region where local cultures have long had their own standards of appropriate hygiene. Western Europe had a health revolution in the nineteenth century—ironically, abetted by new soaps made from oils obtained in tropical Africa—that led to a doubling of life expectancy. Basic tenets of hygiene that are accepted by most people in societies considered "modern" are slow to penetrate many of the world's poorest countries. This is largely because good hygiene requires lots of clean water, is made simpler by modern technology, and is expensive.

Modou S. Joof, "DOSH Officials on Food Safety and Hygiene in Barra," *The Voice*, February 13–15, 2009.

People living in Barra are on edge these days, more so even than in other places, partly because of the government inspections of health facilities, restaurants, and bakeries (the latter rumored to be in response to Jammeh's opening his own bakeries and wanting to make things rough on their competition) and partly because of the

Photo 20   **"No, Mr., Not Here": A newspaper cartoon supporting The Gambia's new, comprehensive, anti-littering law.**

witch hunts that so recently hauled away unsuspecting citizens for exorcism. Wanting neither food nor any part in rites of exorcism, Doris and I board a *gellie-gellie* and head for a distant corner of Niumi where modernity (and political intimidation, we hope) are less evident. We do not escape quickly, however. Outside of Essau, heading east on the main road, we are stopped at a checkpoint by soldiers with guns, one appearing to be an automatic. They do not speak, but instead walk around the car, peering in sternly at the group of us seated inside. We know not to make eye contact. After a minute, one soldier waves his hand for the driver to proceed.

Ever since we arrived in The Gambia, people had been talking about the previous season's rains. Across West Africa, the drought that had been so devastating to crops and herds for more than thirty years seemed to have broken. "1974 was the last year before this one when more rain fell here," said Barry Wells, the U.S. ambassador to The Gambia.[1] For the traveler in the middle of the next dry season, the most obvious effect of the rains is on the roads: they are a mess. Many that run off the main, east-west blacktop simply washed away in the August and

September storms. Rather than wait for road repairs, which might not come for years, Gambian drivers find other paths to get to the same places, so we feel as if we are being taken all over the North Bank region just to get where we want to go. Even going the long way around, the roads are horribly rutted and slow going. Vehicles are in as bad shape as ever, too. Leaving Essau, we follow a Gambia Public Transportation Corporation bus that is so out of alignment that it appears to be going sideways, its rear racing its front. Even the Gambian riders, who know bad vehicles, stare and laugh.

Soon we notice effects of the continuing communications revolution. There are many more cell-phone towers than a few years before and young boys wear strips of phone cards across their chests like ammunition belts as they stand outside the ferry terminal and at spots where taxis stop in villages, hoping for a sale. The cards are such a perceived necessity that they stand on racks beside the tinned milk, matches, and canned sardines in every hole-in-the-wall store in every village. We are told there is at least one cell phone in every compound in every Niumi village, an exaggeration perhaps. Even where reception is bad, there is somewhere in the village, or just outside, where a person standing on a roof or a pile of chaff or even a termite mound can place and receive a call.

As we ride along, we notice the absence of peanut marketing. At this time of year not many years before, we would have seen people outside villages, standing in clouds of chaff, winnowing peanuts, and passed overloaded trucks hauling sacks of peanuts to depots or to the ferry. It is not by chance that we see none of this. "The peanut trucks are on the roads going into Senegal," one person tells us. "Buying is finished in Gambia."

As we pass through villages, we see paintings of the country's president on the walls of buildings in the center of town. One has written above it, "In Jammeh We Trust."

After a while, we come to a village with a new secondary school and decide to pay it a visit. The apprentice, who travels with the *gellie-gellie* to attract passengers and collect fares, bangs the side to notify the driver to stop so we can get off. We have driven off the tarred road, so dust settles over us in a cloud. It is mid-morning and already hot.

Schools in Banjul and its heavily populated suburbs are hives of activity—children outside playing, teachers pointing to lessons on blackboards, and happy chatter in the nearly constant recitation and play. In Niumi, this is not the case. In this school, as in another we visited earlier, a general torpor characterizes administrators, teachers, and pupils. We see a large group of girls hanging around in the shade of a massive mango tree, which looks like God created it for that purpose alone, and most of the teachers sitting under another. There appear to be as many female students as male, and the girls, some in *hijâb*, signifying Islamic consciousness, seem feisty and assertive. There is a mosque on the grounds and classes break for prayers. We notice not a single overweight student, and most are painfully skinny. The World Food Program furnishes lunch for all primary-school students, which is a big factor in parents' decisions about their children's attendance, but secondary students must provide their own. Emphasizing the skinny appearance are school uniforms that are either hand-me-downs from much older siblings or bought many sizes too big so they will last through all of the child's growth spurts. Many of the uniforms are badly worn and faded.

In the principal's office we find the *oustass*—the individual who teaches the Qur'an—in company with several women, one with a nursing child. He tells us the principal has stepped out for a while. He is happy to get a senior teacher to show us around.

We go first to the domestic science classroom, where several electric stoves sit covered with a layer of dust. Perhaps they are not used because women in Niumi cook outside, over charcoal fires. The lesson on the blackboard stresses cleanliness in food preparation and reminds students to wash hands thoroughly before dealing with food, but the appearance of the kitchen and the classroom suggests the advice is not well heeded. "Do boys take this course?" I ask. The teacher laughs, "No. Girls are here. Boys use the next classroom." We walk there and find what looks to be a woodworking and metal shop. All of the machines in the shop are in disrepair. The teacher seems apologetic and feigns optimism: "We are awaiting parts so we can fix the tools," he says.

The school has a computer lab, which our guide shows us with apparent pride, but we learn that the half-dozen PCs (also covered with dust), which were donated new in 2007, have not worked since September 2008. "For security, the computers were taken to another location when school was not in session, and when they came back, they did not work," the teacher says. Only now, in February 2009, has the headmaster been able to get a technician to have a look at them. His tools are a hammer and a screwdriver. When the computers work, off a small diesel generator, they have no connection to the Internet. "We called Gamtel [Gambia Telephone], they came to fix the connection, and it lasted three days," the teacher says. "We called again and could not get them to come back. So we use the computers just to teach basic skills." I assumed that meant word processing, but I saw no printers.

The library is a sadder place yet. We enter to find the librarian resting, prone, on a mat. Dust, again, covers everything and what books there are—maybe a few hundred total—are scattered, lying flat on tables and shelves and in no apparent order. A quick look through the books available for these secondary-level students shows basic science books written before humans reached the moon and books written for children of a much younger age. At the far end of the library a group of students is looking at a big map of the world. "The United States is so big," one of them says to Doris. "And The Gambia is so small," says another, bringing laughter.

The part of the school that appears to be operating most efficiently, and the one in which teachers take the most pride, is the garden, a large plot taking up one whole, sun-drenched corner of the grounds. Mango and cashew trees stand along one edge and cassava plants sprout in the middle. It has not rained here in over three months, so the plants must be watered every morning and evening with water from the school well at the entrance to the grounds, sixty feet away. Over school vacations, students from the community are responsible for coming to the school and watering. "This is part of our agricultural curriculum," says the teacher. "We are teaching our students life skills." Young people growing up in Niumi learned these "life skills" at home, of course, long before there was a school. Later, a parent explains that teachers emphasize the agricultural curriculum because they sell the garden's produce to supplement their meager salaries. Beginning teachers make only 900 dalasi a month, about $35. A person with little or no education who can get work as a cleaner of rooms in a tourist hotel across the river makes four times as much.

Back with the *oustass* and friends in the principal's office, we are told that the government has built these new secondary schools but leaves them with no budget for equipment or maintenance. "Government pays our salaries," one teacher says, "but we have to raise money ourselves to keep things operating." This comment brings knowing glances among our hosts, which I take as an indication of their lack of success at fund-raising.

Before we leave, several teachers pull us aside and want to find out what we can do to enhance their prospects for getting to America. "Does your university sponsor foreign students?" one asks. "Write down for me, please, your university's name." He seems disappointed when I explain I am retired from teaching. "Is there someone there I can write to who remembers you?" he asks.

As we walk from the school to the health center on the other side of the village, we catch up with three secondary-school students on their way home. Classes were dismissed in early afternoon, we learn, so preparations can be made for a day of athletics still a week away. The most talkative one of the bunch wants to be a historian, he says, and study Gambian history. When he learns we are Americans, he asks, "What are obstacles for gaining admission to American universities?" He has heard of Harvard and asks about its admission policies. I tell him Harvard would be a long shot, but we are reluctant to be honest about his circumstances, the value of the education he is getting, or the narrowness of the life he is likely to lead as an adult. His hometown is a village some miles to the north, near Senegal. He is boarding with an uncle in the village with the school and proud that his family pays for him to have a private tutor. "They don't teach you in school," he says. "Everybody knows you must have a tutor to learn."

So long as the one boy is with us and talking, the others do not say much, but when he heads off toward his uncle's compound, another boy tells us that he plans to leave the country for an education and return to be a minister of state. We wish him luck.

Once at the health center, we are impressed as we walk past a new building containing rooms where women can give birth. That is about all we are impressed with, however. We find the head nurse in his office, finishing lunch—the same oily-rice dish that nearly everyone eats. He is proud of the new building and the fact that he now supervises a staff of six. A physician visits the center only occasionally, but the head nurse, perhaps from necessity, insists, "We get along without one." This center deals mostly with prenatal care and deliveries, but also with malaria, gastrointestinal disorders, and cuts and scrapes requiring first aid. There is no laboratory, so patients whose condition is not evident from physical examination or those with more serious health problems must be sent across the river to Banjul, a hard, half-day trip even when a car is available. This visit takes me back to the sad case of an old friend, Jerre Manneh, who died in 2001 of complications from asthma. He experienced "a bad breathing spell" that worsened in the health center, his daughter told me, and by the time they got him to Banjul it was too late to save his life. Respiratory problems are chronic across sub-Saharan Africa, with people breathing smoke from cooking fires, bush fires in the dry season, and burning rubbish.

"Delivery of babies is a problem, too," the head nurse says. "You know, for some reason, most women deliver at night, so we need lights. We have solar panels, but they have never worked right. We have a generator, but I only have two gallons of fuel and the government will not buy any more. I write and call for assistance, but it does not come." The head nurse's existence here is bleak by our standards. The health center sits out in the open in a big yard of dry earth, no trees. The sun beats down on the corrugated tin roofs, so the heat builds up inside. When there is no breeze, it is stifling.

I know a family in a village down the road, and to drive us there we are able to round up a person with an old Mercedes diesel, which starts in a cloud of foul-smelling, dark smoke after young boys push it to life. The family we visit is large. In the same compound live the patriarch and his three wives, two of his sons (one with two wives, the other with one) and their families, the children of another son who is living in the capital, and two children of a daughter who also lives across the river. There are also three "apprentices"—young boys whose families cannot afford to feed them and are happy to turn them over to a family that can. The boys are not mistreated, but they end up doing most of the low-level labor around the compound. "All together we feed twenty-five a day," says one of the sons. "A [100-pound] bag of rice lasts two weeks."

Soon after our arrival, the patriarch assembles the family and formally states their condolences over my brother's death the previous June. They never knew him, but learned of his death from a village resident living in the United States. They consider Doris and me as family, which is easy since such relationships are forever vague. All over Niumi are "aunties" or "cousins," "brothers" or "uncles," terms seeming to connote a close relationship that only sometimes involves common DNA.

Like families everywhere, this one has its dramas. At their core is conflict between parents wanting their children to live in a certain fashion and their offspring having other ideas. Two daughters wearing school uniforms, already at a marrying age, have tasted—through school, television, talk with Gambians who have been to

Europe or America—another version of life than that lived in the family compound. They know that women who marry and remain in a Niumi village face a life of child rearing, hard work, and isolation. Maybe they will be allowed to go to Banjul to pursue nursing or teacher training or to get a job in the civil service (if they know someone) or a bank. They talk about this "all the time" with their friends. None of them wants to stay in the village. Their reason is not so much the hard work as it is that once educated, girls do not want to raise children in an isolated village. For their offspring, they want a different experience.

An older brother in the family has more freedom, but the drama is still there. He got his education at Muslim High School in Banjul, followed it with a two-year degree in accounting from The Gambia's technical school, and now lives outside Banjul, where he has a decent job in a bank. He has friends living in the United States, but he does not want to leave The Gambia. He is generous with his paycheck (a factor, no doubt, in the girls' clean, new school uniforms) and, a good Muslim, follows many of the ways of his parents. But he will not go back to the village to live. He is currently under intense pressure to "find a wife," fully aware how marriage would complicate his plans of going to the University of The Gambia for a four-year degree. As a consequence, he sends money through friends, but does not visit much. "They do not understand my situation," he says, "and they cannot leave me alone."

With a couple more places to visit and not wanting to miss the last ferry back to Banjul, we hail a passing *gellie-gellie* and find ourselves sitting next to a Gambian man, perspiring heavily in a double-breasted suit, conducting some kind of business on his cell phone, loudly and, we think, at least partly for show. "I back you 100 percent," he tells someone, "so proceed with the transaction."

We get the van to stop near trees holding bats' nests overhanging the Essau-Kerewan road near milepost 18. We are hoping to find Fatou Faye, an especially gregarious and forthcoming woman we spoke to in her garden, nearby, in 2003. We walk the quarter mile off the road to where her garden was located, but it is not there. A young woman working nearby knows Faye and says she can walk us to Faye's new spot. Like so many Gambian women, she has a gliding gait, a rolling of the hips without movement of the upper body, necessitated by carrying pails of water on her head. It looks like she is going slowly, but we have difficulty keeping up. When we get to Faye's plot, our guide gestures at it with one hand and then slips away quietly.

Three young girls working nearby tell us that Faye is attending her new grand-daughter's naming ceremony in the village, two miles away. One of the girls calls on her cell phone and reports that the ceremony is nearly over. We walk toward the village in the noonday sun and soon meet Faye, carrying a pink, plastic bucket and heading for the garden. She remembers us, she says, almost without breaking stride, and we talk on the tiring walk back. "I go to the garden every day," says the sixty-two-year-old Faye, "and I stay and work till near dark. These days I even take my breakfast with me, and I don't come home till evening."

Photo 21   **Gardener Fatou Faye** (second from left), **her son** (left), **and three garden helpers** (two of them her granddaughters) **in their garden in rural Niumi.**

By the time we reach the garden again, two of Faye's granddaughters and one older woman with very bad teeth are readying for work. We are not there long before Faye's son rides up on a cart drawn by a dapple horse. Faye lays a cloth over a log for Doris and me to sit on and overturns her bucket to use as a seat. Her son squats on his haunches and the three women stand nearby as Faye talks. It is soon clear that she is not as happy and spirited as she was six years earlier, and this is not entirely a matter of her aging.

Faye spent much of her adult life rearing children and doing the domestic work in her husband's compound. She gave birth to ten children, five of whom died in infancy and another in adolescence. Now, within the last two years, two more have died. One "went to a shop around nightfall, got bitten by a snake on the way, and died," she says, matter of factly, and a month later a daughter, a teacher in Essau, "got a sudden stomach ache, was admitted to the Health Center, and died the next day." Faye's husband, a farmer, is too old to work. "All he can do is keep animals out of the crops," she says. Her remaining daughter, who finished grade twelve in Kuntair "and then sat in the village for four years without a job," is now working in a primary school west of Banjul. Her remaining son, lacking any education, farms in the rainy season and does nothing in the dry season. He has lately borrowed money to buy the horse and cart, hoping to make money to pay off the loan by hauling women's vegetables to market. For the feast at the naming ceremony, as tradition obligates, the family bought a goat on credit for 1,500 dalasi, about $60. Faye was counting on the guests to leave cash gifts large enough to pay off the loan. She does not appear optimistic about these prospects. Her son's wife is now cooking for the extended family, so Faye can devote her days to gardening. For families like hers, small bits of cash from vegetable sales make a big difference.

In some ways Faye is a modern gardener and in some ways she is not. The Green Revolution is not lost on her: she takes the ferry and a taxi to a market outside of Banjul to buy seeds imported from Holland, but they are expensive and not always available. She also buys fertilizer when she can afford it. "Government gives other villages fertilizer and sends experts to diagnose problems with the vegetables and offer solutions, but we don't get those," she says, hinting at what everyone knows: that Jammeh rewards those who support him and punishes those who do not.

For Faye and all gardeners, the most taxing effort involves watering the plants twice each day. She does this by hauling water up from a deep well, hand over hand; filling a plastic bucket; lugging it the twenty yards to her garden plot; filling a can; and watering seedlings and plants. Her fondest dreams are of mechanical pumps, but she says, "We need simpler things like watering cans." Faye uses a standard-looking can for her seedlings, but to water established plants she fills a large tomato can with nail holes perforating its bottom, holds the can by its lip, and moves it back and forth. International economists call this irrigation.

Marketing the vegetables was Faye's biggest headache in 2003. "I grow good vegetables, but I can't control what happens to them," she told me then. But as gardening has continued to spread along the river's north bank and as demand for vegetables has grown with Gambians' changing notion of what is a proper meal, marketing the vegetables has become easier. (Many vegetables consumed by tourists in fancy restaurants and hotels across the river are still imported from Europe.) Middlemen (actually women) come from the capital region and from Fass, near the Senegal border, to buy vegetables. When they fail to come, Faye takes ripe vegetables to the *lumo*, the weekly market in Ndugu Kebbe, usually via *gellie-gellie*. (Her son raises his eyebrows at this, his way of noting that he can save her the fare by taking her on his new horse and cart.) "I get between 50 and 70 dalasi for a bucket of bitter tomatoes from the middlemen," she says, "and I get 75 dalasi for the same thing in the *lumo*."

Faye says she is under stress to come up with money for the family. "I have nine grandchildren. Three of them are in school," she says, "and they have no outside support. Without money, they can't stay in school. I've had to stop buying fertilizer. I use horse manure when I can get it." Some of the children are her son's, and he seems less concerned.

There is no doubt that Faye's advancing age is a factor in her gardening. "I can no longer grow potatoes or carrots," she admits, "because digging them is hard. My body hurts and I can't do as much work." This is why she asks her granddaughters to help in the garden. Her other problems involve animals and insects. "Without decent fencing, monkeys and cows get in and eat everything," she says. The fence

Photo 22 **Miriama, Fatumata, and Binta, three teenage gardeners, pause from their work, breaking clods in a new garden near Ker Wale in Lower Niumi.**

around her plot is made of logs and limbs, adequate, but not strong. "And this year the bugs have been in the bitter tomatoes and onions."

I remembered the last time talking to Faye about the television programs she watched, on a television powered by an eight-volt battery, so I ask if she still watches the same programs. "There's no time now for television," she says. "I'm here all the time. We don't have a television any more, anyway."

Faye looks sad and seems to want to get to work, so we walk down the way to speak to three girls who are doing the arduous work of breaking up hard clods of plowed earth with short-handled hoes, standing shoeless (but in socks) and bending at the waist to hack the clods. Mariama, Fatumata, and Binta are fourteen, fifteen, and seventeen. They have been working in the gardens since their families moved to Niumi from Baddibu, immediately east of Niumi, five years ago. They moved, the girls tell us, because there was nothing for women to do in Baddibu but grow rice during the rainy season, whereas here, with more water available, women can grow vegetables and thus gain income in the dry season as well. All the women in the compound are gardeners, they say. The men grow millet and peanuts, watermelon, maize, and peppers during the rains, but now, Fatumata says, "the men are all back at the compound."

"Do you attend school?" I ask. "No," says Binta. "This is our livelihood. We would have liked to go to school, but we could not. Now, if we could do school, it would be *madrassa* [a Qur'anic school], but we cannot even do that. We garden the year around." Work seems to fill up not only their waking hours, but also their dreams. When we asked what they would most like in life, their answers are fencing material (because "there is something in the squirrel family, but big and tough, that is eating our vegetables"), more wells closer to the garden, and assistance growing permanent crops—oranges, mangos, and cashews. A question about television elicits the first smiles we see from them. They have a color set. Fatumata says she likes seeing and listening to the American-born singer Maria De Angelis. Mariama likes the Argentine drama series *Esmeralda* and *Ruby*. On an impulse, I ask if they are married. They show no embarrassment in answering that they are not. Boys and young men, who have more freedom to go as they please and are almost expected to seek their fortunes elsewhere, at least for a while, are off in the city or elsewhere. One girl puts it simply: "Men are not forthcoming."

The girls do not want their photos taken because they are in their working clothes, but they make a few adjustments and consent. As we leave, I ask if they know who Barack Obama is. They all smile and one says, "Yes, his father is from Gambia and his mother is a *toubab* [white person]."

Fatou Faye's son appears again as we are saying good-bye to his mother and offers to take us to the road on his cart. We go around two cows butting heads, reach the road, say our good-byes, and within a few minutes are in yet another *gellie-gellie*. I have one more stop in mind, Berending, and a visit with another friend, Imam Karamo Njie, leader of the town's Muslim community. When we arrive, however, we learn that Njie has been ill and is staying with family across the river, close to the Royal Victoria Hospital so he can receive treatment. We go, instead, to speak with the imam's brother, Amadou Njie, director of the new Center for Traditional Medicine in Berending. The Gambia's president considers himself a gifted healer (asthma, kidney problems, and infertility, as well as HIV/AIDS, are in his repertoire), and he is using money from the Jammeh Foundation for Peace, funded by sources of dubious legality, to set up and staff local centers like this one. Njie proudly shows off his certificate as a practitioner of traditional medicine, signed by the president. It required no proof of training or testing, only payment of a fee.

He is eager to show us around the center. It is far better equipped than the health center we visited a few hours earlier, though it surpasses any place we've seen in its dust and clutter. We walk by wheelchairs and then see a room where patients receive diagnosis and treatment, a room with beds for those requiring overnight stays, and a cooking room where Njie prepares his traditional remedies. In addition to a stove, there is a large, wooden mortar and pestle for grinding herbs. In back of this room is a separate, small, windowless room holding jerry cans that contain his prepared medicines. Hanging from the ceiling in the back is a massive hive full of bees that he uses in the preparations. We meet two apprentices, friendly young men studying the traditional medicinal arts with Njie. One hands me a record of the names of people who have come to the center for treatment and their afflictions: "private parts pain, pain in liver, eye problems, pain in stomach," it reads. Each person has experienced the problem for "one or two years"; treatments are uniformly "successful."

We are pretty well spent by this time, so we welcome Njie's offer for one of his students to drive us the seven miles to Barra and the ferry. At the terminal gate, with the evening heat bearing down, I discard my everyman ethos, summon the guard, show him my college ID, and tell him I am on an approved visit to Niumi "educational institutions." He acts incredulous for a minute before allowing us to walk through the gate and out to the end of the pier, where there is a breeze off the river's estuary. Just about everyone else has found a way to get past the guard for cooler waiting than is available in the stuffy terminal.

We sidle up to a gaggle of U.S. Peace Corps volunteers, always easy to spot in a crowd, these just back from a softball tournament in Dakar. As we wait for the ferry, I ask the group about events in their villages. One says that the school in Berending has a new principal who "is getting things done." She believes "the principal is key. If he [and they all seem to be he rather than she] has lots of energy and drive, he can turn a school around fast." This is something I had not witnessed.

Another volunteer speaks of stress induced by "Jammeh clamping down!" He explains: "A teacher from our school was pulled away at night and brought to the police station. They took him to Banjul and held him for two weeks. All the time he was asking, 'What did I do?' It turns out he has a brother in Nigeria who said something about the Gambian government. Jammeh just won't allow any opposition to become effective. There are plenty of people opposed to him in my village, but they are afraid to act."

"How do Gambians deal with the stress?" I ask.

One volunteer answers quickly: "Pot!"

They all laugh, and when I shake my head in a skeptical way, another adds, "He's right. Men head to the farms every day with their bag. It gets them through. They can't drink alcohol. Pot is the most popular drug by far. Nobody bothers to hide it. They sit and smoke in front of the *alkalo*'s."

"There are dangerous escapes, too," says one. "A lot of young people do crazy things to get the hell out. Every week, I swear, a pirogue leaves one of those creeks over there [pointing upriver], full of boys hoping to get to Europe. Each one pays twenty or thirty dalasi to the skipper, who is responsible for giving them rice and two liters of water a day. It's really open. Every one of us knows someone who has tried to go to Spain by boat."

It comes on me like a cold slap when I remember that rice and two liters of water a day are close to the provisions on an eighteenth-century slaving vessel heading for the Americas.

"How many of them make it?" I ask.

"A lot don't, but enough to keep more wanting to risk the trip" is the answer.*

---

*Six weeks after this conversation, twenty-seven Gambians died when a boat taking them from Libya to Italy capsized. To the journalist writing the story, they are "irregular immigrants." "27 Gambians Feared Dead in Libyan Tragedy," *The Point,* April 6, 2009, http://thepoint.gm/africa/gambia/article/27-gambians-feared-dead-in-libya-tragedy.

We fall silent for a few minutes, watching Gambian children playing soccer on a strip of packed sand below us. As I notice the ferry churning through the water not far away, I ask, finally, "How is the recession affecting people here?"

They look at each other, apparently perplexed. One finally offers, "The global economy gets only lip service here. When the price of rice skyrockets, we'll hear a lot more. Maybe in the Kombos [the wealthy area around the capital] there is a noticeable effect. You might see some stalled construction over there. In the Niumis, the only thing I know is that less money in remittances is coming in. These are important and I think families are getting less because their sons or daughters living overseas have lost their jobs."

Before we can talk more, the ferry swings in and strong young fellows tie it to the pier. Though the boat will be here at least half an hour, unloading and loading, there is a rush of people to get off and others to get on that creates a human gridlock that stalls all movement. As crazy as this is, we join the rush and eventually get on board, climb to the top level, and find seats not far from the captain's cabin. Once under way, lulled into drowsiness by the setting sun and the steady throb of the ferry's diesels, I use the time to mull over Niumi's long history. Darkest Africa? Remote? Isolated? Hardly, I thought. Niumi has been part of a long globalization process, connected to a steadily widening world and part of one or another elaborate world system, for a thousand years and more. Its people have had been relying on products from distant places, its leaders living off long-distance trade and its culture changing because of influences from afar, into the distant past. I wondered if the world-system theory applied as much today as it did in the past, but much of the rest still seemed valid. World economic fluctuations, global warming, epidemics, improved technologies, advances in health care—all were affecting people's lives in Niumi by degrees, but were these people in this small place not still locked into the same basic economic circumstance they had endured for a thousand years or longer? I wondered.

And now, added on, are problems brought on by a tyrannical leader. For me, the Jammeh phenomenon is bracing and confusing. In the first two editions of this book I was confident that Niumi's place in a wider world had always been the single most important factor determining the nature of human existence there. Now, with tyranny literally at its doorstep, touching the lives of many residents and bringing harm and fear to its most apparent victims and their families, I was no longer so sure.

As before, my thoughts on the Islamic element troubled me, too. I knew that Islam had benefited people in the state in ways beyond the spiritual: in the nineteenth century, influential Muslims led the uprisings against the domineering ruling lineages, and in the twentieth century Islam was an important cultural force that gave Niumi's residents a sense of self-worth when European rules and customs were leading them to think otherwise. But in the face of the present situation of poverty and oppression, I was not so sure Islam was altogether a beneficial force. The resignation before "Allah's will" seemed to be keeping people from asking the right questions about their plight, much as an otherworldly Christianity led African-American slaves to suffer bondage on earth because theirs would be the kingdom of heaven. Most Niumi residents resign themselves to their living circumstances because they see Allah's hand in their poverty, hunger, illness, and short lives; in their lack of sufficient medical care and educational facilities; and in their loss of personal freedoms. I, on the other hand, blame the works of man, spending probably too much time wondering if it is the global or the local aspects of such works that are more responsible for the difficult lives of so many people who reside in Niumi.

The question such thinking always leads to is what—especially in this era of heightened globalization, when we know so much about the plight of the world's poor—should decent people of adequate means try to do about it? Those who speak from an ethical and humanitarian point of view focus on donations of aid. Philosopher Peter Singer, citing Thomas Aquinas's principle of "whatever a man has in super-abundance is owed, of natural right, to the poor for their sustenance," figures that "all it would take to put the world on track to eliminate global poverty . . . would be the modest sum of 1 percent of annual income—if everyone who can afford it were to give." Taking a more conservative, economic (and, they would add, pragmatic) approach are those who argue that the straight giving of aid not only does not end poverty, but causes harm. Former Goldman Sachs economist and Zambian national Dambisa Moyo believes that aid leads to corruption and stamps out initiative; she prefers that African nations enter the bond market and attract, from the outside, commercial investment. Though closer to Singer's position than Moyo's—his book's foreword was written by Bono, one of those Moyo criticizes for using their celebrity status to drum up aid for African nations—Columbia University economist and UN advisor Jeffrey D. Sachs takes a middle position, advocating for sufficient, targeted aid (toward building infrastructure, for example) from the world's wealthier nations to bring the poorest nations onto "the ladder of development."[2]

Just as I (once more) begin to feel I am close to working out the right solution to the problem of Africa's—and The Gambia's and Niumi's—poverty, about a mile out from the Banjul terminal, a tall, skinny young man from a Niumi family walks by and recognizes me from a lecture that I gave, and he attended, one evening at the University of The Gambia. When I tell him that Doris and I are doing some final investigating for this book and, in fact, had been in his village earlier in the day, he asks, "Tell me, prof, how much change do you see since your last time there, four years ago?"

"Well, the school now goes to the senior-secondary level," I answer, and after thinking some I add, "and the mosque looks like it has a fresh coat of whitewash." When he nods, I pause to think more, and the pause is lengthened by an amiable guy hawking perfume, spraying samples that leave wrists smelling like pungent flowers, and then lengthened again by an even more amiable, disabled man, who crawls up on stumps of knees to which he has tied flip-flops, asking for "charity" and saying in good English, "I will pray for your success and happiness; money given as charity is never wasted."

Back on the subject, I finally shake my head and admit, "I can't really think of anything else."

"That's what I thought," he says.

Once the ferry is tied to the pier, we face the hubbub of disembarking, joining women with enamel bowls of oranges balanced on their heads, men pushing homemade carts filled with everything from bags of commodities to old bicycles, businessmen in suits and ties, girls carrying the bags of peanuts and boys toting the bags of Kool-Aid-like flavored water that they spent the day offering "at good price," and heavily tattooed Europeans led along by Gambian men sporting dreadlocks, all rushing alongside massive trucks with brakes hissing and pipes belching foul exhaust, followed by SUVs full of Lebanese merchants and driven by impatient Africans with one hand on the wheel and the other hitting the horn, moving at a halting pace in the direction of the far gate. After passing through, we brave ranks of hawkers' stalls, then a regiment of boys selling DVDs, until we come to the street full of more taxis and people rushing every which way.

The tall young man from the ferry accompanies us through the hubbub and kindly offers a ride to our apartment, west of the city. He has come a long way, figuratively and literally, from the Niumi village of his youth. He works nights in a busy restaurant on the tourist strip, a job that allows him by day to pursue a bachelor's degree at the university. ("I only need three and one-half hours' sleep to function well," he says). The job has also enabled him to buy a small car, which is parked on the street two blocks away. As we get in, buckle up, and pull away, he apologizes for the loud clanking noise coming from the car's rear end. "I had an accident," he says. "Someone hit me from the rear and it has caused the noise."

"Do you have insurance that will pay for getting it fixed?" Doris asks.

"Yes," he says.

"But you haven't gotten it fixed?" she asks.

"No," he says, smiling wryly. "As you know, nothing in Gambia is ever finished."

After he drops us off, he drives down the sandy road and turns the corner. Even after he is out of sight, we hear the clank and squeak coming from the car's rear end. "Nothing in The Gambia," Doris repeats, "is ever finished." Nor is this story, we are sure.

NOTES

Part I. Background: Before A.D. 1446

1. Gomes Eanes de Azurara, *The Chronicle of the Discovery and Conquest of Guinea*, ed. C.R. Beazley and E. Prestage, 2 vols. (London: Hakluyt Society, 1896–1899), 252–257.

2. Alvise da Cadamosto, "The Voyages of Cadamosto," in *The Voyages of Cadamosto and Other Documents in Western Africa in the Second Half of the Fifteenth Century*, ed. G.R. Crone (London: Hakluyt Society, 1937), 97–100.

Chapter 1. The Global Setting for Niumi's History: Before A.D. 1446

1. William H. McNeill, "The *Rise of the West* after Twenty-five Years," *Journal of World History* 1 (1990): 10.

2. Lynda N. Shaffer, "Southernization," *Journal of World History* 5 (1994): 1–21.

3. Literature on globalization has filled publishers' booklists over the past decade. Thomas L. Friedman brought popular attention to the topic with *The Lexus and the Olive Tree*, 2nd ed. (New York: Anchor Books, 2000), and in *The World Is Flat: A Brief History of the Twenty-First Century* (New York: Farrar, Straus and Giroux, 2005). Friedman shows again his enthusiasm for the benefits that the process is capable of bringing to the people of the world. Joseph E. Stiglitz, *Globalization and Its Discontents* (New York: Norton, 2002) is more balanced. In the World Bank's *Globalization, Growth, and Poverty: Building an Inclusive World Economy* (Washington, DC: World Bank, and New York: Oxford University Press, 2002), a team of World Bank economists, led by Stiglitz, points out how globalization is failing to help some 2 billion of the world's people. A relevant essay for this book is Frederick Cooper, "What Is the Concept of Globalization Good For? An African Historian's Perspective," *African Affairs* 100 (2001): 189–213. Paul Collier, in *The Bottom Billion: Why the Poorest Countries Are Failing and What Can Be Done About It* (New York: Oxford University Press, 2007), argues that globalization alone is not likely to help the world's neediest people and offers suggestions for things that will. In other recent work are suggestions that there is not one globalization, but many (Barry K. Gillis, "The Turning of the Tide," in *Globalization and After*, ed. Samir Dasgupta and Ray Kiely [Thousand Oaks, CA: Sage, 2006], 13–20), and argument that variants of the term, *glocalization* and *grobalization*, are necessary for identifying "broad and important types" of globalization (George Ritzer and Michael Ryan, "The Globalization of Nothing," in *The Changing Face of Globalization*, ed. Samir Dasgupta [Thousand Oaks, CA: Sage, 2004], 298–317).

4. McNeill, "The *Rise of the West* after Twenty-five Years," 19; see also McNeill's *The Rise of the West* (Chicago: University of Chicago Press, 1963).

5. In recent literature, Jurgen Osterhammel and Niels P. Peterson consider the major forms taken by premodern and modern globalization in *Globalization: A Short History* (Princeton: Princeton University Press, 2003), 31–35, and in *Africa and the New Globalization* (Burlington, VT: Ashgate, 2008), George Klay Kieh Jr. differentiates between "old globalization" and "new globalization."

6. Immanuel Wallerstein, *The Modern World-System: Capitalist Agriculture and the Origins of the European World-Economy in the Sixteenth Century* (New York: Academic Press, 1974); *The Modern World-System II: Mercantilism and the Consolidation of the*

European World-Economy (New York: Academic Press, 1980); and *The Modern World-System III: The Second Era of Great Expansion of the Capitalist World-Economy* (San Diego: Academic Press, 1988); *World-Systems Analysis: An Introduction* (Durham, NC: Duke University Press, 2004). In "Africa and World-Systems Analysis: A Post-Nationalist Project?" in *Writing African History*, ed. John Edward Phillips (Rochester, NY: University of Rochester Press, 2005), 381, William G. Martin terms Africa and world-systems analysis "a parodoxical relationship."

7. Wallerstein believes that we presently are experiencing an "age of transition" into a new structure, characterized by "chaotic behavior" (Immanuel Wallerstein, "Globalisation or the Age of Transition?" in *Globalisation: One World, Many Voices*, ed. Samit Kar (New Delhi: Rawat Publications, 2004), 47–68. For examples of those who extend the world-system model further into the past, see André Gunder Frank and Barry K. Gillis, eds., *The World System: Five Hundred Years or Five Thousand?* (New York: Routledge, 1993); and Sharon R. Steadman, "Isolation vs. Interaction: Prehistoric Cilicia and Its Role in the Near Eastern World System" (PhD diss., University of California at Berkeley, 1994).

8. A new summary of the theory is Wallerstein, *World-Systems Analysis: An Introduction* (Durham, NC: Duke University Press, 2004).

9. In addition to economic zones labeled "core" and "periphery," Wallerstein's model has an intermediate zone, the "semi-periphery," which includes nations in transition from core to periphery, or vice versa, and consequently shares characteristics with each group. For the sake of simplicity, I omit discussion of the semi-periphery in this brief treatment.

10. Janet Lippman Abu-Lughod, *The World System in the Thirteenth Century: Dead-End or Precursor?* (Washington, DC: American Historical Association, 1993), 4–5. A useful critique of world-systems theory is Vincente Navarro, "The Limits of World-Systems Theory," in *Socialist States in the World System*, ed. Christopher K. Chase-Dunn (Beverly Hills, CA: Sage, 1982).

11. Richard M. Eaton, *Islamic History as Global History* (Washington, DC: American Historical Association, 1990), 43; John O. Voll, "Islam as a Special World System," *Journal of World History* 5 (1994): 213–226.

12. Eaton, *Islamic History*, 44–45.

13. David Wilkinson, "Core, Peripheries, and Civilization," in *Core/Periphery Relations in Precapitalist Worlds*, ed. C. Chase-Dunn and T. Hall (Boulder, CO: Westview Press, 1991), 113–166.

14. Janet L. Abu-Lughod, *Before European Hegemony: The World System A.D. 1250–1350* (New York: Oxford University Press, 1989), 367.

15. Eaton's *Islamic History* is a good, brief discussion of the conflicting interpretations of recent Islamic history.

16. Abu-Lughod, *Before European Hegemony*, 203.

17. The standard, now dated, general treatment of the trans-Saharan trade is E.W. Bovill, *The Golden Trade of the Moors*, 2nd ed. (London: Oxford University Press, 1968). Chapter 2 of Ralph Austen, *African Economic History* (Portsmouth, NH: Heinemann, 1987) is a good summary of the trade based on more recent findings.

18. William H. McNeill suggests a "Chinese primacy between A.D. 1000 and 1500" in *"The Rise of the West* after Twenty-Five Years." Abu-Lughod (*World System in the Thirteenth Century*, 2–11) argues for eight circuits, or subsystems, integrated into the larger world system of the thirteenth century. Recent works that emphasize the early importance of East Asia are R. Bin Wong, *China Transformed: Historical Change and the Limits of European Experience* (Ithaca, NY: Cornell University Press, 1997); André Gunder Frank, *Re-Orient: Global Economy in the Asian Age* (Berkeley: University of California Press, 1998); and Kenneth Pommeranz, *The Great Divergence: China, Europe, and the Making of the Modern World Economy* (Princeton: Princeton University Press, 2000).

19. Abu-Lughod, *World System in the Thirteenth Century*, 3; K.N. Chaudhuri, *Trade and*

Civilisation in the Indian Ocean: An Economic History from the Rise of Islam to 1750 (Cambridge: Cambridge University Press, 1985); K.N. Chaudhuri, *Asia before Europe: Economy and Civilisation in the Indian Ocean from the Rise of Islam to 1750* (Cambridge: Cambridge University Press, 1990); Jung-Pang Lo, "The Emergence of China as a Sea Power during the Late Sung and Early Yuan Periods," *Far Eastern Quarterly* 14 (1955): 489–503.

20. Abu-Lughod, *Before European Hegemony*, ch. 11; *World System in the Thirteenth Century*, 2, 11–18.

21. For Europe's rise to prominence in this early world system, see Abu-Lughod, *Before European Hegemony*, pt. 1; and Fernand Braudel, *Civilization and Capitalism, 15th–18th Century*, vol. 3, *The Perspective of the World* (New York: Harper and Row, 1994), ch. 2.

22. A good discussion of the importance of the Crusades to European commercial and political growth is in William D. Phillips Jr. and Carla Rahn Phillips, *The Worlds of Christopher Columbus* (Cambridge: Cambridge University Press, 1992), 17ff.

23. Abu-Lughod, *Before European Hegemony*, 352–364.

24. Ibid., 108, 116, 118.

25. Discussion of the Black Death is based on William H. McNeill, *Plagues and Peoples* (Garden City, NY: Anchor Books, 1976), 165ff.

26. Jung-Pang Lo, "The Decline of the Early Ming Navy," *Oriens Extrêmus* 5 (1958): 149–168.

27. Abu-Lughod, *Before European Hegemony*, 361.

28. Wallerstein, *Modern World-System*, 37–45; Eric R. Wolff, *Europe and the People Without History* (Berkeley: University of California Press, 1982), ch. 4.

29. For religious motives for European expansion, see Phillips and Phillips, 38–43.

30. Braudel, 138–143, deals with "the unexpected rise of Portugal." Peter Russell, *Prince Henry "the Navigator": A Life* (New Haven, CT: Yale University Press, 2000), explores Henry's activities and the world in which they took place.

31. For the problems Europeans encountered trying to sail into the Atlantic and the technological discoveries that enabled them to do so, see Philip D. Curtin, "The Slave Trade and the Atlantic Basin: Intercontinental Perspectives," in *Key Issues in the Afro-American Experience*, 2 vols., ed. Nathan I. Huggins, Martin Kilson, and Daniel M. Fox (New York: Harcourt Brace Jovanovich, 1971), 1:77–80; John Thornton, *Africa and Africans in the Making of the Atlantic World, 1400–1680*, 2nd ed. (New York: Cambridge University Press, 1998), ch. 1; and Phillips and Phillips, *Worlds of Christopher Columbus*, ch. 4.

32. Thornton, *Africa and Africans*, 22–23.

33. Ibid., 24–29.

34. Austen, *African Economic History*, 36 and Appendix A3.

35. Andrew Watson, *Agricultural Innovation in the Early Islamic World: The Diffusion of Crops and Farming Techniques, 700–1100* (Cambridge: Cambridge University Press, 1983), ch. 6; Colleen Kriger, "Mapping the History of Cotton Textile Production in Precolonial West Africa," *African Economic History* 33 (2005): 94–96.

36. Eaton, *Islamic History*, 27.

37. Ibid., 25–26; Thomas C. Hunter, "The Development of an Islamic Tradition of Learning among the Jahanke of West Africa" (PhD diss., University of Chicago, 1977).

38. For the formation of states in the western Sudan, see Nehemia Levtzion, "The Sahara and the Sudan from the Arab Conquest of the Maghrib to the Rise of the Almoravids," in *The Cambridge History of Africa*, vol. 2, *From c. 500 B.C. to c. A.D. 1500*, ed. J.D. Fage (Cambridge: Cambridge University Press, 1978), 637–684. Roland Oliver offers useful thoughts on the issue in *The African Experience: Major Themes in African History from Earliest Times to the Present* (London: Weidenfeld & Nicholson, 1991), 93–95.

39. George E. Brooks, *Landlords and Strangers: Ecology, Society, and Trade in Western Africa, 1000–1530* (Boulder, CO: Westview Press, 1993), 7.

40. Nehemia Levtzion, *Ancient Ghana and Mali* (London: Methuen, 1973), ch. 5.

41. Robin Law, "Slaves, Trade, and Taxes: The Material Basis of Political Power in Precolonial West Africa," *Research in Economic Anthropology* 1 (1978): 37–52.

Chapter 2. Niumi in a Restructuring World System: Before A.D. 1446

1. Olga Linares de Sapir, "Shell-Middens of Lower Casamance and Diola Protohistory," *West Africa Journal of Archaeology* 1 (1971): 41.

2. Brooks, *Landlords and Strangers*, 12.

3. A good, concise discussion of the region's physical geography is in Brooks, ibid., ch. 1.

4. Annual Report, North Bank Province, June 1921, CSO 1/163.

5. Donald R. Wright, "What Do You Mean There Were No Tribes in Africa? Thoughts on Boundaries—and Related Matters—in Precolonial Africa," *History in Africa* 26 (1999): 409–426.

6. J.R. Harlan, J.J.J. de Wet, and A.B.L. Stemler, eds., *Origins of African Plant Domestication* (The Hague: Mouton, 1976).

7. Philip D. Curtin, *Economic Change in Precolonial Africa: Senegambia in the Era of the Slave Trade* (Madison: University of Wisconsin Press, 1975), 218–219.

8. Philip D. Curtin discusses "Killing Diseases of the Tropical World" in *Death by Migration: Europe's Encounter with the Tropical World in the Nineteenth Century* (Cambridge: Cambridge University Press, 1995), ch. 5.

9. UNDP, *Human Development Report 1991* (New York: Oxford University Press, 1991), 123, 127; *World Tables 1995* (Baltimore: Johns Hopkins University Press, 1995), 295.

10. Except where otherwise noted, information on Gambian society is from Brooks, *Landlords and Strangers*, 33–47; Curtin, *Economic Change*, 29–37; or Donald R. Wright, "Niumi: The History of a Western Mandinka State through the Eighteenth Century" (PhD diss., Indiana University, 1976), 16–27.

11. For a good discussion of West African ethnicity and the role colonial officials played in defining African ethnic groups, see David C. Conrad and Barbara E. Frank, "*Nyamakalaya*: Contradiction and Ambiguity in Mande Society," in *Status and Identity in West Africa: Nyamakalaw of Mande*, ed. David C. Conrad and Barbara E. Frank (Bloomington: Indiana University Press, 1995), 7–10.

12. This describes a patrilocal society, as most Senegambian societies are today. Evidence from oral tradition hints that society in Niumi may have been matrilocal, and perhaps matrilineal, a long time ago, but this is impossible to determine.

13. F. Lafont, "Le Gandoul et les Niominkas," *Bulletin du Comité des études historiques et scientifique de l'Afrique occidentale française* 21 (1938): 414; Paul Pélissier, *Les paysans du Sénégal: Les civilisations agraires du Cayor à la Casamance* (Paris: Imprimerie Fabrèque, 1966), 411.

14. Brooks, *Landlords and Strangers*, 4, 45–46.

15. Curtin, *Economic Change*, 29–37. Peter Weil offers an extended discussion of Mandinka classes in "Slavery, Groundnuts, and European Capitalism in the Wuli Kingdom of Senegambia, 1820–1930," *Research in Economic Anthropology* 6 (1984): 77–119.

16. Conrad and Frank, "*Nyamakalaya*," 10–16; Tal Tamari, "The Development of Caste Systems in West Africa," *Journal of African History* 32 (1991): 221–250.

17. Brooks, *Landlords and Strangers*, 73–77.

18. Good sources for precolonial African slavery are Paul E. Lovejoy, *Transformations in Slavery: A History of Slavery in Africa*, 2nd ed. (Cambridge: Cambridge University Press, 2000); Claude Meillassoux, *The Anthropology of Slavery: The Womb of Iron and Gold*, trans. Alide Dasnois (Chicago: University of Chicago Press, 1986); Suzanne Meirs and Igor Kopytoff, eds., *Slavery in Africa: Historical and Anthropological Perspectives* (Madison: University of Wisconsin Press, 1977); and Arthur Tuden and Leonard Plotnicov, *Social Stratification in Africa* (New York: Free Press, 1970).

19. Martin A. Klein summarizes some of these data in "The Demography of Slavery in the Western Sudan in the Late Nineteenth Century," in *African Population and Capitalism: Historical Perspectives*, ed. Joel Gregory and Dennis Cordell (Boulder, CO: Westview Press, 1987), 50–62.

20. Tuden and Plotnicov, *Social Stratification*, 12.

21. Meirs and Kopytoff, *Slavery in Africa*, Introduction.

22. Thornton, *Africa and Africans*, ch. 3.

23. Ibid., 74.

24. Ibid., 86.

25. Martin A. Klein, "Women in Slavery in the Western Sudan," in *Women and Slavery in Africa*, ed. Claire C. Robertson and Martin A. Klein (Madison: University of Wisconsin Press, 1983), 67–92.

26. Curtin, *Economic Change*, 154–155.

27. Walter Rodney, *A History of the Upper Guinea Coast, 1545–1800* (Oxford: Oxford University Press, 1970), 258ff.

28. During a drought at the end of the eighteenth century, Scottish physician and explorer Mungo Park noticed women who had turned over their children to local rulers in exchange for provisions to keep themselves alive. He related: "There are many instances of freemen voluntarily surrendering up their liberty to save their lives. During a great scarcity, which lasted for three years in the countries of the Gambia, great numbers of people became slaves in this manner." *Travels in the Interior of Africa* (London: Cassell, 1887), 57, 108.

29. Carol Spindel discusses the importance of age groupings in the past and shows how they are considerably less important today in a part-Mande village in northern Ivory Coast in *In the Shadow of the Sacred Grove* (New York: Vintage Books, 1989), 93, 124–127.

30. Brooks, *Landlords and Strangers*, 44–46, 73–77.

31. Ibid., 74.

32. Ibid., 38–39; V.R. Dorjahn and Christopher Fyfe, "Landlord and Stranger: Change in Tenancy Relations in Sierra Leone," *Journal of African History* 3 (1962): 391–397.

33. Cadamosto, "Voyages," 69.

34. Stephan Bühnen, "Place Names as an Historical Source: An Introduction with Examples from Southern Senegambia and Germany," *History in Africa: A Journal of Method* 19 (1992): 1–57. This argument is supported generally by Jean Giraud, *L'or du Bambouk: une dynamique de civilisation ouest-africaine: du royaume de Gabou à la Casamance* (Geneva: Georg Editeur, 1992).

35. Curtin, *Economic Change*, 19–22; Pélissier, *Les paysans du Sénégal*, 192–196; Wright, "Niumi," 9–12.

36. Cadamosto, "Voyages," 70–71.

37. Felipe Tejada, "The Ñiominka" (unpublished paper, Indiana University, c. 1980), 2–4.

38. Philip D. Curtin, *Cross-Cultural Trade in World History* (Cambridge: Cambridge University Press, 1984), 1–2, 17–18, 26–28, 38–39; Curtin, *Economic Change*, ch. 2; Abner Cohen, "Cultural Strategies in the Organization of Trading Diasporas," in *The Development of Indigenous Trade and Markets in West Africa*, ed. Claude Meillassoux (Oxford: Oxford University Press, 1971), 267ff.

39. Giraud, *L'or du Bambouk*, passim.

40. Leon Pales, *Les sels alimentaires: sels minéraux, problème des sels alimentaires en AOF* (Dakar: Direction Général de la Santé Publique, 1950), 13–14, 39, 93–96.

41. George Brooks calls attention to the importance of the kola nut trade in "Kola Nuts and State-Building: Upper Guinea Coast and Senegambia, 15th–17th Centuries" (Working Paper, No. 38, African Studies Center Boston University, 1980). The trading of kola is a principal theme of Brooks, *Landlords and Strangers*.

42. Giraud, *L'or du Bambouk*, passim.

43. Diogo Gomes argued over religion with a Muslim from one such establishment in Niumi and visited an emporium in Cantor, a commercial hub far up the Gambia. Diogo Gomes, "The Voyages of Diogo Gomes," in *Voyages of Cadamosto . . .* , 92–95.

44. Evidence that the state's rulers were not Mandinka and, indeed, were Atlantic-oriented Niuminka is from oral traditions and Diogo Gomes, who, when in the Gambia River in 1457, sent the ruler of Niumi "many presents by his own men in his own canoes, which were going for salt to his own country." Such salt, which "was plentiful there, and of a red colour," was in the coastal territory occupied by the Niuminka. Gomes, "Voyages," 97.

45. Wright, "What Do You Mean?" 414–416.

46. Here, again, one can get bogged down by European concepts of political independence. Virtually every state had relationships of reciprocity and dependence with others in its neighborhood, through marriage alliances and other mutual obligations. To say that the state of Niumi was "apparently independent" in the middle of the fifteenth century simply means that the Portuguese did not refer to its owing allegiance, including payment of tax or tribute, in any formal way to another political authority.

47. Cadamosto, "Voyages," 67.

48. Ivana Elbl, "Cross-Cultural Trade and Diplomacy: Portuguese Relations with West Africa, 1441–1521," *Journal of World History* 3 (1992): 174–175.

Chapter 3. Niumi Between Two Systems: Waxing Atlantic Trade, Continuing Sudanic Trade, 1446–1600

1. Alfred W. Crosby, *Germs, Seeds, and Animals: Studies in Ecological History* (Armonk, NY: M.E. Sharpe, 1994), esp. chs. 1 and 9; A.J.R. Russell Wood, *World on the Move: The Portuguese in Africa, Asia, and America, 1415–1808* (New York: St. Martin's Press, 1992), ch. 5.

2. Bovill, *Golden Trade*, 87–88.

3. C.R. Boxer, *The Portuguese Seaborne Empire, 1415–1825* (New York: Knopf, 1975), 8.

4. Cadamosto, "Voyages," 68.

5. Gomes, "Voyages of Diogo Gomes," 95.

6. Boxer, *Portuguese Seaborne Empire*, 18–19, 24; Curtin, *Economic Change*, 198–206.

7. Philip D. Curtin, *The Rise and Fall of the Plantation Complex* (Cambridge: Cambridge University Press, 1989), 42–43.

8. Curtin has written the clearest treatments of the plantation complex: *The Tropical Atlantic in the Age of the Slave Trade* (Washington, DC: American Historical Association, 1991) is a short description; *Rise and Fall* is a more complete account. Discussion here is based on Curtin's work.

9. Crosby, *Germs, Seeds, and Animals*, 36–37 and ch. 3. Curtin ties disease factors to the centuries-long existence of the Atlantic slave trade in "Epidemiology and the Slave Trade," *Political Science Quarterly* 83 (1968): 190–216.

10. Curtin, *Economic Change*, 155–156; Brooks, *Landlords and Strangers*, 130.

11. Suggesting that it was the Portuguese horse trade that set the stage for Senegambia's fifteenth-century political upheaval are Robin Law, *The Horse in West Africa: The Role of the Horse in the Societies of Pre-Colonial West Africa* (Oxford: Oxford University Press, 1980), 52–53; and Jean Boulègue, *Le grand Jolof (xviiie–xvie siècle)* (Paris: Diffusion Karthala, 1987), 72–77. Ivana Elbl argues otherwise effectively in "The Horse in Fifteenth-Century Senegambia," *International Journal of African Historical Studies* 24 (1991): 85–110.

12. Sources for the early history of Senegambia are Brooks, *Landlords and Strangers*; Curtin, *Economic Change*, ch. 1; Boulègue, *Le grand Jolof*; James F. Searing, *West African Slavery and Atlantic Commerce: The Senegal River Valley, 1700–1860* (Cambridge: Cam-

bridge University Press, 1993), ch. 1; and James L.A. Webb Jr., *Desert Frontier: Ecological and Economic Change along the Western Sahel, 1600–1850* (Madison: University of Wisconsin Press, 1995), chs. 1 and 2.

13. Law, *Horse in West Africa;* Webb, *Desert Frontier*, ch. 4; and Elbl, "Horse in Fifteenth-Century Senegambia."

14. Cadamosto, "Voyages," 49.

15. Webb, *Desert Frontier*, 70–72.

16. Gomes's account shows how quickly the Portuguese recognized the importance of the horse trade and got involved. In 1458, on his way home from his first Senegambian voyage, Gomes admonished the ruler of the island of Gorée, just off Cape Verde, telling him, "It would be better for him to make peace with [the Christians], and that both might exchange merchandise, so that he might have horses, &c., as Burbuck [Walo] and Badamel [Kayor], and other lords of the negroes had." In 1460 Gomes made a second voyage to West Africa. When he arrived at Joal, the major Atlantic port of the state of Siin, immediately north of Niumi, he found two caravels, one commanded by a Portuguese and the other by a Genoese, each "conveying horses thither." Gomes, "Voyages of Diogo Gomes," 99–101.

17. Much of the information on Kaabu is from oral traditions. Summaries and interpretations are in Brooks, *Landlords and Strangers*, 109–113; B.K. Sidibe, *A Brief History of Kaabu and Fuladu, 1300–1930: A Narrative Based on Some Oral Traditions of the Senegambia* (Banjul: Oral History and Antiquities Division, 1974); and Mamadou Mané, "Contribution à l'histoire du Kaabu, des origines au xix siècle," *Bulletin de l'Institut Fondamental d'Afrique Noire*, Series B, 40 (1978): 87–159.

18. A representative sampling of these oral data is in Donald R. Wright, *Oral Traditions from The Gambia*, vol. 1, *Mandinka Griots*, and vol. 2, *Family Elders* (Athens: Ohio University Center for International Studies, 1979, 1980).

19. Some of my earlier ideas of these events are in Donald R. Wright, *The Early History of Niumi: Settlement and Foundation of a Mandinka State on the Gambia River* (Athens: Ohio University Center for International Studies, 1977), ch. 3.

20. Landing Nima Sonko, interview, Berending, Lower Niumi District, November 1, 1974.

21. Jack Goody, *Technology, Tradition, and the State in Africa* (London: Oxford University Press, 1971), chs. 2 and 3.

22. It is a problem discussing Mandinka kinship groupings using the English terms "clan" and "lineage," for such terms are imprecise. Here a clan constitutes all individuals with the same surname who share a sense of having descended from a common ancestor, often a mythical figure who lived in the distant past. Lineages of the same clan can be spread across broad areas of the western savannas. Clan members do not necessarily have personal acquaintance with one another. A lineage is a smaller grouping of people with the same surname, normally several extended families in the same village that know one another and share common descent from an ancestor they can identify from not so long ago.

23. Curtin, *Economic Change*, 66.

24. Jack Goody, "The Impact of Islamic Writing on the Oral Cultures of West Africa," *Cahiers d'Etudes Africaines* 11 (1971): 455–466.

25. Brooks, *Landlords and Strangers*, 129; Gomes, "Voyages of Diogo Gomes," 97.

26. European accounts and maps that include discussion or listing of Muslim clerical towns (*morecunda*) usually include one or more in Niumi. For the Jahanka and their trading network from the upper Gambia, see Lamin O. Sanneh, *The Jahanke: The History of an Islamic Clerical People of the Senegambia* (London: Oxford University Press, 1979); and Curtin, *Economic Change*, 67, 75–83. Hunter's dissertation contains information on divination, charm making, and the supernatural.

27. Much of the information on early Portuguese and *lançado* activities is from Brooks, *Landlords and Strangers*, chs. 7–9. Also useful are Jean Boulègue, *Les Luso-Africains en Séné-*

gambie, xvie–xixe siècle (Lisbon: Instituto de Investigação Cientifica Tropical, 1989); and Peter Mark, *"Portuguese" Style and Luso-African Identity: Precolonial Senegambia, Sixteenth–Nineteenth Centuries* (Bloomington: Indiana University Press, 2002), chs. 1 and 2.

28. Elbl, "Horse in Fifteenth-Century Senegambia," 102.

29. Cadamosto, "Voyages," 49.

30. Brooks, *Landlords and Strangers*, 165.

31. Ibid., 189–192.

32. J.W. Blake, *Europeans in West Africa, 1450–1560* (London: Hakluyt Society, 1942), vol. 1, 213–217.

33. Bakary Tall, interview, Juffure, Upper Niumi District, December 15, 1974.

34. Ivana Elbl, "Cross-Cultural Trade," *Journal of World History* 3 (1992): 177–181.

35. Records of such payments are in the Gambia Castle Charge Book, 1737, T 70/1452.

36. François Froger, *Relation d'un voyage . . . aux côtes d'Afrique* (Amsterdam: Chez les Heritiers d'Antoine Shelte, 1702), 31; Jean-Baptiste Labat, *Nouvelle rélation de l'Afrique occidentale* (Paris: Chez Guilaume Cavalier, 1728), 5:312–314.

37. Mark, in *"Portuguese" Style*, 23, argues for the development of a Luso-African ethnic group along the Upper Guinea Coast and discusses how in Senegambian cultures identity formation was "flexible, malleable, and based on cultural and socioeconomic factors."

38. Peter Mark, "Constructing Identity: Sixteenth- and Seventeenth-Century Architecture in the Gambia-Geba Region and the Articulation of Luso-African Ethnicity," *History in Africa: A Journal of Method* 22 (1995): 310–311, 315; Valentim Fernandes, *Description de la côte occidentale d'Afrique (Sénégal au Cap de Monte, Archipels)*, ed. and trans. Theodore Monod et al. (Bissau: Centro de Estudos da Guiné Portuguesa, 1951), 37; André Alvares de Almada, *Tratado breve dos Rios de Guiné*, trans. P.E.H. Hair, 2 vols. (Liverpool: University of Liverpool, 1984), 1:43–44.

39. Mark, *"Portuguese" Style*, ch. 2.

40. According to Brooks, the word *pirogue* "derives from sixteenth-century European usage of *pirague*, a Galibi Indian word from Brazil." It clearly was brought to Senegambia by the Portuguese; see *Landlords and Strangers*, 209. One can still see pirogues in the Gambia's estuary and along the adjacent Atlantic coast, small ones launched in the morning offshore breeze and larger motorized adaptations conducting fishing operations in deeper water.

41. Much of the discussion on introductions of plants is based on Stanley B. Alpern, "The European Introduction of Crops Into West Africa in Precolonial Times," *History in Africa: A Journal of Method* 19 (1992): 13–43.

42. Brooks, *Landlords and Strangers*, 7.

43. An interesting sidelight to Gambians' sixteenth-century dietary changes, which involved including American peppers to make stews spicier, is a current change in the opposite direction. To accommodate the tastes of European tourists, who find high levels of pepper in Gambian food unacceptable, Gambian cooks are leaving out the pepper, rendering dishes long considered traditional without their identifying taste.

44. Alpern, "European Introduction of Crops," n.1; Stanley B. Alpern, "What Africans Got for Their Slaves: A Master List of European Trade Goods," *History in Africa: A Journal of Method* 22 (1995): 12–13.

45. Curtin, *Economic Change*, 154–156.

Chapter 4. Niumi at the Height of the Atlantic Complex: Seventeenth and Eighteenth Centuries

1. J.B.L. Durand, *A Voyage to Senegal* (London: Printed for Richard Phillips, 1806), 40.

2. Curtin, *Economic Change*, 309–311.

3. Hugh Trevor-Roper on the BBC program *Listener*, November 28, 1963.

4. John M. Gray, *A History of the Gambia* (London: Frank Cass, 1940), 326–327. Gray refers to Niumi's *mansa* as a "king," but encloses the title in quotation marks to indicate that the ruler was hardly a sovereign in the European sense.

5. Compare Sharon E. Nicholson, "Climatic Variations in the Sahel and Other African Regions during the Past Five Centuries," *Journal of Arid Environments* 1 (1978): 3–24, with Brooks, *Landlords and Strangers*, ch. 1.

6. Webb, *Desert Frontier*, 5–9.

7. Before the twentieth century, it was commonplace for residents of an agricultural village in West Africa to move the village. Reasons for such movement were numerous, but mostly they had to do with declining fertility of farming land, decreasing healthfulness of the site because of accumulation of waste or growing presence of disease factors, or general depletion through use of the resources in the neighborhood of the village. Such natural events as fire destroying a village, which occurred with frequency in a land where dry-season burning of brush was the first step in the annual agricultural cycle, or a fierce storm leveling a portion of a village, often precipitated a decision to move. Regular movement was expected, and houses thus were constructed as temporary dwellings rather than as permanent structures.

8. Webb, *Desert Frontier*, 8.

9. In his diaries and quarterly reports from colonial Gambia's North Bank Province in the 1920s, Commissioner Emilius Hopkinson regularly commented on the difficulty of keeping horses alive in Niumi.

10. This segment relies heavily on Curtin, *Rise and Fall of the Plantation Complex*, chs. 6 and 7.

11. "The Transatlantic Slave Trade Database," www.slavevoyages.org/tast/index. faces.

12. Alfred W. Crosby, "The Potato Connection," *World History Bulletin* 12 (1996): 1–5; Crosby, *Germs, Seeds, and Animals*, 92 and ch. 9.

13. Curtin, "Slave Trade and the Atlantic Basin," 90.

14. Gray, *History of the Gambia*, ch. 5.

15. Eaton, *Islamic History*, 27–29, 40–41; Nehemia Levtzion, "Patterns of Islamization in West Africa," in *Conversion to Islam*, ed. Nehemia Levtzion (New York: Holmes & Meier, 1979), 207–216.

16. The English reference to Nandanko's activities is in Joseph Debat and Robert Coulton to the Committee, James Fort, December 8, 1760, T 70/30, 388.

17. Difficulty is inherent in discussing the way things were a long time ago in African societies. Most evidence of state structures and functions is from oral tradition, which presents a formalized ideal rather than an accurate sense of a state's workings. And African states were far from static. They changed over time to enable rulers to deal with new economic, social, and political circumstances. It is almost impossible to discuss with precision the evolutionary nature of a state's governmental apparatus because evidence for gradual institutional change does not exist. I have needed to infer a good bit to make the descriptive comments that follow. In addition to oral data, they are based on contemporary European accounts and anthropological studies. Specific citations to these are in Wright, "Niumi," ch. 4.

18. This official's title in Niumi was *bukenek*. Mandinka states typically had no such official, but Wolof polities did. The *bukenek*'s existence in Niumi suggests the kind of borrowing and assimilation that went on over time—in political structure and most other cultural manifestations—where people mixed and mingled.

19. Landing Jammeh, interview, Brikama, Kombo Central District, December 13, 1974.

20. William Wilkinson, *Systema Africanum; or a Treatise Discovering the Intrigues and Arbitrary Proceedings of the Guiney Company* (London: 1690), 11–12, as quoted in Gray, *History of the Gambia*, 96.

21. M. St. Vendrille, commandant of the frigate *Mutiné*, River Gambia, September 20, 1702, B$_4$23, 391.

22. Minutes of Council, James Fort, November 18, 1722, Rawlinson MS, C-745–7, 580; Gambia Castle Charge Book, 1736, T 70/1452.

23. See, for example, Journal for the Factory on James Island in the River of Gambia, January 9, 1664, T 70/544; Gambia Journal, James Island, August 31, 1693–November 30, 1699, T 70/546; Account-Ledger, Gambia, 1728, T 70/838; Gambia Castle Charge Book, 1737, T 70/1452.

24. Gambia Journal, James Island, August 31, 1693–November 30, 1699, T 70/546; Gambia Castle Charge Book, 1737, T 70/1452; M. Blain to Commandant Particulier à Gorée, July 18, 1846, 13$_G$317, 51.

25. Accounts and Charges, James Fort, 1734, T 70/1451.

26. Francis Moore, *Travels into the Inland Parts of Africa* (London: Edward Cave, 1738); Gambia Castle Charge Book, 1736, T 70/1452.

27. Evidence of the importance of regional marriage linkages is mostly from oral traditions, but some contemporary written evidence is informative. In 1737 and 1738 payments appear in Gambia Castle Charge Books to "Jay Sunco," apparently one of the *mansa*'s daughters, who is identified as "a great Fidalgo and Head Wife of the late King of Bursally [Saloum]." The Charge Books are in T 70/1452–3.

28. A considerable body of evidence describes the process a European vessel had to go through to enter and trade in the Gambia River. The requirements changed over time, of course. See, for example, Abbé Demanet, *Nouvelle histoire de l'Afrique Françoise*, 2 vols. (Paris: Duchesne, 1767), 1:133–134; Thomas Weaver to Royal African Company, James Island, May 4, 1704, T 70/13, 78; or A. & P., 1789, LXXXIV (646a), pt. 1 (Privy Council Report), Captain Heatley, quoted in Roger Anstey, *The Atlantic Slave Trade and British Abolition, 1760–1810* (Cambridge: Cambridge University Press, 1975), 20.

29. James Skinner et al. to the Committee, James Fort, March 12, 1754, T 70/30, 76; Anth. Rogers and Thos. Harrison to Royal African Company, James Fort, February 12, 1732, T 70/7, 192.

30. John Snow to Royal African Company, Gambia, May 8, 1708, T 70/18, 21; Skinner et al. to the Committee, James Fort, January 28, 1752, T 70/29/34.

31. Goody, *Technology, Tradition, and the State in Africa*, ch. 2.

32. Oral traditions contain considerable information relating to such activity, though without a sense of when it took place. Information in "Details sur l'établissement des française dans la rivière de Gambie et sûr le caractere de quesques rois de ce pays," c. 1776, C$_6$17, suggests that the depredations of rulers and their entourages began earlier, perhaps in the middle of the eighteenth century. George Brooks treats the disappearance of Luso-Africans along the Gambia in *Eurafricans in Western Africa: Commerce, Social Status, Gender, and Religious Observance from the Sixteenth to the Eighteenth Century* (Athens: Ohio University Press, 2003), 280–287.

33. Alpern, "What Africans Got for Their Slaves," 6; Curtin, *Economic Change*, 172.

34. Alpern, "What Africans Got for Their Slaves," 23; Curtin, *Economic Change*, 315–319. Demanet, *Nouvelle histoire de l'Afrique Françoise*, 1:242–250, is a discussion of merchandise in demand along Africa's Guinea Coast by a man who spent time in Niumi.

35. Richard Jobson, *The Golden Trade* (London: Dawsons of Pall Mall, 1623), 113; Colleen E. Kriger, *Cloth in West Africa* (Lanham, MD: AltaMira Press, 2006), 132.

36. Watson, *Agricultural Innovation*, ch. 6; Marion Johnson, "Cloth as Money: The Cloth Strip Currencies of Africa," in *Textiles in Africa*, ed. Dale Idiens and K.G. Ponting (London: Pasold Research Fund, 1980), 193–202.

37. B.W. Hodder, "Indigenous Cloth Trade and Markets in Africa," in *Textiles in Africa*, 205–206.

38. In addition to showing that the *mansa* of Niumi's sister married the ruler of sometime-

enemy Saloum, these records offer evidence that the *mansa* had wives and children residing about the state and beyond, and that the *mansa*'s "people" helped the "Emperor of Fogny," across the river, fight against his neighbors. English letters attest to the importance and pervasiveness of marital obligations. David Francis wrote to the Royal African Company on August 30, 1715 (T 70/6/22), "The French . . . at Albreda . . . are married to the Chief women of the country, who having canoes & boats up the river, prevent the merchants coming down with their trade." And Thomas Rutherford wrote to William Knox from the African Office in London, September 23, 1778 (CO 267/17), "The Castle Slaves [employed by the English on James Island] are so closely connected with the People of the Country by Marriages and other Social Ties, that an Attempt to remove any of the former would infallibly occasion very great Disturbances and Insurrections among the Natives, and render the Safety of the Forts and Settlements highly precarious, as their Defense depends more on the Attachment of the Slaves than on the feeble Force in Civil and Military Servants."

39. Curtin, *Economic Change*, 207–215, 240–241, 312–314; Alpern, "What Africans Got for Their Slaves," 12–16; Demanet, *Nouvelle histoire de l'Afrique Françoise*, 1:242.

40. R.A. Kea notes similar use of firearms on the Gold and Slave coasts in "Firearms and Warfare on the Gold and Slave Coasts from the Sixteenth to the Nineteenth Centuries," *Journal of African History* 12 (1971): 185–213. Disagreement continues over uses of firearms and their role in the enslaving process, as indicated by J.E. Inikori, "The Import of Firearms into West Africa, 1750–1807: A Quantitative Analysis," *Journal of African History* 18 (1977): 339–368. See, too, Alpern, "What Africans Got for Their Slaves," 18–22, and Curtin, *Economic Change*, 324–325. Demanet, *Nouvelle histoire*, 1: 249, reported that guns were "only for the Kings and the big men of the court."

41. James Island journals and log books, T 70/544 and 550; Alexander Cleeve to Royal African Company, James Island, August 24, 1680, T 70/20, 53; Curtin, *Economic Change*, 323; and Alpern, "What Africans Got for Their Slaves," 24–25. The availability of so much strong spirits must have had an adverse effect on Senegambian society. Moore, 85, offers evidence: "The King [of Saloum] and all his Attendance profess the *Mahometan* Religion, notwithstanding they drink so much Strong Liquors; and when he is sober, or not quite fuddled, he prays."

42. Boulègue, *Les Luso-Africains en Sénégambie*; Curtin, *Economic Change*, 95–100; Brooks, *Landlords and Strangers*, 188–196; Brooks, *Eurafricans in Western Africa*; and Mark, *"Portuguese" Style and Luso-African Identity*.

43. Ledger for the Factory on James Island, begun January 9, 1664, by Capt. John Ladd, T 70/827; Moore, *Travels Into the Inland Parts of Africa*, 55.

44. Labat, *Nouvelle rélation de l'Afrique occidentale*, 5:377–378; Prosper Cultru, *Premier voyage de Sieur de la Courbe fait à la coste d'Afrique en 1685* (Paris: Emile Larose, 1913), 196.

45. Accounts and Charges, James Fort, and Gambia Castle Charge Books, 1733–8, T 70/1451–3.

46. Ledger for the Factory on James Island, 1664, T 70/827; Journal of the Factory on James Island, 1665, T 70/545; Natives Employed as Linguisters and Messengers, James Fort, 1720, T 70/1450; Accounts and Charges, James Fort, T 70/1451.

47. Accounts and Charges, James Fort, 1733, T 70/1451; Relation veritable de Jean Baptiste Benoist cy dessous Commandant en Gambia en 1723 et 1724, May 10, 1720, $C_6$29; Gambia Castle Charge Book, 1735, T 70/1452.

48. Curtin, *Economic Change*, 100; Boulègue, *Les Luso-Africains en Sénégambie*, 66–67, 87; various Accounts and Ledgers, James Fort, 1758–9, T 70/582, 868; Demanet, *Nouvelle histoire de l'Afrique Françoise*, 1:122–224; Brooks, *Eurafricans in Western Africa*, ch. 9.

49. Nehemia Levtzion, "The Eighteenth Century: Background to the Islamic Revolutions in West Africa," in *Eighteenth-Century Renewal and Reform in Islam*, ed. Nehemia Levtzion and John O. Voll (Syracuse, NY: Syracuse University Press, 1987), 28.

50. Interview with Afang Seku Fati in Aljamdu, Upper Niumi District, December 14, 1974.

51. "The Minister of the King of Niumi is named Faudé, is a Marabout—or a Mohammedan Priest." M. Poncet de la Riviere à Government, Gorée, May 25, 1764, C₆15.

52. Philip D. Curtin, "Jihad in West Africa: Early Phases and Inter-Relations in Mauritania and Senegal," *Journal of African History* 12 (1971): 11–24; Levtzion, "Eighteenth Century."

53. Donald R. Wright, "The Epic of Kelefa Saane as a Guide to the Nature of Precolonial Senegambian Society—and Vice Versa," *History in Africa: A Journal of Method* 14 (1987): 307–327. John Iliffe, *Honour in African History* (New York: Cambridge University Press, 2005), ch 2.

54. Kathryn L. Green describes the formation of a Mande-speaking group of *soninke* (Sonongui) in northern Côte d'Ivoire in the eighteenth century in "Dyula and Sonongui Roles in the Islamization of the Region of Kong," in *Rural and Urban Islam in West Africa*, ed. Nehemia Levtzion and Humphrey J. Fisher (Boulder, CO: Lynne Rienner, 1987), 97–117.

55. Evidence for heightened class solidarity and identification is from oral traditions, but corroboration exists in contemporary written records. In 1734, a "great warrior," Toggomoi Fall, who was the "Prince of Biole" (Baol, a Wolof state north of Niumi) and a brother to the ruler of Kayor, on Baol's north, paid a visit to James Island. Coming in his company were Maunkey Njie, "a Jelleware [*guelowar*, the Wolof equivalent of *soninke*] of Colar [Kular]" and the "King of Niumi's people" to make proper introductions. It was a delegation from the ruling strata of a significant part of western Senegambia. Accounts and Charges, James Fort, 1734, T 70/1451.

56. This argument does not agree with the ideas of historians who believe the Senegambian ruling elites became predatory with their subjects only after the Atlantic slave trade ended, thereby reducing royal revenues. See, for example, Boubacar Barry, "Senegambia from the Sixteenth to the Eighteenth Century: Evolution of the Wolof, Sereer, and 'Tukulor,'" in *General History of Africa*, vol. 5, *Africa from the Sixteenth to the Eighteenth Century*, ed. B.A. Ogot (Paris: UNESCO, 1992), 262–299; and Martin A. Klein, "Social and Economic Factors in the Muslim Revolution in Senegambia," *Journal of African History* 13 (1972): 419–441. Curtin argues that royal revenues did not decline with the ending of the Atlantic slave trade in Senegambia and that evidence is not sufficient to postulate increased slave raiding and lawlessness on the part of the ruling groups in "The Abolition of the Slave Trade from Senegambia," in *The Abolition of the Atlantic Slave Trade: Origins and Effects in Europe, Africa, and the Americas*, ed. David Eltis and James Walvin (Madison: University of Wisconsin Press, 1981), 83–97.

57. Curtin, *Economic Change*, 325–327.

58. Gambia Journal, July 1–December 31, 1741, T 70/576. Account and Charge Books from James Island (T 70/545 and 1451-2) provide evidence for grain purchases.

59. Charles O'Hara to Lord of the Treasury, Fort Lewis, Senegal, September 15, 1768, CO 267/14; Matthias McNamara to Earl of Dartmouth, James Fort, June 8, 1775, CO 267/16.

Chapter 5. A Time of Transition in Niumi: 1816–1965

1. D'Arcy to Major Mackey, Bathurst, July 5, 1866, CSO 1/13.

2. Extracts from Previous Annual Reports, 1894–1920, CSO 9/134.

3. Walter Rodney, *How Europe Underdeveloped Africa* (London: Bogle-l'Ouverture, 1972); Basil Davidson, *Black Mother: Africa and the Atlantic Slave Trade*, rev. ed. (Harmondsworth, UK: Penguin, 1980).

4. Immanuel Wallerstein, "Africa and the World-Economy," in *General History of Africa*, vol. 6, *Africa in the Nineteenth Century Until the 1880s*, ed. J.F. Ade Ajayi (Paris: UNESCO, 1989), 23–39. Similarly, J. Forbes Munro points to the period between 1800 and

1870 as a time when "older connexions with the international economy were cast off and new ones evolved" and when "new systems of production and exchange" brought a greater extent, and a different kind, of "African integration into the international economy," in *Africa and the International Economy: An Introduction to the Modern Economic History of Africa South of the Sahara* (Totowa, NJ: Rowman and Littlefield, 1976), 41.

5. Peter M. Stearns, *Interpreting the Industrial Revolution* (Washington, DC: American Historical Association, 1991), ch. 5.

6. Vaclav Smil, *Energy in World History* (Boulder, CO: Westview Press, 1994), ch. 5 passim.

7. Daniel P. Headrick, *The Tools of Empire: Technology and European Imperialism in the Nineteenth Century* (New York: Oxford University Press, 1981).

8. Michael P. Adas, *Machines as the Measure of Men: Science, Technology, and Ideologies of Western Dominance* (Ithaca: Cornell University Press, 1989), ch. 5 passim. "The White Man's Burden" is in Rudyard Kipling, *Complete Verse: Definitive Edition* (New York: Doubleday, 1940), 321–323.

9. John Ralph Willis, "Introduction: Reflections on the Diffusion of Islam in West Africa," in *Studies in West African Islamic History*, vol. 1, *The Cultivators of Islam*, ed. John Ralph Willis (London: Frank Cass, 1979), 1–39.

10. Ibid., 2.

11. By the mid-nineteenth century at least some members of Niumi's ruling elite were Muslims, though perhaps not good ones. In January 1834, the ruling lineages put off the installation of Demba Sonko as the new *mansa* because it was the holy month of Ramadan (Rendall to Hay, Bathurst, January 17, 1834, CO 87/10). Three decades later an English official labeled the *suma* of Essau, who was leading Niumi's *soninke* forces against Muslims from Niumi and Baddibu, "a Marabout-Soninke" because he claimed to be a Muslim and said his prayers but did not want to give up political control to the Muslims. Of course, nearly all of Niumi's *mansa* and their entourages drank heavily. Nineteenth-century British officials believed that the most obvious trait separating non-Muslims from Muslims was the latter's abstinence from alcohol.

12. Curtin, "Jihad in West Africa," 11–24; Boubacar Barry, *Le royaume du Waalo: Le Sénégal avant la conquête* (Paris: François Maspero, 1972), 137–142 and pt. 2, ch. 2 passim. Barry contends that the *toubenan* was an Islamic uprising against slave trading of the traditional ruling elites.

13. Levtzion, "Patterns of Islamization in West Africa," 207–216. Levtzion provides other information relevant to the discussion that follows in Nehemia Levtzion, *Islam in West Africa: Religion, Society and Politics to 1800* (Aldershot, UK: Variorum, 1994), 1–38.

14. These figures are from Curtin, *Economic Change*, 164, Table 4.3. Curtin divides the numbers into French and British exports. I have assumed that most of the British exports listed are from the Gambia River. Because British traders obtained slaves from elsewhere in Senegambia, my average figures are high, especially for the 1760s and 1770s. Nevertheless, they show trends from one decade to another.

15. Curtin, "Abolition of the Slave Trade from Senegambia," 85–92.

16. Lucie G. Colvin, "Interstate Relations in Precolonial Senegambia," paper presented at the annual meeting of the African Studies Association, Syracuse, NY, 1973.

17. Col. A. Grant to Gen. McCarthy, St. Mary's [River Gambia], June 24, 1816, CO 26/42.

18. "Extract from a letter from Lt. Col. Alexander Grant to R.W. Hay, Esq., Under Secretary of State," November 25, 1825, CSO 1/2, 297–302.

19. Gov. Turner to Earl of Bathurst, July 4, 1825, Freetown, CSO 2/2; Alexander Grant to Earl of Bathurst, October 26 and November 26, 1820, CO 267/51.

20. Paul Mbaeyi, *British Military and Naval Forces in West African History, 1807–1874* (New York: Nok, 1978), 71–73.

21. Sir Neil Campbell to Earl of Bathurst, Freetown, August 3, 1827, CSO 2/2.

22. Col. Alexander Findlay to R.W. Hay, Bathurst, March 1, 1829, CO 87/2; Lt. Gov. Rendall to R.W. Hay, Bathurst, April 28, 1830, CO 87/3.

23. A summary of what the British termed "The Barra War" is in letters from Rendall to Lord Viscount Goderich, Bathurst, August 24, 1831–January 30, 1832, CO 87/5, 46–60.

24. Rendall to Goderich, Bathurst, January 30, 1832, CO 87/6.

25. This treaty is in CSO 1/4.

26. The history of early peanut production along the Gambia River is based on George E. Brooks, "Peanuts and Colonialism: Consequences of the Commercialization of Peanuts in West Africa, 1830–1870," *Journal of African History* 16 (1975): 29–54; and Kenneth Swindell and Alieu Jeng, *Migrants, Credit, and Climate: The Gambian Groundnut Trade, 1834–1934* (Boston: Brill, 2006), ch. 1.

27. Martin A. Klein, *Islam and Imperialism in Senegal: Sine-Saloum, 1847–1914* (Stanford, CA: Stanford University Press, 1968), 36–37; Hazel R. Barrett, *The Marketing of Foodstuffs in The Gambia, 1400–1980* (Aldershot, UK: Avebury, 1988), 37.

28. Barrett, *Marketing of Foodstuffs*, 36–39; Curtin, *Economic Change*, 14, 231; Charlotte A. Quinn, *Mandingo Kingdoms of the Senegambia: Traditionalism, Islam, and European Expansion* (Evanston, IL: Northwestern University Press, 1977), 77; Gambia Ground-Nut Trade Statistics, CSO 54/157.

29. Munro, *Africa and the International Economy*, 45. Historians continue to argue related points. See John Thornton, "Precolonial African Industry and the Atlantic Trade, 1500–1800"; responses to Thornton by Ralph A. Austen, Patrick Manning, Jan S. Hogendorn and H.A. Gemery, and E. Ann McDougall; and Thornton's rejoinder, all in *African Economic History* 19 (1990): 1–54.

30. Jan S. Hogendorn, "The 'Vent-for-Surplus' Model and African Cash Agriculture to 1914," *Savanna* 5 (1976): 15–28.

31. Swindell and Jeng, *Migrants, Climate, and Credit*, ch. 2.

32. Curtin, *Economic Change*, 171, 230.

33. Extracts from Annual Reports, 1894–1920, CSO 9/134.

34. [Col. George A.K. d'Arcy], "Gambia Colony and the Civil War," *Colburn's United Service Magazine*, 419–420 (1863): 405.

35. Klein, "Social and Economic Factors in the Muslim Revolution," 419–41; Curtin, "Abolition of the Slave Trade from Senegambia," 83–97.

36. David Robinson, "Abdul Qadir and Shaykh Umar: A Continuing Tradition of Islamic Leadership in Futa Toro," *International Journal of African Historical Studies* 6 (1973): 286–303; David Robinson, *The Holy War of Umar Tal: The Western Sudan in the Mid-Nineteenth Century* (Oxford: Clarendon Press, 1985).

37. Charlotte Alison Quinn, "Maba Diakhou and the Gambian *Jihad*, 1850–1890," in *Studies in West African Islamic History*, ed. John Ralph Willis (London: Frank Cass, 1979), 233–258.

38. H. Ingram to Lord Stanley, Bathurst, December 2, 1841, CO 87/28; O'Connor to Secretary of State for Colonies, Bathurst, August 28, 1854, CO 85/57.

39. O'Connor to Secretary, December 2, 1841, CO 87/57; O'Connor to H. Labouchere, Bathurst, January 12, 1857, CO 87/64.

40. British Blue Books from Gambia show that in the decade of the 1830s, for example, nearly 100,000 firearms and 23,000 barrels of gunpowder passed through the customs post at Bathurst. CO 90/4–13.

41. d'Arcy, "Gambia Colony and the Civil War," 238.

42. As late as 1975, residents of Tubab Kolong could show visitors the massive, old silk-cotton tree with the gouge in the side made by a British cannonball. Evidence for the "Tubab Kolong War" is in letters and reports from d'Arcy to his superiors in CSO 1/12 and 1/13.

43. Mahmood Bah to the Queen of England, Powas, Baddibu, June 20, 1871, CO 87/100; W. Boreham to Henry Fowler, Fort Bullen, April 24, 1871, CO 87/99.

44. Michael Adas, *"High" Imperialism and the "New" History* (Washington, DC: American Historical Association, 1995) treats recent thinking on late-nineteenth-century imperialism, including the takeover of Africa.

45. Harry A. Gailey, *A History of the Gambia* (New York: Praeger, 1965), chs. 5 and 6.

46. Extracts from Annual Reports, CSO 9/134.

47. Swindell and Jeng, *Migrants, Climate, and Credit,* 87–98. O'Connor's statement is in O'Connor to Labouchere, May 31, 1857, CO 87/63. Information on the operation of the export-import and credit systems is in various early annual reports of British commissioners. See, for example, Traveling Commissioner's Report, North Bank Province, 1893, CSO 60/1.

48. Swindell and Jeng, *Migrants, Climate, and Credit,* 115 passim. Information on the operation of the export-import and credit systems is in early annual reports of British commissioners, for example: Traveling Commissioner's Report, North Bank Province, 1893, CSO 60/1.

49. Swindell and Jeng, *Migrants, Climate, and Credit,* 35–37; Traveling Commissioner's Report, North Bank Province, 1901, CSO 9/134.

Chapter 6. Niumi as Part of the Gambia Colony and Protectorate: 1897–1965

1. Monthly Diary, Traveling Commissioner, North Bank Province, January 31, 1921, CSO 2/460.

2. Annual Report, North Bank Province, 1929, CSO 1/168.

3. "Agreement Entered into Between Administrator R.B. Llewelyn and Maranta Sonko, King of Niumi," April 7, 1893, CSO 9/824; Treaty of Protection, January 2, 1897, CSO 9/824.

4. Denton to Secretary of State, November 6, 1903, CO 87/170; Annual Report, North Bank Province, 1905 (CO 87/74), 1908 (CSO 2/123), 1911 (CSO 60/2), and 1912 (CSO 60/2).

5. Munro, *Africa and the International Economy*, ch. 5.

6. Michael Crowder, "The First World War and Its Consequences," in *General History of Africa*, vol. 7, *Africa Under Colonial Domination, 1880–1935*, ed. A. Adu Boahen (Paris: UNESCO, 1985), 283.

7. S.M. Martin, "The Long Depression: West African Export Producers and the World Economy, 1914–1945," in *The Economies of Africa and Asia in the Inter-War Depression*, ed. Ian Brown (New York: Routledge, 1989), 74–94.

8. Quoted in William Roger Louis, *Imperialism at Bay: The United States and the Decolonization of the British Empire, 1941–1945* (New York: Oxford University Press, 1978), 200.

9. After 1893, Niumi's Ceded Mile, while technically part of the colony, was administered as protectorate. Once Niumi joined the protectorate, the Ceded Mile's special status was all but forgotten.

10. Lord Lugard, *The Dual Mandate in British Tropical Africa* (London: Blackwood and Sons, 1922).

11. Jan Hogendorn explains the theory behind such taxes in "Economic Initiative and African Cash Farming: Pre-Colonial Origins of Early Colonial Developments," in *Colonialism in Africa, 1870–1914*, vol. 4, *The Economics of Colonialism*, ed. Peter Duignan and L.H. Gann (Cambridge: Cambridge University Press, 1975), 302.

12. Annual Report, North Bank Province, 1899, CO 87/159.

13. Annual Report, North Bank Province, 1919, CSO 60/2.

14. Extracts from Annual Reports, 1901, CSO 9/134.

15. Lamin Sowe, interview, Berending, Lower Niumi District, March 16, 1996.

16. Gailey, *History of the Gambia*, 115–117.

17. H. Lloyd Pryce, "The Laws and Customs of the Mandingos of the North Bank Province of the Gambia Protectorate," unpublished report, 1906, CSO 1/151.

18. Traveling Commissioner's Report, North Bank Province, 1893, CSO 60/1.

19. Traveling Commissioner's Report, North Bank Province, 1894, CSO 60/1.

20. Traveling Commissioner's Report, North Bank Province, 1896, CSO 60/1.

21. Denton to Secretary of State, Bathurst, March 30, 1903, CO 87/168.

22. P.H.S. Hatton, "The Gambia, the Colonial Office, and the Opening Months of the First World War," *Journal of African History* 7 (1966): 123–124; Peanut export statistics are in Swindell and Jeng, *Migrants, Credit, and Climate,* 16, 24, 102, 149, and 201.

23. See, for example, G.C.B. Parish to Commissioner, North Bank Province, February 19, 1932; and R.W. Macklin to Colonial Secretary, January 22, 1932, CSO 2/1167.

24. Archibald J. Brooks, Report by the Director of Agriculture, October 22, 1930, CSO 75/11.

25. At one point in 1921, commissioners discussed taking silver ornaments that people were wearing in repayment of the debt. Information on the debt problem is in Commissioners' Conferences, CSO 56/1; Annual Report, North Bank Province, 1921, CSO 1/163; "Increased Export Duty on Groundnuts," 1922, CSO 3/49; and "Rice and Seed-Nut Debt," March 26, 1924, CSO 1/166.

26. Gailey, *History of the Gambia*, 167–169; Annual Report, North Bank Province, 1922, CSO 1/163.

27. "Increased Export Duty on Groundnuts," 1922, CSO 3/49.

28. R.W. Cohen to Undersecretary of State for Colonies, London, January 3, 1930, CSO 4/33.

29. Maj. John Bingham to Mr. Stanley, Edinburgh, August 29, 1943, CO 87/255/7.

30. H.R. Palmer to Legislative Council, Bathurst, December 14, 1932, CO 89/23.

31. Palmer, Address on Legislative Council, June 27, 1934, CO 63/10.

32. Quarterly Report, North Bank Province, June 30, 1937, CSO 2/1632.

33. Quarterly Report, North Bank Province, September 30, 1936, CSO 2/1589.

34. Annual Report, Western Division, 1951 (CSO 63/9) and 1952 (CSO 63/10).

35. Oliver, *African Experience*, 187.

36. Gailey, *History of the Gambia*, 166.

37. Ibid., ch. 5.

38. Ibid., 166.

39. Denton to Secretary of State, April 19, 1904, Bathurst, CO 87/171.

40. C.H. Armitage to Secretary of State for Colonies, May 26, 1921, CO 87/213.

41. Annual Report, North Bank Province, 1931, CO 87/236/11; "Lower Niumi District—Medical and Health Matters," CSO 9/421.

42. Minutes of Gambia Legislative Council, November 22, 1929, CO 87/213.

43. Gailey, *History of the Gambia*, 177.

44. "Establishment of Mission Station and School at Essau by St. Mary's Church Body," 1931, CSO 2/1142.

45. "Essau School," CSO 6/43.

46. "Berending School," CSO 6/59.

47. Gailey, *History of the Gambia*, 152–157.

48. J.C. Froelich, "Essai sur les causes et méthods de l'Islamisation de l'Afrique de l'Ouest du xie au xxe siècle," in *Islam in Tropical Africa*, ed. I.M. Lewis (London: Oxford University Press, 1966), 166.

49. A. Quellien, *La politique Musulmane dans l'Afrique occidentale française* (Paris:

Larose, 1910), 100, cited in Donal Cruise O'Brien, "Toward an 'Islamic Policy' in French West Africa, 1854–1914," *Journal of African History* 8 (1967): 305. Discussion of the influence of Comte on colonial Islamic policy is in Peter B. Clarke, *West Africa and Islam: A Study of Religious Development from the 8th to the 20th Century* (London: Edward Arnold, 1982), 189–190.

50. Clarke, *West Africa and Islam,* 202–212; Donal Cruise O'Brien, *The Mourides of Senegal* (Oxford: Oxford University Press, 1971); Cheikh Anta Babou, *Fighting the Greater Jihad: Amadu Bamba and the Founding of the Muridiyya of Senegal, 1853–1913* (Athens, OH: Ohio University Press, 2007).

51. Information in this paragraph and subsequent discussion of the village of Aljamdu is based on information from interviews in Aljamdu, Tubab Kolong, and Sika in 1974 and 1975.

52. Quarterly Report, North Bank Province, September 30, 1939, CSO 2/1777.

53. Myron Echenberg, *Colonial Conscripts: The Tirrailleurs Sénégalais in French West Africa, 1857–1960* (Portsmouth, NH: Heinemann, 1991), 29–31; Quarterly Commissioner's Diary, North Bank Province, November–December 1914, CSO 2/167.

54. Hatton, "Gambia, the Colonial Office, and the Opening Months of the First World War," 123–131; "Trade of the Gambia," September 14, 1914, CSO 1/156; Annual Report, North Bank Province, 1915, CSO 1/157.

55. "Military Report on the Gambia," December 12, 1923, CSO 1/164.

56. "The Gambia Company in East Africa," May 31, 1918, CSO 1/159.

57. "Military Report on the Gambia," December 12, 1923, CSO 1/164.

58. Governor of Gambia to Secretary of State for Colonies, June 10, 1917, CSO 1/159; Annual Report, South Bank Province, 1917, CO 87/205.

59. Annual Report, North Bank Province, 1917, CSO 60/2; Commissioner's Diary, North Bank Province, June 30, 1917, CSO 2/167.

60. Extracts from Previous Annual Reports, North Bank Province, 1917, CSO 9/134.

61. "Military Report on the Gambia," December 12, 1923, CSO 1/164; Annual Report, North Bank Province, June 1921, CSO 1/163.

62. John M. Barry, *The Great Influenza: The Epic Story of the Deadliest Plague in History* (New York: Penguin, 2004), 397.

63. Information on flu and its effects in Gambia and Niumi is in Annual Report, North Bank Province, 1919, CSO 1/162; H. Heaton to Secretary of State for the Colonies, Bathurst, November 8, 1918, CO 87/208.

64. Intelligence Report, North Bank Province, August 31, 1939, CSO 75/4. British propaganda involved showing Ministry of Information photos of successful Allied activities, which impressed Gambians, if not always as intended. Commissioner George Lorimer showed photos in one Niumi village and overheard: "The British are fighting with guns and beating the enemy, and all the time they are taking photos!" But the overall effect was as intended. After hearing Hitler speak on radio, a Niumi villager described the Führer as "a man whose head crack." Intelligence Report, North Bank Province, January 31, 1941, CSO 75/4.

65. Bingham to Stanley, CO 87/255/7.

66. Intelligence Report No. 8, North Bank Province, September 26, 1941, CSO 4/241; Provincial Bulletin, North Bank Province, April 30, 1944, CSO 9/224.

67. Intelligence Report, North Bank Province, January 31, 1941, CSO 75/4; Provincial Bulletin, North Bank Province, August 15, 1944, CSO 9/224; Governor, Gambia, to Wagon, Nigeria, March 28, 1942, CSO 4/302; H.R. Oke, Address to Legislative Council, November 19, 1940, CSO 89/23.

68. Annual Confidential Report, North Bank Province, CSO 3/156.

69. "Local Effects of the War in the North Bank Province," 1941, CSO 3/246.

70. "Report from a District Commissioner in the Senegal," 2nd Quarter, 1941, CSO 75/20.

71. Quarterly Report, North Bank Province, 1940, CSO 2/1861. (Colonial authorities never doubted the loyalty of their Gambian subjects as represented by appointed chiefs. When told of the collapse of France and the threat to Great Britain from German attack, chiefs in Niumi collected over £200 from residents for the War Charities Fund and the Spitfire Fund.)

72. Intelligence Report No. 2, North Bank Province, June 1941, CSO 4/241; "Report from a District Commissioner in the Senegal," 2nd Qtr., 1941, CSO 75/20; David Killingray, "Labour Mobilisation in British Colonial Africa for the War Effort, 1939–46," in *Africa and the Second World War*, ed. David Killingray and Richard Rathbone (London: Macmillan, 1986), 72.

73. "Future of the Home Guard," October 8, 1943, CSO 4/250; "Gambia Local Defense Volunteers," 1942, CSO 4/254; "Local Defense Volunteers," 1943, CSO 2/1919.

74. "Local Effects of the War," CSO 3/246.

75. Intelligence Report No. 6, North Bank Province, July 1941, CSO 4/241.

76. Compulsory Service Ordinance, October 31, 1942, CSO 4/131.

77. "Relations with the Military in North Bank Province," 1943, CSO 3/415.

78. Intelligence Report, North Bank Province, 1942, CSO 4/241; Hilary Blood, Address to Legislative Council, October 15, 1942, CO 89/30.

79. "Relations with the French and Local Effects of the War," 1943, CSO 3/246.

80. Provincial Bulletin, North Bank Province, April 30, 1944, 9/224.

81. Provincial Bulletin, North Bank Province, July 31, 1944, CSO 9/224; Interview with Sowe, March 16, 1996.

82. Resident Minister, Gold Coast, to Sir Hilary Blood, Accra, March 19, 1945, CSO 4/480.

83. K.W. Blackburne to G.W. Lorimer, July 30, 1942, CSO 75/20.

84. North Bank Divisional Bulletin, February 1946, CSO 9/224; Annual Report, North Bank Division, 1946, CSO 75/26.

85. Secretary of State for the Colonies to Governor, Gambia, July 9, 1949, CSO 116/37.

86. "Economic Crisis," 1947, CSO 85/54.

87. "Resettlement of African Soldiers After the War," 1947, CSO 2/2831.

88. Information on Small's early life is from "Extract from Confidential Despatch to the Secretary of State," May 7, 1921, CSO 2/165; and Nana Grey-Johnson, *Edward Francis Small: Watchdog of The Gambia* (Kanifing, The Gambia: BPMRU, 2002), 1–16. J. Ayodele Langley, *Pan-Africanism and Nationalism in West Africa, 1900–1945: A Study in Ideology and Social Classes* (Oxford: Clarendon Press, 1973), treats Small's activities in the context of twentieth-century West African nationalism.

89. Quoted in Grey-Johnson, *Edward Francis Small*, 11.

90. National Council for British West Africa, Gambia Committee, June 18, 1921, CSO 1/163; Commissioners' Conferences, CSO 56/1.

91. In 1924, for example, when peanuts were bringing 4/3 a bushel in Liverpool, Gambian farmers received only 2/6 per bushel. Annual General Report, 1924, CSO 1/166.

92. Small, n.d. [first page of letter missing], CSO 54/231.

93. Colonial Secretary minute, May 19, 1937, SCO 3/291, quoted in Langley, *Pan-Africanism*, 137.

94. Commissioner's Diary, North Bank Province, March 1930, July 1930, CSO 3/147.

95. Small to R.W. Macklin, Bathurst, February 5, 1932, CSO 54/231.

96. For insight into early political movements in Gambia, see Ndey Tupha Sosseh's interview with Alhaji A.E. Cham-Joof, *Daily Observer*, February 17, 2003.

97. Gailey, *History of the Gambia*, ch. 10. The optimism was not limited to Africans. Respected journalist and historian Michael Crowder expresses optimism in "Rice Revolution in the Gambia," a piece he wrote for the *Times British Colonies Review*, 3rd Quarter,

1956, and 4th Quarter, 1957, reprinted in Michael Crowder, *Colonial West Africa: Selected Essays* (London: Frank Cass, 1978), 263–268.

98. Gailey, *History of the Gambia*, 183.

Part IV. The Post-Colonial Period: Independence or In Dependence? 1965–2009

1. UNDP Human Development Report, 2007–2008, http://hdr.undp.org/en/media/HDR_20072008_EN_Complete.pdf; Halifa Sallah, "Portrait of The Gambia After 38 Years of Commemoration: Independence or Growing Dependence?" *Foroyaa*, February 20–23, 2003.

Chapter 7. Independent Niumi in the First Republic of The Gambia: 1965–1994

1. Berkeley Rice, *Enter Gambia: The Birth of an Improbable Nation* (Boston: Houghton Mifflin, 1967), ch. 2.

2. Ibid., 60.

3. Discussion of global events of the last half-century follows arguments in L.S. Stavrianos, *Lifelines from Our Past: A New World History* (Armonk, NY: M.E. Sharpe, 1989), esp. 132–146.

4. It speaks of the racism of the times that one of the reasons the Bretton Woods inn was selected for the meetings was that, unlike many other managers of New England resorts, the person in charge of the Bretton Woods establishment agreed to provide a room for U.S. Secretary of the Treasury Henry Morgenthau, who was Jewish. James Gerstenzang, "Bretton Woods: The Economic Equivalent to D-Day Invasion: World Trade Conference's Policies Led to Post-War Prosperity, But Are Changes Needed?" *Los Angeles Times*, home edition, July 31, 1994. See also Stiglitz, *Globalization and Its Discontents*, 11–12.

5. International Bank for Reconstruction and Development, *Charter*.

6. Craig Emms, interview, Abuko, Kombo North, The Gambia, January 30, 2003; Catherine Brahic, "Africa Trapped in Mega-Drought Cycle," *New Scientist*, April 16, 2009, www.newscientist.com/article/dn16967-africa-trapped-in-megadrought-cycle.html; Torgeir Fyhri, "The Gambia: The Complexity of Modernising the Agricultural Sector in Africa," Thesis in Geography of Resources, University of Oslo, 1998, ch. 4; Richard A. Schroeder, *Shady Practices: Agroforestry and Gender Politics in The Gambia* (Berkeley: University of California Press, 1999), 16.

7. L.S. Stavrianos, *Global Rift: The Third World Comes of Age* (New York: William Morrow, 1981), 472; *New York Times*, "World Bank Warns of Third World Debt," December 16, 1991. As of December 1991, the World Bank calculated Third World debt to be $1.3 trillion.

8. Trevor W. Parfitt, "Adjustment for Stabilisation or Growth? Ghana and The Gambia," *Review of African Political Economy* 22 (March 1995): 55–72.

9. Full treatment of Jawara's background and political life is in Arnold Hughes and David Perfect, *Political History of The Gambia, 1816–1994* (Rochester, NY: University of Rochester Press, 2006), 136–149 passim.

10. "Matchet's Diary," *West Africa*, January 20, 1965, 195.

11. "Grappling with the Gambia's Problems," *West Africa*, July 16, 1966, 791.

12. "A Bank in Disarray," *West Africa*, April 6, 1987, 658–661; "One-Half of Gambia's Population Affected by Drought," *West Africa*, March 22, 1969, 339.

13. "The Gambia: Debt Exploitation," *West Africa*, February 12, 1988, 249–250.

14. "Stocktaking in Bathurst," *West Africa*, July 27, 1968, 864.

15. Christine Jones and Steven C. Radelet, "The Groundnut Sector," in *Economic*

Recovery in The Gambia: Insights for Adjustment in Sub-Saharan Africa, ed. Malcolm F. McPherson and Steven C. Radelet (Cambridge, MA: Harvard Institute for International Development, 1995), 207–208; Tijan M. Sallah, "Economics and Politics in The Gambia," *Journal of Modern African Studies* 28 (1990): 625.

16. Discussion of the economic plan and its effects is based on Steven Radelet, "Reform Without Revolt: The Political Economy of Economic Reform in The Gambia," *World Development* 20 (1992): 1087–1099; McPherson and Radelet, chs. 1 and 2; and *Economic Management: Sector Adjustment Loan (SECAL)* (Banjul: Government of The Gambia, 1994), 18–21.

17. "Bank in Disarray," 661.

18. Jones and Radelet, "Groundnut Sector," 207.

19. World Bank, *Basic Needs in The Gambia* (Washington, DC: World Bank, 1981), 1.

20. "The Gambia: Debt Exploitation," 249–250; Radelet, "Reform Without Revolt," 1089–1090.

21. Jones and Radelet, "Groundnut Sector," 208.

22. *Country Profile: The Gambia*; *Mauritania* (London: Economist Intelligence Unit, 1995–96), 12, 21.

23. Susan Katz Miller, "Gambia Weathers Senegal Split," *Christian Science Monitor*, July 19, 1990; *Economic Management (SECAL)*, 19–20; Peter Da Costa, "The Squeeze on The Gambia," *Africa Report* 39 (March/April 1994): 16–17.

24. Donald R. Wright, "That Hell-Hole of Yours," *American Heritage* 46 (October 1995): 47–58.

25. Halifa Sallah, "The Negative Socio-Cultural Impact of Tourism in The Gambia and the Fairness of the Trade: An Overview," paper presented at workshop organized by Gambia Tourism Concern, Banjul, November 25, 1998, www.subrosa.uk.com/tourism/html/impact7.htm; B. Harrell-Bond, "Tourism in Gambia," *Review of African Political Economy* 6 (1979): 78–90.

26. Alex Haley, *Roots: The Saga of an American Family* (Garden City, NY: Doubleday, 1976); Donald R. Wright, "Uprooting Kunta Kinte: On the Perils of Relying on Encyclopedic Informants," *History in Africa: A Journal of Method* 8 (1981): 205–217; David A. Gerber, "Haley's *Roots* and Our Own: An Inquiry Into the Nature of a Popular Phenomenon," *Journal of Ethnic Studies* 5 (1977): 87–88.

27. Haley, *Roots*, chs. 118–120.

28. Ibid., 579.

29. Ibid., 584.

30. Mark, *"Portuguese" Style and Luso-African Identity*, chs. 1 and 2, shows that such villages, heavily involved in the Atlantic trade and experiencing cross-cultural influences, were more likely in the eighteenth century to have had square houses in the "Portuguese" style rather than round houses more typical of Mandinka villages some distance inland.

31. Stephen Buckley, "From 'Roots' to Riches?" *Washington Post*, May 19, 1995; Alex Haley, "Return to the Land of *Roots*," *GEO* 3 (November 1981): 104–122.

32. Buckley, "From 'Roots' to Riches?"

33. Figures cited are for the entire North Bank Division, which includes the former state of Baddibu with Niumi. Data for Niumi are not significantly different. They are in *1993 Household Economic Survey Report: The Gambia* (Banjul: Central Statistics Department, Ministry of Finance and Economic Affairs, 1994), ch. 3.

34. Discussion of change in farming is based on Kathleen M. Baker, "Traditional Farming Practices and Environmental Decline, with Special Reference to The Gambia," in *Agricultural Change, Environment and Economy: Essays in Honour of W.B. Morgan*, ed. Keith Hoggart (London: Mansell, 1992), 180–202. Half of the villages that Baker studied in 1990 and 1991 are in Niumi.

35. *Round Table Conference: Strategy for Poverty Alleviation* (Banjul: Government of The Gambia, 1994), 19.

36. Figures extrapolated from *1993 Household Economic Survey Report*, 54–55.

37. *Round Table Conference*, 1, 17–19; Baker, "Traditional Farming Practices," 191–193.

38. Baker, "Traditional Farming Practices," 185–186.

39. Ibid., 193.

40. Quoted in Judith Carney, "Struggles Over Land and Crops in an Irrigated Rice Scheme: The Gambia," in *Agriculture, Women, and Land*, ed. Jean Davidson (Boulder, CO: Westview Press, 1988), 59–78.

41. Baker, "Traditional Farming Practices," 197–200; Schroeder, *Shady Practices*, ch. 2.

42. *1993 Household Economic Survey Report*, 4–5; UNPD, *Human Development Report 1991*, 123, 127.

43. "Face-to-Face with Farmers," *West Africa*, November 30, 1988, 2186; *Health Sector Requirement Studies, Phase II Report* (Banjul: The Republic of The Gambia Ministry of Health, Social Welfare and Women's Affairs, 1995), ch. 4.

44. UNPD, *Human Development Report 1991*, 121.

45. Jerre Manneh, interview, Bunyadu, Lower Niumi, March 16, 1996.

Chapter 8. Niumi in the Recent Wave of Globalization: The Second Republic, 1994–2009

1. Samuel P. Huntington, *The Third Wave: Democratization in the Late Twentieth Century* (Norman, OK: University of Oklahoma Press, 1993). For Gambians' reactions to the coup, see Arnold Hughes and David Perfect, *A Political History of The Gambia, 1816–1994*, (Rochester, NY: University of Rochester Press, 2006), ch. 11.

2. Among the president's "Honours" listed on the Gambia State House website are seven awards purchased from the American Biographical Institute of Raleigh, NC, including a "Millennium Medal of Honor" and a "World Lifetime Achievement Award." These and others are listed at www.statehouse.gm/cv/biography.html. Jammeh's claim of curing HIV/AIDS received broad coverage. See BBC News, "Gambia's UN Envoy Expelled," February 23, 2007, http://news.bbc.co.uk/2/hi/africa/6390319.stm.

3. World Bank, *Globalization, Growth, and Poverty*, 23.

4. Stiglitz, *Globalization and Its Discontents,* 11–12, 213; William Finnegan, "The Economics of Empire: Notes on the Washington Consensus," *Harper's*, May 2003, 41–54. It is too soon to know if measures taken by wealthy nations to increase investment, combat unemployment, and lift their economies out of the 2008–2009 recession will lead back toward government intervention in the economy over the long term.

5. Friedman, *Lexus and Olive Tree,* ch. 7; Finnegan, "Economics of Empire," 41–54.

6. Paul Collier, *The Bottom Billion: Why the Poorest Countries Are Failing and What Can Be Done About It* (New York: Oxford University Press, 2007), 3; Finnegan, "Economics of Empire," 43; World Bank, *Globalization, Growth, and Poverty*, 5.

7. The international lending institutions do nothing to raise confidence in their reasoning when they make such statements as one attributed to a 2001 IMF report that "things are going well in The Gambia, although inequity and poverty seem to be on the rise," cited in "The Gambia Said to Experience a Favourable Economic Development," *afrol News, 2001,* www.afrol.com/News2001/gam001_econ.poverty.htm.

8. Hughes and Perfect, *Political History*, ch. 11; Abdoulaye Saine, *The Paradox of Third-Wave Democratization in Africa: The Gambia Under AFPRC-APRC Rule, 1994–2008* (Lanham, MD: Lexington Books, 2009), ch. 3. The latest, full title Jammeh insists on people using is "His Excellency President Sheikh Professor Alhaji Dr. Yahya Jammeh." "Sheikh" is an honorific title for patriarchs or those especially learned in Islamic society. The head of the Gambia Supreme Islamic Council bestowed the title on Jammeh in May

2009. Jammeh uses the title "Professor" because he is *ex officio* chancellor of the University of The Gambia. "Alhaji" is a title assumed by all those who have made the *hajj*, the pilgrimage to Mecca. And Jammeh is "Dr." by virtue of honorary doctorates awarded him by the university and St. Mary's College of Maryland, which has a thriving overseas study program in The Gambia.

9. Saine, *Paradox*, 31–32.

10. "The Gambia Tackles Poor Governance," *afrol News*, August 2002, www.afrol.com/Countries/Gambia/backgr_governance.htm; Jimmy D. Kandeh, "What Does the 'Militariat' Do When It Rules? Military Regimes: The Gambia, Sierra Leone and Liberia," *Review of African Political Economy* 23 (1996): 387–404.

11. Abdoulaye Saine, "The October 2001 Presidential Election in The Gambia: A Critical Analysis," *The Point*, February 24, 2003.

12. Saine, *Paradox*, chs. 4–6.

13. IMF, "Debt Relief Under the Heavily Indebted Poor Countries Initiative," www.imf.org/external/np/exr/facts/hipc.htm.

14. Saine, *Paradox*, 91–93.

15. Jammeh made the ironic statement that the zoo would enable Gambians to "experience African wildlife." His initial efforts with the zoo were as disastrous for the animals as for the Gambian budget. Elephants, giraffes, and lions, all imported from southern Africa at considerable expense, either wandered away or were killed by predators or local hunters. Crocodiles moved to the zoo from their natural, protected habitat at the Abuko Game Preserve died from insufficient food. My source for this information asked not to be identified.

16. *Independent*, "Jammeh Explains Government's Poor Performance," March 10, 2003.

17. "Statement to the Nation on Oil Exploration," February 13, 2004, www.statehouse.gm/president-statemnt-feb13.htm; BBC News, "Country Profile: The Gambia," http://news.bbc.co.uk/2/hi/africa/country_profiles/1032156.stm.

18. Tania Bernath, "Gambia, Fear Rules," Amnesty International, November 11, 2008, www.amnesty.org/en/library/info/AFR27/003/2008/en.

19. Saine, *Paradox*, 28; *Freedom Newspaper*, "Yahya Jammeh Did Not Win," September 25, 2006, www.freedomnewspaper.com/Homepage/tabid/36/mid/367/newsid367/1060/Yahya-Jammeh-did-not-winIECS-Carayol-not-a-smart-thiefmath-of-voter-turn-out-reveals-more/Default.aspx.

20. *Southeast Farm Press*, "Demise of Peanut Program Reflects Realities of 2002," April 3, 2002, http://southeastfarmpress.com/ar/farming_demise_peanut_program. Most people who owned peanut quotas in the United States did not even raise peanuts—they sold their quotas to growers at a good profit. The biggest holder of American peanut quotas in 2003 was the John Hancock Mutual Life Insurance Company of Boston. See Elizabeth Becker, "Peanut Proposals Put a New Wrinkle on Farm Subsidies," *New York Times*, March 4, 2003; and Public Citizen, "Fast Track Will Exacerbate NAFTA's Damage to U.S. Peanut Farmers," 2002, www.citizen.org/documents/Peanuts.pdf.

21. Torgeir Fyhri, "The Gambia: The Complexity of Modernising the Agricultural Sector in Africa," Thesis in Geography of Resources, University of Oslo, 1998, ch. 4, www.afrol.com/library/Fyhri_1998/fyhri(98).htm.

22. Ibid., ch. 5.

23. *Foroyaa*, "President Jammeh Should Stop Misleading the Nation Regarding His Powers," February 17–19, 2003; *The Point*, "Our Nuts Would Not Move—Farmers," January 8, 2003; IRIN, "Gambia: Can Peanut Farming Bounce Back?" April 3, 2009, www.alertnet.org/thenews/newsdesk/IRIN/150fca0e3c198dc71a0ff7f3f1918743.htm28; "The Gambia Tackles Poor Governance," *afrol News*, August 2002; Pa Malick Faye and J.T. Brown, "Farmers to Benefit from Government Subsidies," *Daily Observer*, January 29, 2003.

24. Faye and Brown, "Farmers to Benefit."

25. Osman Kargbo, "AGOA to Stimulate Economic Growth in The Gambia," *The Point*, February 8, 2003.

26. "AGOA.Info," www.agoa.info/index.php?view=country_info&country=gm.

27. BBC News, "Gambia Struggles with Economic Reform," October 18, 2001, http://news.bbc.co.uk/2/hi/business/1600624.stm; interview with U.S. Ambassador to The Gambia, Jackson McDonald, Fajara, January 31, 2003; Sallah, "Portrait of The Gambia," see pt. IV, n. 1; "Gambia Round Table Conference: From Entrepot to Exporter to Eco-Tourism," 2008, www.gm.undp.org/rtable/if_summary.pdf.

28. Desmond Davies, "Tourism Sector Prepares for the Future," *West Africa*, February 17–23, 2003, 16; Peter U.C. Dieke, "The Political Economy of Tourism in The Gambia," *Review of African Political Economy* 21 (1994): 611–626; "Tourist Statistics for Gambia," www.accessgambia.com/information/tourism-statistics.html; *The Point*, "GTA Monthly Tourist Arrival Statistics Released," June 11, 2009. Because of the global recession, the number of tourists in 2008–2009 dropped 20 percent, to approximately 110,000.

29. Brooke Oppenheimer, interview, Kanifing, February 8, 2003; David Gamble, personal communication, October 20, 2000. See Gamble's unpublished manuscript, "Postmortem: A Study of the Gambian Section of Alex Haley's *Roots*," c. 2000; and Donald R. Wright, "History, Memory, and Fiction: Criticism and Commodification of Alex Haley's *Roots*," unpublished paper, 1998.

30. Craig Emms, interview, Abuko, Kombo North, January 30, 2003; Jibril Camara, interview, Jinak Kajata, Lower Niumi, February 5, 2003; Buba Sonko, interview, Kanuma, Lower Niumi, February 5, 2003; Pa Modou Fall and Fama Sey, "4 Vessels Caught Fishing in Wrong Waters," *Daily Observer*, January 30, 2003.

31. Camara, interview; Craig Emms and Linda Barnett, *The Gambia: The Bradt Travel Guide* (Chalfont St. Peter, UK: Bradt Travel Guides, 2001), 193–194.

32. Camara, interview.

33. One of the boats in service in 1996, the *Banjul*, sits on the riverbank, stripped of everything removable except its flaking paint and losing a battle with rust. Gambians will tell you, "That one is finished."

34. *Daily Observer*, "D27.5 Million GTA Complex Commissioned," July 25, 2009.

35. Landing Bondi, "Synchronise the Tempo of EFA Drive," *Gambia Daily*, February 24, 2003; UNICEF, "At a Glance: Gambia," 2009, www.unicef.org/infobycountry/gambia_statistics.html; UNDP, "Tracking the Millennium Development Goals," www.mdgmonitor.org/factsheets_00.cfm?c=GMB&cd43.

36. "Gambian Health Facilities," www.dosh.gm/hmis/facilities.htm; Baboucarr Jeng and Adelle Sock, interview, Bakau, February 25, 2003; Oppenheimer interview; *Gambia Daily*, "President Reaffirms Government's Resolve to Fight HIV/AIDS," December 2, 2002; UNICEF, "At a Glance: Gambia," 2009, www.unicef.org/infobycountry/gambia_statistics.html.

37. Gibril M.S. Jassey, "DoSE Employs More Teachers," *Daily Observer*, January 27, 2003.

38. Oppenheimer, interview; Jeng and Sock, interview.2003.

39. Oppenheimer interview; UNICEF, "Girls' Education in The Gambia," www.unicef.org/programme/girlseducation/action/ed_profiles/gambiafinal.pdf; Saloum Sheriff Janko, "GTU Holds Workshop to 'Upgrade' Gambian Teachers," *Today*, February 10, 2009, p. 7; Chris Honeycutt and Peter O'Neall, interview, February 5, 2009, Fajara.

40. Information on the university is derived from Gambia faculty and students during visits to the university over several years; Honeycutt and O'Neall, interview, February 18, 2009, Fajara.

41. Alan Guttmacher Institute, "Many Women in Rural Gambia Have Reproductive Health Problems, But Few of Them Seek Treatment," *International Family Planning Perspectives* 27 (December 2001); Sallah, "Portrait of The Gambia," see pt. IV, n. 1; "Women

in Decision-Making Roles and Indicators of Women's Health in Selected Countries: The Gambia," APHA International Health Section, www.apha-ih.org; UNICEF, "At a Glance: Gambia," 2007, www.unicef.org/infobycountry/gambia_statistics.html.

42. WHO Statistical Information System, www.who.int/whosis/en/; UNDP, "Tracking the Millennium Development Goals," 52.

43. Henry C. Lucas Jr. and Richard Sylla, in "The Global Impact of the Internet: Widening the Economic Gap Between Wealthy and Poor Nations?" *Prometheus* 21 (2003): 3–22, argue that the Internet contributes to global economic inequality since developing countries, lacking sufficient information technology, will fall further and further behind.

44. WHO Statistical Information System, www.who.int/whosis/en/.

45. Oppenheimer, interview.

46. Sheldon J. Segal, *Under the Banyan Tree: A Population Scientist's Odyssey* (New York: Oxford University Press, 2003), 10; *Foroyaa*, "Rapid Population Growth and Sustainable Development," January 30–February 2, 2003, 6. Population data are from U.S. Census Bureau, International Data Base: The Gambia, www.census.gov/ipc/www/idb/country.php.

47. WHO Statistical Information System, www.who.int/whosis/en/.

48. *Gambia Daily*, "The State of World Population, 2002," January 17, 2003.

49. Mariama Khan, "Addressing Population Concerns Critical to Meeting MDGs," *Gambia Daily*, January 17, 2003.

50. International Monetary Fund, World Economic Outlook Database, April 2009, www.imf.org/external/pubs/ft/weo/2009/01/weodata/weorept.aspx.

51. Manneh family, interview, Bunyadu, Lower Niumi, January 19, 2003.

52. *Gambia Daily*, "'Only By Investing in Women Can We Expect to Get There,' Says Kofi Annan," March 7, 2003; Segal, *Under the Banyan Tree*, 208.

53. Oppenheimer, interview.

54. Discussion of FGM in The Gambia is in Ylva Hernlund, "Cutting without Ritual and Ritual without Cutting: Female 'Circumcision' and the Re-Ritualization of Initiation in the Gambia," in *Female "Circumcision" in Africa: Culture, Controversy, and Change*, ed. Bettina Shell-Duncan and Ylva Hernlund (Boulder, CO: Lynne Rienner, 2000), 235–252. Unless otherwise indicated, information provided on FGM is from Hernlund.

55. "Tostan: Community-Led Development," www.tostan.org; anonymous interview, February 2003; anonymous interviews, February and March 2003; U.S. Department of State, "The Gambia: Report on Female Genital Mutilation or Female Genital Cutting," www.state.gov/s/wi/rls/rep/crfgm/1009/htm; IRIN, "Gambia: Reaching the FGM/C Tipping Point," June 18, 2009, http://allafrica.com/stories/200906180635.html; IRIN, "Tipping Point"; Hernlund, "Cutting Without Ritual," 239.

56. Amnesty International, National Report 2000, The Gambia, http://web.amnesty.org/web/ar2000web.nsf/0/274996726930d5ad802568f200552 923?opendocument; IRIN, "Tipping Point"; *Senegambia News*, "President Jammeh Threatens Imam Baba Leigh," http://senegambianews.com/article.cfm?articleID=18700.

57. UNICEF, "Girls' Education in The Gambia"; WHO Statistical Information System; UNICEF, "At a Glance: Gambia," 2009.

58. UNICEF, "At a Glance: Gambia, Mothers Seize the Right to Education for Their Daughters and Themselves," 2004, www.unicef.org/infobycountry/gambia_17474.html.

59. Schroeder, *Shady Practices*, 34. Discussion of women's gardens is based on Schroeder's study.

60. A "North-Bank Gardener," quoted in Schroeder, *Shady Practices*, 56.

61. "Rio Declaration on Environment and Development," www.unep.org/Documents.Multilingual/Default.asp?documentID=78&articleID=1163; Schroeder, *Shady Practices*, 106.

62. Schroeder, *Shady Practices*, 106.

63. Hughes and Perfect, *Political History*, 292, 271.

64. Peter Baldeh, "'How I Was Abducted by Witch Hunters': A Victim Explains His Ordeal," *Foroyaa*, April 30, 2009. As many as 1,000 Gambians went through this ordeal, with reports of five additional deaths and untold other people suffering serious physical ills. See Adam Nossiter, "Witch Hunts and Foul Potions Heighten Fear of Leader in Gambia," *New York Times*, May 20, 2009.

65. Nossiter, "Witch Hunts."

66. Amnesty International, "Day of Action Takes Place for Freedom in Gambia," July 20, 2009, www.amnesty.org/en/news-and-updates/news/day-action-takes-place-freedom-gambia-20090720.

67. Reuters, "US Demands Release of Convicted Reporters in Gambia," August 7, 2009, www.reuters.com/article/mediaNews/idUSN0741347020090807.

68. Nossiter, "Witch Hunts."

69. Bala (pseudonym), interview, Banjul, February 16, 2003.

70. Honeycutt and O'Neall, interview, February 5, 2009.

71. Information on Atlanta's Gambian community is from interviews conducted, most anonymously at the interviewee's request, in Atlanta, July 3–5, 2009.

72. Honeycutt and O'Neall, interview, February 5, 2009.

73. Gambian Association of Minnesota, www.mingam.org.

74. International PEN, "Gambia: Fatou Jaw Manneh Given Prison Sentence; Fined and Released," August 26, 2008, www.internationalpen.org.uk/index.cfm?objectid=FFE7AE63-E0C4-ED84-0E40EB4504AD9260.

Epilogue: Niumi, 2009: Global Recession, Local Oppression

1. Barry L. Wells, interview, U.S. Embassy, Fajara, February 4, 2009.

2. Peter Singer, *One World: The Ethics of Globalization* (New Haven, CT: Yale University Press, 2002), 195; Dambisa Moyo, *Dead Aid: Why Aid Is Not Working and How There Is a Better Way for Africa* (New York: Farrar, Straus and Giroux, 2009); Jeffrey D. Sachs, *The End of Poverty: Economic Possibilities for Our Time* (New York: Penguin Books, 2005).

BIBLIOGRAPHY

Unpublished Sources

Archives and Libraries

Archives Nationales de France, Paris. These include records of French traders under "Colonies:Sénégal et Côte Occidentale d'Afrique" (prefix B_4) and "Marine: Service General" (prefix C_6).

Archives Nationales de Sénégal, Dakar. These include correspondence relating to the French post at Albreda (prefix 13_G).

Bodleian Library, Oxford. The Rawlinson Manuscripts, which include Minutes of Council from James Fort in the eighteenth century (prefix C745–7).

The Gambia National Archives, Banjul. These documents are identified with the prefix CSO. They include British records from the nineteenth and twentieth centuries and a small number of documents relating to the postindependence period.

Public Record Office, Kew Gardens, London. These include records of the Treasury (African Companies, prefix T 70) from the seventeenth and eighteenth centuries and the Colonial Office (Gambia, General Correspondence, prefix CO 87, and Sierra Leone, General Correspondence, prefix CO 267) from the nineteenth and twentieth centuries. Some documents from the CO series are duplicated in The Gambia National Archives. I cite the source I used.

Dissertations and Manuscripts

Colvin, Lucie G. "Interstate Relations in Precolonial Senegambia." Paper presented at the Annual Meeting of the African Studies Association. Syracuse, New York, 1973.

Fyhri, Torgeir. "The Gambia: The Complexity of Modernising the Agricultural Sector in Africa." Thesis, University of Oslo, 1998.

Gamble, David P. "Postmortem: A Study of the Gambian Section of Alex Haley's *Roots.*" Unpublished paper, c. 2000.

Hunter, Thomas C. "The Development of an Islamic Tradition of Learning among the Jahanke of West Africa." PhD diss., University of Chicago, 1977.

Sallah, Halifa. "The Negative Socio-Cultural Impact of Tourism in The Gambia and the Fairness of the Trade: An Overview." Paper presented at workshop organized by Gambia Tourism Concern. Banjul, The Gambia, November 25, 1998. www.subrosa.uk.com/tourism.html/impact7.htm.

Steadman, Sharon R. "Isolation vs. Interaction: Prehistoric Cilicia and Its Role in the Near Eastern World System." PhD diss., University of California at Berkeley, 1994.

Tejada, Felipe. "The Ñiuminka." Unpublished paper, Indiana University, c. 1980.

Wright, Donald R. "History, Memory, and Fiction: Criticism and Commodification of Alex Haley's *Roots.*" Unpublished paper, 1998.

———. "Niumi: The History of a Western Mandinka State Through the Eighteenth Century." PhD diss., Indiana University, 1976.

295

Oral Interviews

Unless otherwise noted, all oral interviews were conducted in The Gambia by the author.

Abella, Nancy. Consul for Political and Economic Affairs, American Embassy. Interviewed January 24, 2003, in Fajara, Kombo-St. Mary District.

Barnett, Linda. President of Mankasutu Wildlife Trust, residing in Abuko. Interviewed January 30, 2003, in Abuko, Kombo North District.

Camara, Jibril. Caretaker of Niumi National Park, residing in Jinak Kajata. Interviewed February 5, 2003, in Jinak Kajata, Lower Niumi District.

Colley, Safiatou. Market woman and gardener, residing in Banjulinding. Interviewed January 26, 2003, in Banjulinding, Kombo North District.

Drammeh, Demba. Market woman, residing in Ndugu Kebbe. Interviewed February 15, 2003, in Ndugu Kebbe, Lower Niumi District.

Eller, Emily. Community Liaison Officer, U.S. Embassy. Interviewed February 4, 2009, in Fajara, Kombo-St. Mary District.

Emms, Craig. Executive Director of Mankasutu Wildlife Trust, residing in Abuko. Interviewed January 30, 2003, in Abuko, Kombo North District.

Fati, Afang Seku. Marabout, residing in Aljamdu. Interviewed December 14, 1974, in Aljamdu, Lower Niumi District.

Faye, Fatou. Gardener, residing in Ker Wale. Interviewed January 29, 2003, and February 21, 2009, near Ker Wale, Lower Niumi District.

Forster, Hannah. Executive Director of African Centre for Democracy and Human Rights Studies. Interviewed February 7, 2003, in Kololi, Kombo-St. Mary District.

Gomez, Francisco. Gardener, residing in Ker Wale. Interviewed January 29, 2003, near Ker Wale, Lower Niumi District.

Honeycutt, Chris. U.S. Peace Corps volunteer. Interviewed February 5 and February 18, 2009, in Fajara.

Jallow, Pa Alieu. Internet café owner in Kololi, residing in Bundung, Serrekunda. Interviewed February 20, 2003, in Kololi, Kombo-St. Mary District.

Jallow, Sulayman. Former bumster (unofficial tourist guide), residing in Kololi. Interviewed March 7, 2003, in Kololi, Kombo-St. Mary District.

Jammeh, Landing. Retired farmer from Bakindiki Koto, residing in Brikama. Interviewed December 13, 1974, in Brikama, Kombo Central District.

Jeng, Baboucarr. General Secretary of the Gambia Teachers' Union. Interviewed February 25, 2003, in Bakau, Kombo-St. Mary District.

Keita, Amadou. Seventeen-year-old student in eighth grade, residing in Kanuma. Interviewed February 5, 2003, in Kanuma, Lower Niumi District.

Manneh, Baboucar. Son of Jerre Manneh and employee of Gambia Marine, residing in Bunyadu. Interviewed January 19, 2003, in Bunyadu, Lower Niumi District.

Manneh, Jerre. Farmer in Bunyadu, deceased. Interviewed March 16, 1996, in Bunyadu, Lower Niumi District.

Manneh, Omar. Fifteen-year-old grandson of Jerre Manneh and student in ninth grade, residing in Bunyadu. Interviewed February 15, 2003, in Bunyadu, Lower Niumi District.

Mbur, Omar. President of the Gambia Teachers' Union. Interviewed February 25, 2003, in Bakau, Kombo-St. Mary District.

McDonald, Jackson. U.S. ambassador to The Gambia. Interviewed January 31, 2003, in the U.S. Embassy, Fajara, Kombo-St. Mary District, and June 2005 in the U.S. Embassy, Conakry, Guinea.

Mills, David. U.S. Peace Corps volunteer and teacher, residing in Essau. Interviewed March 1, 2003, in Fajara, Kombo-St. Mary District.

Ndow, Adama. Fourteen-year-old gardener, residing in Medina Sering Mas. Interviewed January 29, 2003, near Ker Wale, Lower Niumi District.

Njie, Alhaji Karamo. Imam of Berending Mosque, residing in Berending. Interviewed January 19, 2003, in Berending, Lower Niumi District.

Njie, Amadou. Director of the Center for Traditional Medicine, Berending. Interviewed February 21, 2009, in Berending, Lower Niumi District.

O'Neall, Peter. U.S. Peace Corps volunteer. Interviewed February 5 and February 18, 2009, in Fajara, Kombo-St. Mary District.

Oppenheimer, Brooke. U.S. Peace Corps volunteer and teacher. Interviewed February 8, 2003, in Kanifing, Kombo-St. Mary District.

Sey, Kabba. Gardener and market woman, residing in Kerr Mama. Interviewed February 15, 2003, in Ndugu Kebbe, Lower Niumi District.

Sidibe, Bakary. Retired director of The Gambia National Council of Arts and Culture, residing in Churchill's Town, Serrekunda. Interviewed February 4, 2003, in Serrekunda, Kombo-St. Mary District.

Sock, Adele. Vice principal of St. Joseph's School for Girls (Banjul) and first vice president of the Gambia Teachers Union, residing in Kanifing. Interviewed February 25, 2003, in Bakau, Kombo-St. Mary District.

Sonko, Buba Jariatou. Farmer, residing in Kanuma. Interviewed February 5, 2003, in Kanuma, Lower Niumi District.

Sonko, Landing Nima. Farmer in Berending, deceased. Interviewed November 1, 1974, in Berending, Lower Niumi District.

Sowe, Lamin. Farmer and artist residing in Berending, deceased. Interviewed March 16, 1996, in Berending, Lower Niumi District.

Strehlow, Adrian. U.S. Peace Corps volunteer in health care, residing in Medina Sering Mas. Interviewed February 8, 2003, in Serrekunda, Kombo-St. Mary District.

Sumare, Binta. Gardener, residing in Banjulinding. Interviewed January 26, 2003, in Banjulinding, Kombo North District.

Sumareh, Janke. Gardener, residing in Banjulinding. Interviewed January 26, 2003, in Banjulinding, Kombo North District.

Tall, Bakary. Farmer, residing in Juffure. Interviewed December 15, 1974, in Juffure, Upper Niumi District.

Wells, Barry L. U.S. ambassador to The Gambia. Interviewed February 4, 2009, at the U.S. Embassy, Fajara, Kombo-St. Mary District.

Newspapers and Periodicals

Africa Report, March/April 1994.

Christian Science Monitor, July 19, 1990.

Daily Observer [Bakau, The Gambia], December 2002–March 2003, January–August 2009.

Foroyaa (Freedom) [Serrekunda, The Gambia], December 2002–March 2003, January–August 2009.

Gambia Daily [Banjul, The Gambia], December 2002–March 2003.

Independent [Banjul, The Gambia], December 2002–March 2003.

Los Angeles Times, July 31, 1994.

New York Times, March 31, 1976; August 24, 1976; December 16, 1991; August 28, 1994; February 29, 1996; March 4, 2003; May 20, 2009.

Point [Banjul, The Gambia], December 2002–March 2003, January–August 2009.

Wall Street Journal, December 13, 1993.

Washington Post, May 19, 1995.

West Africa, January 20, 1965; July 16, 1966; July 27, 1968; March 22, 1969; April 6, 1987; February 12, 1988; July 16, 2001; August 27, 2001; October 18, 2001; February 18, 2002; February 17, 2003; June 2, 2003.

Books and Articles

Abu-Lughod, Janet L. *Before European Hegemony: The World System* A.D. *1250–1350*. New York: Oxford University Press, 1989.

———. *The World System in the Thirteenth Century: Dead-End or Precursor?* Washington, DC: American Historical Association, 1993.

Adas, Michael P. *"High" Imperialism and the "New" History*. Washington, DC: American Historical Association, 1995.

———. *Machines as the Measure of Men: Science, Technology, and Ideologies of Western Dominance*. Ithaca, NY: Cornell University Press, 1989.

Alford, Terry. *The Fortunate Slave*. New York: Oxford University Press, 1977.

Almada, André Alvares de. *Tratado breve dos Rios de Guiné*. 1594. Trans. P.E.H. Hair. 2 vols. Liverpool: University of Liverpool, 1984.

Alpern, Stanley B. "The European Introduction of Crops Into West Africa in Precolonial Times." *History in Africa: A Journal of Method* 19 (1992): 13–43.

———. "What Africans Got for Their Slaves: A Master List of European Trade Goods." *History in Africa: A Journal of Method* 22 (1995): 5–43.

Anderson, Sarah, ed. *Views from the South: The Effects of Globalization and the WTO on Third World Countries*. San Francisco: International Forum on Globalization, 1999.

Anstey, Roger. *The Atlantic Slave Trade and British Abolition, 1760–1810*. Cambridge: Cambridge University Press, 1975.

Austen, Ralph A. *African Economic History*. Portsmouth, NH: Heinemann, 1987.

Azurara, Gomes Eanes de. *The Chronicle of the Discovery and Conquest of Guinea*, ed. C.R. Beazley and E. Prestage. 2 vols. London: Hakluyt Society, 1896–1899.

Babou, Cheikh Anta. *Fighting the Greater Jihad: Amadu Bamba and the Founding of the Muridiyya of Senegal, 1853–1913*. Athens: Ohio University Press, 2007.

Baker, Kathleen M. "Traditional Farming Practices and Environmental Decline, with Special Reference to The Gambia." In *Agricultural Change, Environment and Economy: Essays in Honour of W.B. Morgan*, ed. Keith Hoggart, 180–202. London: Mansell, 1992.

Barrett, Hazel R. *The Marketing of Foodstuffs in The Gambia, 1400–1980*. Aldershot, UK: Avebury, 1988.

Barry, Boubacar. *Le royaume du Waalo: Le Sénégal avant la conquête*. Paris: François Maspero, 1972.

———. "Senegambia from the Sixteenth to the Eighteenth Century: Evolution of the Wolof, Sereer, and 'Tukulor.'" In *General History of Africa*. Vol. 5, *Africa from the Sixteenth to the Eighteenth Century*, ed. B.A. Ogot, 262–299. Paris: UNESCO, 1992.

Barry, John M. *The Great Influenza: The Epic Story of the Deadliest Plague in History*. New York: Penguin, 2004.

Beinart, William. "Beyond the Colonial Paradigm: African History and Environmental History in Large-Scale Perspective." In *The Environment in World History*, ed. Edmund Burke III and Kenneth Pomeranz. Berkeley: University of California Press, 2009.

Blake, J.W. *Europeans in West Africa, 1450–1560*. 2 vols. London: Hakluyt Society, 1942.

Boulègue, Jean. *Le grand Jolof (xiiie–xvie siècle)*. Paris: Diffusion Karthala, 1987.

———. *Les Luso-Africains en Sénégambie, xvie–xixe siècle*. Lisbon: Instituto de Investigação Cientifica Tropical, 1989.

Bovill, E.W. *The Golden Trade of the Moors*. 2nd ed. London: Oxford University Press, 1968.

Boxer, C.R. *The Portuguese Seaborne Empire, 1415–1825*. New York: Knopf, 1975.

Braudel, Fernand. *Civilisation and Capitalism, 15th–18th Century*. Vol. 3, *The Perspective of the World*. New York: Harper and Row, 1994.

Brooks, George E. *Eurafricans in Western Africa: Commerce, Social Status, Gender, and Religious Observance from the Sixteenth to the Eighteenth Century.* Athens: Ohio University Press, 2003.

———. "Kola Nuts and State-Building: Upper Guinea Coast and Senegambia, 15th–17th Centuries." Working Paper No. 38, African Studies Center, Boston University, 1980.

———. *Landlords and Strangers: Ecology, Society, and Trade in Western Africa, 1000–1530.* Boulder, CO: Westview Press, 1993.

———. "Peanuts and Colonialism: Consequences of the Commercialization of Peanuts in West Africa, 1830–1870." *Journal of African History* 16 (1975): 29–54.

Bühnen, Stephan. "Place Names as an Historical Source: An Introduction with Examples from Southern Senegambia and Germany." *History in Africa: A Journal of Method* 19 (1992): 1–57.

Cadamosto, Alvise da. "The Voyages of Cadamosto." In *The Voyages of Cadamosto and Other Documents in Western Africa in the Second Half of the Fifteenth Century*, ed. G.R. Crone, 1–84. London: Hakluyt Society, 1937.

Carney, Judith. *Black Rice: The African Origins of Rice Cultivation in the Americas.* Cambridge, MA: Harvard University Press, 2001.

———. "Struggles Over Land and Crops in an Irrigated Rice Scheme: The Gambia." In *Agriculture, Women, and Land*, ed. Jean Davidson, 59–78. Boulder, CO: Westview Press, 1988.

Caufield, Catherine. *Masters of Illusion: The World Bank and the Poverty of Nations.* New York: Henry Holt, 1996.

Chaudhuri, K.N. *Asia Before Europe: Economy and Civilisation in the Indian Ocean from the Rise of Islam to 1750.* Cambridge: Cambridge University Press, 1990.

———. *Trade and Civilisation in the Indian Ocean: An Economic History from the Rise of Islam to 1750.* Cambridge: Cambridge University Press, 1985.

Chen, Shaohua, and Martin Ravallion. "How Did the World's Poorest Fare in the 1990s?" World Bank Group, Policy Research Working Paper, August 2000. http://econ.worldbank.org/docs/1164.pdf.

Clark, Emma. "Gambia Struggles with Economic Reform." BBC News, October 18, 2001. www.bbc.co.uk/2/hi/business/1600624.stm.

Clarke, Peter B. *West Africa and Islam: A Study of Religious Development from the 8th to the 20th Century.* London: Edward Arnold, 1982.

Cohen, Abner. "Cultural Strategies in the Organization of Trade Diasporas." In *The Development of Indigenous Trade and Markets in West Africa*, ed. Claude Meillassoux, 266–284. Oxford: Oxford University Press, 1971.

Collier, Paul. *The Bottom Billion: Why the Poorest Countries Are Failing and What Can Be Done About It.* New York: Oxford University Press, 2007.

Conrad, David C., and Barbara E. Frank. "*Nyamakalaya:* Contradiction and Ambiguity in Mande Society." In *Status and Identity in West Africa:* Nyamakalaw *of Mande,* ed. David C. Conrad and Barbara E. Frank, 1–23. Bloomington: Indiana University Press, 1995.

Cooper, Frederick. "What Is the Concept of Globalization Good For? An African Historian's Perspective." *African Affairs* 100 (2001): 189–213.

Country Profile: The Gambia; Mauritania. London: Economist Intelligence Unit, 1995–1996.

Crosby, Alfred W. *Germs, Seeds, & Animals: Studies in Ecological History.* Armonk, NY: M.E. Sharpe, 1994.

———. "The Potato Connection." *World History Bulletin* 12 (1996): 1–5.

Crowder, Michael. *Colonial West Africa: Selected Essays.* London: Frank Cass, 1978.

———. "The First World War and Its Consequences." In *General History of Africa.* Vol. 7, *Africa Under Colonial Domination, 1880–1935,* ed. A. Adu Boahen, 283–311. Paris: UNESCO, 1985.

Cultru, Prosper. *Premier Voyage de Sieur de la Courbe fait à la coste d'Afrique en 1685.* Paris: Emile Larose, 1913.

Curtin, Philip D. "The Abolition of the Slave Trade from Senegambia." In *The Abolition of the Slave Trade: Origins and Effects in Europe, Africa, and the Americas*, ed. David Eltis and James Walvin, 83–97. Madison: University of Wisconsin Press, 1981.

———. *The Atlantic Slave Trade: A Census.* Madison: University of Wisconsin Press, 1969.

———. *Cross-Cultural Trade in World History.* Cambridge: Cambridge University Press, 1984.

———. *Death by Migration: Europe's Encounter with the Tropical World in the Nineteenth Century.* Cambridge: Cambridge University Press, 1995.

———. *Economic Change in Precolonial Africa: Senegambia in the Era of the Slave Trade.* Madison: University of Wisconsin Press, 1975.

———. "Epidemiology and the Slave Trade." *Political Science Quarterly* 83 (1968): 190–216.

———. "Jihad in West Africa: Early Phases and Inter-Relations in Mauritania and Senegal." *Journal of African History* 12 (1971): 11–24.

———. *The Rise and Fall of the Plantation Complex.* Cambridge: Cambridge University Press, 1989.

———. "The Slave Trade and the Atlantic Basin: Intercontinental Perspectives." In *Key Issues in the Afro-American Experience*, ed. Nathan I. Huggins, Martin Kilson, and Daniel M. Fox, 1:74–93. New York: Harcourt Brace Jovanovich, 1971.

———. *The Tropical Atlantic in the Age of the Slave Trade.* Washington, DC: American Historical Association, 1991.

[d'Arcy, Col. George A.K.]. "Gambia Colony and the Civil War." *Colburn's United Service Magazine* 419–420 (1863): 236–258, 401–418, 498–508.

Dasgupta, Samir, ed. *The Changing Face of Globalization.* Thousand Oaks, CA: Sage, 2004.

Davidson, Basil. *Black Mother: Africa and the Atlantic Slave Trade.* Rev. ed. Harmondsworth, UK: Penguin, 1980.

Demanet, Abbé. *Nouvelle histoire de l'Afrique Françoise.* 2 vols. Paris: Duchesne, 1767.

Dey, Jennie. "Gambian Women: Unequal Partners in Rice Development Projects." *Journal of Development Studies* 17 (1981): 109–122.

Dieke, Peter U.C. "The Political Economy of Tourism in The Gambia." *Review of African Political Economy* 21 (1994): 611–626.

Dorjahn, V.R., and Christopher Fyfe, "Landlord and Stranger: Change in Tenancy Relations in Sierra Leone." *Journal of African History* 3 (1962): 391–397.

Durand, J.B.L. *A Voyage to Senegal.* London: Printed for Richard Phillips, 1806.

Eaton, Richard M. *Islamic History as Global History.* Washington, DC: American Historical Association, 1990.

Echenberg, Myron. *Colonial Conscripts: The Tirailleurs Sénégalais in French West Africa, 1857–1960.* Portsmouth, NH: Heinemann, 1991.

Economic Management: Sector Adjustment Loan (SECAL). Banjul: Government of The Gambia, 1994.

Elbl, Ivana. "Cross-Cultural Trade and Diplomacy: Portuguese Relations with West Africa, 1441–1521." *Journal of World History* 3 (1992): 165–204.

———. "The Horse in Fifteenth-Century Senegambia." *International Journal of African Historical Studies* 24 (1991): 85–110.

Emms, Craig. "Exploring The Gambia's Wild Places: Jinak Island." *Wildlife News* 4 (Winter 2002): 5.

Emms, Craig, and Linda Barnett. *The Gambia: The Bradt Travel Guide.* Chalfont St. Peter, UK: Bradt Travel Guides Ltd., 2001.

"EU Pays 11 Million Euros to Alimenta to Settle Groundnut Crisis." *Africast.com News List,* February 6, 2001.

Fage, J.D. *On the Nature of African History.* Birmingham, UK: Birmingham University Press, 1965.

Fernandes, Valentim. *Description de la côte occidentale d'Afrique (Sénégal au Cap de Monte, Archipels),* ed. and trans. Theodore Monod et al. Bissau: Centro de Estudos da Guiné Portuguesa, 1951.

Finnegan, William. "The Economics of Empire: Notes on the Washington Consensus." *Harper's Magazine,* May 2003, 41–54.

Fitch Ratings. "The Gambia: 2002." www.state.gov/p/af/scr/16107.htm.

Frank, André Gunder. *Re-Orient: Global Economy in the Asian Age.* Berkeley: University of California Press, 1998.

———, and Barry K. Gillis, eds. *The World System: Five Hundred Years or Five Thousand?* New York: Routledge, 1993.

Friedman, Thomas L. *The Lexus and the Olive Tree.* 2nd ed. New York: Anchor Books, 2000.

———. *The World Is Flat: A Brief History of the Twenty-First Century.* New York: Farrar, Straus and Giroux, 2005.

Froelich, J.C. "Essai sur les causes et méthods de l'Islamisation de l'Afrique de l'Ouest du xiᵉ au xxᵉ siècle." In *Islam in Tropical Africa,* ed. I.M. Lewis, 160–173. London: Oxford University Press, 1966.

Froger, François. *Relation d'un voyage . . . aux côtes d'Afrique.* Amsterdam: Chez les Heritiers d'Antoine Shelte, 1702.

Gailey, Harry A. *A History of the Gambia.* New York: Praeger, 1965.

Gambia Tourism Concern. "The Bumster Syndrome: A Closer Look." www.subrosa.uk.com/tourism/html/bumst1.htm.

Gerber, David A. "Haley's *Roots* and Our Own: An Inquiry Into the Nature of a Popular Phenomenon." *Journal of Ethnic Studies* 5 (1977): 87–111.

Gillis, Barry K. "The Turning of the Tide." In *Globalization and After,* ed. Samir Dasgupta and Ray Kiely, 13–20. Thousand Oaks, CA: Sage, 2006.

Giraud, Jean. *L'or du Bambouk: une dynamique de civilisation ouest-africaine: du royaume de Gabou à la Casamance.* Geneva: Georg Editeur, 1992.

Gomes, Diogo. "The Voyages of Diogo Gomes." In *The Voyages of Cadamosto and Other Documents in Western Africa in the Second Half of the Fifteenth Century,* ed. G.R. Crone, 91–102. London: Hakluyt Society, 1937.

Goody, Jack. "The Impact of Islamic Writing on the Oral Cultures of West Africa." *Cahiers d'Etudes Africaines* 11 (1971): 455–466.

———. *Technology, Tradition, and the State in Africa.* London: Oxford University Press, 1971.

Gray, John M. *A History of the Gambia.* London: Frank Cass, 1940.

Green, Kathryn L. "Dyula and Sonongui Roles in the Islamization of the Region of Kong." In *Rural and Urban Islam in West Africa,* ed. Nehemia Levtzion and Humphrey J. Fisher, 97–117. Boulder, CO: Lynne Rienner, 1987.

Grey-Johnson, Nana. *Edward Francis Small: Watchdog of The Gambia.* Kanifing, The Gambia: BPMRU, 2002.

Haley, Alex. "Return to the Land of *Roots.*" *GEO* 3 (1981): 104–122.

———. *Roots: The Saga of an American Family.* Garden City, NY: Doubleday, 1976.

Harlan, J.R., J.J.J. de Wet, and A.B.L. Stemler, eds. *Origins of African Plant Domestication.* The Hague: Mouton, 1976.

Harrell-Bond, B. "Tourism and Gambia." *Review of African Political Economy* 6 (1979): 78–90.

Hatton, P.H.S. "The Gambia, the Colonial Office, and the Opening Months of the First World War." *Journal of African History* 7 (1966): 123–131.

Headrick, Daniel P. *The Tools of Empire: Technology and European Imperialism in the Nineteenth Century.* New York: Oxford University Press, 1981.

Health Sector Requirement Studies, Phase II Report. Banjul: The Republic of The Gambia Ministry of Health, Social Welfare and Women's Affairs, 1995.

Hernlund, Ylva, "Cutting without Ritual and Ritual without Cutting: Female 'Circumcision' and the Re-Ritualization of Initiation in The Gambia." In *Female "Circumcision" in Africa: Culture, Controversy, and Change*, ed. Bettina Shell-Duncan and Ylva Hernlund. Boulder, CO: Lynne Rienner, 2000.

Hodder, B.W. "Indigenous Cloth Trade and Markets in Africa." In *Textiles in Africa*, ed. Dale Idiens and K.G. Ponting, 201–210. London: Pasold Research Fund, 1980.

Hogendorn, Jan S. "Economic Initiative and African Cash Farming: Pre-Colonial Origins of Early Colonial Developments." In *Colonialism in Africa, 1870–1914.* Vol. 4, *The Economics of Colonialism*, ed. Peter Duignan and L.H. Gann, 283–328. Cambridge: Cambridge University Press, 1975.

———. "The 'Vent-for-Surplus' Model and African Cash Agriculture to 1914." *Savanna* 5 (1976): 15–28.

Hoggart, Keith, ed. *Agricultural Change, Environment and Economy: Essays in Honour of W.B. Morgan.* London: Mansell, 1992.

Hopkins, A.G. *Globalization in World History.* New York: Norton, 2002.

Household Economic Survey Report, 1993: The Gambia. Banjul: Central Statistics Department, Ministry of Finance and Economic Affairs, 1994.

Hughes, Arnold, and David Perfect. *A Political History of The Gambia, 1816–1994.* Rochester, NY: University of Rochester Press, 2006.

Huntington, Samuel P. *The Third Wave: Democratization in the Late Twentieth Century.* Norman: University of Oklahoma Press, 1993.

Huxley, Elspeth. *Four Guineas: A Journey Through West Africa.* London: Chatto and Windus, 1954.

Iliffe, John. *Honour in African History.* New York: Cambridge University Press, 2005.

Inikori, J.E. "The Import of Firearms Into West Africa, 1750–1807: A Quantitative Analysis." *Journal of African History* 18 (1977): 339–368.

Jobson, Richard. *The Golden Trade.* London: Dawsons of Pall Mall, 1623.

Johnson, Marion. "Cloth as Money: The Cloth Strip Currencies of Africa." In *Textiles in Africa*, ed. Dale Idiens and K.G. Ponting, 193–202. London: Pasold Research Fund, 1980.

Jones, Christine, and Stephen C. Radelet, "The Groundnut Sector." In *Economic Recovery in The Gambia: Insights for Adjustment in Sub-Saharan Africa*, ed. Malcolm F. McPherson and Steven C. Radelet. Cambridge, MA: Harvard Institute for International Development, 1995.

Kandeh, Jimmy D. "What Does the 'Militariat' Do When It Rules? Military Regimes: The Gambia, Sierra Leone and Liberia." *Review of African Political Economy* 23 (1996): 387–404.

Kar, Samit, ed. *Globalization: One World, Many Voices: Essays in Honor of Prof. Ramkrishna Mukherjee.* New Delhi: Rawat Publications, 2004.

Kea, Ray E. "Firearms and Warfare on the Gold and Slave Coasts from the Sixteenth to the Nineteenth Centuries." *Journal of African History* 12 (1971): 185–213.

Kieh, George Klay, Jr. *Africa and the New Globalization.* Burlington, VT: Ashgate, 2008.

Killingray, David, "Labour Mobilisation in British Colonial Africa for the War Effort, 1939–46." In *Africa and the Second World War*, ed. David Killingray and Richard Rathbone. London: Macmillan, 1986.

Kipling, Rudyard. *Complete Verse: Definitive Edition.* New York: Doubleday, 1940.

Klein, Martin A. "The Demography of Slavery in the Western Sudan in the Late Nineteenth Century." In *African Population and Capitalism: Historical Perspectives*, ed. Joel Gregory and Dennis Cordell, 50–62. Boulder, CO: Westview Press, 1987.

———. *Islam and Imperialism in Senegal: Sine-Saloum, 1847–1914.* Stanford, CA: Stanford University Press, 1968.

———. "Social and Economic Factors in the Muslim Revolution in Senegambia." *Journal of African History* 13 (1972): 419–441.

———. "Women in Slavery in the Western Sudan." In *Women and Slavery in Africa*, ed. Claire C. Robertson and Martin A. Klein, 67–92. Madison: University of Wisconsin Press, 1983.

Kriger, Colleen E. *Cloth in West African History.* Lanham, MD: AltaMira Press, 2006.

———. "Mapping the History of Cotton Textile Production in Precolonial West Africa." *African Economic History* 33 (2005): 87–116.

Labat, Jean-Baptiste. *Nouvelle rélation de l'Afrique occidentale.* 5 vols. Paris: Chez Guilaume Cavalier, 1728.

Lafont, F. "Le Gandoul et les Niominkas." *Bulletin du comité des études historiques et scientifiques de l'Afrique occidentale française* 21 (1938): 385–458.

Langley, J. Ayodele. *Pan-Africanism and Nationalism in West Africa, 1900–1945: A Study in Ideology and Social Classes.* Oxford: Clarendon Press, 1973.

Law, Robin. *The Horse in West Africa: The Role of the Horse in the Societies of Pre-Colonial West Africa.* Oxford: Oxford University Press, 1980.

———. "Slaves, Trade, and Taxes: The Material Basis of Political Power in Precolonial West Africa." *Research in Economic Anthropology* 1 (1978): 37–52.

Leonard, David K., and Scott Straus. *Africa's Stalled Development: International Causes and Cures.* Boulder, CO: Lynne Rienner, 2003.

Levtzion, Nehemia. *Ancient Ghana and Mali.* London: Methuen, 1973.

———. "The Eighteenth Century: Background to the Islamic Revolutions in West Africa." In *Eighteenth-Century Renewal and Reform in Islam*, ed. Nehemia Levtzion and John O. Voll, 21–38. Syracuse, NY: Syracuse University Press, 1987.

———. *Islam in West Africa: Religion, Society and Politics to 1800.* Aldershot, UK: Variorum, 1994.

———. "Patterns of Islamization in West Africa." In *Conversion to Islam*, ed. Nehemia Levtzion, 206–219. New York: Holmes & Meier, 1979.

———. "The Sahara and the Sudan from the Arab Conquest of the Maghrib to the Rise of the Almoravids." In *The Cambridge History of Africa.* Vol. 2: *From c. 500 B.C. to c. A.D. 1500*, ed. J.D. Fage, 637–684. Cambridge: Cambridge University Press, 1978.

Lo, Jung-Pang. "The Decline of the Early Ming Navy." *Oriens Extrêmus* 5 (1958): 1499–1568.

———. "The Emergence of China as a Sea Power During the Late Sung and Early Yuan Periods." *Far Eastern Quarterly* 14 (1955): 489–503.

Louis, William Roger. *Imperialism at Bay: The United States and the Decolonization of the British Empire, 1941–1945.* New York: Oxford University Press, 1978.

Lovejoy, Paul. *Transformations in Slavery: A History of Slavery in Africa.* 2nd ed. Cambridge: Cambridge University Press, 2000.

Lucas, Henry C., Jr., and Richard Sylla. "The Global Impact of the Internet: Widening the Economic Gap Between Wealthy and Poor Nations?" *Prometheus* 21 (2003): 3–22.

Lugard, Lord. *The Dual Mandate in British Tropical Africa.* London: Blackwood and Sons, 1922.

Mané, Mamadou. "Contribution à l'histoire du Kaabu, des origines au xix siècle." *Bulletin de l'Institut Fondamental d'Afrique Noire,* Series B 40 (1978): 87–159.

Mark, Peter. "Constructing Identity: Sixteenth- and Seventeenth-Century Architecture in the Gambia-Geba Region and the Articulation of Luso-African Ethnicity." *History in Africa: A Journal of Method* 22 (1995): 307–327.

———. *"Portuguese" Style and Luso-African Identity: Precolonial Senegambia, Sixteenth–Nineteenth Centuries.* Bloomington: Indiana University Press, 2002.

Martin, S.M. "The Long Depression: West African Export Producers and the World Economy, 1914–1945." In *The Economies of Africa and Asia in the Inter-War Depression*, ed. Ian Brown, 74–94. New York: Routledge, 1989.

Martin, William G. "Africa and World-Systems Analysis: A Post-Nationalist Project?" In *Writing African History*, ed. John Edward Phillips, 381–402. Rochester, NY: University of Rochester Press, 2005.

Mbaeyi, Paul. *British Military and Naval Forces in West African History, 1807–1874.* New York: Nok, 1978.

McNeill, William H. "Afterword: World History and Globalization." In *Global History: Interactions Between the Universal and the Local*, ed. A.G. Hopkins. New York: Palgrave Macmillan, 2006.

———. *Plagues and Peoples.* Garden City, NY: Anchor Books, 1976.

———. *The Rise of the West.* Chicago: University of Chicago Press, 1963.

———. "The Rise of the West After Twenty-Five Years." *Journal of World History* 1 (1990): 1–21.

McPherson, Malcolm F., and Steven C. Radelet, eds. *Economic Recovery in The Gambia: Insights for Adjustment in Sub-Saharan Africa.* Cambridge, MA: Harvard Institute for International Development, 1995.

Meillassoux, Claude. *The Anthropology of Slavery: The Womb of Iron and Gold*, trans. Alide Dasnois. Chicago: University of Chicago Press, 1986.

Meirs, Suzanne, and Igor Kopytoff, eds. *Slavery in Africa: Historical and Anthropological Perspectives.* Madison: University of Wisconsin Press, 1977.

Moore, Francis. *Travels Into the Inland Parts of Africa.* London: Edward Cave, 1738.

Moyo, Dambisa. *Dead Aid: Why Aid Is Not Working and How There Is a Better Way for Africa.* New York: Farrar, Straus and Giroux, 2009.

Munro, J. Forbes. *Africa and the International Economy: An Introduction to the Modern Economic History of Africa South of the Sahara.* Totowa, NJ: Rowman and Littlefield, 1976.

Nicholson, Sharon E. "Climatic Variations in the Sahel and Other African Regions During the Past Five Centuries." *Journal of Arid Environments* 1 (1978): 3–24.

O'Brien, Donal Cruise. *The Mourides of Senegal.* Oxford: Oxford University Press, 1971.

———. "Toward an 'Islamic Policy' in French West Africa, 1854–1914." *Journal of African History* 8 (1967): 303–316.

Oliver, Roland. *The African Experience: Major Themes in African History from Earliest Times to the Present.* London: Weidenfeld & Nicholson, 1991.

Osterhammel, Jürgen, and Niels P. Petersson. *Globalization: A Short History.* Princeton: Princeton University Press, 2003.

Pales, Leon. *Les sels alimentaires: sels minéraux, problème des sels alimentaires en AOF.* Dakar: Direction Général de la Santé Publique, 1950.

Parfitt, Trevor W. "Adjustment for Stabilisation or Growth? Ghana and The Gambia." *Review of African Political Economy* 22 (March 1995): 55–72.

Park, Mungo. *Travels in the Interior of Africa.* London: Cassell, 1887.

Pélissier, Paul. *Les paysans du Sénégal: Les civilisations agraires du Cayor à la Casamance.* Paris: Imprimerie Fabrèque, 1966.

Phillips, William D., Jr., and Phillips, Carla Rahn. *The Worlds of Christopher Columbus.* Cambridge: Cambridge University Press, 1992.

Pilcher, Jeffrey M. *Food in World History.* New York: Routledge, 2006.

Pogge, Thomas. *World Poverty and Human Rights: Cosmopolitan Responsibilities and Reforms.* Cambridge: Blackwell, 2002.

Pommeranz, Kenneth. *The Great Divergence: China, Europe, and the Making of the Modern World Economy.* Princeton: Princeton University Press, 2000.

Quinn, Charlotte A. "Maba Diakhou and the Gambian *Jihad,* 1850–1890." In *Studies in West African Islamic History.* Vol. 1, *The Cultivators of Islam*, ed. John Ralph Willis, 233–258. London: Frank Cass, 1979.

———. *Mandingo Kingdoms of the Senegambia: Traditionalism, Islam, and European Expansion.* Evanston, IL: Northwestern University Press, 1977.

Radelet, Stephen C. "Reform Without Revolt: The Political Economy of Economic Reform in The Gambia." *World Development* 20 (1992): 1087–1099.

Ragin, Charles, and Chirot, Daniel. "The World System of Immanuel Wallerstein: Sociology and Politics as History." In *Vision and Method in Historical Sociology*, ed. Theda Skocpol, 276–312. Cambridge: Cambridge University Press, 1984.

Rice, Berkeley. *Enter Gambia: The Birth of an Improbable Nation.* Boston: Houghton Mifflin, 1967.

Rippel, Barbara. "Not Just Peanuts." *Consumer Alert* (March 1998). www.consumeralert. org/pubs/research/march98.htm.

Ritzer, George, and Michael Ryan. "The Globalization of Nothing." In *The Changing Face of Globalization*, 298–317. Thousand Oaks, CA: Sage, 2004.

Roberts, Bill, Janet Haugaard, and Pam Hicks. *Together in Friendship: M'be karafaring nyoma.* St. Mary's City, MD: Kent Hall Press, 2001.

Robinson, David. "Abdul Qadir and Shaykh Umar: A Continuing Tradition of Islamic Leadership in Futa Toro." *International Journal of Africa Historical Studies* 6 (1973): 286–303.

———. *The Holy War of Umar Tal: The Western Sudan in the Mid-Nineteenth Century.* Oxford: Clarendon Press, 1985.

Rodney, Walter. *A History of the Upper Guinea Coast, 1545–1800.* Oxford: Oxford University Press, 1970.

———. *How Europe Underdeveloped Africa.* London: Bogle-l'Ouverture, 1972.

Round Table Conference: Strategy for Poverty Alleviation. Banjul: The Government of The Gambia, 1994.

Russell, Peter. *Prince Henry "the Navigator": A Life.* New Haven: Yale University Press, 2000.

Russell-Wood, A.J.R. *World on the Move: The Portuguese in Africa, Asia, and America, 1415–1808.* New York: St Martin's Press, 1992.

Sachs, Jeffrey D. *The End of Poverty: Economic Possibilities for Our Time.* New York: Penguin Books, 2005.

Saine, Abdoulaye. *The Paradox of Third-Wave Democratization in Africa: The Gambia Under AFPRC-APRC Rule, 1994–2008.* Lanham, MD: Lexington Books, 2009.

Sallah, Tijan M. "Economics and Politics in The Gambia." *Journal of Modern African Studies* 28 (1990): 621–648.

Sanneh, Lamin O. *The Jahanke: The History of an Islamic Clerical People of the Senegambia.* London: Oxford University Press, 1979.

Sapir, Olga Linares de. "Shell-Middens of Lower Casamance and Diola Protohistory." *West African Journal of Archaeology* 1 (1971): 23–54.

Schroeder, Richard A. *Shady Practices: Agroforestry and Gender Politics in The Gambia.* Berkeley: University of California Press, 1999.

Searing, James F. *West African Slavery and Atlantic Commerce: The Senegal River Valley, 1700–1860.* Cambridge: Cambridge University Press, 1993.

Segal, Sheldon J. *Under the Banyan Tree: A Population Scientist's Odyssey.* New York: Oxford University Press, 2003.

Shaffer, Lynda N. "Southernization." *Journal of World History* 5 (1994): 1–21.

Shannon, Thomas Richard. *An Introduction to the World-System Perspective.* Boulder, CO: Westview Press, 1989.

Sidibe, B.K. *A Brief History of Kaabu and Fuladu, 1300–1930: A Narrative Based on Some Oral Traditions of the Senegambia.* Banjul: Oral History and Antiquities Division, 1974.

Singer, Peter. *One World: The Ethics of Globalization.* New Haven, CT: Yale University Press, 2002.

Smil, Vaclav. *Energy in World History.* Boulder, CO: Westview Press, 1994.

Spindel, Carol. *In the Shadow of the Sacred Grove*. New York: Vintage, 1989.

Stavrianos, L.S. *Global Rift: The Third World Comes of Age*. New York: William Morrow, 1981.

———. *Lifelines from Our Past: A New World History*. Armonk, NY: M.E. Sharpe, 1989.

Stearns, Peter. *Interpreting the Industrial Revolution*. Washington, DC: American Historical Association, 1991.

Stiglitz, Joseph E. *Globalization and Its Discontents*. New York: Norton, 2002.

Swindell, Kenneth. "African Food Imports and Agricultural Development: Peanut Basins and Rice Bowls in The Gambia, 1843–1933," in *Agricultural Change, Environment and Economy: Essays in Honour of W.B. Morgan*, ed. Keith Hoggart. London: Mansell, 1992, 159–179.

———, and Alieu Jeng. *Migrants, Credit, and Climate: The Gambian Groundnut Trade, 1834–1934*. Boston: Brill, 2006.

Tamari, Tal. "The Development of Caste Systems in West Africa." *Journal of African History* 32 (1991): 221–250.

Thornton, John. *Africa and Africans in the Making of the Atlantic World, 1400–1680*. 2nd ed. New York: Cambridge University Press, 1998.

———. "Precolonial African Industry and the Atlantic Trade, 1500–1800." *African Economic History* 19 (1990): 1–54.

The Transatlantic Slave Trade Database. www.slavevoyages.org/tast/index.faces.

Tuden, Arthur, and Leonard Plotnicov. *Social Stratification in Africa*. New York: Free Press, 1970.

United Nations Development Programme. *Human Development Report 1991*. New York: Oxford University Press.

———. *Human Development Report 2002*. www.undp.org/hdr2002.

U.S. Department of Agriculture, Farm Service Agency. "Farm Bill 2002: Frequently Asked Questions, Peanuts." June 6, 2002. www.fsa.usda.gov/pas/farmbill/readfaqs. asp?catcode=5&faqid=93.

Voll, John O. "Islam as a Special World System." *Journal of World History* 5 (1994): 213–226.

Wallerstein, Immanuel. "Africa and the World-Economy." In *General History of Africa*. Vol. 6, *Africa in the Nineteenth Century Until the 1880s*, ed. J.F. Ade Ajayi, 23–39. Paris: UNESCO, 1989.

———. *The Modern World-System: Capitalist Agriculture and the Origins of the European World-Economy in the Sixteenth Century*. New York: Academic Press, 1974.

———. *The Modern World-System II: Mercantilism and the Consolidation of the European World-Economy*. New York: Academic Press, 1980.

———. *The Modern World-System III: The Second Era of Great Expansion of the Capitalist World Economy*. San Diego: Academic Press, 1988.

———. *World-Systems Analysis: An Introduction*. Durham, NC: Duke University Press, 2004.

Watson, Andrew. *Agricultural Innovation in the Early Islamic World: The Diffusion of Crops and Farming Techniques, 700–1100*. Cambridge: Cambridge University Press, 1983.

Webb, James L.A. *Desert Frontier: Ecological and Economic Change along the Western Sahel, 1600–1850*. Madison: University of Wisconsin Press, 1995.

———. "Ecological and Economic Change Along the Middle Reaches of the Gambia River, 1945–1985." *African Affairs* 91 (1992): 543–565.

Weil, Peter. "Slavery, Groundnuts, and European Capitalism in the Wuli Kingdom of Senegambia, 1820–1930." *Research in Economic Anthropology* 6 (1984): 77–119.

Wilkinson, David. "Core, Peripheries, and Civilization." In *Core/Periphery Relations in Precapitalist Worlds*, ed. C. Chase-Dunn and T. Hall, 113–166. Boulder, CO: Westview Press, 1991.

Willis, John Ralph. "Introduction: Reflections on the Diffusion of Islam in West Africa." In *Studies in West African Islamic History.* Vol. 1, *The Cultivators of Islam*, ed. John Ralph Willis, 1–39. London: Frank Cass, 1979.

Wolff, Eric R. *Europe and the People Without History.* Berkeley: University of California Press, 1982.

Wong, R. Bin. *China Transformed: Historical Change and the Limits of European Experience.* Ithaca, NY: Cornell University Press, 1997.

World Bank. *Assessing Aid: What Works, What Doesn't, and Why?* New York: Oxford University Press, 1998.

———. *Basic Needs in The Gambia.* Washington, DC: World Bank, 1981.

———. *Globalization, Growth, and Poverty: Building an Inclusive World Economy.* Washington, DC: World Bank, and New York: Oxford University Press, 2002.

———. *World Development Report 2002.* New York: Oxford University Press, 2001. http://encon.worldbank.org/wdr/structured_doc.php?pr=2391&doc_id=2394.

World Tables 1995. Baltimore: Johns Hopkins University Press, 1995.

World Trade Organization. "The WTO in Brief." www.wto.org/english/thewto_e/whatis_e/inbrief_e/inbr00_ e.htm.

Wright, Donald R. *The Early History of Niumi: Settlement and Foundation of a Mandinka State on the Gambia River.* Athens: Ohio University Center for International Studies, 1977.

———. "The Epic of Kelefa Saane as a Guide to the Nature of Precolonial Senegambian Society—and Vice Versa." *History in Africa: A Journal of Method* 14 (1987): 307–327.

———. *Oral Traditions from The Gambia.* 2 vols. Athens: Ohio University Center for International Studies, 1979, 1980.

———. "That Hell-Hole of Yours." *American Heritage* 46 (1995): 47–58.

———. "Uprooting Kunta Kinte: On the Perils of Relying on Encyclopedic Informants." *History in Africa: A Journal of Method* 8 (1981): 205–217.

———. "What Do You Mean There Were No Tribes in Africa? Thoughts on Boundaries—and Related Matters—in Precolonial Africa." *History in Africa: A Journal of Method* 26 (1999): 409–426.

INDEX

ABOUT THE AUTHOR

Donald R. Wright is Distinguished Teaching Professor of History, Emeritus, at the State University of New York–Cortland. A student of Gambian history for over forty years, he holds MA and PhD degrees in history from Indiana University and a BA from DePauw University. Dr. Wright has received Fulbright-Hays, NEH, and SUNY fellowships for research in Africa; was a scholar-in-residence at the Rockefeller Foundation's Study and Conference Center in Bellagio, Italy, in 2003; has lectured at universities in South Africa and China; and in 2005–2006 held the Mark W. Clark Distinguished Visiting Chair of History at The Citadel. Dr. Wright has published two books on early African American history and a two-volume collection of oral traditions from The Gambia; he is co-author of *The Atlantic World: A History* (2007). He lives with his wife, Doris, in Homer, New York.